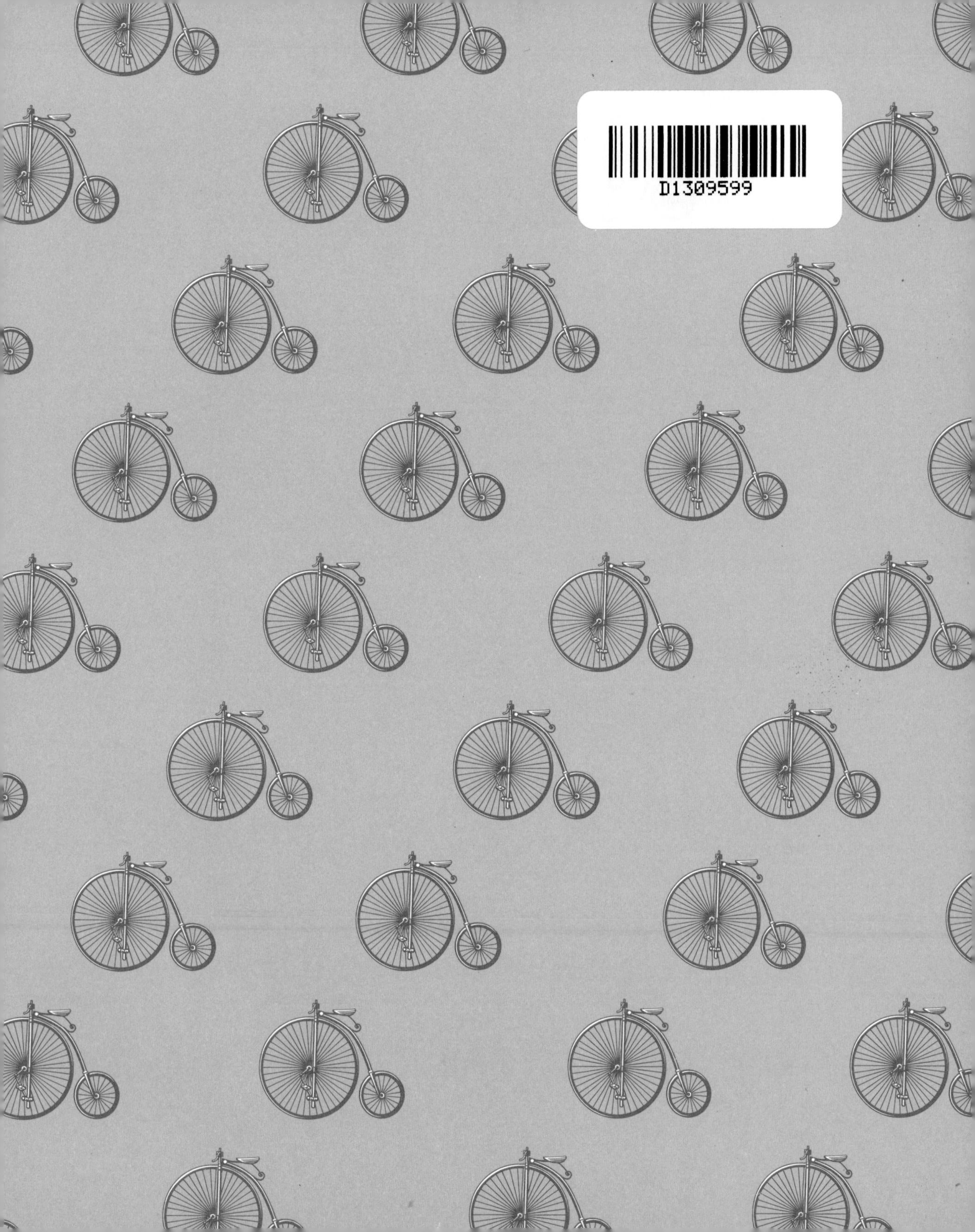

Wonders of Our World

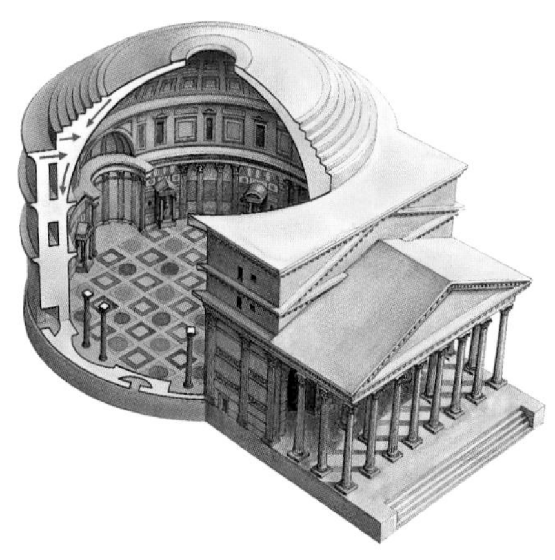

TIME® LIFE BOOKS

Time-Life Books is a division of Time Life Inc.
Time-Life is a trademark of Time Warner Inc.
and affiliated companies.

Conceived and produced by Weldon Owen Pty Limited
59 Victoria Street, McMahons Point, NSW, 2060, Australia
A member of the Weldon Owen Group of Companies
Sydney • San Francisco • London

TIME LIFE INC.
Chairman and Chief Executive Officer: Jim Nelson
President and Chief Operating Officer: Steven Janas
Senior Executive Vice President and Chief Operations Officer: Mary Davis Holt
Senior Vice President and Chief Financial Officer: Christopher Hearing

TIME-LIFE BOOKS
President: Larry Jellen
Senior Vice President, New Markets: Bridget Boel
Vice President, Home and Hearth Markets: Nicholas M. DiMarco
Vice President, Content Development: Jennifer L. Pearce

TIME-LIFE TRADE PUBLISHING
Vice President and Publisher: Neil S. Levin
Senior Sales Director: Richard J. Vreeland
Director, Marketing and Publicity: Inger Forland
Director of Trade Sales: Dana Hobson
Director of Custom Publishing: John Lalor
Director of Rights and Licensing: Olga Vezeris

WONDERS OF OUR WORLD
Director of New Product Development: Carolyn M. Clark
Senior Editor: Robert Somerville
Director of Design: Tina Taylor
Project Manager: Jennifer L. Ward
Production Manager: Virginia Reardon

WELDON OWEN PUBLISHING
Chief Executive Officer: John Owen
President: Terry Newell
Publisher: Sheena Coupe
Associate Publisher: Lynn Humphries
Art Director: Sue Burk
Editorial Coordinator: Sarah Anderson
Production Manager: Helen Creeke
Production Assistant: Kylie Lawson
Vice President International Sales: Stuart Laurence

Managing Editor: Rosemary McDonald
Project Editors: Helen Bateman, Ann B. Bingaman, Jean Coppendale, Kathy Gerrard, Selena Quintrell
Text Editors: Jane Bowring, Claire Craig, Gillian Gillett, Tracy Tucker
Educational Consultants: Richard L. Needham, Deborah A. Powell
Designers: Juliet Cohen, Lyndel Donaldson, Kathy Gammon, Kylie Mulquin, Mark Nichols
Assistant Designers: Gary Fletcher, Robyn Latimer, Angela Pelizzari, Regina Safro, Melissa Wilton,
Visual Research Coordinator: Jenny Mills
Visual Researchers: Peter Barker, Karen Burgess, Annette Crueger, Carel Fillmer, Kathy Gerrard, Fran Meagher, Kristina Sturm, Amanda Weir

Text: Ian Graham, Terry Gwynn-Jones, Anne Lynch, Steve Parker, Richard Wood

Illustrators: Susanna Addario; Graham Back; Kenn Backhaus; David Boehm; Gregory Bridges; Colin Brown/Garden Studio; Sam Burgess; Leslye Cole; Lynette R. Cook; Dr. Levent Efe/CMI; Christer Eriksson; Alan Ewart; Rod Ferring; John Foerster/Foerster Illustration, Inc; Chris Forsey; Greg Gillespie; Mike Golding; Mike Gorman; Ray Grinaway; Terry Hadler; Langdon G. Halls; Adam Hook/Bernard Thornton Artists, UK; Christa Hook/Bernard Thornton Artists, UK; Richard Hook/Bernard Thornton Artists, UK; Gillian Jenkins; Janet Jones; David Kirshner; Mike Lamble; Alex Lavroff; Connell Lee; Kent Leech; Ulrich Lehmann; Chris Lyon/Brihton Illustration; Martin Macrae/Folio; Iain McKellar; David Mathews/ Brihton Illustration; Peter Mennim; David Nelson; Darren Pattenden/Garden Studio; R. Spencer Phippen; Oliver Rennert; John Richards; Trevor Ruth; Michael Saunders; Stephen Seymour/Bernard Thornton Artists, UK; Christine Shafner/K.E. Sweeney Illustration; Nick Shewring/Garden Studio; Ray Sim; Mark Sofilas; Roger Stewart/Brihton Illustration; Kate Sweeney/K.E. Sweeney Illustration; Kevin Stead; Steve Trevaskis; Ross Watton/Garden Studio; Rod Westblade; Steve Weston/Linden Artists; David Wood; Ann Winterbotham

Color reproduction by Colourscan Co Pte Ltd
Printed by LeeFung-Asco Printers
Printed in China
10 9 8 7 6 5 4 3 2 1

School and library distribution by Time-Life Education, P.O. Box 85026, Richmond, Virginia 23285-5026.

CIP data available upon request:
Librarian, Time-Life Books
2000 Duke Street
Alexandria, VA 22314

ISBN 0-7370-1008-8

A Weldon Owen Production

Wonders of Our World

CONSULTING EDITORS

Eryl Davies
Donald Lopez
Anne Lynch
Alison Porter
Marie Rose
Richard Wood

Contents

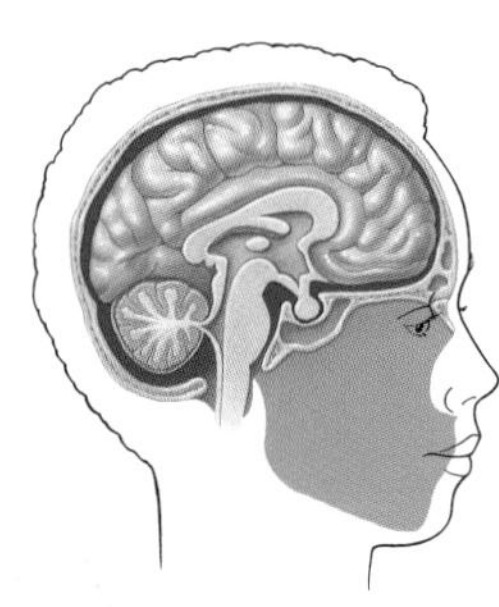

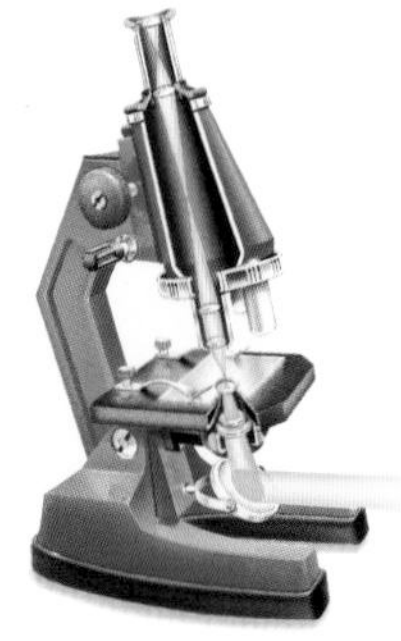

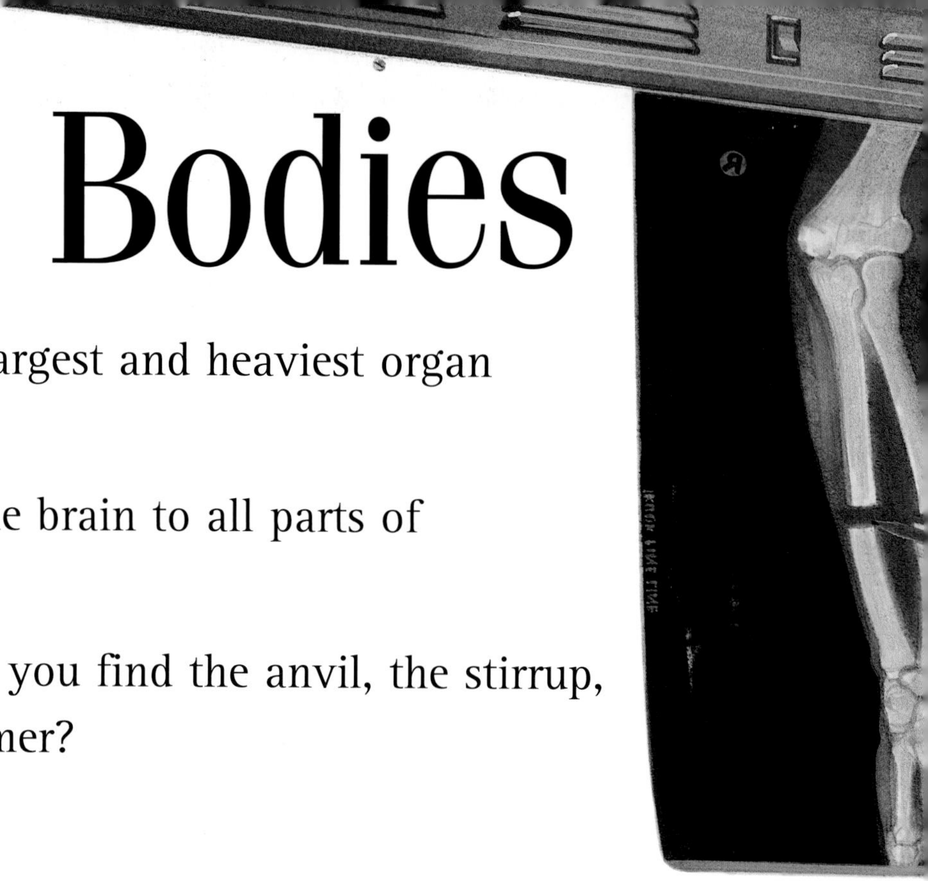

Our Bodies

- What is the largest and heaviest organ in the body?
- What links the brain to all parts of the body?
- Where would you find the anvil, the stirrup, and the hammer?

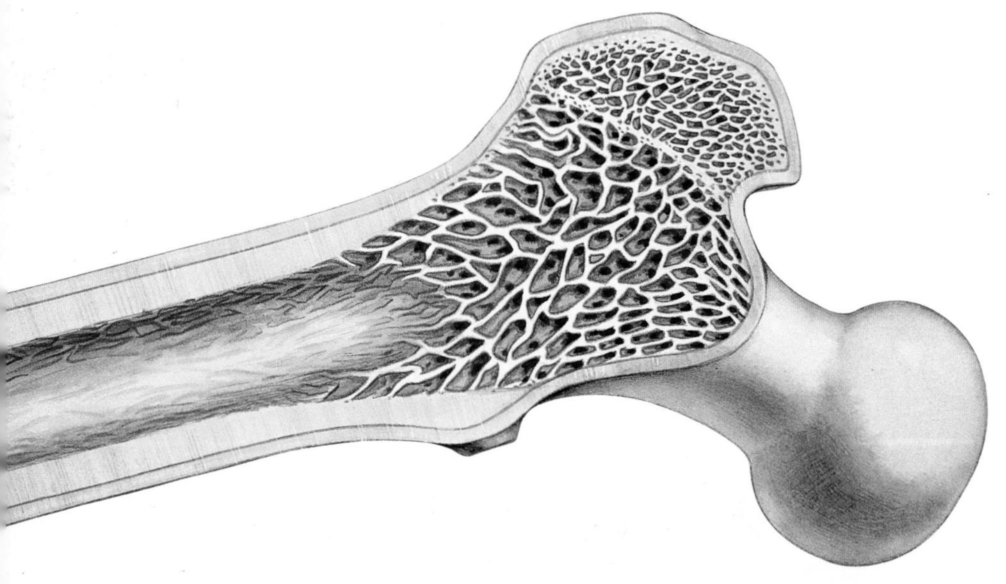

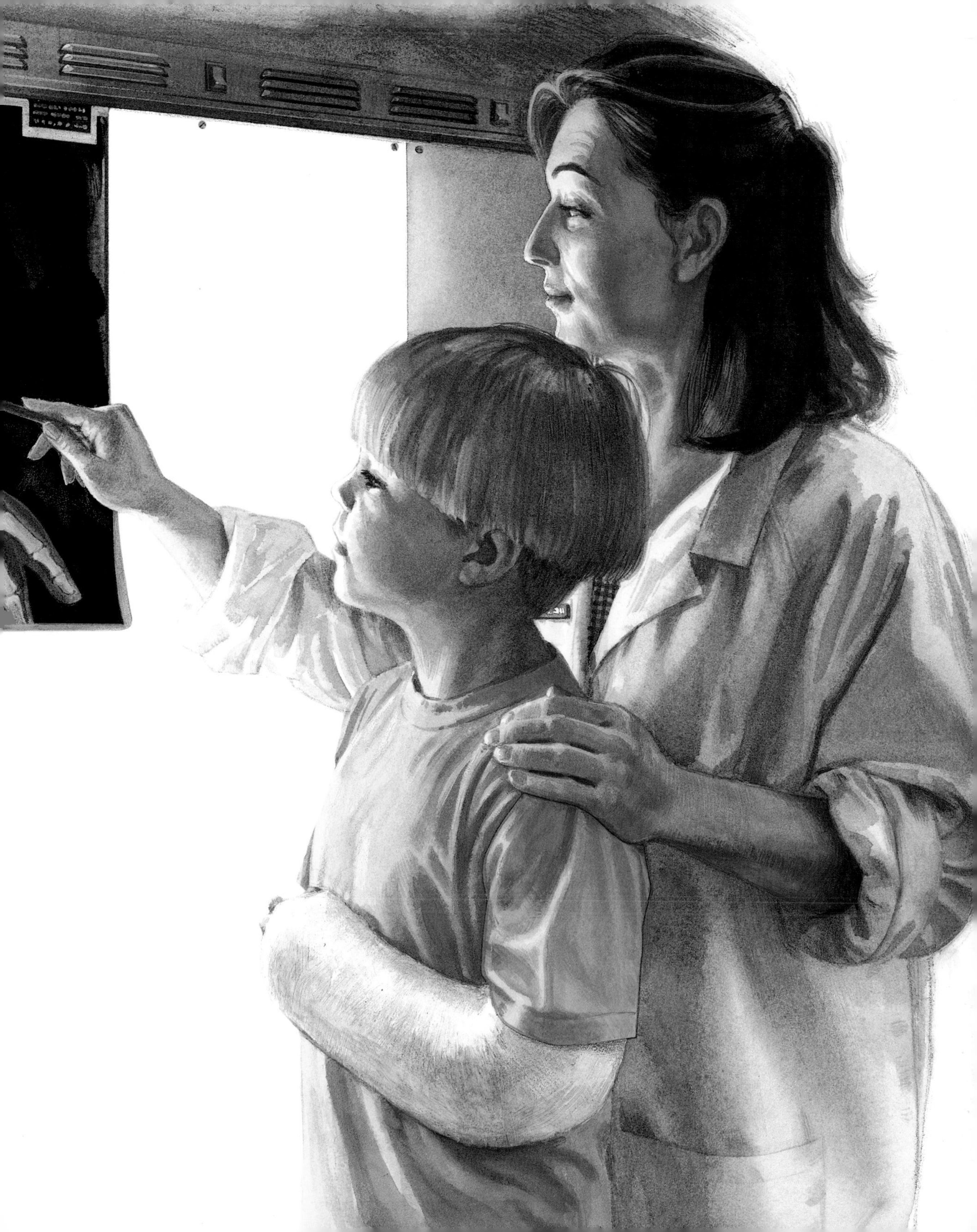

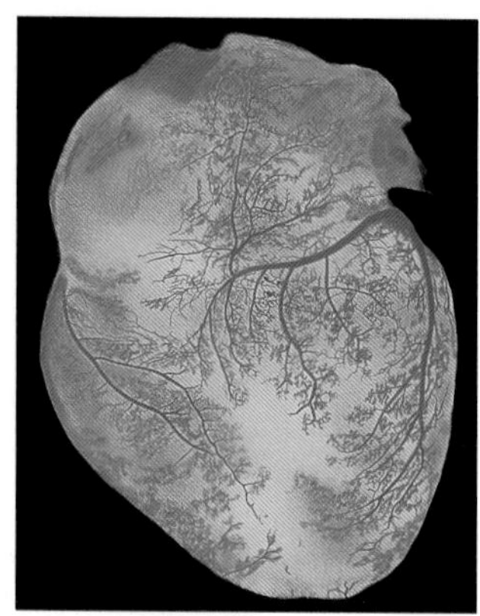

BRANCHES OF BLOOD
The thick, muscular walls of the heart work nonstop. To do this, they need their own blood supply for nourishment and energy. This comes from arteries that branch over the outside of the heart.

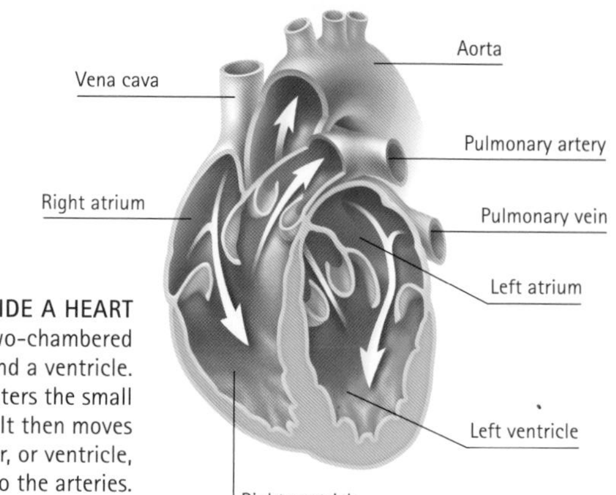

INSIDE A HEART
Each side of the heart is a two-chambered pump made up of an atrium and a ventricle. Blood flowing from veins enters the small upper chamber, or atrium. It then moves into the large lower chamber, or ventricle, which squeezes it into the arteries.

• THE VITAL SYSTEMS •

From the Heart

OLD HEARTS
Ancient Egyptians believed that the heart was the home of all thoughts, feelings and memories. They placed heart amulets (above) with the dead to help them on their journey to the afterlife.

Your heart is about the same size as your fist. This bag of muscle filled with blood squeezes tirelessly once every second of your life to pump blood around your body. The heart is made up of two pumps, which lie side by side. The right pump sends blood through the lungs to pick up the vital oxygen needed by all the cells in the body. The left pump sends blood around the body to deliver the oxygen. The blood then returns to the right pump and so on, round and round the double loop of the circulatory system. The heart pushes blood into tubes called arteries, which carry the blood around the body. When the heart relaxes, it fills with blood that comes back from the body along floppy tubes called veins. A heartbeat occurs every time the heart squeezes and relaxes.

A HELPING HEART
Some people with heart disease need a new heart. Surgeons are able to remove a healthy heart from someone who has just died and put it into the body of someone who needs it. People of all ages, such as this group (left), have undergone successful heart transplants.

Did You Know?

When an embryo is four weeks old, its heart starts beating. By the time it is eight weeks old, the heart is fully developed.

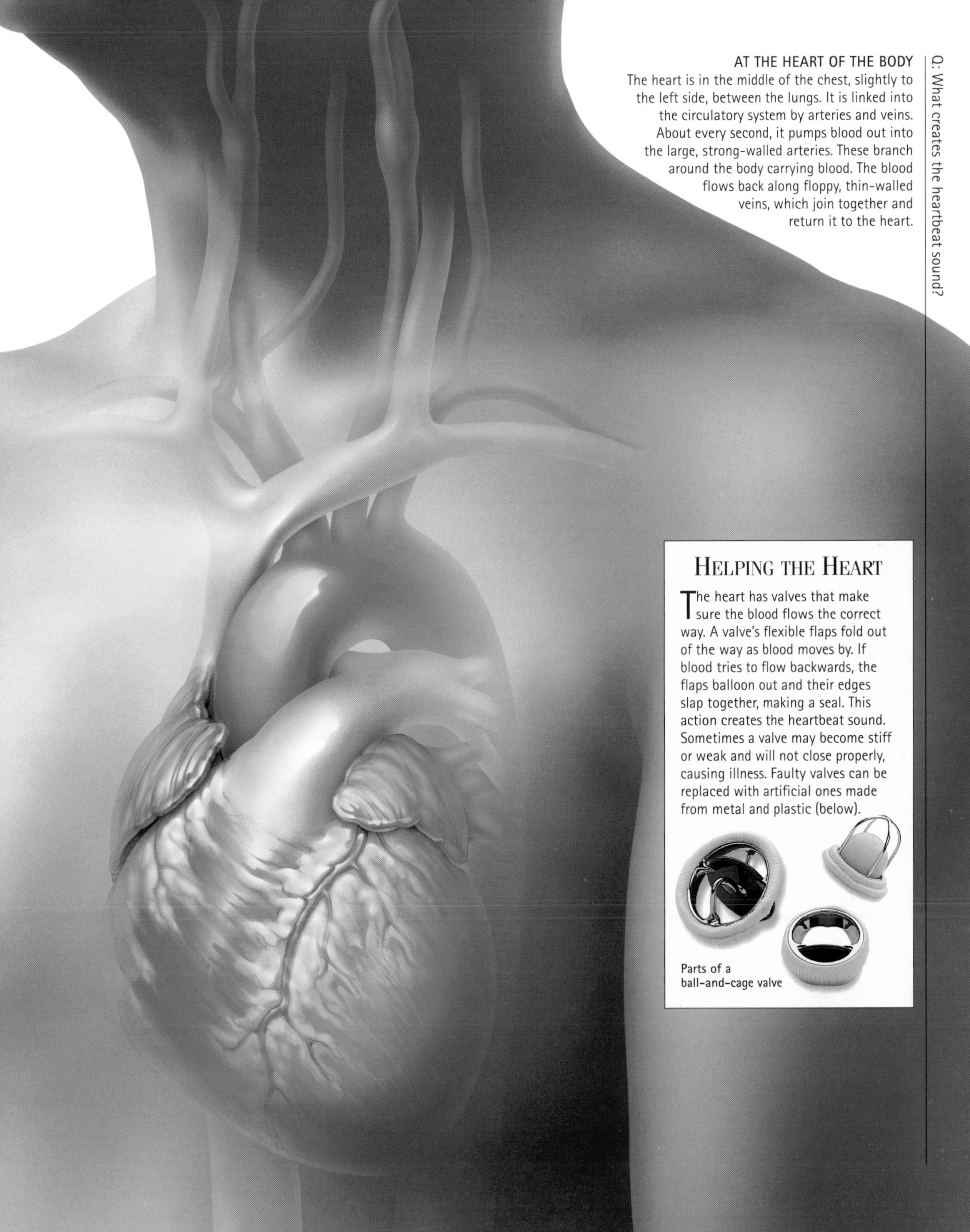

AT THE HEART OF THE BODY

The heart is in the middle of the chest, slightly to the left side, between the lungs. It is linked into the circulatory system by arteries and veins. About every second, it pumps blood out into the large, strong-walled arteries. These branch around the body carrying blood. The blood flows back along floppy, thin-walled veins, which join together and return it to the heart.

Helping the Heart

The heart has valves that make sure the blood flows the correct way. A valve's flexible flaps fold out of the way as blood moves by. If blood tries to flow backwards, the flaps balloon out and their edges slap together, making a seal. This action creates the heartbeat sound. Sometimes a valve may become stiff or weak and will not close properly, causing illness. Faulty valves can be replaced with artificial ones made from metal and plastic (below).

Parts of a ball-and-cage valve

Moving Things Around

Blood flows from the heart along arteries. These have thick, tough, stretchy walls that withstand the surge of blood pressure with each heartbeat. Arteries divide many times as they spread around the body, and form millions of micro-blood vessels called capillaries. The walls of the capillaries are so thin that vital substances in blood–oxygen, nutrients, high-energy sugars and hormones (chemical messengers)–can seep through to surrounding cells. Carbon dioxide and other wastes from the cells can pass into blood, which takes them away to be removed from the body by the lungs, kidneys and liver. The capillaries join to make larger, thin-walled veins, which return the blood to the heart. Blood carries white cells that fight germs and disease. It also clots to seal leaks and wounds, and it spreads warmth evenly around the body.

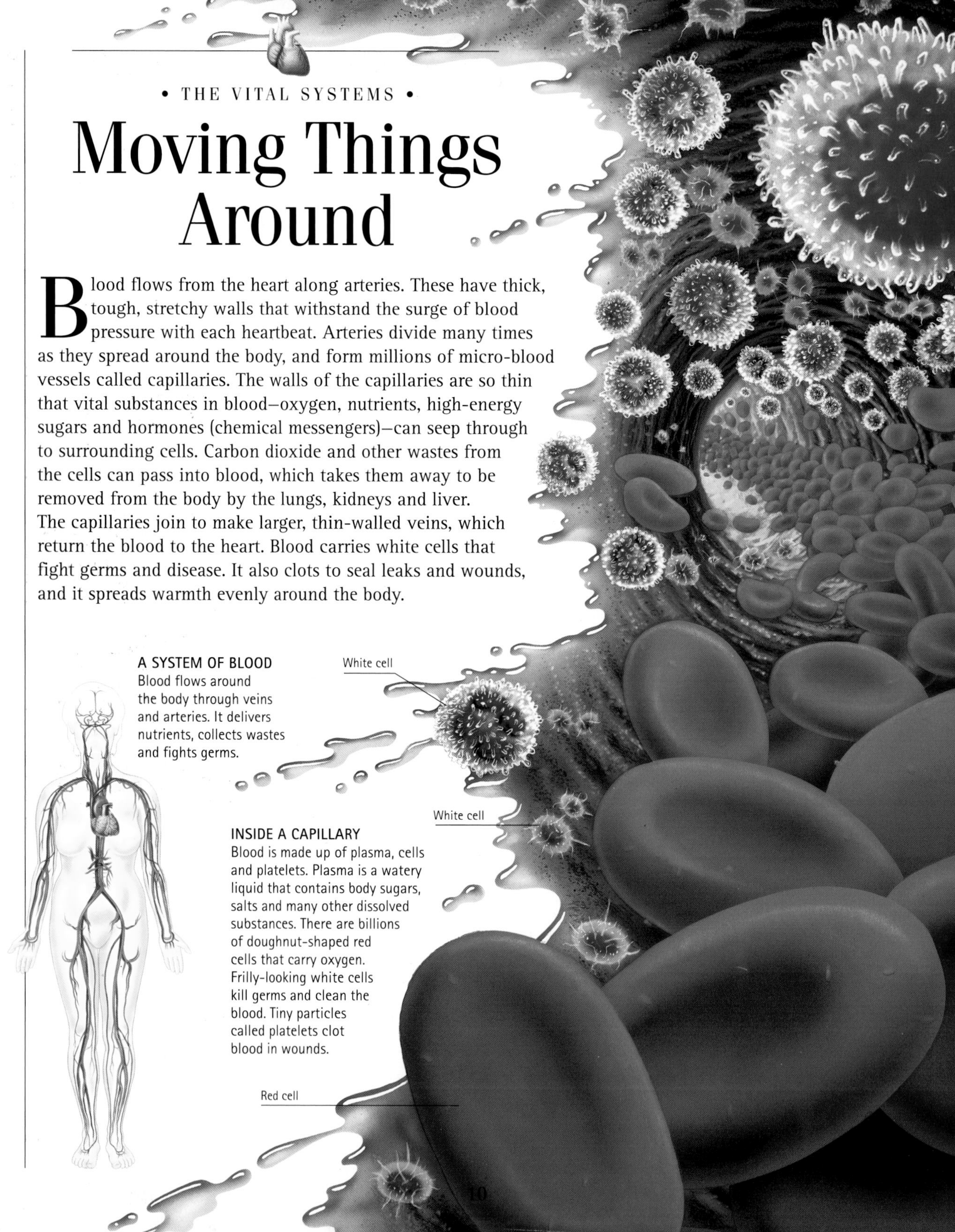

A SYSTEM OF BLOOD
Blood flows around the body through veins and arteries. It delivers nutrients, collects wastes and fights germs.

INSIDE A CAPILLARY
Blood is made up of plasma, cells and platelets. Plasma is a watery liquid that contains body sugars, salts and many other dissolved substances. There are billions of doughnut-shaped red cells that carry oxygen. Frilly-looking white cells kill germs and clean the blood. Tiny particles called platelets clot blood in wounds.

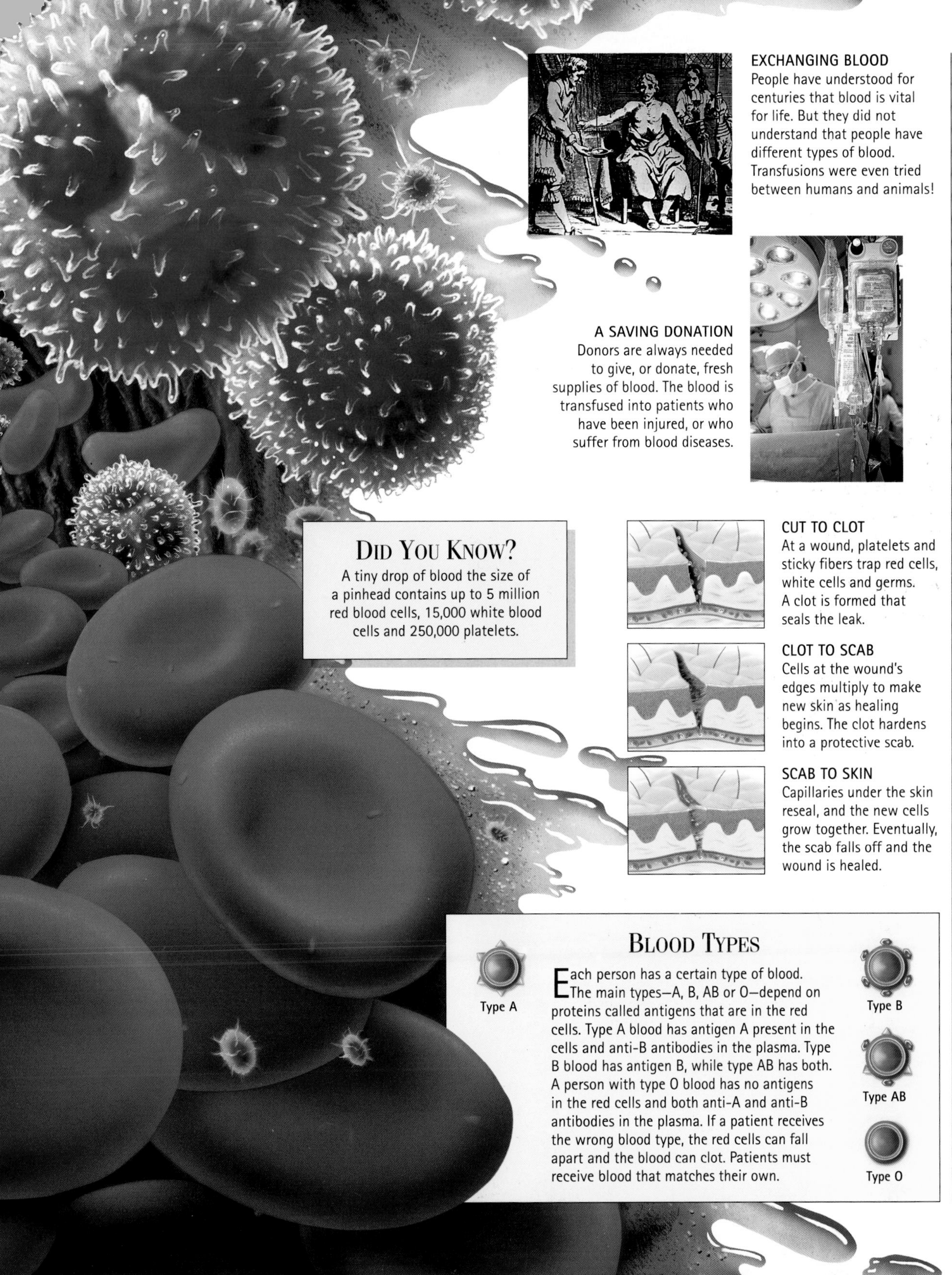

EXCHANGING BLOOD
People have understood for centuries that blood is vital for life. But they did not understand that people have different types of blood. Transfusions were even tried between humans and animals!

A SAVING DONATION
Donors are always needed to give, or donate, fresh supplies of blood. The blood is transfused into patients who have been injured, or who suffer from blood diseases.

Did You Know?

A tiny drop of blood the size of a pinhead contains up to 5 million red blood cells, 15,000 white blood cells and 250,000 platelets.

CUT TO CLOT
At a wound, platelets and sticky fibers trap red cells, white cells and germs. A clot is formed that seals the leak.

CLOT TO SCAB
Cells at the wound's edges multiply to make new skin as healing begins. The clot hardens into a protective scab.

SCAB TO SKIN
Capillaries under the skin reseal, and the new cells grow together. Eventually, the scab falls off and the wound is healed.

Blood Types

Each person has a certain type of blood. The main types—A, B, AB or O—depend on proteins called antigens that are in the red cells. Type A blood has antigen A present in the cells and anti-B antibodies in the plasma. Type B blood has antigen B, while type AB has both. A person with type O blood has no antigens in the red cells and both anti-A and anti-B antibodies in the plasma. If a patient receives the wrong blood type, the red cells can fall apart and the blood can clot. Patients must receive blood that matches their own.

Type A

Type B

Type AB

Type O

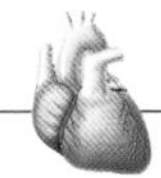

A Deep Breath

You breathe in one pint (half a liter) of air every few seconds when you are resting. The air enters through the nose and mouth, goes down the throat and into the windpipe, called the trachea, before entering the two spongy lungs. The lungs absorb oxygen, which makes up one-fifth of normal air. Oxygen is vital because it is an essential part of the energy-giving chemical reactions inside each cell. The lungs pass the oxygen into the blood, which carries it to all body cells. The body's main waste substance, called carbon dioxide, passes in the opposite direction, from the blood to the air in the lungs. You then breathe this up the windpipe and out—before breathing in new air. The body cannot store much oxygen, so you need to keep breathing to stay alive.

Did You Know?

Each lung contains more than 300 million alveoli, or "air bubbles," which give it a light and spongy texture. The alveoli provide a huge surface area to absorb oxygen. They would cover half a tennis court if they were flattened out.

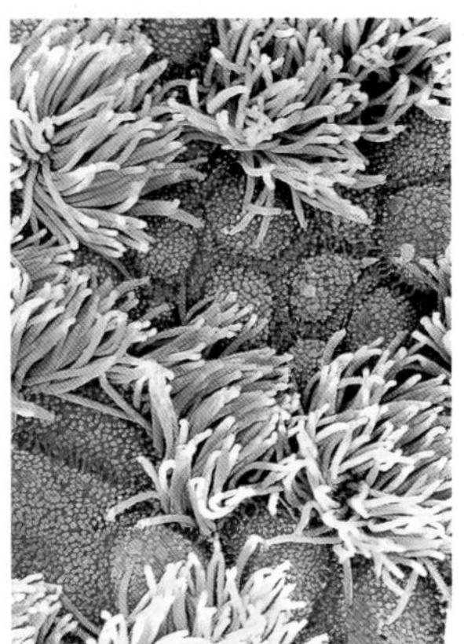

THE DUST REMOVERS
Sticky mucus lines the airways of the nose, throat, windpipe and lungs. It traps dust, dirt and other airborne particles. In the lining of the lungs and windpipe, microscopic hairs called cilia (left) wave to and fro. They push the dirty mucus up to the throat, where it is swallowed.

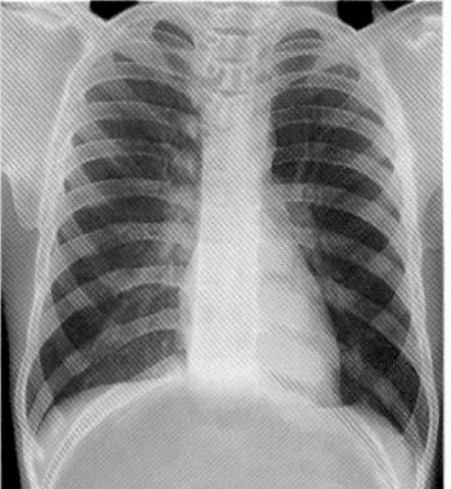

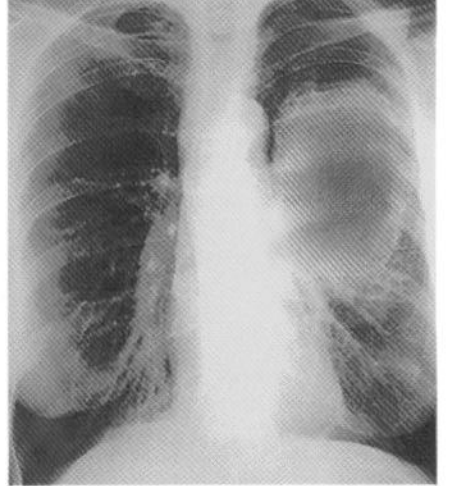

IN THE CLEAR
On an X-ray photograph, healthy lungs (left) show up as faint shapes. Shadowy areas (right) show lungs that have been damaged, for example, by smoking.

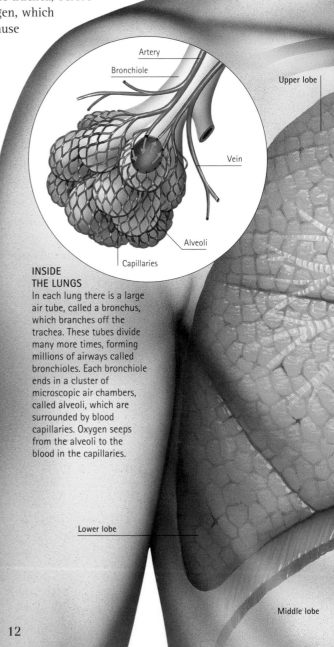

Artery
Bronchiole
Vein
Alveoli
Capillaries
Upper lobe
Lower lobe
Middle lobe

INSIDE THE LUNGS
In each lung there is a large air tube, called a bronchus, which branches off the trachea. These tubes divide many more times, forming millions of airways called bronchioles. Each bronchiole ends in a cluster of microscopic air chambers, called alveoli, which are surrounded by blood capillaries. Oxygen seeps from the alveoli to the blood in the capillaries.

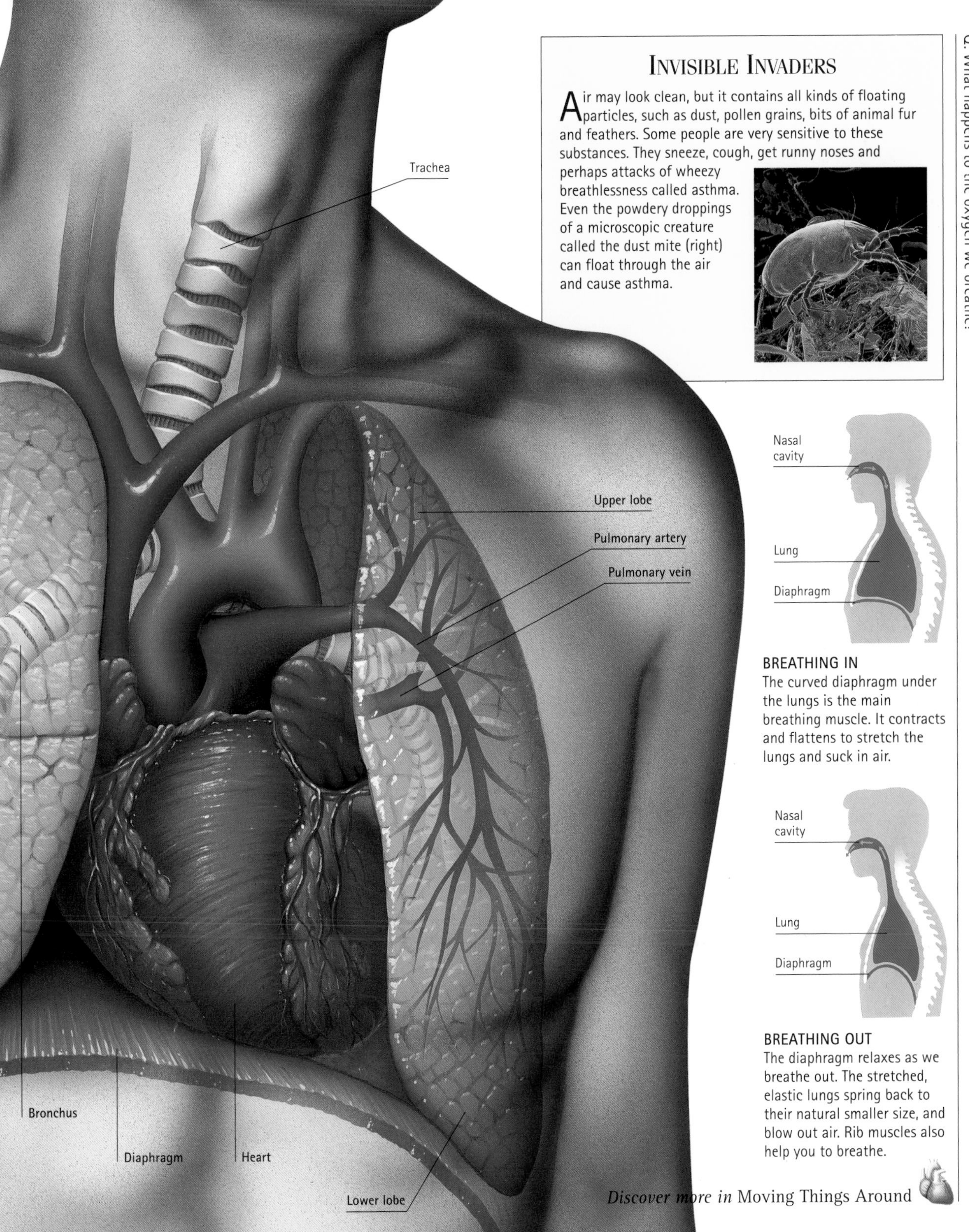

Invisible Invaders

Air may look clean, but it contains all kinds of floating particles, such as dust, pollen grains, bits of animal fur and feathers. Some people are very sensitive to these substances. They sneeze, cough, get runny noses and perhaps attacks of wheezy breathlessness called asthma. Even the powdery droppings of a microscopic creature called the dust mite (right) can float through the air and cause asthma.

BREATHING IN
The curved diaphragm under the lungs is the main breathing muscle. It contracts and flattens to stretch the lungs and suck in air.

BREATHING OUT
The diaphragm relaxes as we breathe out. The stretched, elastic lungs spring back to their natural smaller size, and blow out air. Rib muscles also help you to breathe.

Discover more in Moving Things Around

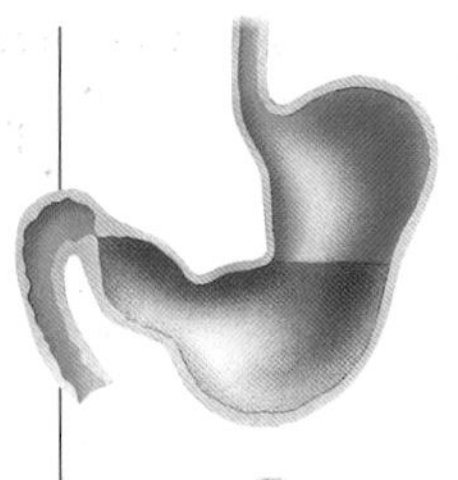

JUST SWALLOWED
The stomach's muscular walls squeeze and squirm to mash food (coloured blue). Its lining produces powerful digestive juices that break down food.

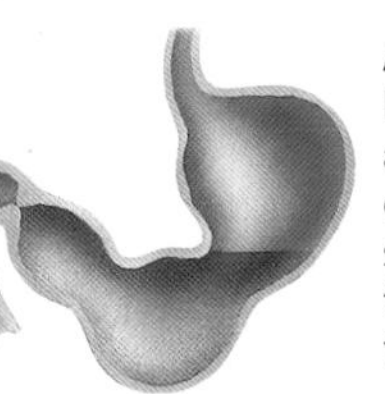

AFTER ONE HOUR
Food is turned into a lumpy soup called chyme. Starchy and sugary foods digest fastest, while fatty foods are the slowest.

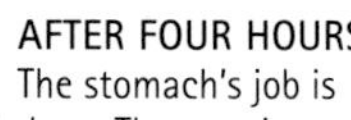

AFTER FOUR HOURS
The stomach's job is done. The remains exit through the sphincter, which opens regularly to allow squirts of chyme into the small intestine.

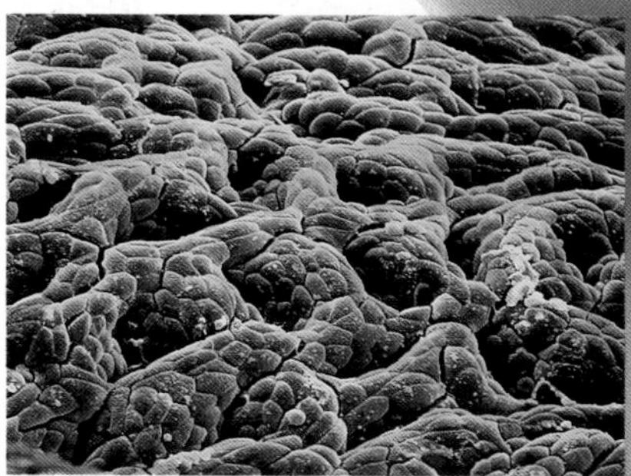

SELF-PROTECTION
The stomach's lining (above) contains tiny glands that make gastric acids, enzymes, and mucus. The lining is coated with thick mucus so that it does not digest itself.

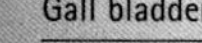

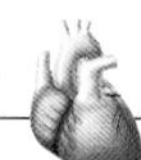

• THE VITAL SYSTEMS •

The Production Line

The first stop for food swallowed down the esophagus is the stomach. The stomach is the widest part of the digestive tract. It is a muscle-walled bag that can expand to hold about 1/2 gallon (2 liters) of food and drink. The stomach breaks up the food with powerful squeezing actions and strong digestive chemicals. The soupy, partly digested food oozes into the next section, called the small intestine. More enzymes are mixed in for further chemical breakdown. The digested nutrients are absorbed into blood flowing through the lining of the small intestine. The large intestine is shorter, but much wider, than the small intestine. Water, body salts and minerals from the undigested food are absorbed here. The brownish, semi-solid remains are called feces and are stored in the rectum. The final stage is when the remains are passed through the anus.

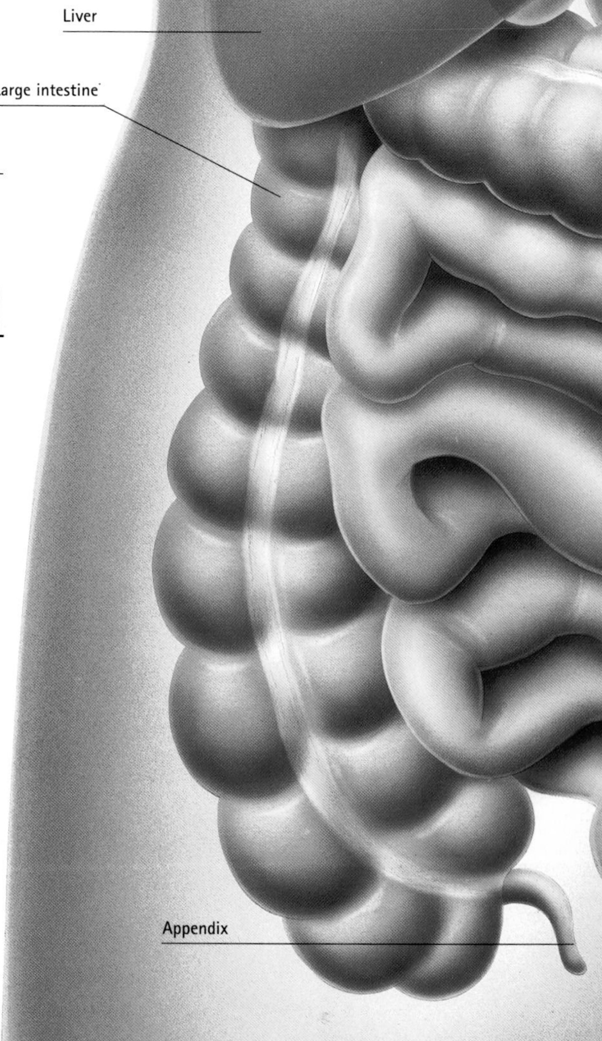

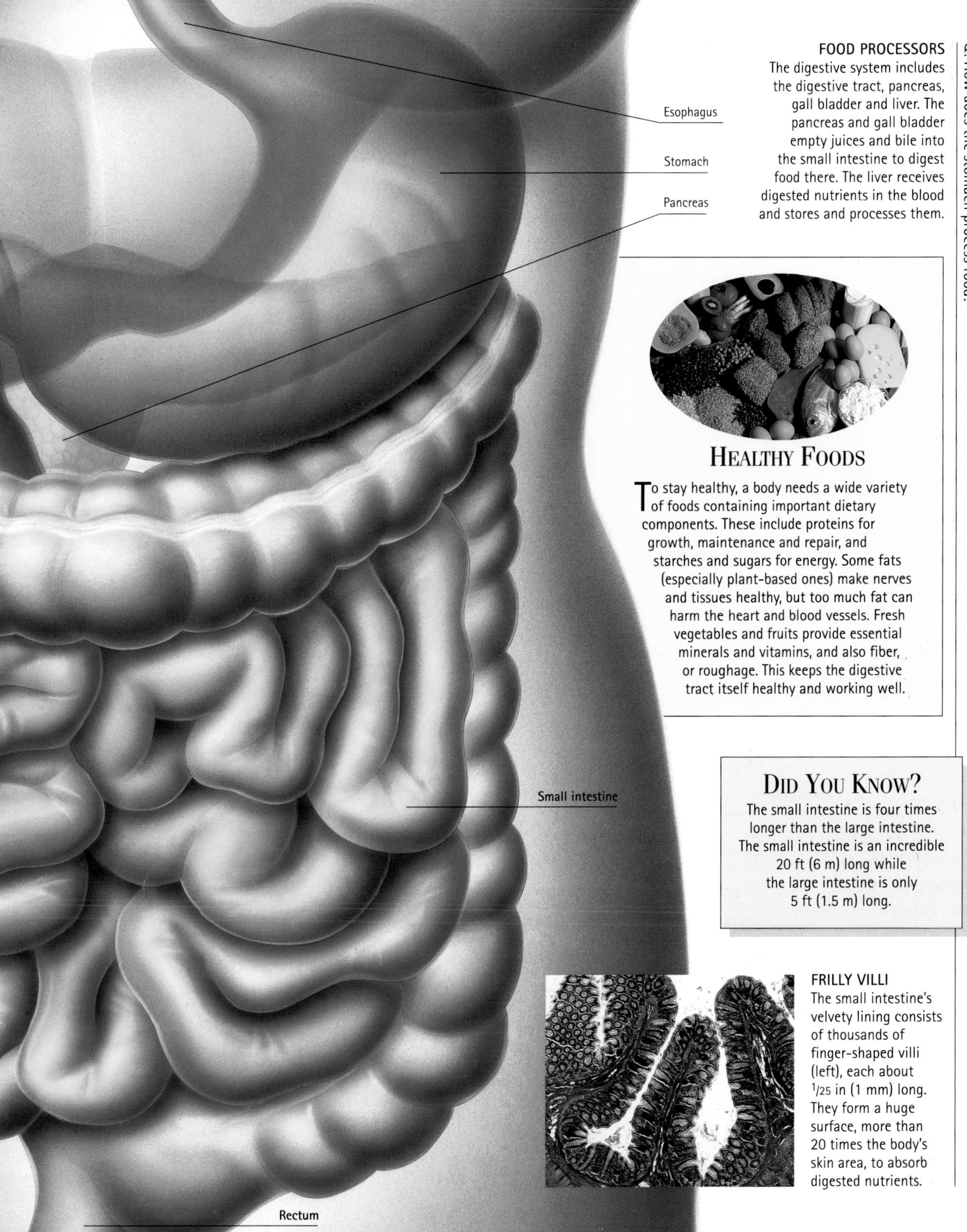

FOOD PROCESSORS
The digestive system includes the digestive tract, pancreas, gall bladder and liver. The pancreas and gall bladder empty juices and bile into the small intestine to digest food there. The liver receives digested nutrients in the blood and stores and processes them.

HEALTHY FOODS

To stay healthy, a body needs a wide variety of foods containing important dietary components. These include proteins for growth, maintenance and repair, and starches and sugars for energy. Some fats (especially plant-based ones) make nerves and tissues healthy, but too much fat can harm the heart and blood vessels. Fresh vegetables and fruits provide essential minerals and vitamins, and also fiber, or roughage. This keeps the digestive tract itself healthy and working well.

DID YOU KNOW?

The small intestine is four times longer than the large intestine. The small intestine is an incredible 20 ft (6 m) long while the large intestine is only 5 ft (1.5 m) long.

FRILLY VILLI
The small intestine's velvety lining consists of thousands of finger-shaped villi (left), each about 1/25 in (1 mm) long. They form a huge surface, more than 20 times the body's skin area, to absorb digested nutrients.

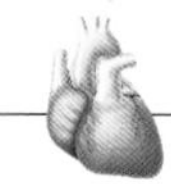

The Work Continues

The digestive system is made up of the digestive tract, the pancreas, the gall bladder and the liver. The wedge-shaped pancreas gland, just behind the stomach, makes strong digestive juices to help food digest in the small intestine. The gall bladder is under the liver. It stores bile, a yellowish fluid made by the liver, which also helps digestion in the small intestine. The liver, next to the stomach, is the largest organ inside the body. It has more than 600 different jobs, mostly processing nutrients and other substances that are brought by the blood from the small intestine. After body cells have used their nutrients, they make waste products such as urea. The blood collects the waste products, and the excretory system—the kidneys, ureters, bladder and urethra—gets rid of them as a yellowish fluid called urine.

Did You Know?

An average adult produces 45 fl oz (1,500 ml) of urine each day. It is 95 per cent water, and 5 per cent wastes such as unwanted salts and minerals. Healthy urine contains no bacteria or other germs.

Liver

Gall bladder

Cortex

Medulla

Renal artery

Renal vein

Renal pelvis

BLOOD'S FILTER
Each kidney's cortex and medulla layers filter blood brought by the renal artery. The filtered blood returns to the heart by the renal vein. Wastes and excess water collect in the renal pelvis as urine.

THE EXCRETORY SYSTEM
The two kidneys are in the upper abdomen, just below the liver and stomach. Urine flows to the bladder in the lower abdomen, then out along the urethra.

TINY FILTERS
Each kidney contains about 1 million microscopic blood-filtering units called nephrons (above). Every day, the kidneys filter about 42 gallons (190 liters) of blood.

JUICES FOR DIGESTION
As you eat a meal, the digestive system prepares for action. Bile flows into the small intestine from the gall bladder along the bile duct. It digests mainly fatty foods. Digestive juices flow from the pancreas, along the pancreatic duct, into the small intestine. They digest mainly proteins.

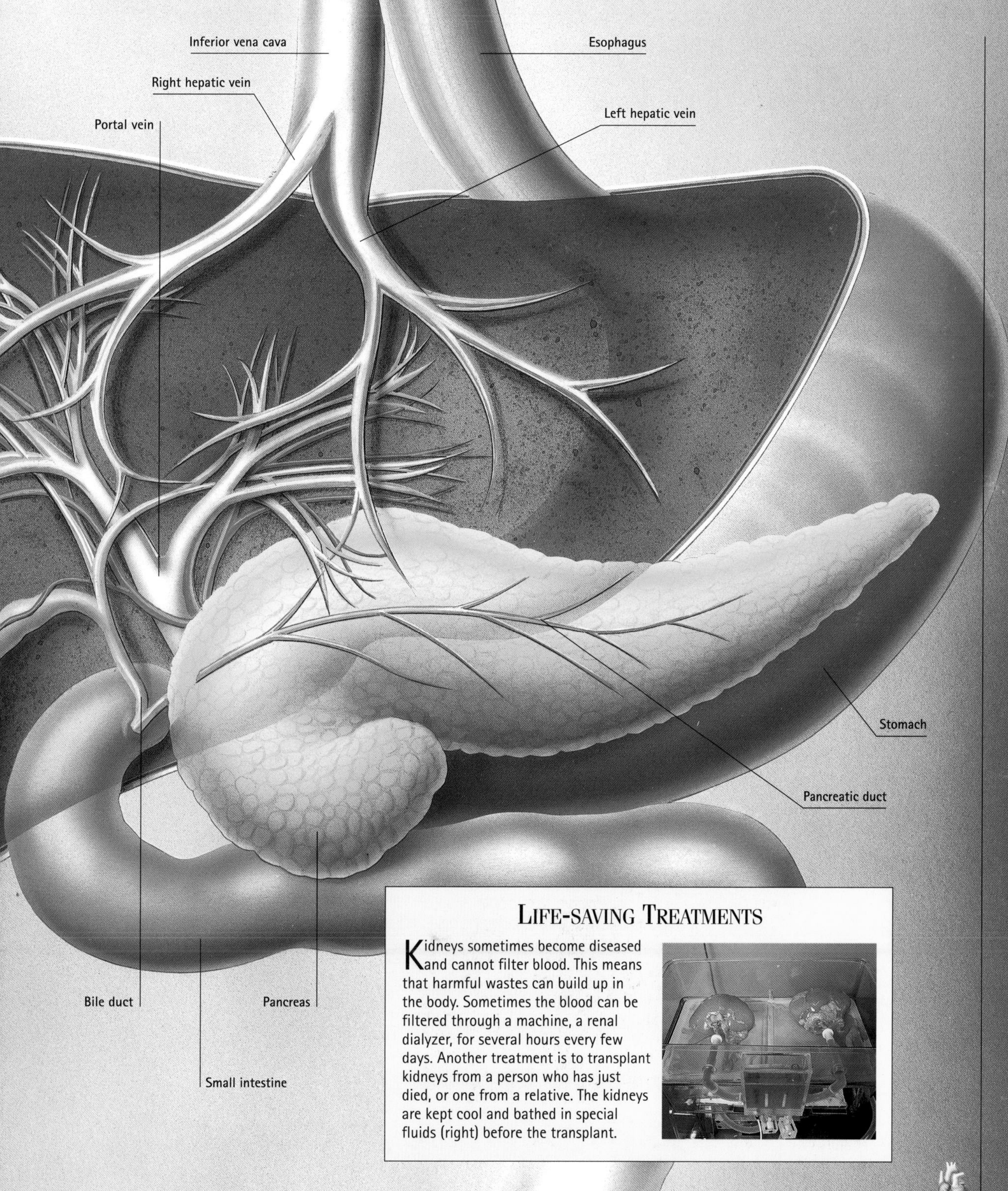

Life-saving Treatments

Kidneys sometimes become diseased and cannot filter blood. This means that harmful wastes can build up in the body. Sometimes the blood can be filtered through a machine, a renal dialyzer, for several hours every few days. Another treatment is to transplant kidneys from a person who has just died, or one from a relative. The kidneys are kept cool and bathed in special fluids (right) before the transplant.

Discover more in The Production Line

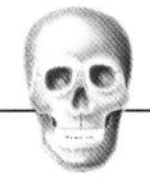

The Bare Bones

Most parts of the body, such as blood vessels, nerves and intestines, are soft and floppy. The whole body can stand up straight and move about because it is held together by a skeleton. This is the inner framework of 206 bones, which are stiff and strong. The skeleton has two main parts. The axial skeleton is the central column, and is made up of the skull, vertebrae (backbones), ribs and sternum. The appendicular skeleton is made up of the bones of the arms and legs. About half of all the body's bones are in the wrists, hands, ankles and feet. Each bone in your body works as a movable beam or lever and is specially shaped to support, protect and withstand stresses and strains. Most bones are linked at flexible joints and pulled by muscles, which allow you to walk, run, jump, and perform more delicate movements.

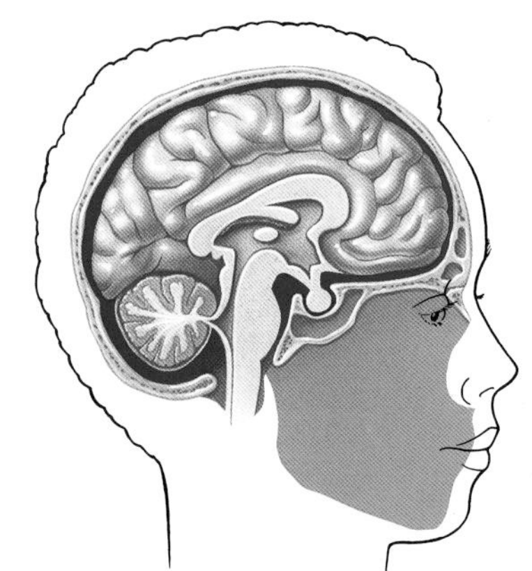

BRAIN PROTECTION
Bones support and protect. The rounded dome of the skull shields the delicate brain from injury. The upper skull, or cranium, is made up of eight curved bones linked firmly at wiggly lines called suture joints.

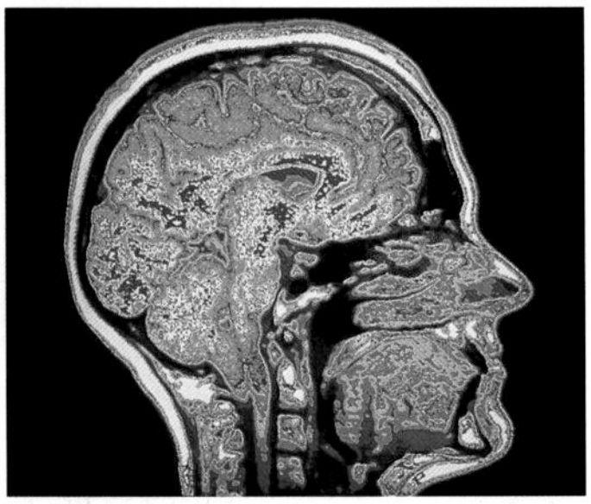

HEAD BONES
The brain is so securely encased in bone that doctors must use scanners to find out if anything is wrong.

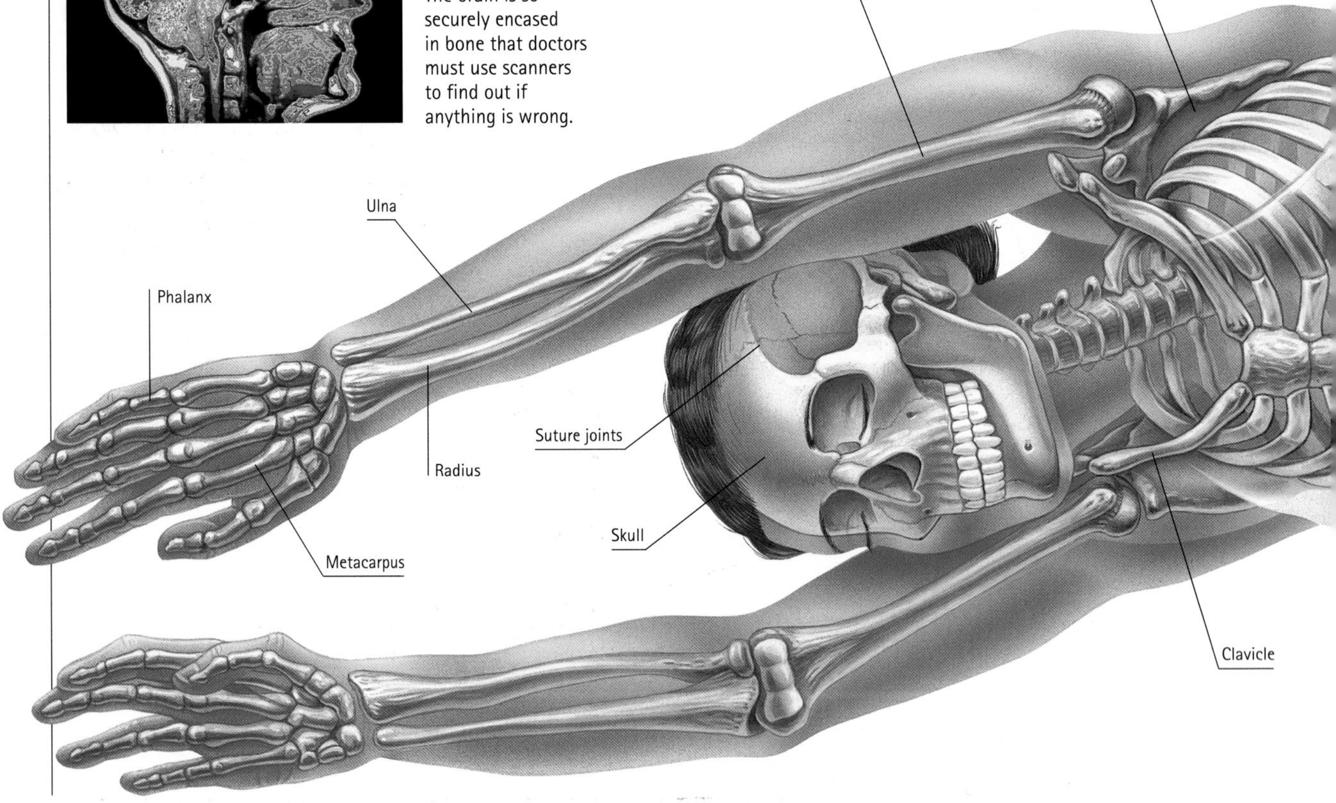

Scapula

Humerus

Ulna

Phalanx

Suture joints

Radius

Skull

Metacarpus

Clavicle

Did You Know?

The spine, or vertebral column, is made up of 24 vertebrae. These have washer-like disks of flexible cartilage (tough, elastic tissue) between them. As you stand and walk, the body's weight squashes each cartilage disk by as much as 2/5 in (1 cm) each day. When you lie down, the disks expand to their normal position.

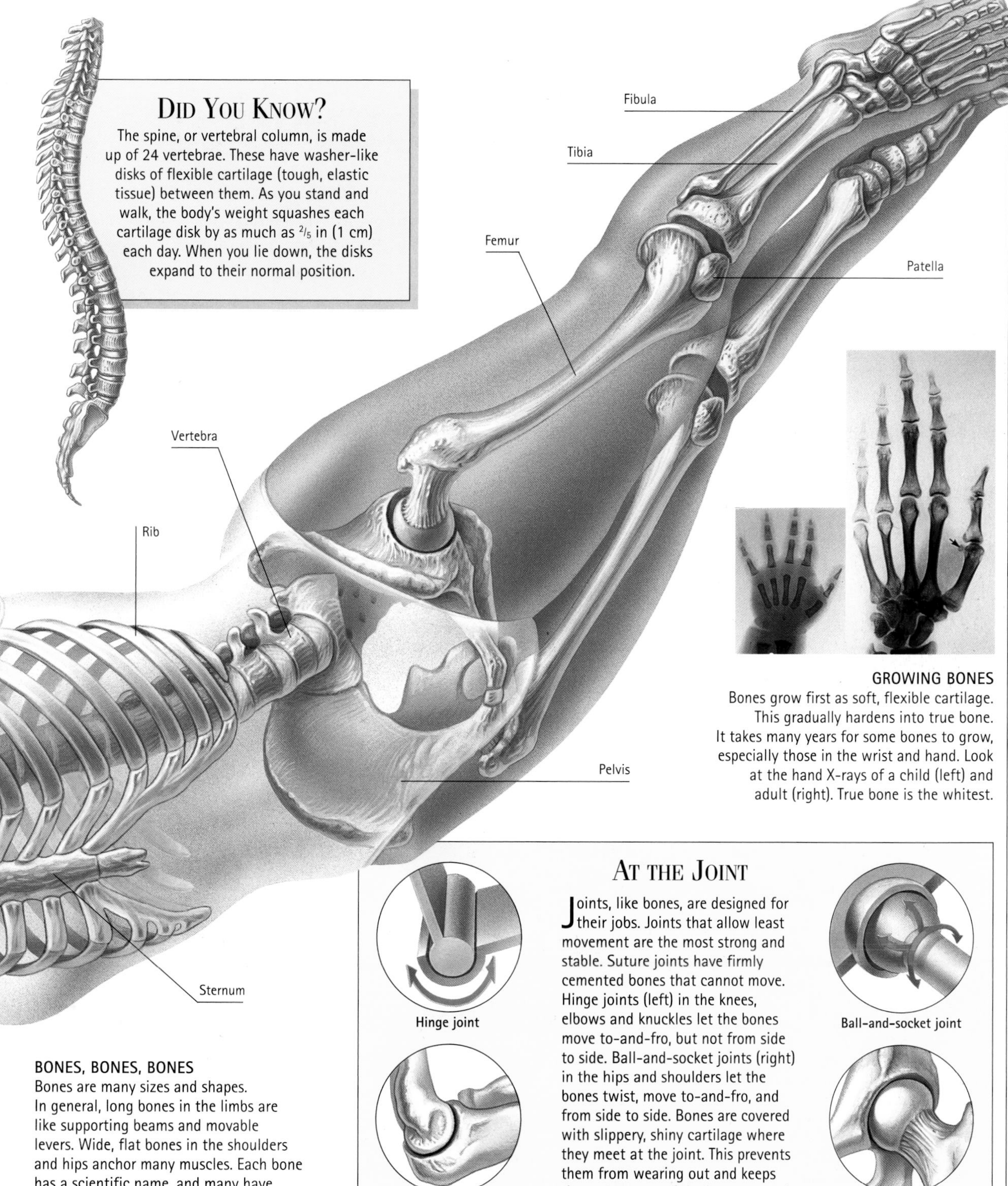

GROWING BONES

Bones grow first as soft, flexible cartilage. This gradually hardens into true bone. It takes many years for some bones to grow, especially those in the wrist and hand. Look at the hand X-rays of a child (left) and adult (right). True bone is the whitest.

At the Joint

Joints, like bones, are designed for their jobs. Joints that allow least movement are the most strong and stable. Suture joints have firmly cemented bones that cannot move. Hinge joints (left) in the knees, elbows and knuckles let the bones move to-and-fro, but not from side to side. Ball-and-socket joints (right) in the hips and shoulders let the bones twist, move to-and-fro, and from side to side. Bones are covered with slippery, shiny cartilage where they meet at the joint. This prevents them from wearing out and keeps the movements of the bones smooth.

BONES, BONES, BONES

Bones are many sizes and shapes. In general, long bones in the limbs are like supporting beams and movable levers. Wide, flat bones in the shoulders and hips anchor many muscles. Each bone has a scientific name, and many have common names, too. The patella, for example, is usually called the kneecap.

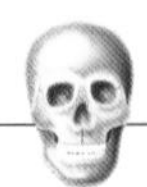

Muscle Power

Every movement you make uses muscles. They allow you to blink, jump, eat, run and sing. Your body has three different kinds of muscles. Cardiac muscle in the heart squeezes life-giving blood around the body. Smooth muscle in the walls of the digestive tract massages food along. The walls of other internal tubes and bags, such as the arteries and lungs, also contain smooth muscle. The most common kind of muscle is skeletal, or striped, muscle. You have about 640 skeletal muscles and these make up two-fifths of your body weight. Some are long, thin and straplike; others bulge in the middle, or are flat and sheet-shaped. Skeletal muscles are joined to bones or to each other. When they contract, they pull on the bones and other tissues, and let you hoist up a huge weight or tie a shoelace.

PULLING TOGETHER
Many muscles work in pairs. For example, the biceps pulls the forearm bone to bend the elbow. Its opposing partner, the triceps, pulls the other way to straighten the elbow. Muscles must shorten, or contract, to create movement.

Biceps contract
Triceps relax
Biceps relax
Triceps contract

Trapezius
Deltoid
Hamstring
Gastrocnemius
Triceps
Gluteus maximus
Rectus abdominis
Achilles tendon

LAYERS OF MUSCLES
Dozens of skeletal muscles lie just under the skin. Their narrowed ends form ropelike tendons that anchor them firmly to bones. The muscles crisscross and intertwine to form layers all over the body.

Did You Know?

The biggest muscle in the body is the gluteus maximus, which is in the buttock and upper thigh.
The smallest muscle is the stapedius. This is attached to the tiny stirrup bone, deep in the ear.

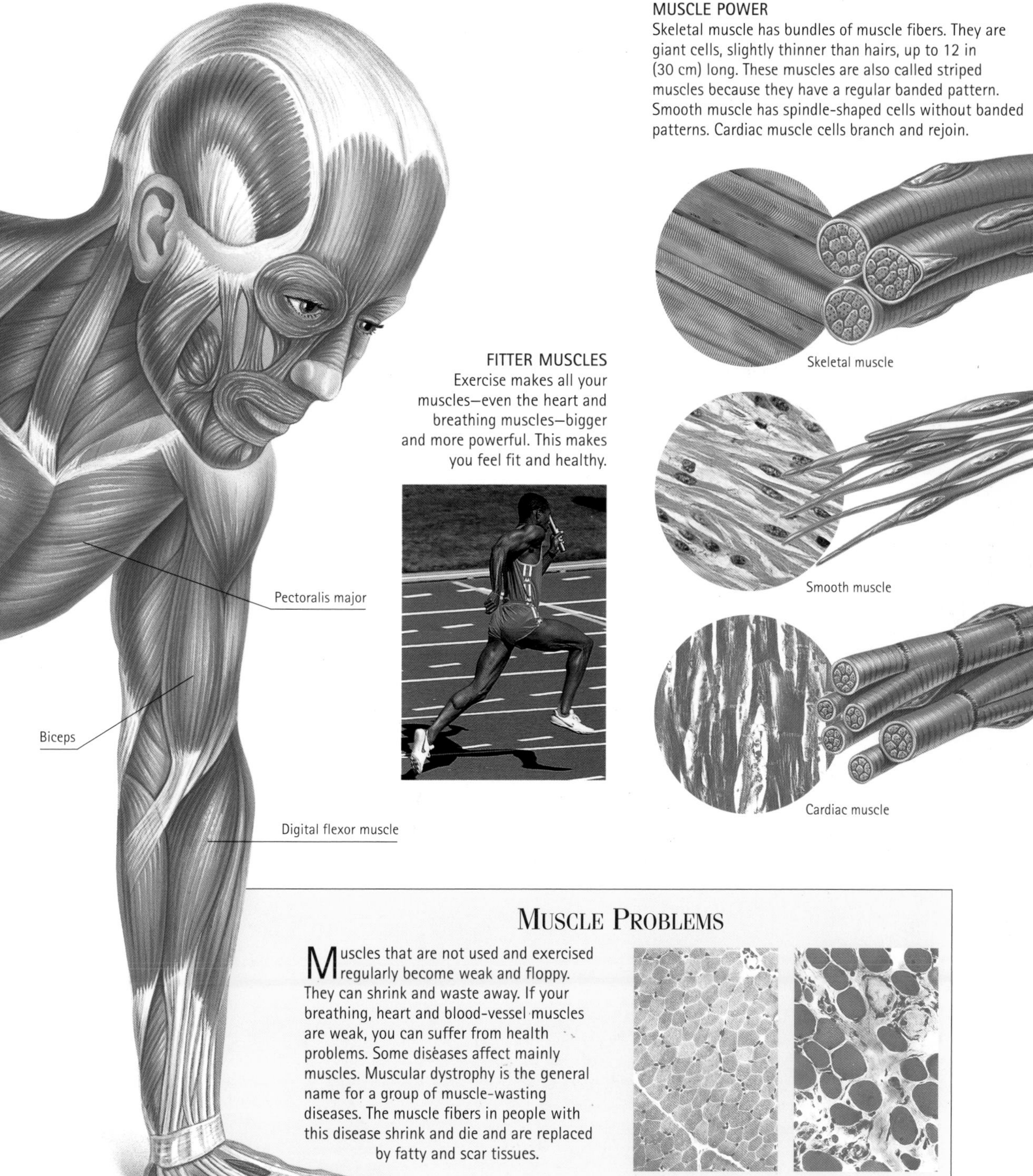

MUSCLE POWER

Skeletal muscle has bundles of muscle fibers. They are giant cells, slightly thinner than hairs, up to 12 in (30 cm) long. These muscles are also called striped muscles because they have a regular banded pattern. Smooth muscle has spindle-shaped cells without banded patterns. Cardiac muscle cells branch and rejoin.

FITTER MUSCLES

Exercise makes all your muscles—even the heart and breathing muscles—bigger and more powerful. This makes you feel fit and healthy.

Muscle Problems

Muscles that are not used and exercised regularly become weak and floppy. They can shrink and waste away. If your breathing, heart and blood-vessel muscles are weak, you can suffer from health problems. Some diseases affect mainly muscles. Muscular dystrophy is the general name for a group of muscle-wasting diseases. The muscle fibers in people with this disease shrink and die and are replaced by fatty and scar tissues.

Healthy muscle

Muscular dystrophy

Discover more in On the Move

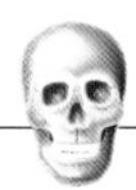

THE ULTIMATE STRUCTURE

Skin Deep

Skin is the body's largest and heaviest organ. It covers almost 21 1/2 sq ft (2 sq m) on an adult, and weighs up to 9 lb (4 kg). It varies in thickness from 1/50 in (0.5 mm) on the eyelids to 1/5 in (5 mm) on the soles of the feet. Skin keeps in body fluids, salts and soft tissues. It keeps out dirt, germs, water and most harmful rays from the sun. It protects the delicate inner parts of the body against wear and tear, knocks and physical damage, and extremes of temperature. Skin also helps the body to maintain a constant temperature of 98.6°F (37°C). It turns flushed and sweaty to lose extra warmth, or goes pale to save heat. It also provides the body's sense of touch, so that we can detect danger and stay out of harm's way.

ONLY ONE YOU

The ridged patterns of fingertip skin are fingerprints. They help to grip small objects and to identify you. No two fingerprints are the same. The skin replaces itself each month, but fingerprints remain through life.

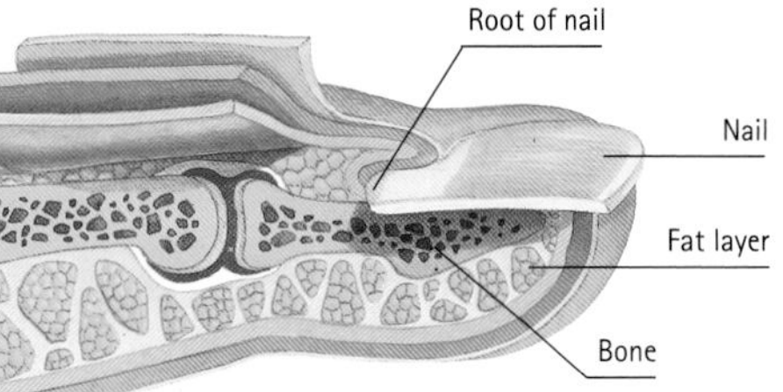

AT YOUR FINGERTIPS

A fingernail grows from a fold in the skin at the nail's root. It stays attached along the nail bed. Like a hair, a nail is dead. The nail bed and surrounding skin feel touch and pressure.

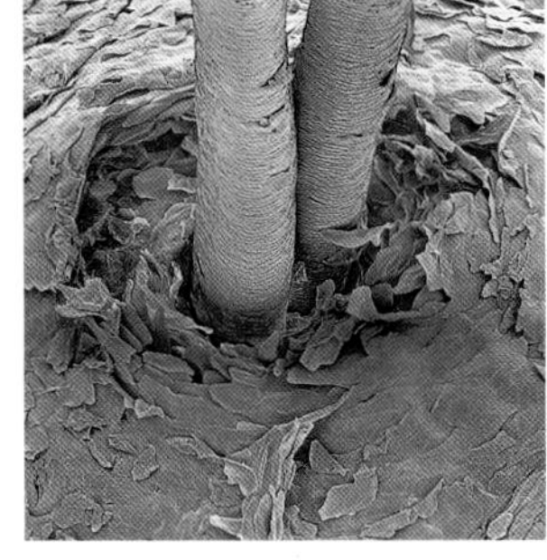

LOSING HAIR

Hairs, nails and the tough, dead cells at the skin's surface are all made from a body protein called keratin. An average scalp hair (above) lives for three years before it falls out and is replaced by a new one.

HAIR TYPES

The kind of hair you have depends mainly on its shape. Viewed under a microscope, a cross section of curly hair looks square, wavy hair looks oval and straight hair is circular. Like skin, hair color is determined by melanin.

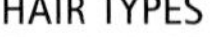

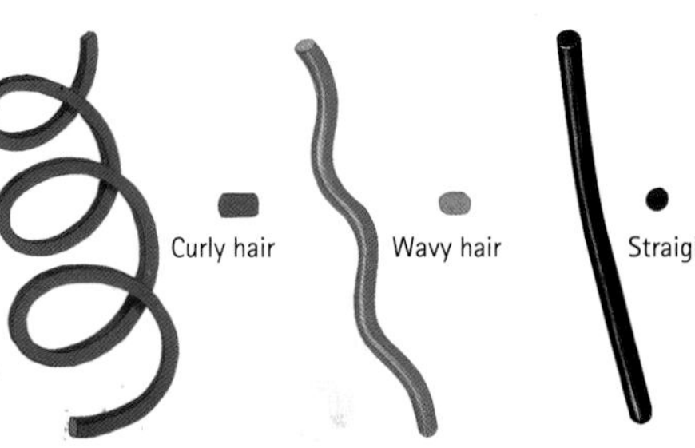

SEEING INTO SKIN

This close-up of skin shows its two main layers. The epidermis is made of hard, tough cells. A top layer of dead cells rubs off and is replaced by cells multiplying below. The dermis contains many tiny parts such as blood vessels and nerves.

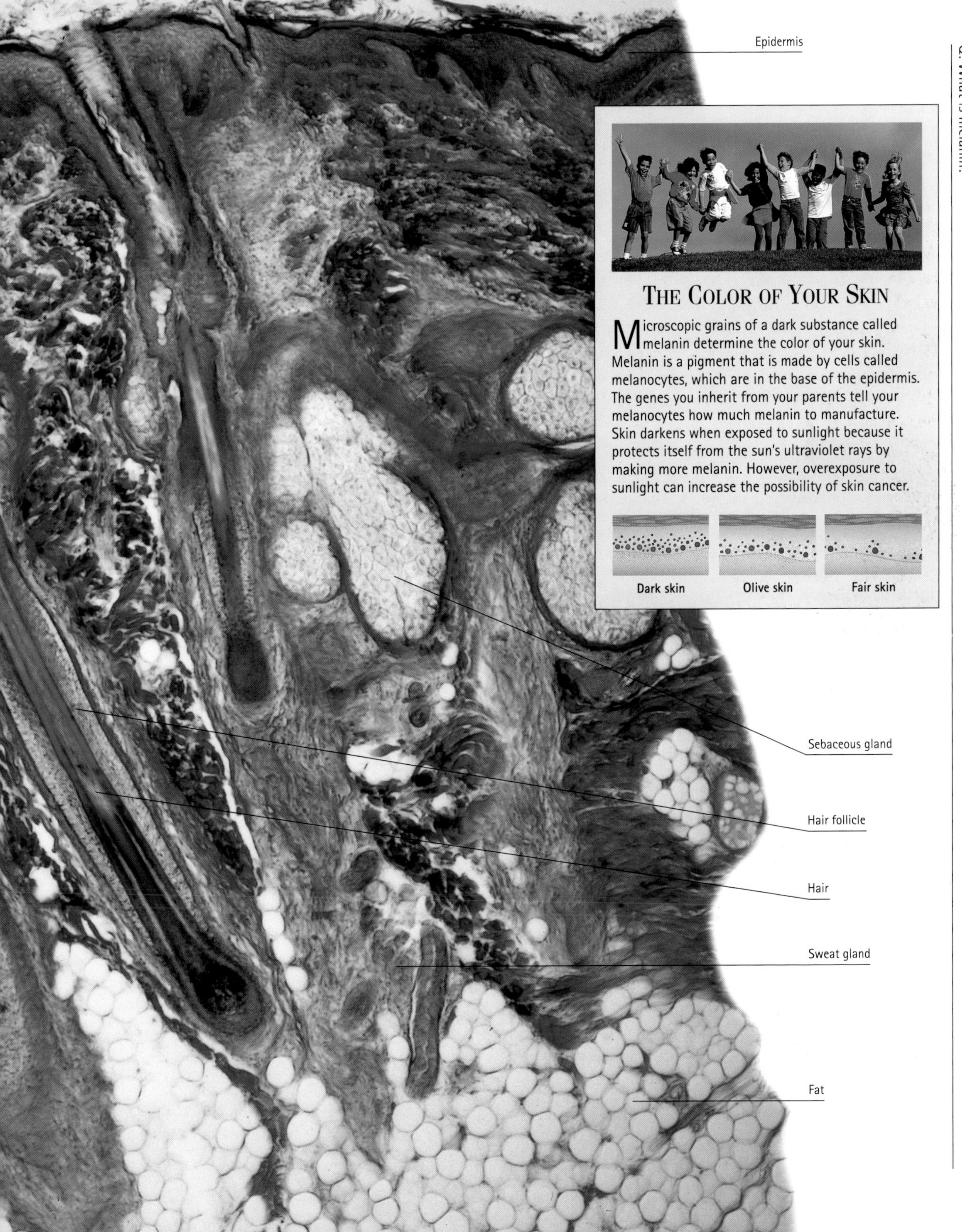

The Color of Your Skin

Microscopic grains of a dark substance called melanin determine the color of your skin. Melanin is a pigment that is made by cells called melanocytes, which are in the base of the epidermis. The genes you inherit from your parents tell your melanocytes how much melanin to manufacture. Skin darkens when exposed to sunlight because it protects itself from the sun's ultraviolet rays by making more melanin. However, overexposure to sunlight can increase the possibility of skin cancer.

• FROM THE OUTSIDE WORLD •

Looking Around

Five main senses tell the body about the outside world: sight, hearing, smell, taste and touch. Sight is the most important. Two-thirds of all the information processed in the human brain comes in through the eyes. Light enters through the clear, domed cornea at the front. It then passes through an adjustable hole, called the pupil, which is situated in a ring of muscle, called the iris. A lens focuses the light rays so that they cast a clear, sharp image on the retina, which lines the back of the eyeball. In the retina, about 130 million light-sensitive cells generate nerve signals when light rays shine on them. Signals are then sent along the optic nerve to the brain. The images formed on the retina are upside down (like those inside a camera), but the brain interprets them the right way up.

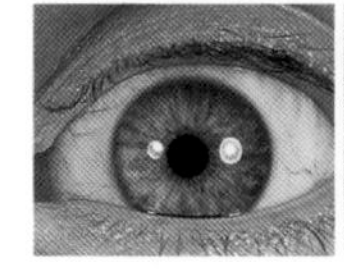

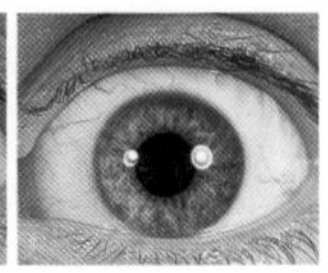

BRIGHT AND DIM
The iris adjusts the pupil. The pupil shrinks in bright conditions to keep too much light from damaging the retina (left), and widens in dim conditions to let in as much light as possible (right).

RETINA REVEALED
A doctor or optician sees into the eye with an ophthalmoscope. This shows the retina and blood vessels branching over the eye (left) and gives the doctor valuable information about the eye's health.

Optic nerve

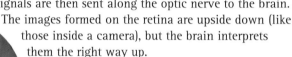

Eye muscle

Retina

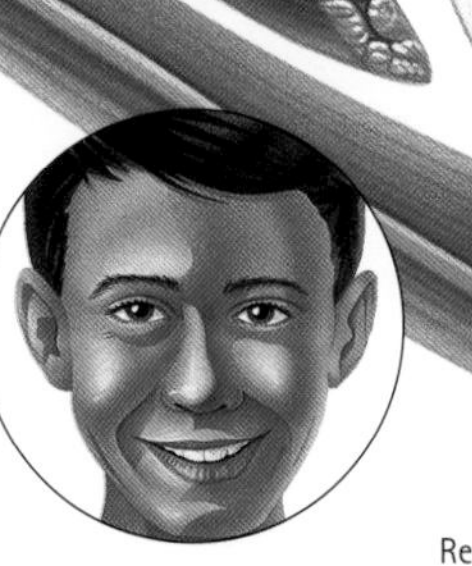

CELLS THAT SEE
The retina has two kinds of light-sensitive cells, called rods (yellow) and cones (blue). Rods work in dim conditions and cannot see colors. Cones can detect colors and fine details, but only function in bright light.

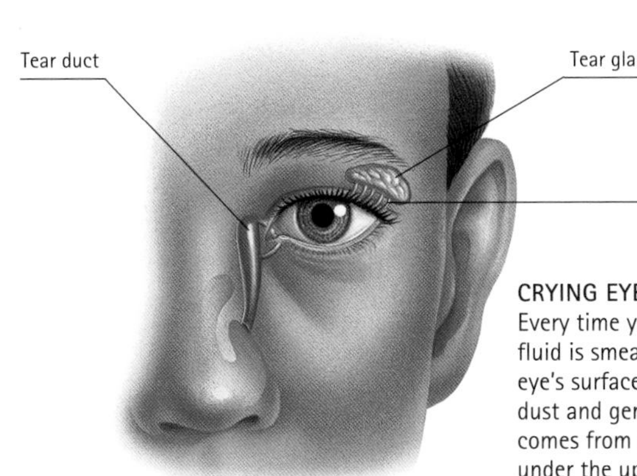

CRYING EYES

Every time you blink, tear fluid is smeared over the eye's surface to wash away dust and germs. The fluid comes from the tear gland, under the upper eyelid. It drains through tear ducts into the nose. This is why crying makes you sniff.

Eye Problems

Sometimes the eyeball is not the correct shape. If the eyeball is too long, the lens is unable to focus on distant objects and this causes near-sightedness (myopia). If the eyeball is too short, it causes far-sightedness (hyperopia). Glasses or contact lenses are used to correct these problems. If the light-sensitive rods and cones in your retina do not work properly, you can have problems seeing colors. This can cause confusion between reds and greens. Tests using dots of different colors (left) can reveal color blindness.

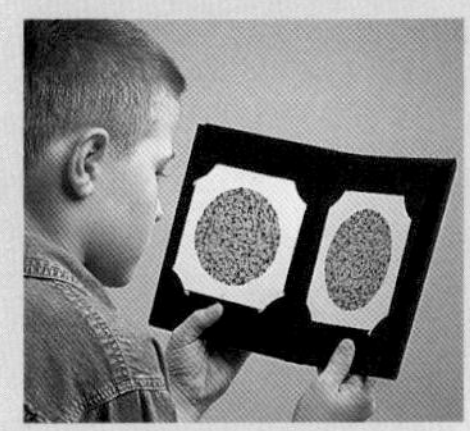

Sclera

Pupil

Iris

Cornea

Lens

LOOKING INSIDE

The main part of the eyeball is filled with a clear, jelly-like fluid, called vitreous humor. It keeps the eye firm and well shaped. The sclera is the eye's "white," its tough outer covering. Eye muscles behind the eyeball move it within its bony socket in the skull.

Did You Know?

The human eye has been a powerful symbol for many cultures through the centuries. Many people believed that dreadful things, such as disease or death, could happen if someone was looked at with the evil eye. Today, some cultures still paint eyes on their fishing boats to ward off the bad luck of evil eyes.

Discover more in The Control Center

• FROM THE OUTSIDE WORLD •

Listening In

Eyes see light, but they cannot see sound. Sound travels as invisible waves of high and low air pressure and is detected by your ears. The outer ear funnels these waves into the ear canal. They bounce off the eardrum, a small flap of taut skin, and make it vibrate. The eardrum is joined to a tiny bone called the hammer. The vibrations pass by the hammer, and two other miniature bones, the anvil and stirrup. After passing through a flexible membrane called the oval window, the vibrations move into a snail-shaped, fluid-filled area called the cochlea. Ripples are created in the cochlea's fluid. The ripples move microscopic hairs that stick out from rows of hair cells in the fluid. The hairs' movements generate nerve signals that pass along the auditory nerve to the brain.

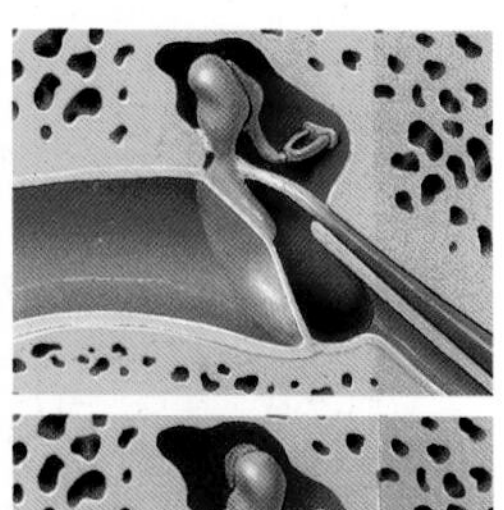

EQUAL PRESSURE
The middle-ear chamber is a tiny air pocket behind the eardrum. The Eustachian tube links it to the throat, and so to outside air.

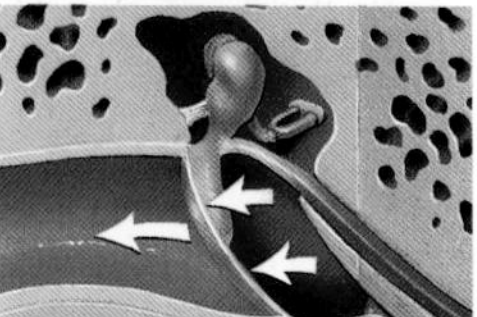

PRESSURE UP
The outside air pressure is less when you are up high. Because the middle-ear pressure stays the same, the eardrum bulges and your hearing fades.

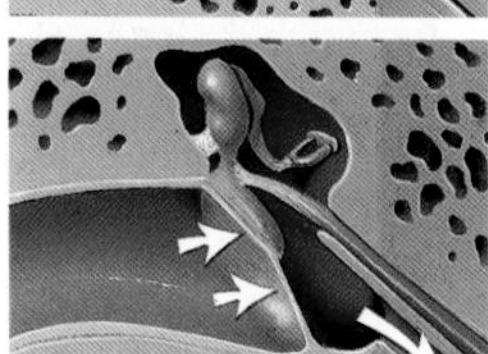

PRESSURE DOWN
If you swallow hard, the Eustachian tube opens. Air rushes out of the middle ear to relieve the pressure. Your eardrum "pops" back to normal.

EYES AND EARS
The ear canal of the outer ear is $1\frac{1}{5}$ in (3 cm) long. This means the delicate hearing parts of the middle and inner ear are set deep in the head, almost behind the eye. They are well protected inside the thick skull bone.

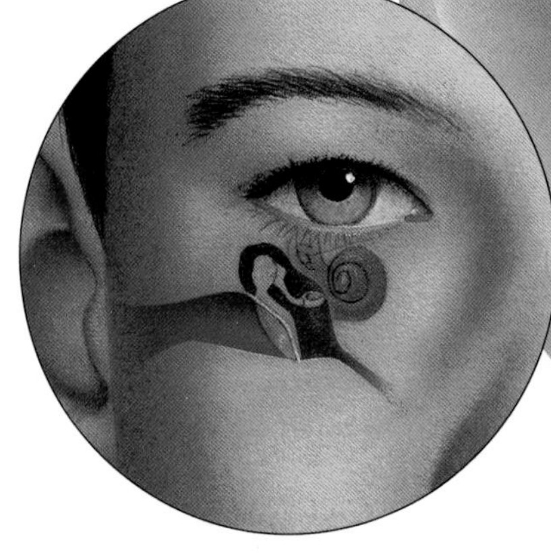

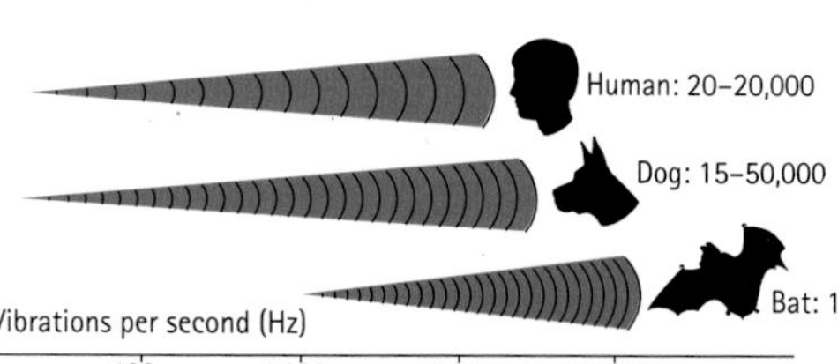

HEARING SILENCE
The pitch or frequency of sound, from low to high, is measured in vibrations per second, or hertz (Hz). Human ears hear about 20 to 20,000 Hz, but animals can hear even higher pitched, or ultrasonic, sounds.

INSIDE THE EAR
The outer ear is large and obvious and guides sound waves into the ear canal. Three tiny ear bones vibrate in the air-filled middle-ear chamber, which is set into the skull bone. The snail-shaped cochlea converts vibrations to nerve signals.

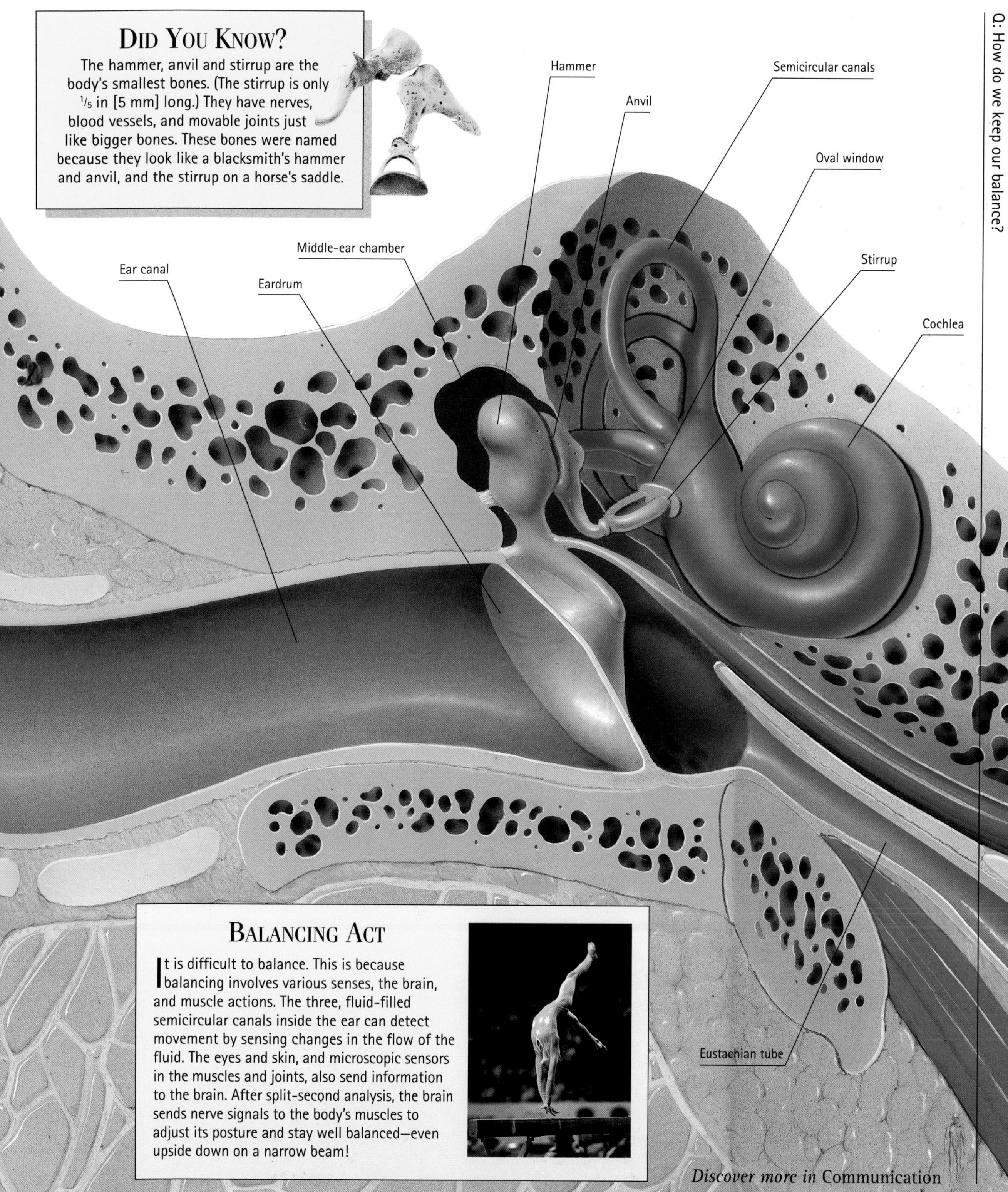

Did You Know?

The hammer, anvil and stirrup are the body's smallest bones. (The stirrup is only $^{1}/_{5}$ in [5 mm] long.) They have nerves, blood vessels, and movable joints just like bigger bones. These bones were named because they look like a blacksmith's hammer and anvil, and the stirrup on a horse's saddle.

Balancing Act

It is difficult to balance. This is because balancing involves various senses, the brain, and muscle actions. The three, fluid-filled semicircular canals inside the ear can detect movement by sensing changes in the flow of the fluid. The eyes and skin, and microscopic sensors in the muscles and joints, also send information to the brain. After split-second analysis, the brain sends nerve signals to the body's muscles to adjust its posture and stay well balanced—even upside down on a narrow beam!

Q: How do we keep our balance?

Discover more in Communication

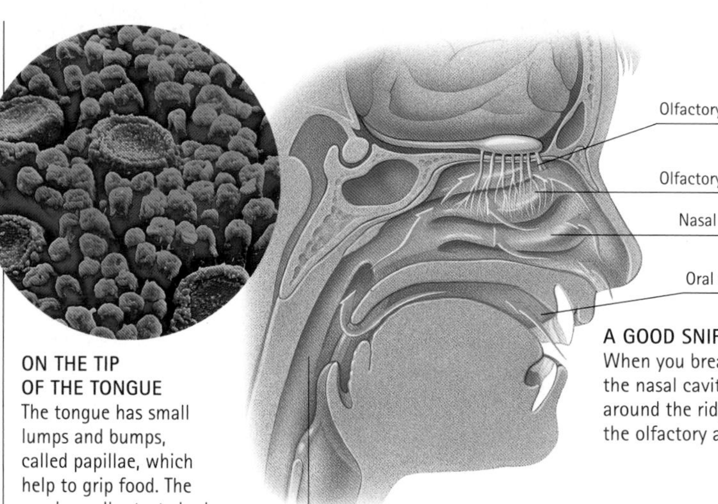

ON THE TIP OF THE TONGUE
The tongue has small lumps and bumps, called papillae, which help to grip food. The much smaller taste buds are set into the surface around their edges.

A GOOD SNIFF
When you breathe normally, air flows into the nasal cavity. To smell or sniff, air swirls around the ridged bones in the nose up to the olfactory areas in the nasal cavity's roof.

DID YOU KNOW?

The flavor-sensing cells in taste buds are replaced after ten days. But as the human body ages, the cell replacement system becomes less efficient. This means that food often tastes bland and without flavor to older people.

• FROM THE OUTSIDE WORLD •

Taste Sensations

Taste and smell work in similar ways. They are both chemosenses, which means they respond to certain chemical substances. Taste detects flavors in food and drink. As you chew, watery saliva dissolves the flavors from foods. These flavors are picked up by more than 8,000 taste buds in the tongue's upper surface. Each taste bud has up to 50 chemical-sensing cells clustered together like segments of an orange. Smell detects odors floating in the air. The different odors around you land on two thumbnail-sized patches inside the top of the nose, called the olfactory areas. Taste and smell can help to warn you if food or drink is bad. They also detect delicious aromas and flavors. Smell alone can also warn you of danger, such as smoke from a fire.

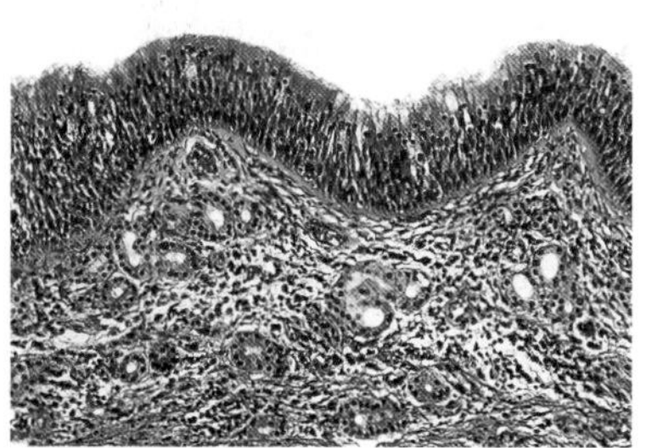

HAIRS THAT SMELL
Each olfactory area has 10 million cells that detect chemicals. Each cell has a tuft of up to 20 long hairs, called cilia. Different smells settle on these hairs and trigger nerve signals. An average person can identify 10,000 different smells.

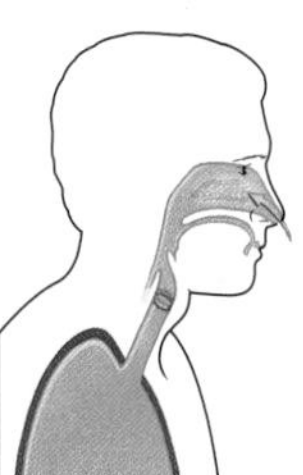

AAAAA...
You sneeze when dust, animal fur or plant pollen irritates the sensitive lining of the nose.

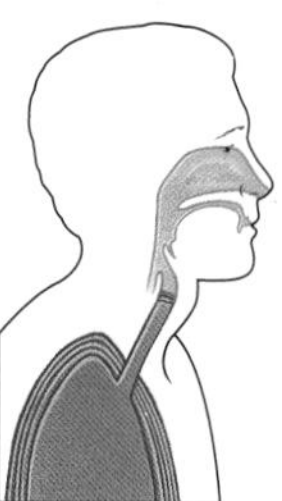

AAAAA...
The throat and windpipe close. Muscles in the chest and abdomen press the lungs and squash the air inside.

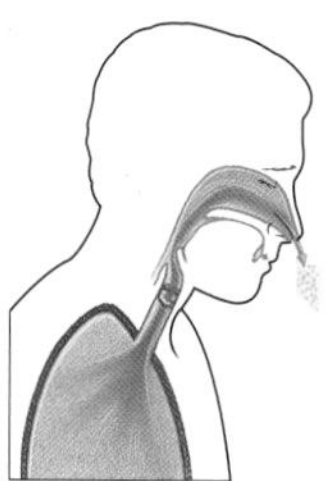

CHOOO!
When the windpipe and throat open again, high-pressure air blasts through the nose to blow away the irritants.

TASTES ON THE BRAIN
When the tongue's taste buds detect certain flavors, they send nerve signals along sensory nerves to the taste centers in the brain. These sort the signals and identify the taste. Smell signals run from the olfactory areas in the top of the nose to the olfactory bulb. This sorts out some of the smells and passes the signals on to the olfactory centers in the brain.

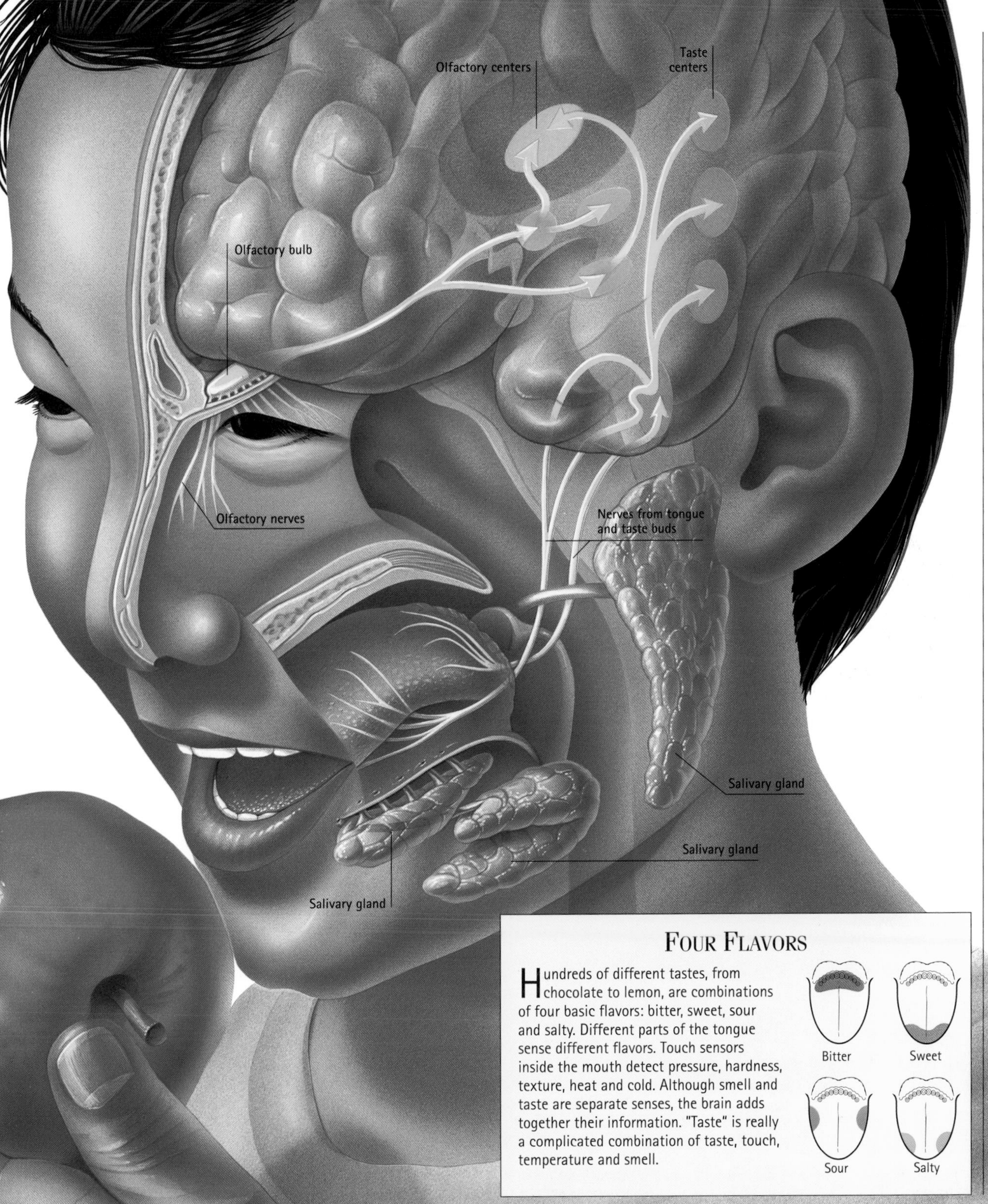

Four Flavors

Hundreds of different tastes, from chocolate to lemon, are combinations of four basic flavors: bitter, sweet, sour and salty. Different parts of the tongue sense different flavors. Touch sensors inside the mouth detect pressure, hardness, texture, heat and cold. Although smell and taste are separate senses, the brain adds together their information. "Taste" is really a complicated combination of taste, touch, temperature and smell.

Q: What are the four basic flavors our tongue can sense?

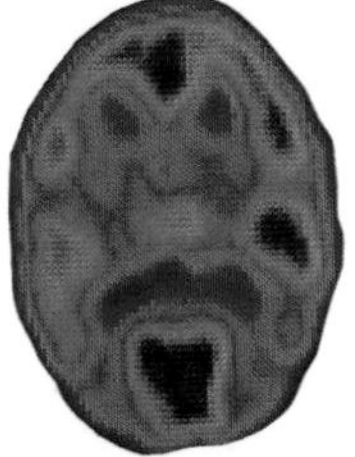

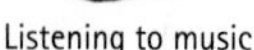

Listening to music

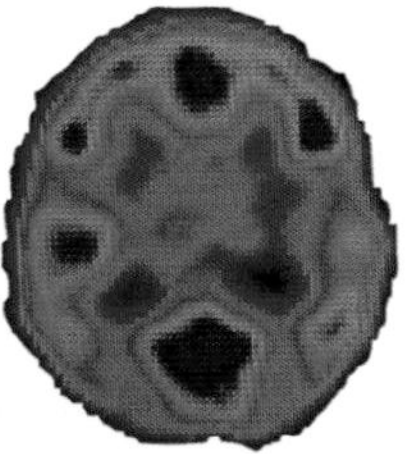

Understanding language

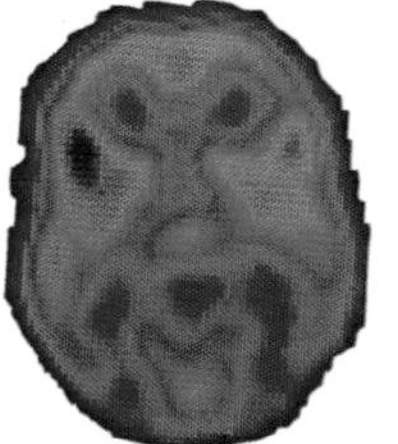

Eyes closed

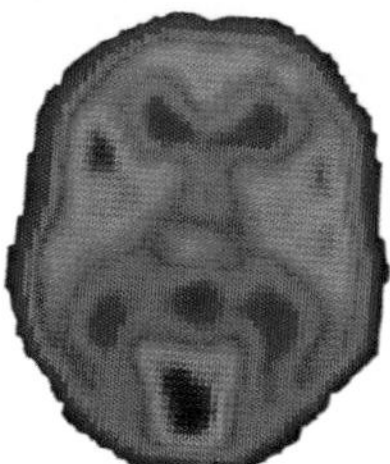

Eyes open

SEEING THINKING
PET (Positron Emission Tomography) scans show which parts of the brain are busiest as the owner carries out different thoughts and actions. They help to "map" the jobs of various brain parts.

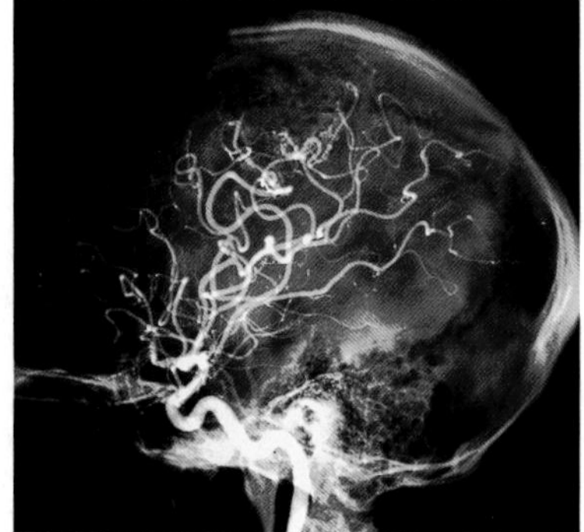

BRAIN'S BLOOD SUPPLY
An angiogram X-ray (above) shows arteries bringing blood to the brain. These angiograms can help to identify problems, such as strokes and brain tumors. If the blood supply to the brain stops for more than just a few minutes, parts of the brain begin to die.

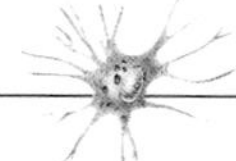

• TOTAL CONTROL •

The Control Center

The brain is the control center of the body. All the nerve signals from the eyes, ears and other sense organs travel to the brain to be sorted and analyzed. These signals tell the brain about conditions outside the body. The brain decides what to do, and sends nerve signals to the muscles that control body movements. There are also sensors inside the body that send nerve signals to the brain, telling it about body conditions such as temperature, blood pressure, and amounts of oxygen, carbon dioxide, nutrients and fluids. The brain automatically controls breathing, heartbeat, digestion and many other inner processes. When nutrients or fluids run low, your brain makes you feel hungry or thirsty. The brain is the place where you think, remember, work out problems, have feelings, imagine and daydream.

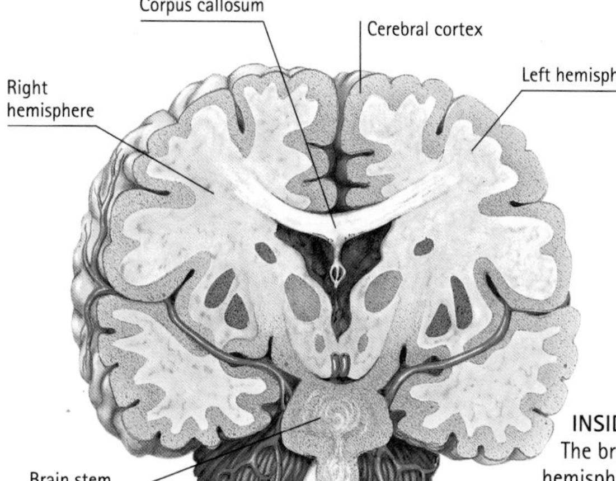

INSIDE THE BRAIN
The brain has two parts called cerebral hemispheres. The two hemispheres are linked by the corpus callosum, a bridge of 100 million nerve fibers. Most conscious thoughts and feelings take place in the outer gray layer, called the cerebral cortex. The cerebellum, at the rear of the brain, helps to keep body movements coordinated. The brain stem connects the brain to the spinal cord.

Did You Know?

The brain is one-fiftieth of the weight of the whole body, but it consumes one-fifth of all the energy used by the body. This means the brain is ten times more energy-hungry than any other body part. Whether you are thinking or fast asleep, your brain is using energy constantly.

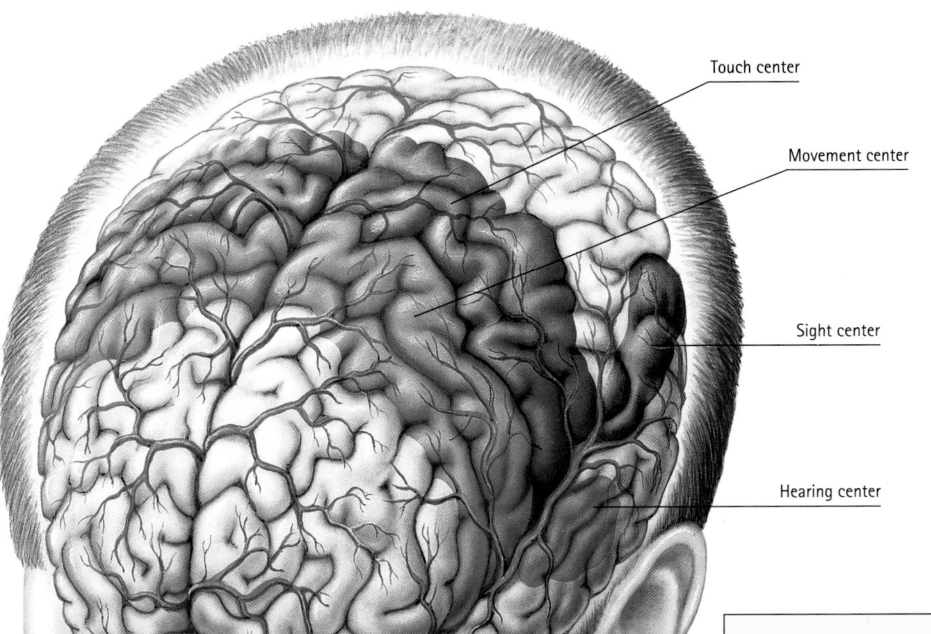

BRAIN CENTERS
The cerebral cortex looks the same all over, but different parts, or centers, do different jobs. The sight center receives and analyzes nerve signals from the eyes. This is where you really "see." Other senses, such as hearing and touch, have their own centers. The movement center sends out signals to the body's muscles.

SMALL BUT COMPLEX

The brain's touch and movement centers are divided into parts. Each part deals with nerve signals coming from a certain area of the body, such as the lips. But the parts are not in proportion to the size of the body area. Small but sensitive areas, such as the lips, can have more brain to deal with their signals than a whole leg does!

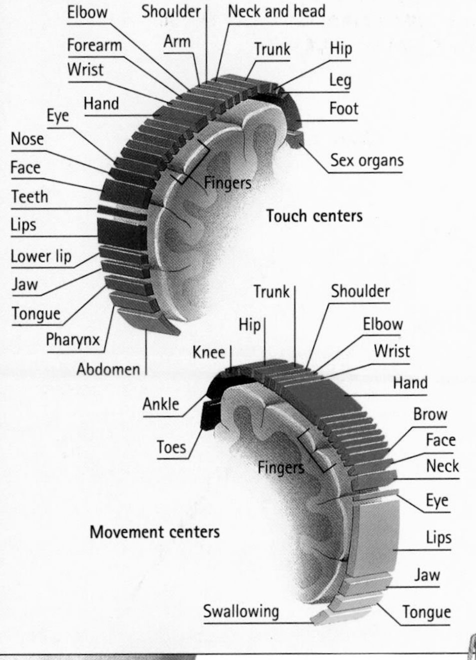

Discover more in On the Move

Q: What are the two main parts of the brain?

HOT FOOT

Long ago, people believed that nerves were tubes of fluid flowing to and from the brain. They thought this fluid carried messages around the body. If you burned your foot, for example, the fluid told your brain to pull your leg away.

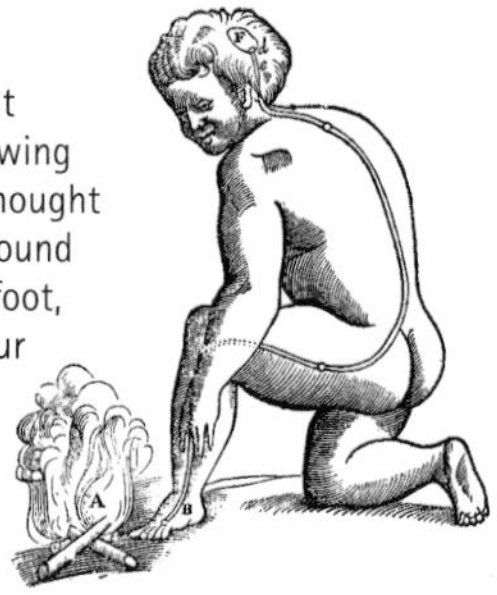

Did You Know?

If you sit in an awkward position, the nerves are sometimes squashed and blood vessels cannot supply vital nutrients and oxygen. A part of your body may "go to sleep," or feel numb. When you change your position, the pressure is relieved, blood flows, and the nerves begin to work again.

What a Nerve!

The brain is not isolated in its curved casket of skull bones. It is linked to all parts of the body by nerves. Nerves are long, pale and thin, like pieces of shiny string. The main nerve is the spinal cord, a bundle of millions of nerve cells with long, wirelike fibers. The spinal cord is about 18 in (45 cm) long, and is as thick as an index finger. Branches of nerves connect it to the skin, muscles and other body parts, and the upper end merges with the brain. The lower end tapers into a stringy cord inside the vertebrae (backbones) of the lower back. The billions of nerve cells in the brain, spinal cord and nerves are linked into a vast web, or network, which carries tiny electrical nerve signals.

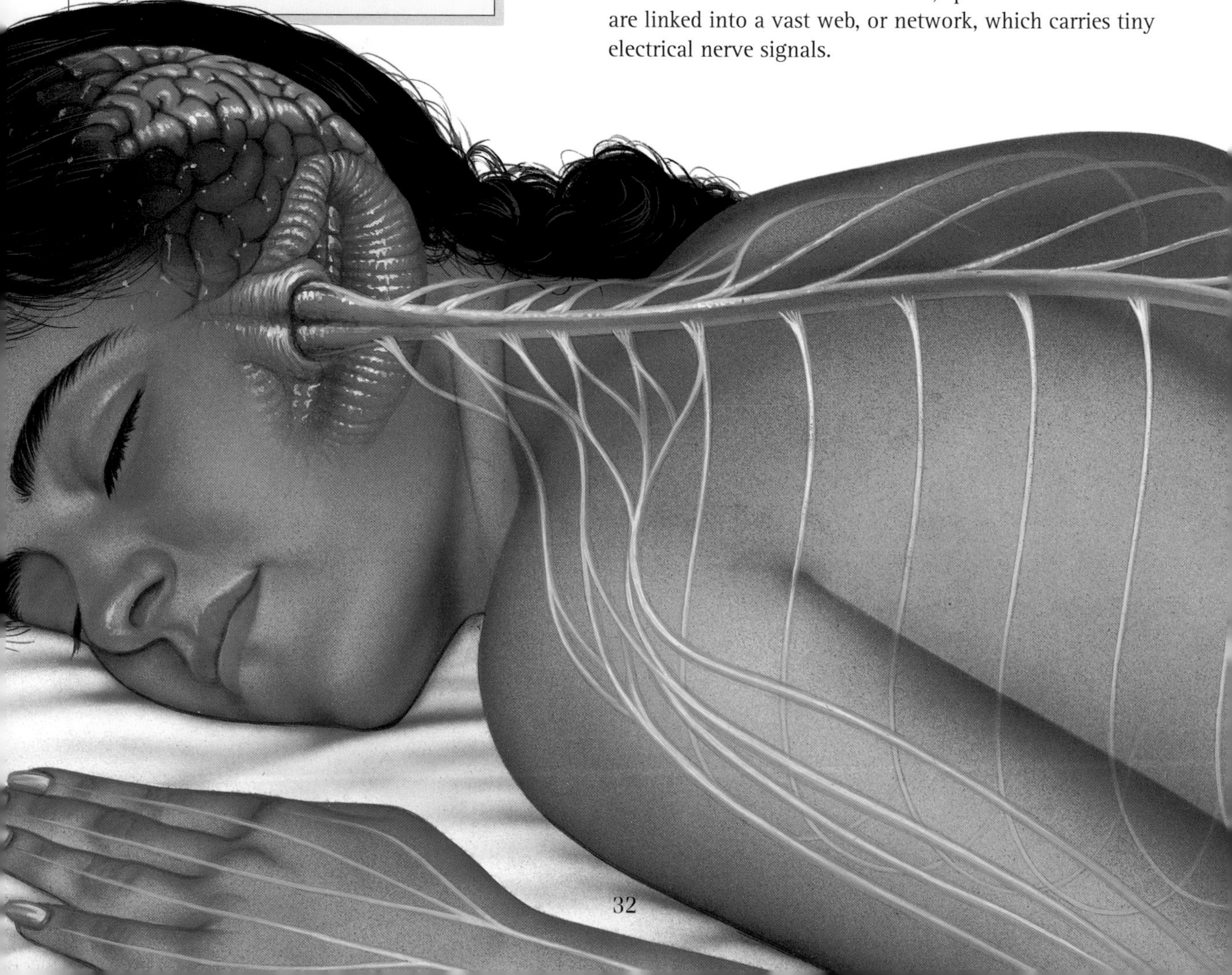

NEURAL NETWORK

Each nerve cell has spidery dendrites that gather signals from other nerve cells at synapses. The signals travel along the cell's main wirelike section, called the axon, before passing on to other nerve cells.

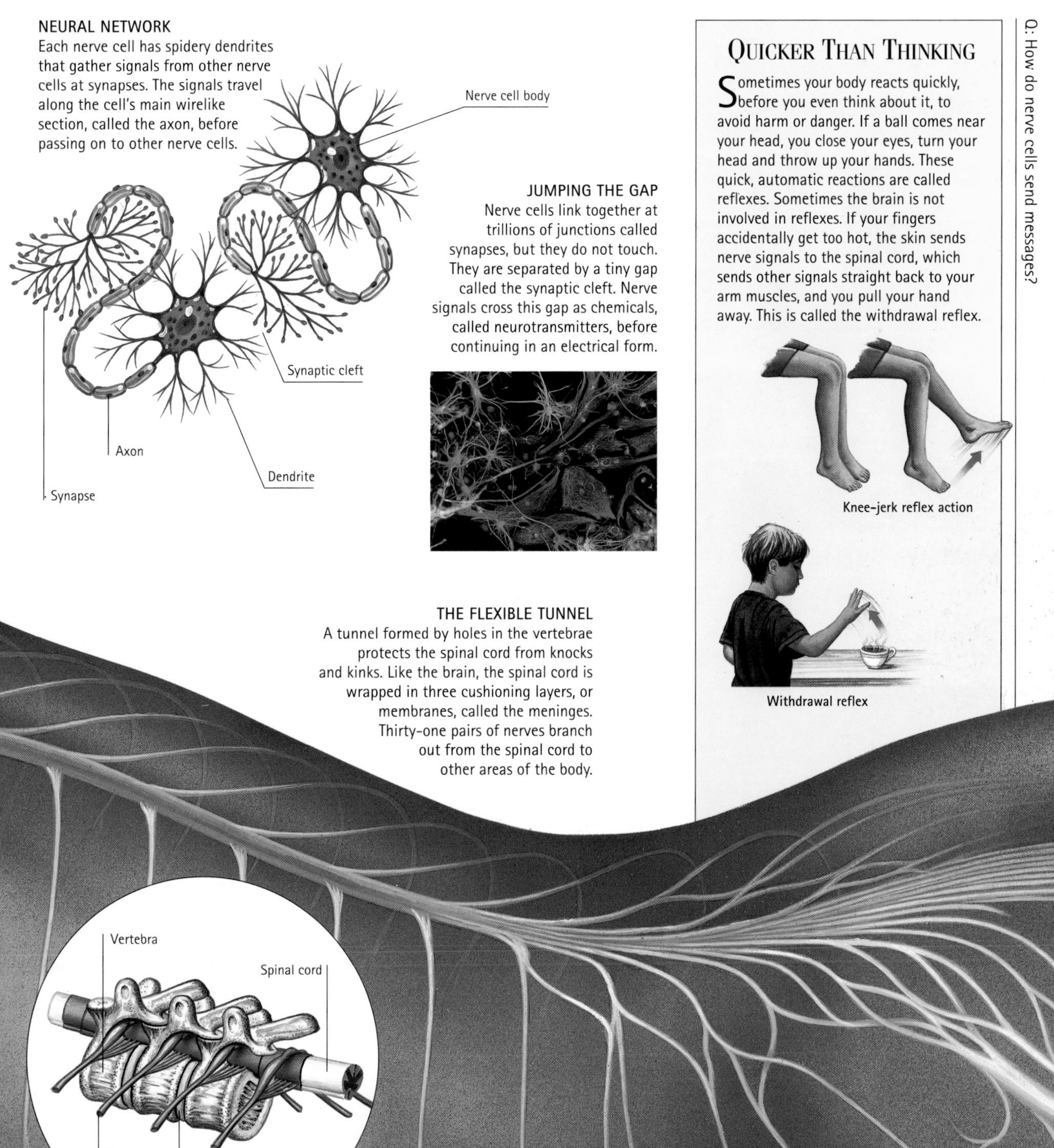

JUMPING THE GAP

Nerve cells link together at trillions of junctions called synapses, but they do not touch. They are separated by a tiny gap called the synaptic cleft. Nerve signals cross this gap as chemicals, called neurotransmitters, before continuing in an electrical form.

THE FLEXIBLE TUNNEL

A tunnel formed by holes in the vertebrae protects the spinal cord from knocks and kinks. Like the brain, the spinal cord is wrapped in three cushioning layers, or membranes, called the meninges. Thirty-one pairs of nerves branch out from the spinal cord to other areas of the body.

Quicker Than Thinking

Sometimes your body reacts quickly, before you even think about it, to avoid harm or danger. If a ball comes near your head, you close your eyes, turn your head and throw up your hands. These quick, automatic reactions are called reflexes. Sometimes the brain is not involved in reflexes. If your fingers accidentally get too hot, the skin sends nerve signals to the spinal cord, which sends other signals straight back to your arm muscles, and you pull your hand away. This is called the withdrawal reflex.

Knee-jerk reflex action

Withdrawal reflex

Q: How do nerve cells send messages?

SILENT SPEECH
Some people who cannot hear and have difficulty learning to speak use sign language. Their hand and finger positions can convey letters, letter groups, words, phrases and other information (left).

LETTERS AND WORDS
There are more than 2,000 different written languages. Most of these have an alphabet of basic units called letters, which are combined into groups known as words. Here are just some of the ways the words "the human body" can be written.

Braille

ΤΟ ΑΝΘΡΩΠΙΝΟΝ ΣΩΜΑ
Greek

ТЕЛО ЧЕЛОВЕКА
Russian

人體
Chinese

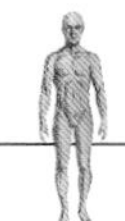

• WORKING TOGETHER •

Communication

Humans communicate with each other every day using sounds and body movements. Most commonly, we share information about the world around us through spoken languages. These are special sounds we make to represent objects, actions, numbers, colors and other features. We use our brains to remember words, put them in the correct order, and make the larynx, or voice box, produce the correct sounds. If a person is unable to speak, he or she can communicate in other ways, often by using sign language. We also have written and pictorial languages, which are signs, symbols and squiggles that represent spoken words. The whole body works together to help us convey our innermost thoughts and feelings through language.

SHAPING SOUNDS
The jaws, tongue, cheeks and lips help to shape sounds, such as words, from the larynx. But not all the sounds from the larynx are words. They can be laughter, sad sobs or screams of pain.

Aaah

Eeee

Oooh

Mmmm

SOUNDS OF SPEECH
The sounds we make come from the larynx at the top of the trachea. It has two vocal cords at its sides. Air passes silently through the wide gap when we breathe normally. When we speak, the muscles pull the cords close together. Air then flows up the trachea making the vocal cords vibrate to produce sounds.

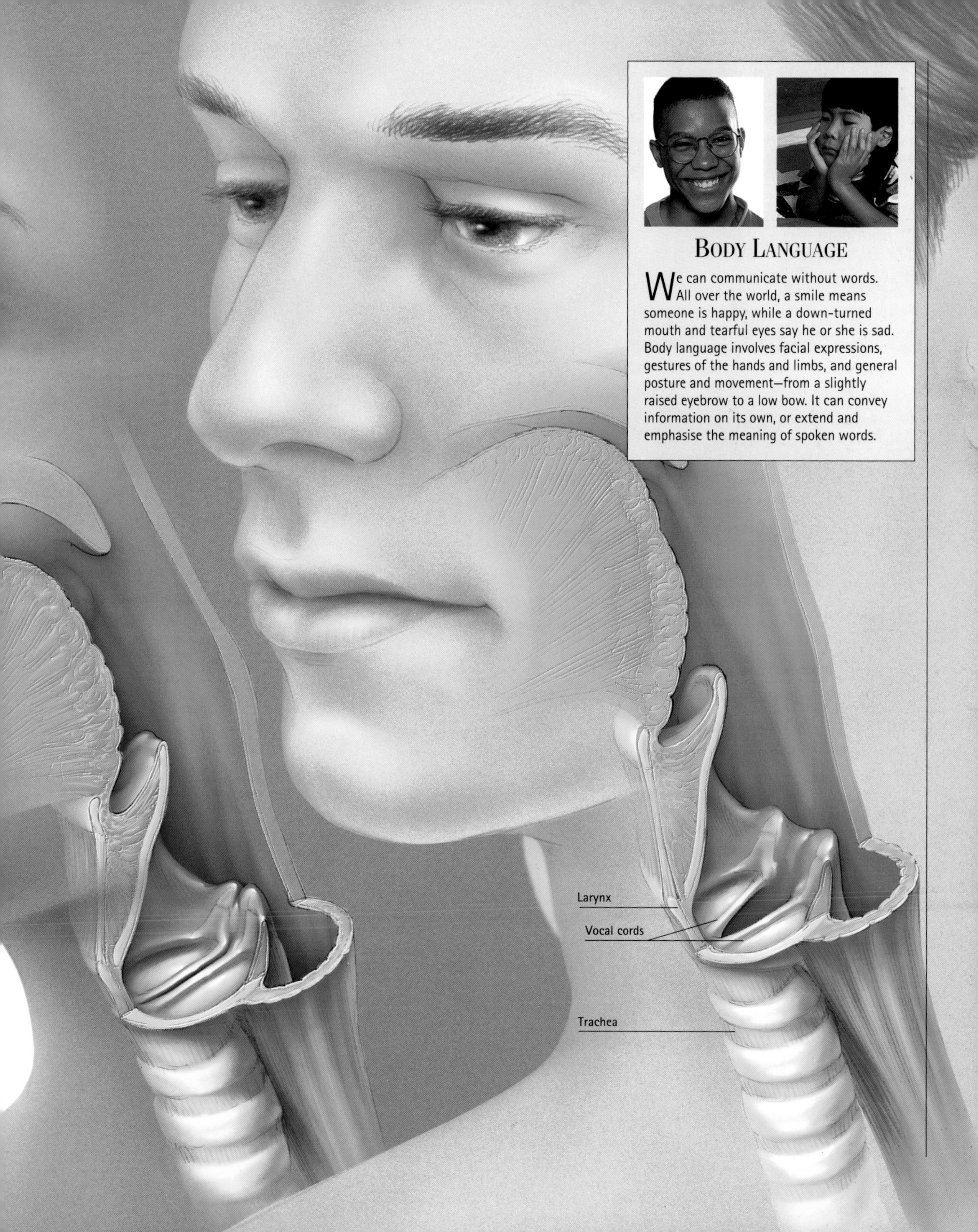

Body Language

We can communicate without words. All over the world, a smile means someone is happy, while a down-turned mouth and tearful eyes say he or she is sad. Body language involves facial expressions, gestures of the hands and limbs, and general posture and movement—from a slightly raised eyebrow to a low bow. It can convey information on its own, or extend and emphasise the meaning of spoken words.

GETTING AROUND
Some people cannot move around easily because they have an injury, a disease or a disability. Wheelchairs and other devices help them to move more freely and to take part in sports.

IN THE SWIM
A dolphin swishes its broad tail with powerful back muscles to surge through the water at high speed. Humans can also swim underwater, but they need the help of diving equipment to stay underwater for long periods.

• WORKING TOGETHER •

On the Move

Your body is constantly on the move. Even when you are resting or sleeping, oxygen, nutrients and other chemicals spread throughout the body, and cells grow, multiply and migrate. The heart pumps blood, lungs breathe and food squeezes through your stomach. When you are awake, your body is also in continuous motion–from glancing quickly to jumping in the air. The body's inner parts work together for movement. The brain sends signals along nerves to muscles, telling them to contract. The muscles need the oxygen and energy-rich sugars that are brought by blood, which is pumped by the heart. The lungs absorb oxygen, while the intestines digest nutrients from food. All of this happens in animals, too. Many animals are built for specialized movements–whales can swim, bats can fly and monkeys can climb. But the human body is probably the best all-rounder. People can do many things and they use their brains to invent special equipment to allow them to do even more.

ON THE RUN
A cheetah can run faster than any other animal. With four long, slim legs and a flexible body, it is built for speed. Humans can run short and long distances, but they are never as fast as the cheetah.

IN THE SKY

Birds can fly because they have extra-light bodies and powerful chest and shoulder muscles. Humans need to use equipment, such as a hang-glider, to fly.

UP THE SLOPE

Sloths hang around in trees all day, and all night, too. Their hooklike claws are made for climbing. Humans can climb, but they often need to use picks, ropes and other equipment.

Sleeping on the Job

Scientists study people to find out what happens when we sleep. They have discovered that the body slows down, and the skeletal muscles are relaxed and still. But the body is still moving and working. The heart pumps blood, lungs breathe air, intestines digest food, kidneys make urine, and millions of electrical signals fly around the brain. Sleep is vital and a person without it will die sooner than a person without food. By the time you are 60, you will have spent 20 years sleeping.

Discover more in Growing Up

• FROM THE BEGINNING •

How Life Begins

The body has systems for digestion, movement and other activities. It also has a system for reproduction. The reproductive system is different in men and women. The parts of the female system are inside the lower abdomen. Glands called ovaries contain egg cells, or ova. The main parts of the male system are just below the lower abdomen. Glands called testicles contain sperm cells, or spermatozoa. Together, one egg and one sperm contain all the information and instructions necessary to create life. The instructions are in the form of genes, which are made from the chemical deoxyribonucleic acid (DNA). When a sperm fertilizes an egg, a baby begins to develop in the woman's womb.

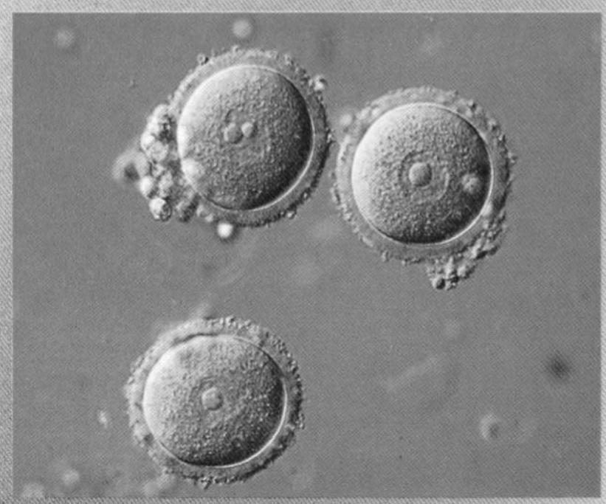

A MASSIVE CELL
The ripe egg is one of the largest cells in the human body. It is full of nutrients for the early stages of a baby's development. Like the sperm, the egg has only a half-set of DNA.

FEMALE PARTS
Each month one ovum, or egg, ripens and passes along the Fallopian tube to the uterus, or womb. The womb lining becomes thick and rich in blood vessels to nourish the fertilized egg as it develops. If the egg is not fertilized, the womb lining is not needed. It breaks down and comes away through the vagina as fluids and blood. This is called menstruation.

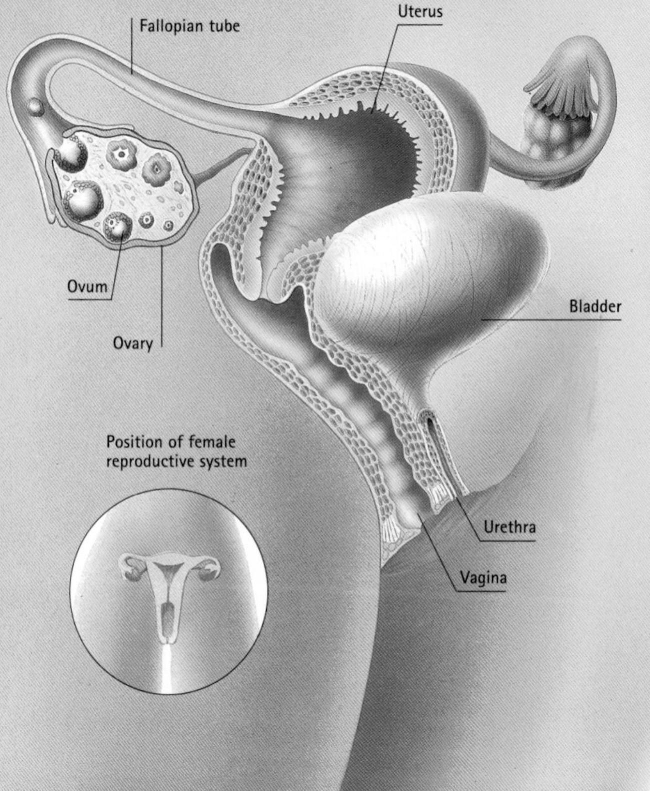

DID YOU KNOW?

An enormous set of instructions—between 100,000 and 200,000 genes—is needed to create a human body.

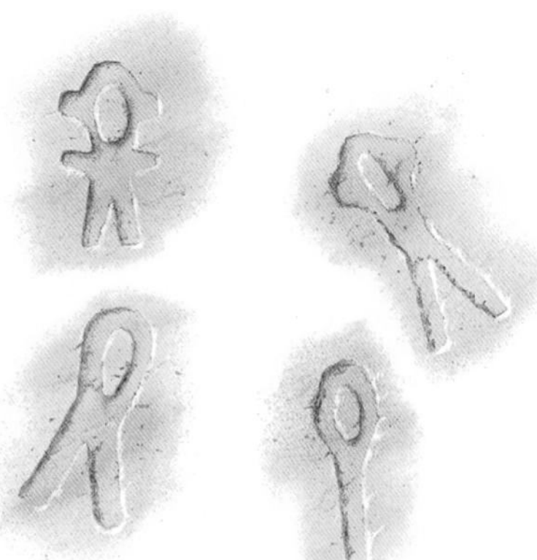

ANCIENT ART
People have always known that babies grew in a mother's uterus, or womb. The ancient Egyptians used hieroglyphs, or picture-symbols, such as these to represent the uterus.

Coils and Supercoils

Every cell contains DNA molecules. These hold all the genetic information, such as height and hair color, that makes you different from every other living thing. A DNA molecule is made up of four chemicals that fit together to form what look like the rungs of a twisting ladder. As a DNA molecule becomes tightly coiled, it forms part of a threadlike object called a chromosome. A sperm and an egg usually have 23 chromosomes each, a half-set of DNA. When they join, every cell in the new human body has 46 chromosomes, a full DNA set.

MALE PARTS

The testicles, or testes, contain cells that continually divide to form millions of sperm cells every day. The sperm are stored in a coiled tube called the epididymis. During sexual intercourse, sperm are forced along the vas deferens and then along the urethra by powerful muscular contractions. About 400 million sperm come out of the urethra in a milky fluid called semen.

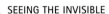

SEEING THE INVISIBLE

People could not see sperm or egg cells until the microscope was invented. Dutchman Anton van Leeuwenhoek made his own microscopes, such as the one below, and drew the first published pictures of sperm (left) in 1677.

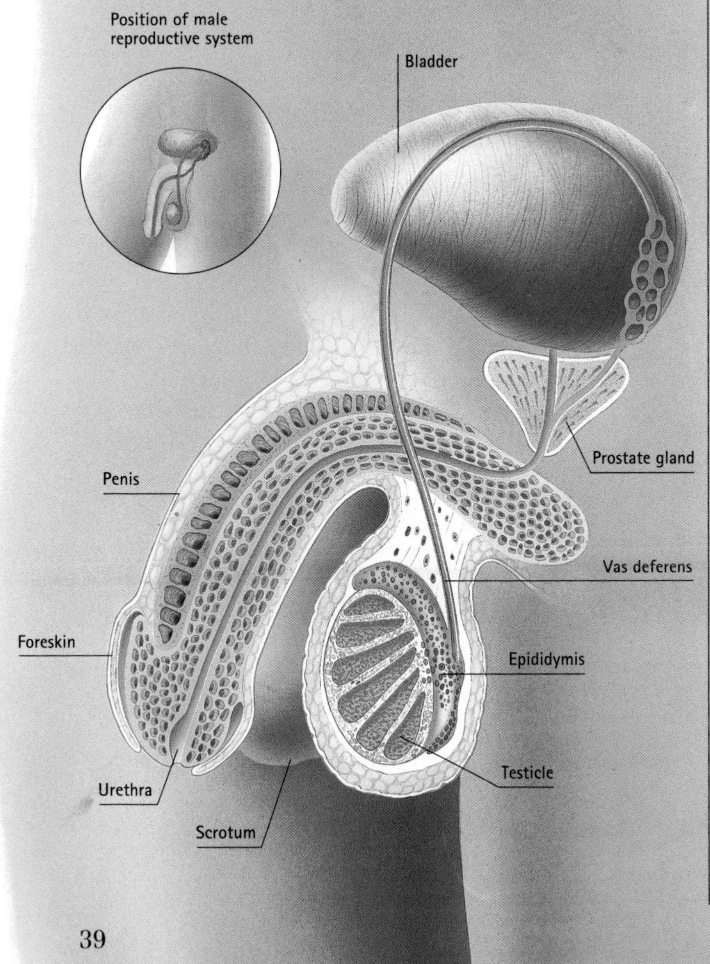

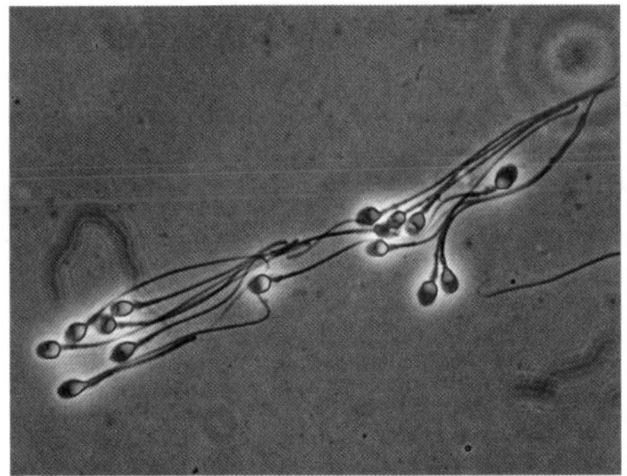

TINY SWIMMERS

Sperm cells are like microscopic tadpoles that swim by lashing their tails. The half-set of DNA that they carry is inside the front end, or head, of the sperm.

Q: How many chromosomes are in a normal body cell?

THE SPERM MEETS THE EGG
Hundreds of sperm cells gather around the egg cell as it moves slowly along the Fallopian tube to the uterus. But only one sperm will merge with, or fertilize, the egg.

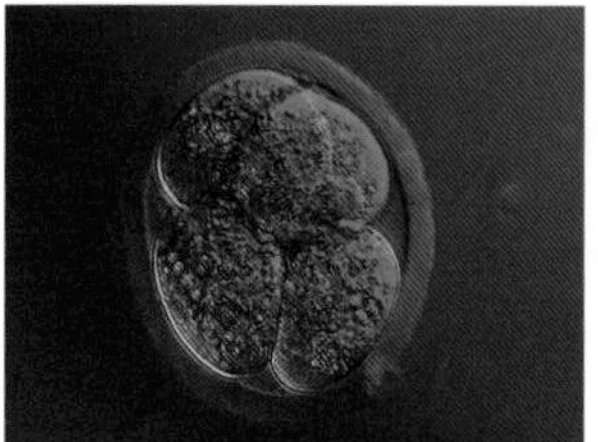

THE CELLS DIVIDE
The fertilized egg divides into two cells. These split into four cells, then eight, and so on. After a few days, there is a ball of dozens of cells.

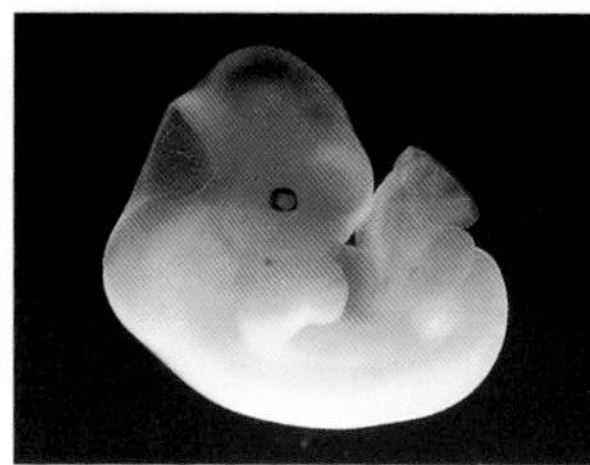

AN EMBRYO FORMS
Four weeks after fertilization, cells are multiplying in their millions and forming tissues and organs, such as the brain, the liver and the heart, which has already started to beat.

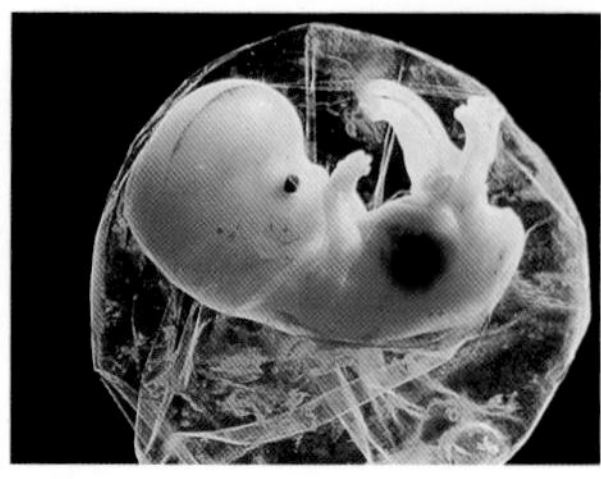

THE BODY SHAPES ITSELF
Six weeks after fertilization, the grape-sized embryo begins to develop arms and legs. The head is bigger than the body and has eyes and ears.

• FROM THE BEGINNING •

Early Life

When the egg and sperm join at fertilization, they form a single cell that is smaller than the head of a pin. The cell divides into a ball of cells that burrows into the blood-rich womb lining, absorbs the nutrients there and starts to grow. This time is called gestation, or pregnancy. From about the fifth month, the mother can feel the foetus kicking and moving about in the bulging uterus. The foetus floats in a pool of fluid, protected and cushioned from knocks and noises. It cannot breathe air or eat food. It obtains oxygen and nutrients from its mother's blood through an organ the size of a dinner plate, called the placenta, which is in the wall of the uterus. The foetus is linked to the placenta by a curly lifeline called the umbilical cord, through which blood flows. Nine months after fertilization the foetus has developed into a baby who is an average of 19 1/2 in (50 cm) long and 7 1/2 lb (3.4 kg) in weight.

Did You Know?

A baby has more than 350 bones in its body. Some of these gradually join together during childhood to form the 206 bones of an adult skeleton.

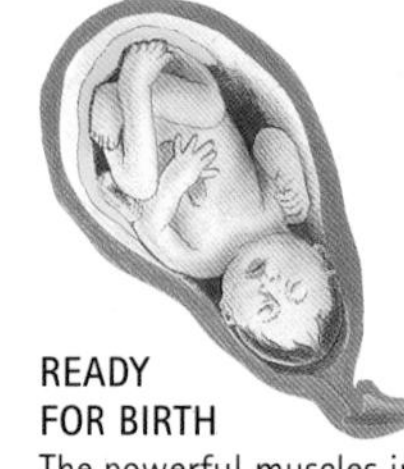

READY FOR BIRTH
The powerful muscles in the walls of the uterus contract during labor. They begin to push the fully developed baby into the birth canal.

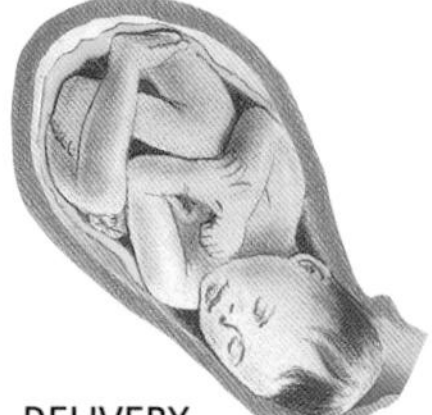

DELIVERY
The baby's head, its widest part, passes through the cervix, or opening of the womb. It emerges from the birth canal.

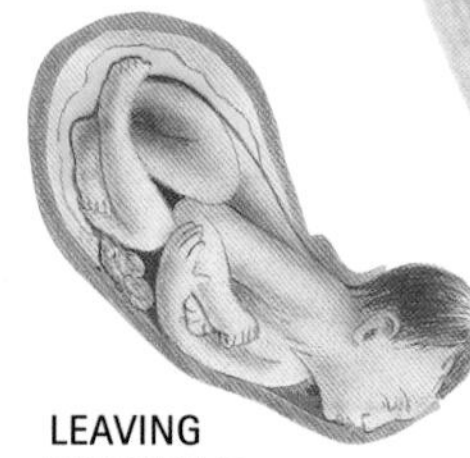

LEAVING THE WOMB
The muscles of the uterus continue to contract. The baby slips from warmth and darkness into the outside world.

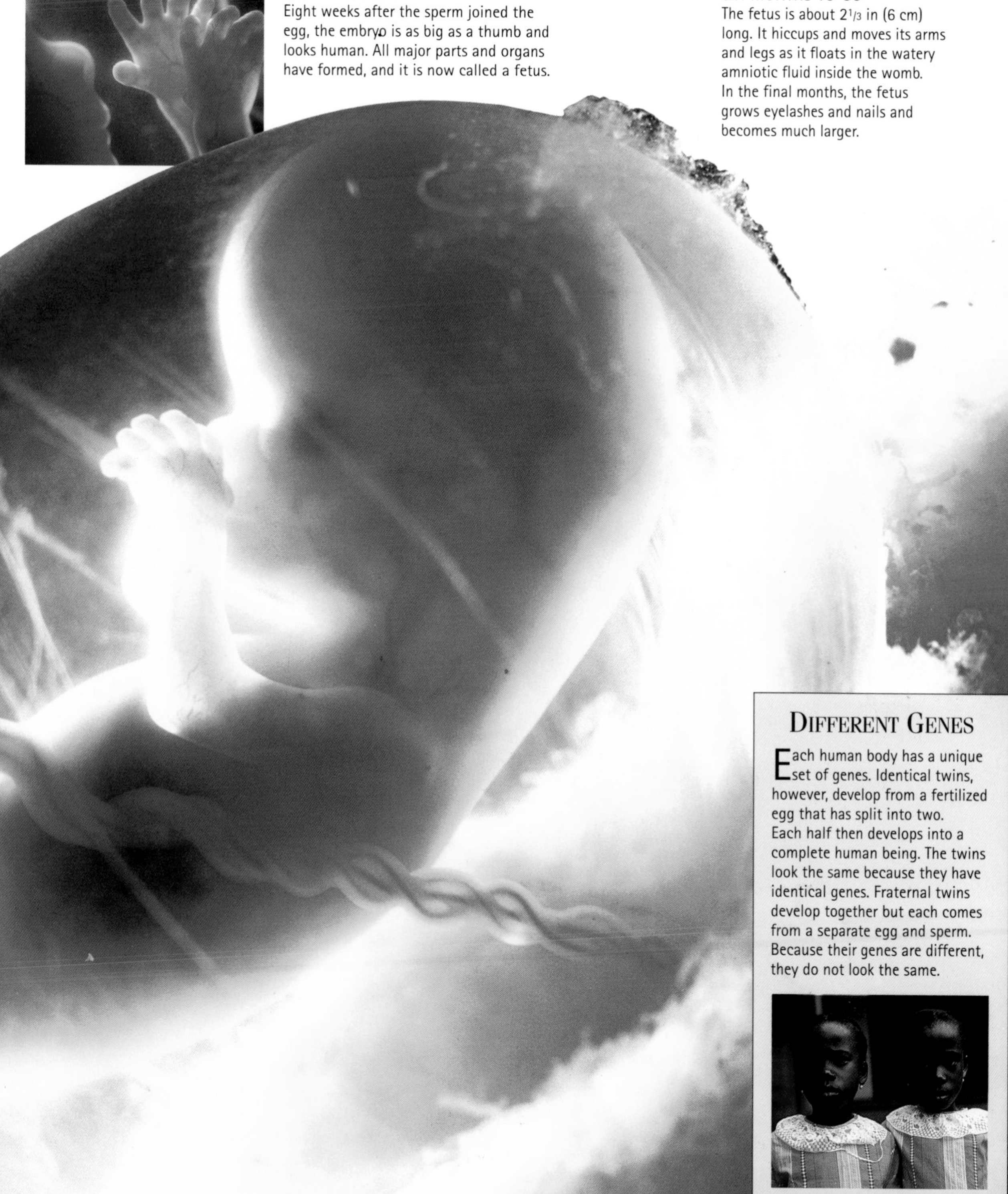

THE FETUS FORMS
Eight weeks after the sperm joined the egg, the embryo is as big as a thumb and looks human. All major parts and organs have formed, and it is now called a fetus.

SIX MONTHS TO GO
The fetus is about 2 1/3 in (6 cm) long. It hiccups and moves its arms and legs as it floats in the watery amniotic fluid inside the womb. In the final months, the fetus grows eyelashes and nails and becomes much larger.

Q: How does a fetus obtain nutrients from its mother?

Different Genes

Each human body has a unique set of genes. Identical twins, however, develop from a fertilized egg that has split into two. Each half then develops into a complete human being. The twins look the same because they have identical genes. Fraternal twins develop together but each comes from a separate egg and sperm. Because their genes are different, they do not look the same.

Growing Up

TALL AND SMALL
People who have an excess of the growth hormone grow too much, while those with too little do not grow enough. Doctors can now treat these conditions to help people grow to a normal size.

The body grows by increasing its cell numbers. Growth is fastest in the mother's womb, and continues very rapidly during the first two years. Then, it begins to slow. Growth is controlled mainly by a growth hormone that is made by the pea-sized pituitary gland below the brain. Sex hormones control physical changes when girls are between 10 and 14 years old and boys are between 12 and 14 years old. A girl develops breasts, rounded hips and other female features. A boy develops a deep voice, facial hair and other male features. The body's final height is due largely to the genes inherited from the parents. However, the human body also needs nutrients, energy and raw materials from healthy food to grow properly. As the body develops, so does the mind. We learn how to communicate and perform hundreds of other day-to-day tasks.

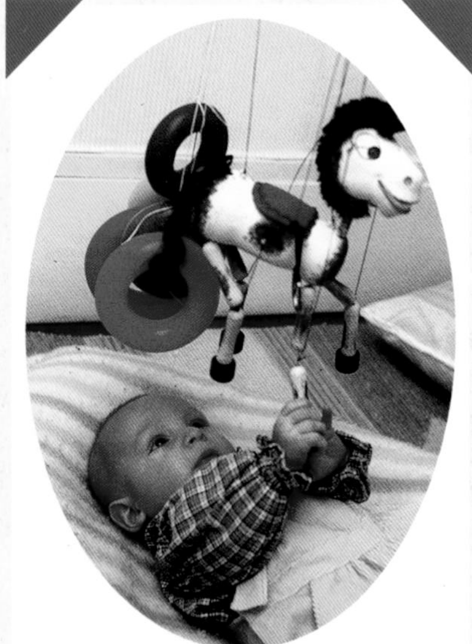

FOR THE FIRST TIME
By the time babies are eight months old, they have learned to move their arms and legs and to sit up. They have also grown teeth.

David, age 6 months

David, age 2 years

ON YOUR FEET
Children grow fastest in their first two years of life. By the age of two, most children can walk and run.

HAND OVER HAND
By the age of seven, children can perform delicate tasks with their hands. They have begun to develop independent thought.

David, age 7 years

Growing Older

The average human body peaks in size and physical fitness at about 20 years of age. The body begins to age after this, but for many years the aging process can hardly be noticed. Gradually the aging signs become more obvious. Hair turns gray, skin becomes wrinkled, reactions become slower, muscle strength decreases, height reduces, senses lose their sharpness, and even memory and concentration become less efficient. However, these signs happen at very different ages and rates in each individual.

Sam, age 4

Sam, age 6

Sam, age 8

SELF-PORTRAITS
Some skills combine your physical and mental abilities. To draw, you have to be able to use a pen or a brush. This involves your brain, nerves and hand muscles and feedback from your eyes. But you also show your understanding and experience of the world in your drawings.

David, age 10 years

MENTAL NOTES
At about the age of ten, a child's growth rate once again increases. The child's mental development is very important at this age.

THE CHANGING YEARS
At 12–14, everyday activities are usually mastered. The body goes through puberty and grows very quickly.

David, age 13 years

David, age 18 years

GROWN UP
At 18–20 years of age, the average person is physically fully grown and is considered adult.

How Things Work

- How does a satellite stay in orbit?
- How does a clock keep time?
- How does a doctor take a picture of a human brain?
- What trick of technology does a television use?

Wind Power

People have used the power of the wind for more than 5,000 years. It propelled their sailing boats over rivers, lakes and oceans; it turned the heavy blades of windmills to grind grain and pump water. Wind has energy because it is always moving in one direction or another. This energy can be caught, or harnessed, by large sails or blades. When electricity was developed in the nineteenth century, wind power did not seem as efficient as this marvelous new source of power, and most windmills disappeared. But wind power is making a comeback. Today, modern versions of windmills called wind turbines are used to generate electricity. Groups of wind turbines with long, thin metal or plastic blades, which look like airplane propellers on top of tall thin towers, are often erected together in wind farms that stretch across the landscape. By the middle of the twenty-first century, one-tenth of the world's electricity could be powered by wind turbines.

WIND FARMS
These are built in very windy areas and are controlled by computers that turn their blades into the wind. When the wind turns the blades, the spinning motion is converted into electricity.

Blades
The blades of the turbine are set at an angle that can be changed to suit the wind's speed or direction.

WIND-ASSISTED TANKER
This ship has stiff fiberglass sails as well as engines. It can save fuel by using sails whenever there is enough wind. Computers calculate the wind speed and indicate when it is time to unfold the sails.

Cables
Underground cables collect the electricity produced by the turbines at a wind farm.

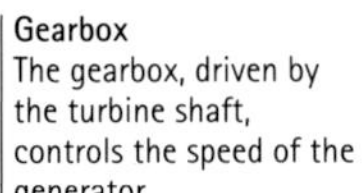

The gearbox, driven by the turbine shaft, controls the speed of the generator.

Turbine shaft
Wind turns the blades, which turn the central turbine shaft. The speed of the shaft varies according to the strength of the wind.

The nacelle (the part that contains the machinery) pivots to keep the blades pointing into the wind. The angle of the blades is set automatically to suit the wind speed.

The tower holds the blades at a safe height above the ground and contains the cables that carry the electricity underground.

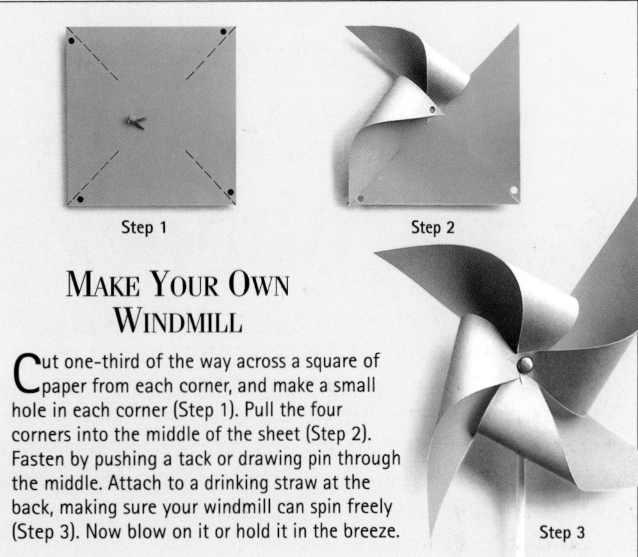

MAKE YOUR OWN WINDMILL

Cut one-third of the way across a square of paper from each corner, and make a small hole in each corner (Step 1). Pull the four corners into the middle of the sheet (Step 2). Fasten by pushing a tack or drawing pin through the middle. Attach to a drinking straw at the back, making sure your windmill can spin freely (Step 3). Now blow on it or hold it in the breeze.

Q: Where would you build a wind farm?

TIMES PAST
This kind of windmill was used many years ago to grind grain.

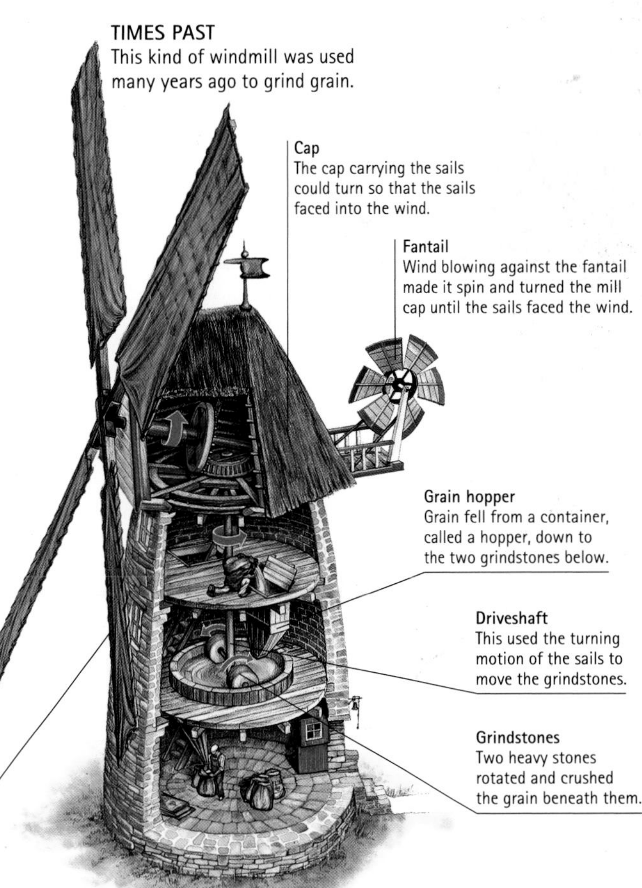

Cap
The cap carrying the sails could turn so that the sails faced into the wind.
Fantail
Wind blowing against the fantail made it spin and turned the mill cap until the sails faced the wind.
Grain hopper
Grain fell from a container, called a hopper, down to the two grindstones below.
Driveshaft
This used the turning motion of the sails to move the grindstones.
Canvas-covered sails
Canvas sheeting stretched over the wooden frame of the sails caught the wind and moved the sails around.
Grindstones
Two heavy stones rotated and crushed the grain beneath them.

The Ways of Water

Water covers more than two-thirds of the Earth's surface and is constantly on the move. It rushes along rivers and streams; it flows into oceans. This endless movement of water creates energy that can be harnessed. For centuries, people have channeled flowing water into waterwheels that turn to grind grain. Hydroelectric power stations use water in a similar way, but to generate electricity. These enormous concrete constructions are usually found in mountainous regions where there is a high rainfall. Engineers build huge dams across steep-sided valleys. Turbines (modern versions of ancient wooden waterwheels) are placed in the path of the water that gushes with force through the dam. This torrent of water strikes the angled blades of the turbines, which begin to spin and extract an incredible amount of energy from the water. The process of producing hydroelectric power is set in motion.

Transmission lines
Strengthened electric cables called transmission lines carry electricity away from the power plant.

Spillway
The spillway gates are opened to release water when the level of water behind the dam is too high.

Control room
The operation of the entire power plant is directed from the control room.

Drift tube
Water leaves the turbines through the drift tube.

WATERING THE LAND
The water for this insectlike irrigation system is coming from the dam of a hydroelectric power station.

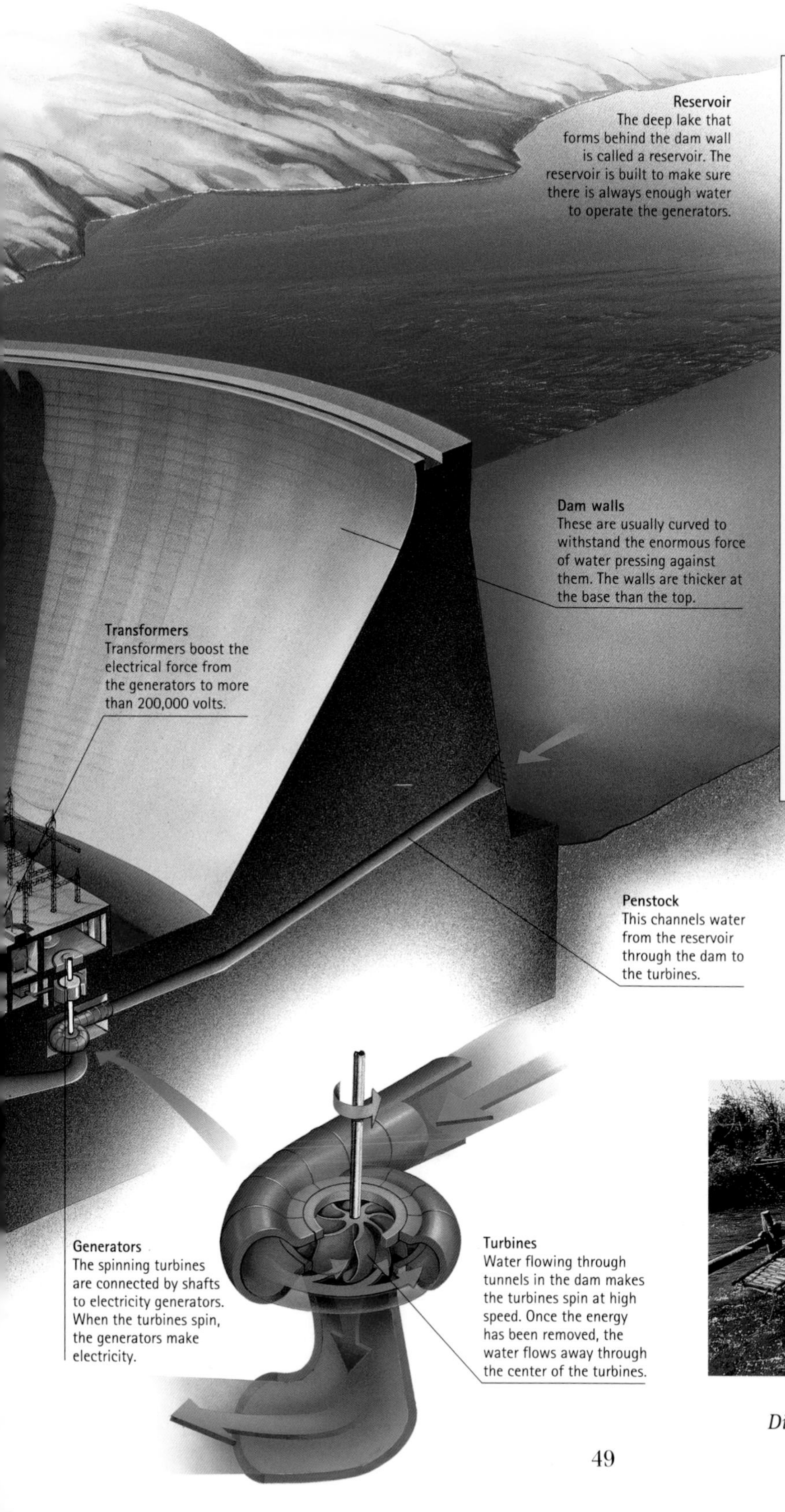

Reservoir
The deep lake that forms behind the dam wall is called a reservoir. The reservoir is built to make sure there is always enough water to operate the generators.

Dam walls
These are usually curved to withstand the enormous force of water pressing against them. The walls are thicker at the base than the top.

Transformers
Transformers boost the electrical force from the generators to more than 200,000 volts.

Penstock
This channels water from the reservoir through the dam to the turbines.

Generators
The spinning turbines are connected by shafts to electricity generators. When the turbines spin, the generators make electricity.

Turbines
Water flowing through tunnels in the dam makes the turbines spin at high speed. Once the energy has been removed, the water flows away through the center of the turbines.

Make Your Own Waterwheel

Cut four pieces of cardboard 1½ in x ¾ in (4 cm x 2 cm) and collect an empty thread spool and drinking straw (Step 1). Glue each piece of cardboard to the thread spool (Step 2) and push the drinking straw through the middle so that your waterwheel can spin easily. Hold the wheel under a running faucet. When water hits the card paddles, the wheel will turn (Step 3).

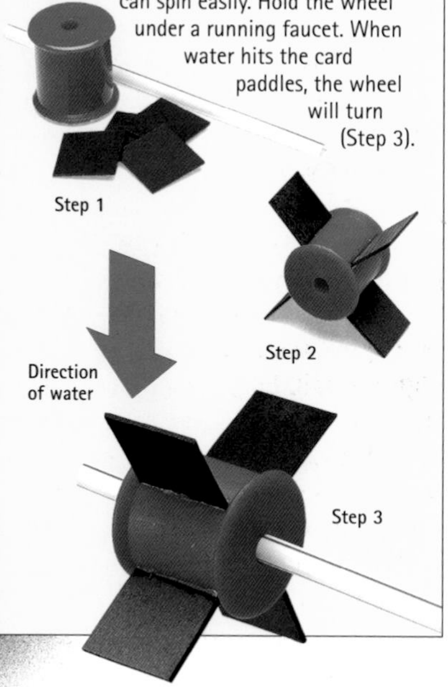

Step 1

Step 2

Direction of water

Step 3

A DAILY GRIND
This water-powered hammer is used in Laos in Southeast Asia to grind rice. When the paddles are turned by the flow of the river, the crossbeam at the end of the axle raises the hammer, then releases it to fall on the rice below.

Q: Why are dam walls usually curved?

Discover more in Roaming the Oceans

Passing on the Power

Electricity has to be sent from the power station where it is made to the homes and businesses where it is used. Whether the power station is nuclear powered, hydroelectric or burns coal, the electricity it makes is distributed in the same way. Transformers at the power station boost the electricity to a very high voltage–hundreds of thousands of volts. The electricity is then carried by metal cables suspended from tall transmission towers, or pylons. It usually ends its journey by passing along underground cables. By the time it reaches your home, transformers have reduced its voltage to a level that depends on which country you live in. Electricity generated in one place can be sent to another part of the country if more power is needed.

TURBOGENERATOR
Electricity is made by a turbogenerator—a generator driven by a turbine. When a wire moves near a magnet, electricity flows along the wire. Inside the generator, strong magnets make electricity flow through coils of wire.

Rotor
The rotor consists of coils of wire that rotate at high speed. Electric current flowing through the coils creates powerful magnetic fields around them.

Anode
A carbon rod acts as the positive electrode.

Electrolyte
This is a chemical paste.

Cathode
The zinc battery case forms the negative electrode.

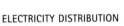

BATTERIES
When a battery is connected to an electric circuit, a chemical reaction between the negative terminal (cathode) and a liquid or paste (electrolyte) creates a current. This current travels round the circuit and returns to the battery at the positive electrode (anode).

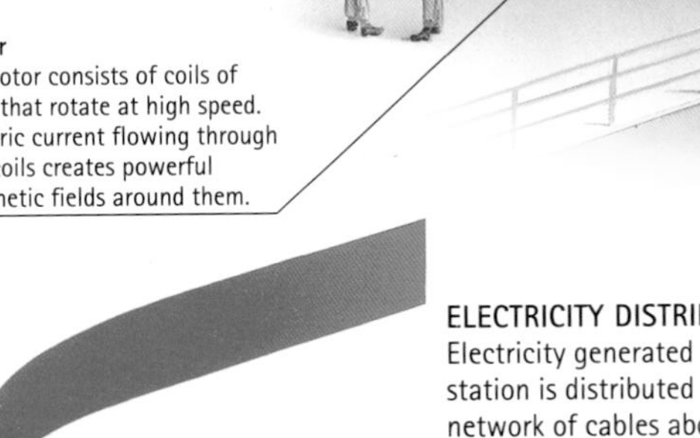

ELECTRICITY DISTRIBUTION
Electricity generated at a power station is distributed through a network of cables above and below the ground.

Transformers
Transformers increase the voltage before electricity is transmitted.

A Bright Idea

Most light bulbs contain a thin coiled wire filament that heats up and glows when an electric current flows through it. They are called incandescent bulbs (left). An energy efficient bulb (right) is a fluorescent tube that needs less electricity to produce the same amount of light as a normal bulb. When an electric current passes through mercury vapor inside the tube, the vapor releases invisible ultraviolet rays, and the coating on the inside of the bulb converts them into visible light.

Stator
The stator, which does not move, is made from coils of wire surrounding the rotor. As the rotor turns, its magnetic fields cut through the stator coils and make an electric current flow through them.

Power take-off cables
Thick cables lead electric current away from the generator.

Did You Know?

Power stations have to be ready to boost electricity production whenever demand suddenly increases. In many countries, television schedules help to predict power demands! At the end of films or major sporting events, the demand for electricity soars as millions of television viewers switch on their electric kettles to make tea or coffee.

Transmission towers
The transmission lines are held high above the ground by tall transmission towers. Glass or ceramic insulators between the metal towers and the cables stop the current from running down the towers into the ground.

Transmission lines
Cables strengthened by steel carry the current.

Street transformer
Before electricity reaches your home, its voltage is reduced by transformers. The voltage level depends on the country you live in.

Home
Electricity enters your home through a meter that measures how much electricity is used.

SAVING ENERGY

An energy-efficient house is designed to minimize energy waste. It generates its own electricity, but it is still connected to the national power grid. If it generates more electricity than it needs, the excess is supplied to the grid. If it needs more electricity, this is supplied by the grid.

Keeping warm
Most of the heat lost by a house escapes through the roof. The roof of an energy-efficient house is lined with insulation material to stop heat from escaping.

Solar panels
When the sun shines on a solar panel, solar energy is converted into electricity to power electrical appliances in the house, such as water heaters or cooling fans.

Harnessing the Sun

The sun is an extraordinarily powerful form of energy. In fact, the Earth receives 20,000 times more energy from the sun than we currently use. If we used much more of this source of heat and light, it could supply all the power needed throughout the world. We can harness energy from the sun, called "solar" energy, in many ways. Satellites in space have large panels covered with solar cells that change sunlight directly into electrical power. Some buildings have solar collectors that use solar energy to heat water. These panels are covered with glass and are painted black inside to absorb as much heat as possible. Some experimental electric cars are even powered by solar panels. Solar energy is a clean fuel, but fossil fuels, such as oil or coal, release harmful substances into the air when they are burned. Fossil fuels will run out eventually, but solar energy will continue to reach the Earth long after the last coal has been mined and the last oil well has run dry.

The sunny side
The house is built with one long side facing the sun so that it can absorb as much solar energy as possible during the day.

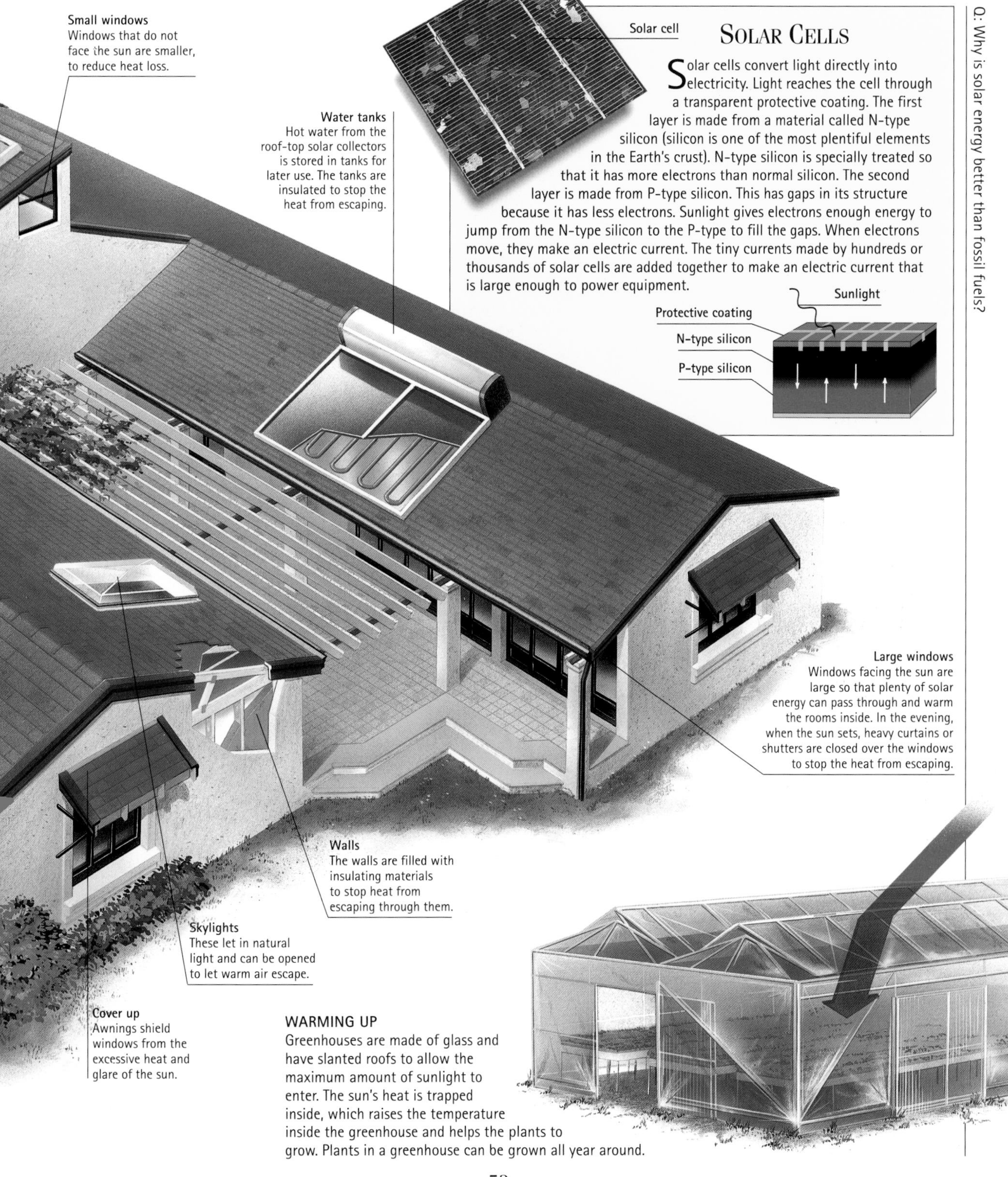

Small windows
Windows that do not face the sun are smaller, to reduce heat loss.
Water tanks
Hot water from the roof-top solar collectors is stored in tanks for later use. The tanks are insulated to stop the heat from escaping.
Solar cell
Sunlight
Protective coating
N-type silicon
P-type silicon
Large windows
Windows facing the sun are large so that plenty of solar energy can pass through and warm the rooms inside. In the evening, when the sun sets, heavy curtains or shutters are closed over the windows to stop the heat from escaping.
Walls
The walls are filled with insulating materials to stop heat from escaping through them.
Skylights
These let in natural light and can be opened to let warm air escape.
Cover up
Awnings shield windows from the excessive heat and glare of the sun.

Solar Cells

Solar cells convert light directly into electricity. Light reaches the cell through a transparent protective coating. The first layer is made from a material called N-type silicon (silicon is one of the most plentiful elements in the Earth's crust). N-type silicon is specially treated so that it has more electrons than normal silicon. The second layer is made from P-type silicon. This has gaps in its structure because it has less electrons. Sunlight gives electrons enough energy to jump from the N-type silicon to the P-type to fill the gaps. When electrons move, they make an electric current. The tiny currents made by hundreds or thousands of solar cells are added together to make an electric current that is large enough to power equipment.

WARMING UP

Greenhouses are made of glass and have slanted roofs to allow the maximum amount of sunlight to enter. The sun's heat is trapped inside, which raises the temperature inside the greenhouse and helps the plants to grow. Plants in a greenhouse can be grown all year around.

Q: Why is solar energy better than fossil fuels?

Did You Know?

People have made instruments to measure the passing of time for at least 3,000 years. The sundial was developed from a simple observation. As the Earth turns, the sun appears to cross the sky and the shadows it casts move across the ground. If the positions of the shadows are marked at regular intervals, they can be used to tell the time.

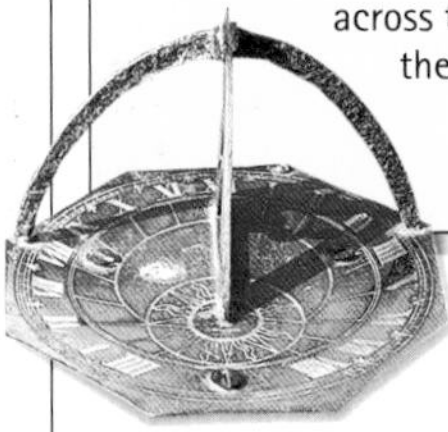

Escapement
This regulates the speed of the clock. It consists of an anchor that rocks from side to side, and an escape wheel that is repeatedly caught and released by the anchor.

Hour hand
The hour hand makes one revolution every 12 hours.

Minute hand
The minute hand moves 12 times faster than the hour hand and makes one revolution every hour.

Pendulum
The swinging pendulum regulates the rocking motion of the anchor.

• MACHINES •

About Time

People have been keeping the time for thousands of years. The first time-keeping devices were very inaccurate. They measured time by the sun, or by the falling levels of water or sand. Mechanical clocks are much more accurate. They have three main parts: an energy supply, a mechanism for regulating the energy and a way of showing the passing of time. The energy is supplied by a coiled spring or a weight. The spring unwinds, or the weight falls, and turns a series of interlocking, toothed wheels. Hands linked to the wheels rotate around a dial. For the clock to be accurate, the hands must turn at a constant speed. In large clocks, a pendulum swings at a constant rate and regulates the movement of the escapement. Digital or electronic watches have a piece of quartz crystal that vibrates at 32,768 times a second. An electronic circuit uses these movements to turn the hands or change numbers on the watch face.

ON YOUR MARK, GET SET, GO!
Athletes often cross the finish line at exactly the same moment and it is difficult to decide who has won the race. Officials accurately record the athletes' race times so that very close finishes can be separated by degrees of a second.

KEEPING TIME
Athletes train hard for their events. Stopwatches can help them monitor their progress by measuring times to within 100th of a second. Some stopwatches can also store up to 100 laps in their memories and even print times using built-in printers.

Gears
These make sure that the minute hand goes around 12 times faster than the hour hand.

Weight
This hangs on a cord wound around a shaft so that the weight turns the shaft to move the gears.

Things in Common

Pendulum clocks and digital watches are very different in size, but they are made from the same basic building blocks. Both have an oscillator that moves or swings at a regular rate (left), a device that turns these movements into time-keeping pulses (center) and a display for showing the time (right).

Pendulum | Escapement | Display

Crystal | Circuit | Display

Q: What does a clock's escapement do?

Discover more in Computer Friendly

VACUUM CLEANER

A vacuum cleaner works in a similar way to a straw. When you drink through a straw you suck out the air and this draws up the fluid. A vacuum cleaner creates a powerful flow of air that sucks up dust and dirt through a hose and traps it inside the machine.

FAST FOOD

A microwave oven uses powerful radio waves of a very short wavelength (microwaves) to cook food very quickly. These waves heat the inside as well as the outside of food immediately. In more traditional ovens, the heat takes longer to cook the inside of the food.

• MACHINES •

Saving Time and Effort

We use machines around the house every day. They make our lives easier and give us time to do other things. Hundreds of years ago, for example, household chores took most of the day. Water was carted from a well, food was cooked over an open fire, and houses were swept with branches. Today, most homes have labor-saving devices, which are designed to make jobs around the home less of an effort. Washing machines automatically wash and rinse clothes, then spin them to force out most of the water. Some even dry the clothes completely. Refrigerators and freezers keep food fresh longer so that we do not need to shop every day. Dishwashers, remote controls for televisions and videos, microwave ovens and vacuum cleaners are some of the appliances found in many homes throughout the world.

Dust bag
Air carries dust and dirt into the dust bag. The air then escapes through tiny holes in the bag and leaves the dust trapped inside. Some vacuum cleaners have a "micro-filter," with even smaller holes in it, to trap the tiniest dust particles.

Fan
A spinning fan sucks air and dust through the flexible hose into the vacuum cleaner.

Motor
The fan is driven by an electric motor. Some vacuum cleaners can vary the speed of the motor so that the suction power can be adjusted to clean different surfaces.

Insulation
The oven is double-walled and insulated. This stops heat from leaking out of the oven.

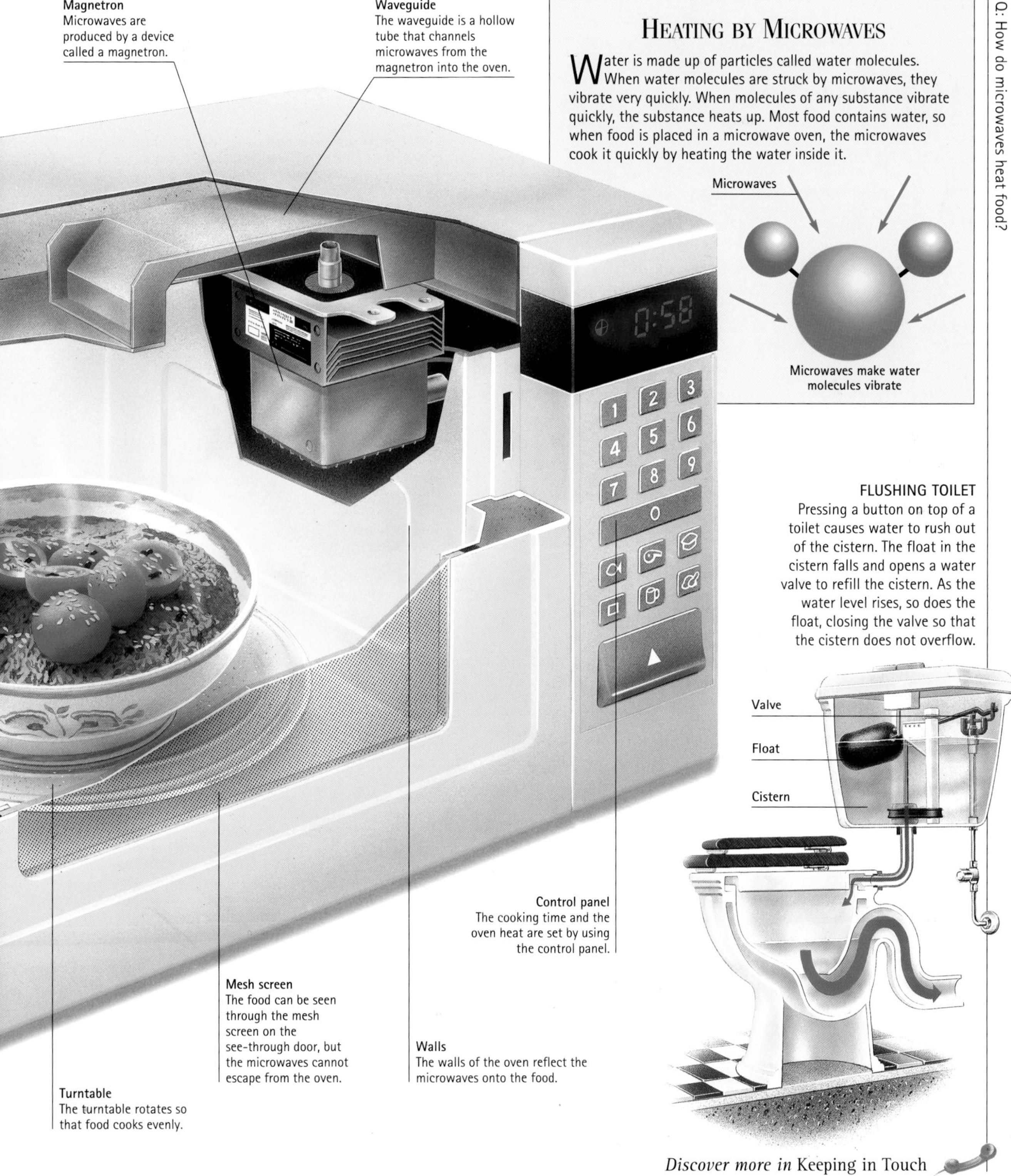

Magnetron
Microwaves are produced by a device called a magnetron.
Waveguide
The waveguide is a hollow tube that channels microwaves from the magnetron into the oven.
0:58
Control panel
The cooking time and the oven heat are set by using the control panel.
Mesh screen
The food can be seen through the mesh screen on the see-through door, but the microwaves cannot escape from the oven.
Walls
The walls of the oven reflect the microwaves onto the food.
Turntable
The turntable rotates so that food cooks evenly.
Valve
Float
Cistern

Heating by Microwaves

Water is made up of particles called water molecules. When water molecules are struck by microwaves, they vibrate very quickly. When molecules of any substance vibrate quickly, the substance heats up. Most food contains water, so when food is placed in a microwave oven, the microwaves cook it quickly by heating the water inside it.

Microwaves make water molecules vibrate

FLUSHING TOILET

Pressing a button on top of a toilet causes water to rush out of the cistern. The float in the cistern falls and opens a water valve to refill the cistern. As the water level rises, so does the float, closing the valve so that the cistern does not overflow.

Q: How do microwaves heat food?

Discover more in Keeping in Touch

Office Essentials

Modern businesses depend on being able to send and receive information quickly. Telephones enable people to talk to each other over long distances, but the worldwide telephone network carries much more than people's voices. Computers and fax machines, for example, use this network to send information to each other. "Fax" is short for "facsimile transmission" (facsimile means copy). A fax machine can transmit a copy of an image on paper—a printed document, handwritten message or drawing—to anywhere in the world within seconds. It does this by changing the information on the paper into electrical signals, then converting these into sounds that are sent along normal telephone lines. Another fax machine receives the sounds and changes them back into a printed copy of the original image. Computers exchange information by telephone in the same way. Some of the information exchanged by computers is called electronic mail or E-mail, because it is an electronic version of the ordinary postal system.

Drum
The rotating drum attracts black toner powder onto itself, then transfers the powder onto the paper. This creates an image on the page.

Print head
A row of lights flashes on and off as the charged drum rotates next to it. The electric charge on the drum is weakened wherever light strikes it. Black toner powder sticks only to the uncharged parts of the drum and forms an image of the transmitted document on it.

Numerical keypad
Telephone numbers are dialed by using this pad.

One-touch keys
Frequently used telephone numbers are keyed into the fax machine and stored in an electronic memory. When a number is selected from the memory, by pressing one of these buttons, the machine dials it automatically.

Image sensor
The electrical signal produced by the photosensor is changed into sounds that are transmitted down a telephone line.

Faxing a Message

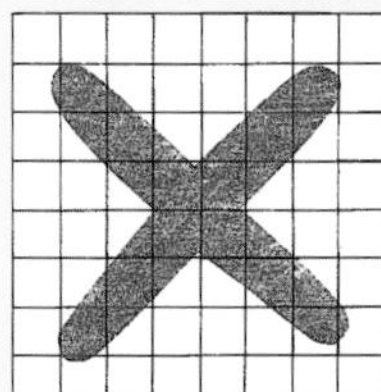

The fax machine divides the image on the paper into a grid of tiny squares and detects whether each square is light or dark.

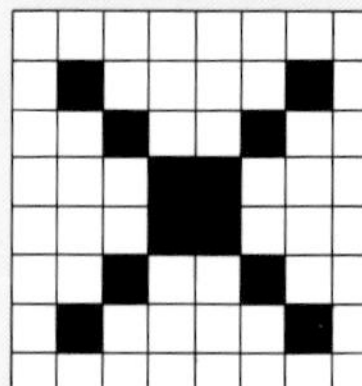

Each square is registered as either completely black or completely white.

The pattern of black and white squares is changed into an electrical signal. A pulse of electricity represents a dark square.

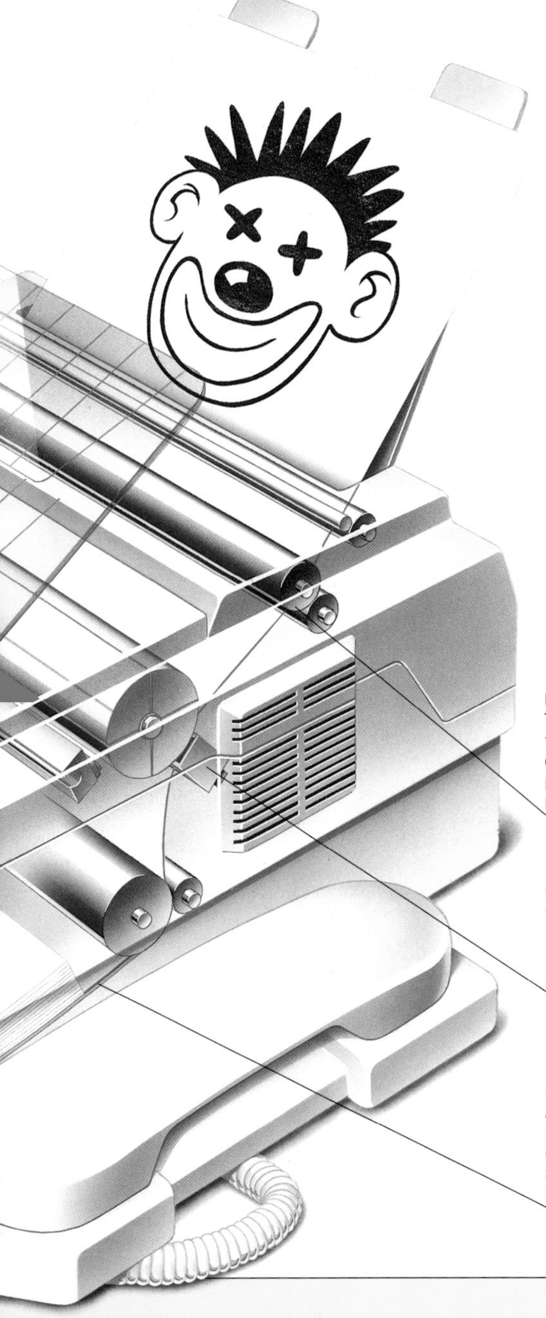

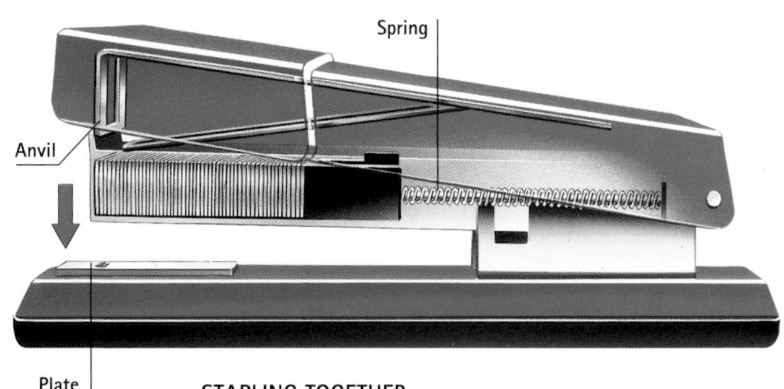

STAPLING TOGETHER

A stapler fastens sheets of paper together with short lengths of wire called staples. The staples are glued in a row, but when the stapler's jaws are pressed down over the paper, one staple is separated from the rest and forced through the paper.
A metal plate with specially shaped grooves in the base bends the ends of the staple inward so that it cannot fall out again.

STICK-ON NOTES

Stick-on notes can be stuck to almost any surface, peeled off again easily and stuck somewhere else. The secret lies in the gum on the back. It is not as sticky as the gum on adhesive tape, and the notes can be peeled off paper without damaging it.

Fuser unit
The paper leaves the machine through the fuser unit, a pair of rollers that melts the toner powder and fuses it to the paper by heat and pressure.

Transfer unit
The transfer unit charges the paper so that it attracts toner powder off the drum and onto the paper.

Paper
A plain paper fax machine prints copies of documents onto sheets of paper that are stored in a tray at the bottom of the machine.

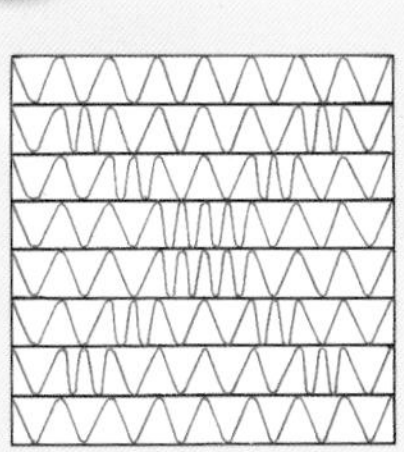

This simple electrical signal is changed into a complex code. As documents are usually printed on white paper, white is given a shorter code than black. The code is changed into sounds that can be sent down a telephone line.

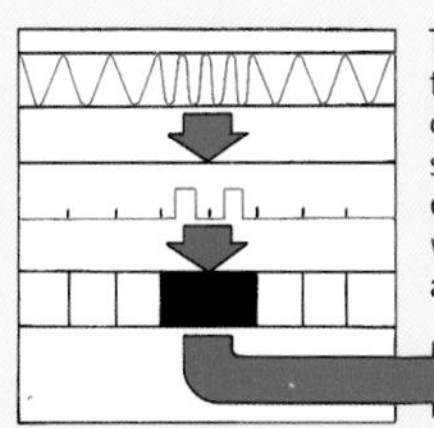

The receiving fax machine changes the sounds into an electrical signal, which controls a printer.

By printing line after line of black spots, the receiving fax machine builds up a copy of the original document.

Jib
The cross arm, or jib, suspends the hook that lifts the load. The jib is suspended by cables or steel rods from the top of the tower.
Counterweight
Concrete slabs on one side of the tower balance the weight of the loads it lifts on the other side.
Operator's cab
The crane operator sits in a cab at the top of the tower and moves the load by operating controls. The front of the cab is made from glass to give the operator a clear view of the hook, from the ground up.

• MACHINES •

Building Upward

Machines are used in the construction industry to lift, move, cut, drill and connect the various materials used. A tower crane, for example, is used to lift heavy materials up to the workers. The horizontal arm of the tower crane is called the jib. This can swing around horizontally, but it cannot be raised or lowered. The crane's hook is raised and lowered by winding the cable it hangs from around a large motorized drum. Thousands of tons of materials have to be delivered to the construction site. One of these materials, concrete, is delivered by concrete mixers. Their drums rotate constantly to stop the concrete inside from setting hard before it is poured out wherever it is needed. Pulleys (wheels with grooves around their rims) are often used on building sites to help move very heavy loads. When a rope or chain is threaded around several pulleys, a pull on the rope or chain is enhanced, or magnified, by the pulleys to enable a small effort to move a heavy load.

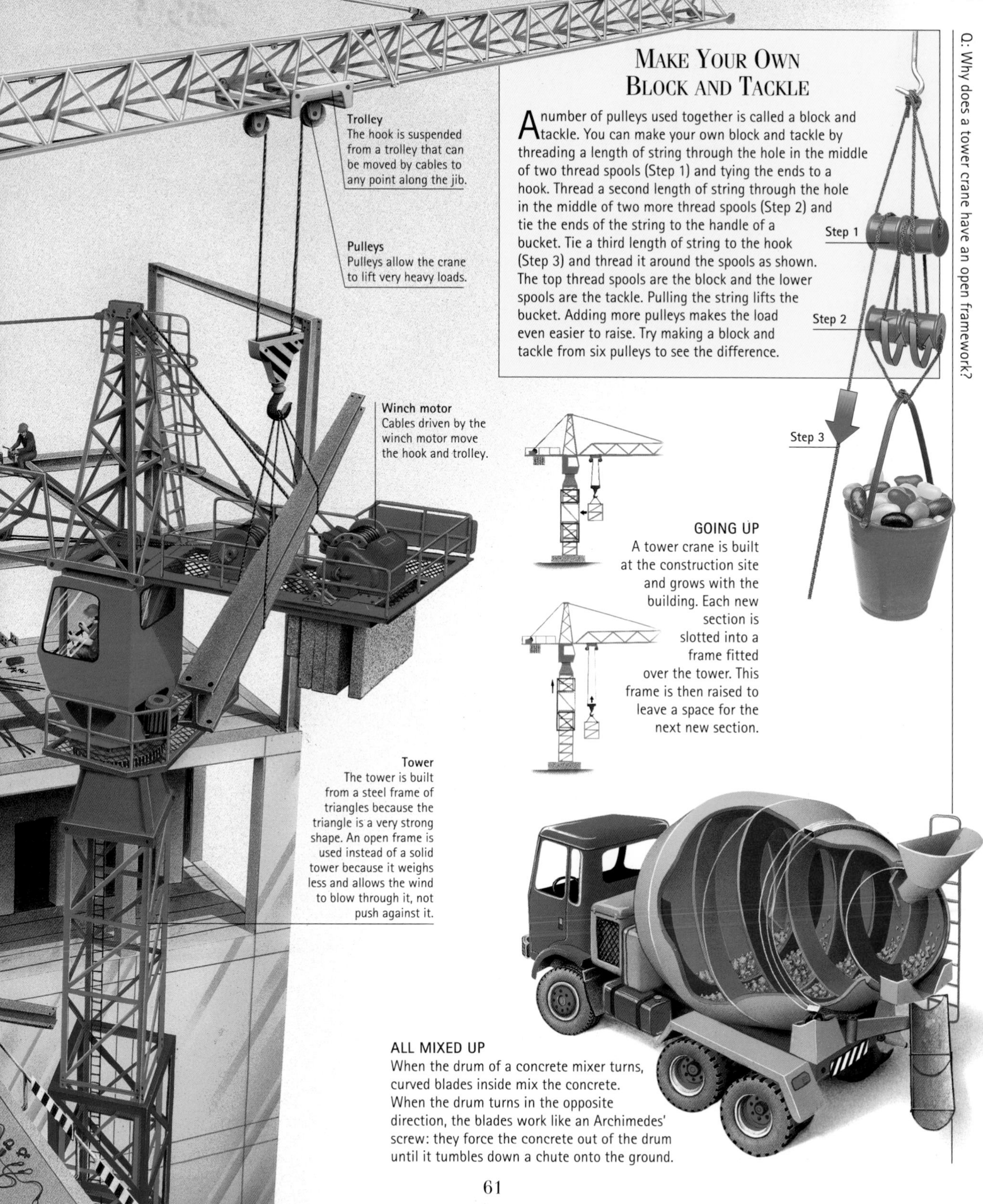

Trolley
The hook is suspended from a trolley that can be moved by cables to any point along the jib.
Pulleys
Pulleys allow the crane to lift very heavy loads.
Winch motor
Cables driven by the winch motor move the hook and trolley.
Tower
The tower is built from a steel frame of triangles because the triangle is a very strong shape. An open frame is used instead of a solid tower because it weighs less and allows the wind to blow through it, not push against it.
Step 1
Step 2
Step 3

MAKE YOUR OWN BLOCK AND TACKLE

A number of pulleys used together is called a block and tackle. You can make your own block and tackle by threading a length of string through the hole in the middle of two thread spools (Step 1) and tying the ends to a hook. Thread a second length of string through the hole in the middle of two more thread spools (Step 2) and tie the ends of the string to the handle of a bucket. Tie a third length of string to the hook (Step 3) and thread it around the spools as shown. The top thread spools are the block and the lower spools are the tackle. Pulling the string lifts the bucket. Adding more pulleys makes the load even easier to raise. Try making a block and tackle from six pulleys to see the difference.

GOING UP
A tower crane is built at the construction site and grows with the building. Each new section is slotted into a frame fitted over the tower. This frame is then raised to leave a space for the next new section.

ALL MIXED UP
When the drum of a concrete mixer turns, curved blades inside mix the concrete. When the drum turns in the opposite direction, the blades work like an Archimedes' screw: they force the concrete out of the drum until it tumbles down a chute onto the ground.

Q: Why does a tower crane have an open framework?

Making Shopping Easy

Technology has made shopping quick and convenient. Automated teller machines (ATMs) give us immediate access to our money and reduce the need to stand in long lines inside the bank. Personal identification numbers (PINs) and cash cards replace passbooks and withdrawal slips. All cash cards have a magnetic strip on their backs. When the code and information stored here match the information in the bank's computer, the machine gives you the requested amount of money. Computers and lasers speed up the service at checkout counters in stores. A laser scans the barcode of every product and tells the computerized cash register how much the product costs. It also records how many of a certain product have sold, so that more stock can be ordered when necessary. Some products have security tags attached to them. If anyone tries to take a tagged product out of the store, sensors at the door detect the tag and sound an alarm.

Did You Know?

The printing on paper currency can be copied by forgers. In 1988, the Commonwealth Reserve Bank of Australia issued a plastic folding banknote that is very difficult to copy.

PRICE SCAN
As the laser beam scans the barcode, a light-sensitive sensor in the handset picks up its reflections. An electric current flows through the sensor and produces electrical pulses in a pattern that matches the barcode's pattern of black lines. A pair of thin lines in the middle divides the barcode in two. The first half of the code contains the manufacturer's name and the second half is the code for the product. The pairs of thin lines at each end of the pattern tell the computer where the code starts and finishes. A barcode computer can always "translate" the code lines because the same standard—the Universal Product Code—is used for barcodes all over the world.

Currency cassettes Banknotes are stored in boxes called cassettes.

Barcode scanner A laser in the handset scans the barcode. The sensor identifies the product and its price, then sends these details to the cash register.

BANKING MADE EASY
An automated teller machine (ATM) enables people to withdraw money from an account. Most ATMs can also show us how much money is in our account and can transfer money from one account to another.

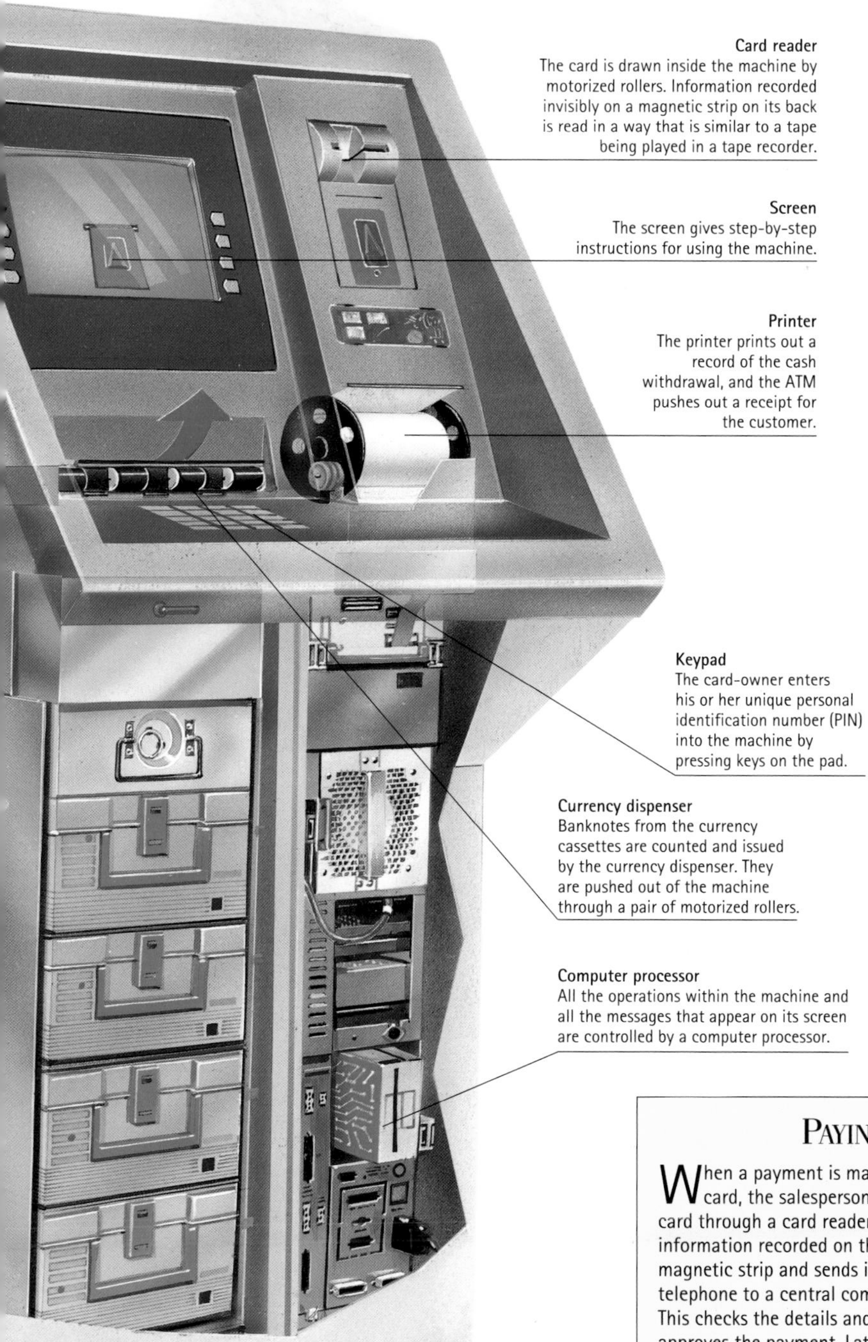

Card reader
The card is drawn inside the machine by motorized rollers. Information recorded invisibly on a magnetic strip on its back is read in a way that is similar to a tape being played in a tape recorder.

Screen
The screen gives step-by-step instructions for using the machine.

Printer
The printer prints out a record of the cash withdrawal, and the ATM pushes out a receipt for the customer.

Keypad
The card-owner enters his or her unique personal identification number (PIN) into the machine by pressing keys on the pad.

Currency dispenser
Banknotes from the currency cassettes are counted and issued by the currency dispenser. They are pushed out of the machine through a pair of motorized rollers.

Computer processor
All the operations within the machine and all the messages that appear on its screen are controlled by a computer processor.

Q: How are lasers used in shops?

SECURITY TAGS
Plastic security tags contain coils of wire that can be detected magnetically or by radio waves when they pass through the sensors at the store entrance.

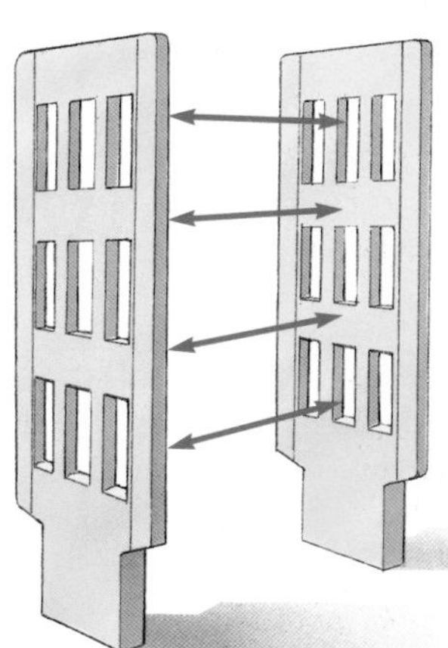

Paying by Credit Card

When a payment is made by credit card, the salesperson slides the card through a card reader. It reads information recorded on the card's magnetic strip and sends it by telephone to a central computer. This checks the details and approves the payment. Later, the card's owner receives a bill for this payment. Payments are also made in this way with debit cards, but the amounts are transferred from the card-owner's bank to the store.

Discover more in Recording Sound

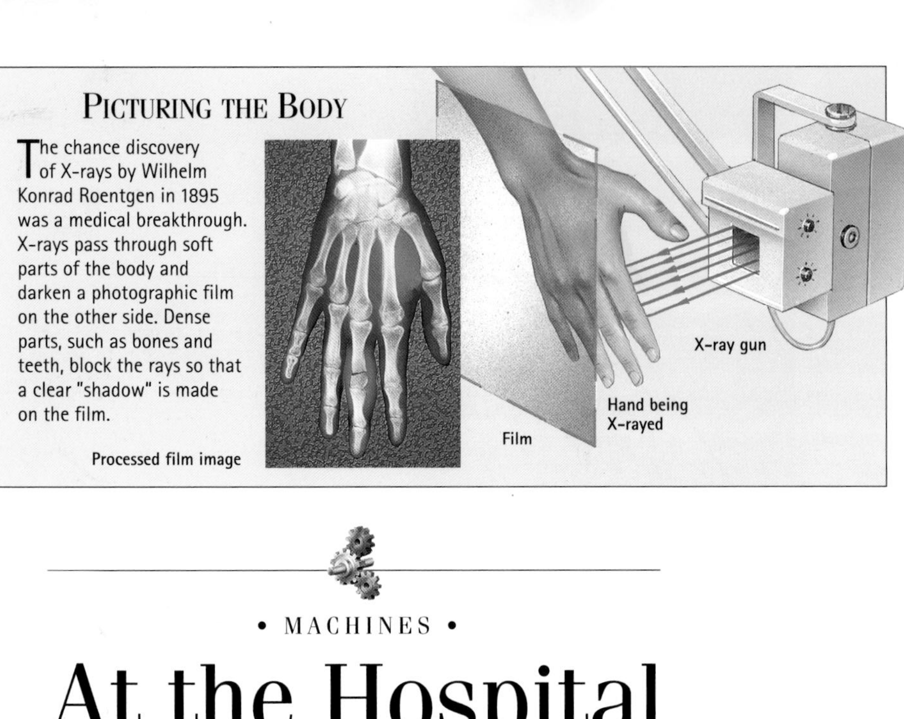

Picturing the Body

The chance discovery of X-rays by Wilhelm Konrad Roentgen in 1895 was a medical breakthrough. X-rays pass through soft parts of the body and darken a photographic film on the other side. Dense parts, such as bones and teeth, block the rays so that a clear "shadow" is made on the film.

• MACHINES •

At the Hospital

In hospitals, medical staff use machines and instruments to help people. Ultrasound scanners, X-ray machines and other medical equipment can be used to diagnose an illness, treat an injury or monitor changes in the patient's condition. More complex scanners use the high-speed processing power of computers to create intricate pictures. These scanners can show cross-sections of a body, three-dimensional views of internal organs, and pictures of the brain showing which parts of it are active while the patient is thinking, seeing, hearing or moving. These pictures can be seen on the scanner's own special screen, and can also be printed out on paper or on film. Such a detailed view of a disease or an injury allows doctors to see all the angles of a medical problem and then figure out the best way to treat it.

Hand-held probe

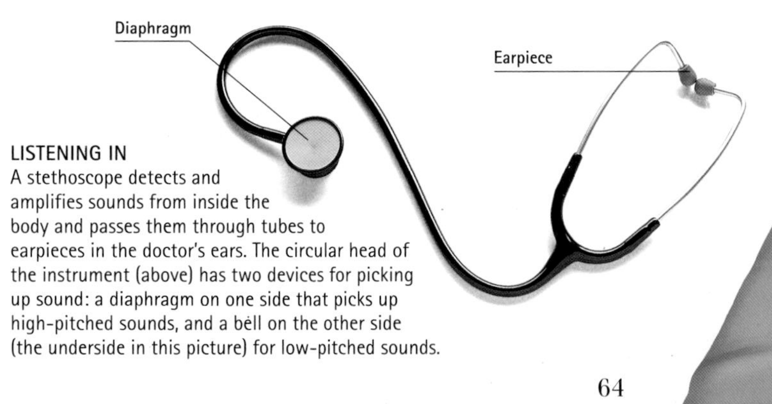

LISTENING IN
A stethoscope detects and amplifies sounds from inside the body and passes them through tubes to earpieces in the doctor's ears. The circular head of the instrument (above) has two devices for picking up sound: a diaphragm on one side that picks up high-pitched sounds, and a bell on the other side (the underside in this picture) for low-pitched sounds.

AN INSIDE VIEW

This woman is having an ultrasound examination of her baby. The probe that is held on her stomach sends bursts of ultrasound down into her body. It also receives the reflections bouncing back again. Reflections from deeper inside the patient take longer to bounce back. The machine records the different "flight times" of the sound waves and produces a picture of a part of the body. Unborn babies are often examined in this way.

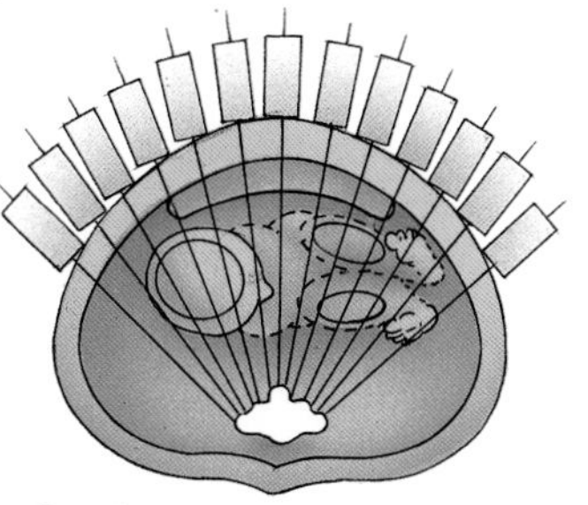

Scanning

The ultrasound probe is moved from side to side, sending ultrasonic vibrations down into the patient's body. When the ultrasound vibrations strike anything inside the body, some are reflected. Others pass through to be reflected by deeper layers.

Generating an image

The ultrasound reflections are received by the probe and combined by a computer to make a picture of the patient's internal organs. If the patient is a pregnant woman, an ultrasound scan shows a picture of her unborn baby and its internal organs.

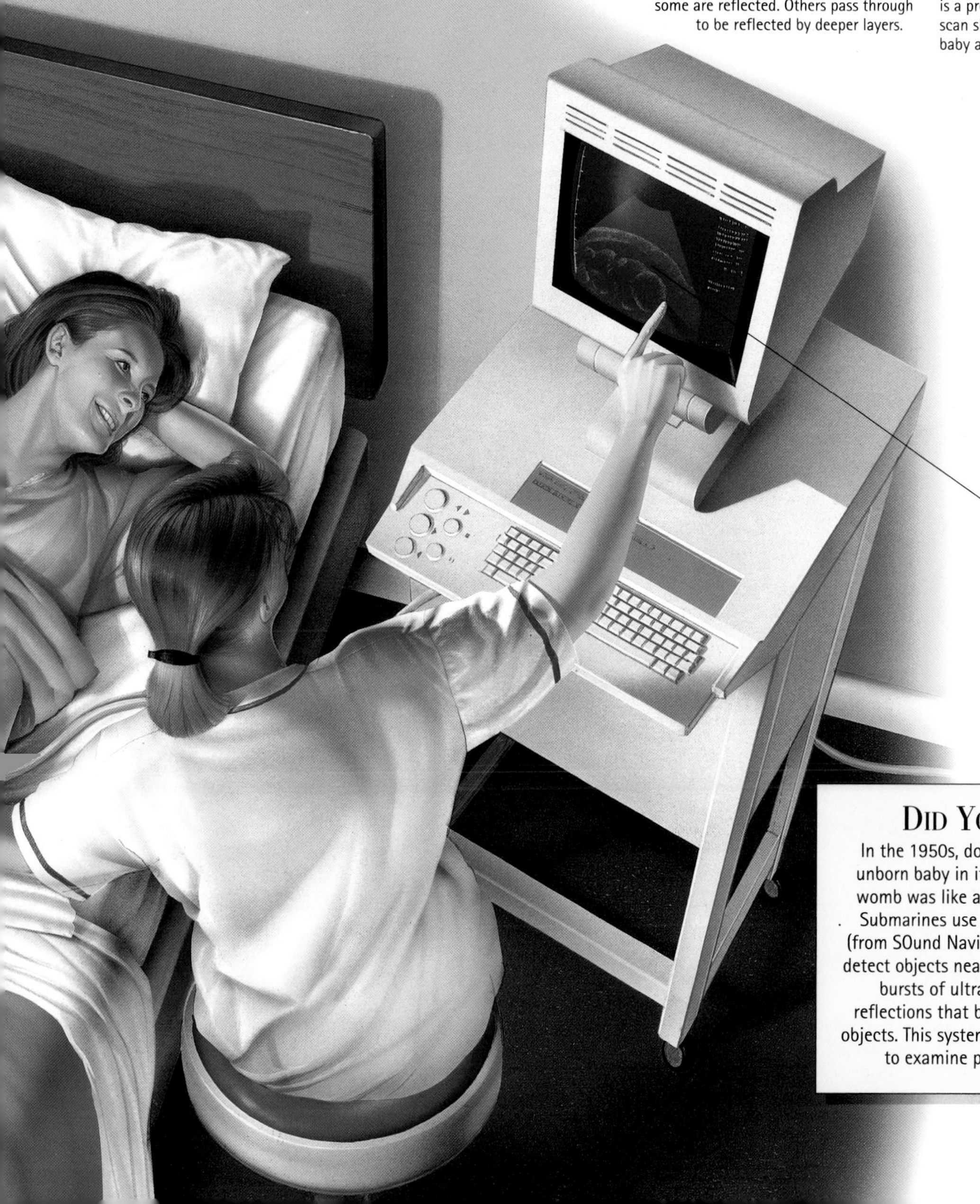

Inside information

An ultrasound operator can tell from the picture on the machine's screen whether an unborn baby is a boy or a girl. He or she can also examine the baby's internal organs, especially the heart, to make sure that the fetus is developing normally. Ultrasound can also confirm the number of babies the mother is carrying.

DID YOU KNOW?

In the 1950s, doctors realized that an unborn baby in its mother's fluid-filled womb was like a submarine in the sea. Submarines use a system called sonar (from SOund Navigation And Ranging) to detect objects near them. Sonar sends out bursts of ultrasound and detects reflections that bounce back from solid objects. This system was adapted and used to examine people in hospitals.

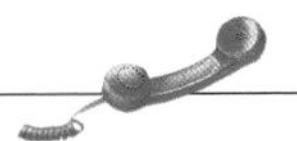

Keeping in Touch

Radio waves are vibrating, invisible waves of energy. They are similar to light waves, and are very useful for carrying information across great distances. Radio and television programs, for example, travel from transmitters all over the world to our homes. As radio waves can travel through outer space, astronauts' voices and information collected by satellites can also be transmitted by radio. Many natural objects in the universe send out radio signals that radio telescopes on Earth can receive. Whatever a radio receiver is used for, it always has the same parts. An aerial, or receiving antenna, picks up the radio signals and feeds them down a cable to the receiver. A tuner selects particular signals and discards all the rest, and an amplifier strengthens the selected signals. A radio telescope receives data, which can be displayed as perhaps pictures or charts; while a radio at home changes the radio signals it receives into sound.

RADIO TELESCOPE
A radio telescope forms images of the sky from very faint radio signals. They are so weak that they cannot be used until a series of amplifiers makes them 1,000 million million times larger. The telescope scans an object in the sky from side to side and builds up a picture of it from a series of horizontal lines.

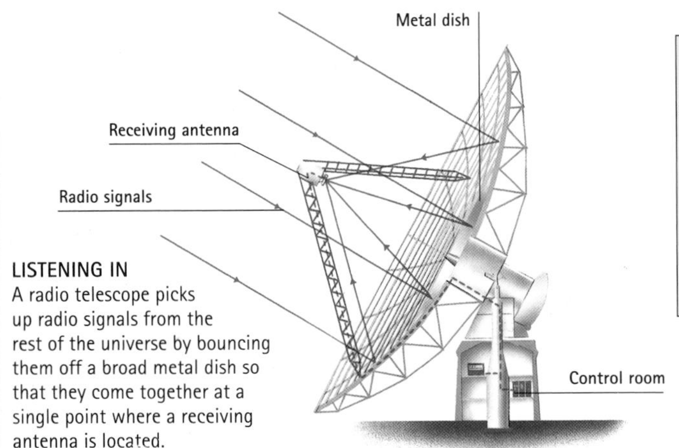

LISTENING IN
A radio telescope picks up radio signals from the rest of the universe by bouncing them off a broad metal dish so that they come together at a single point where a receiving antenna is located.

Did You Know?

The world's largest radio telescope is in Arecibo, Puerto Rico. It was built by lining a natural hollow in the ground with wire mesh to form a reflecting dish 1,000 ft (305 m) across. The Arecibo telescope cannot be moved, but most radio telescopes can be tilted and turned to point at any part of the sky.

When you switch on your radio, you might listen to a tape or a disk, or to someone speaking into a microphone at a studio.

An engineer sitting at a mixing desk adjusts the signals from the studio so that no signal is too large or too small.

Mixing desk

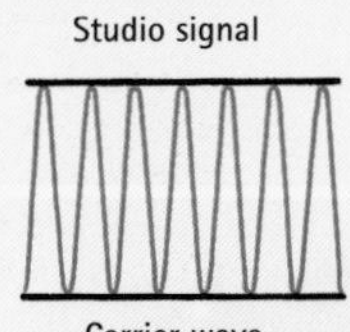

The studio signal is mixed with a high-frequency (rapidly vibrating) signal that is called a carrier wave (it carries the studio signal), and then beamed across the country from a transmitter.

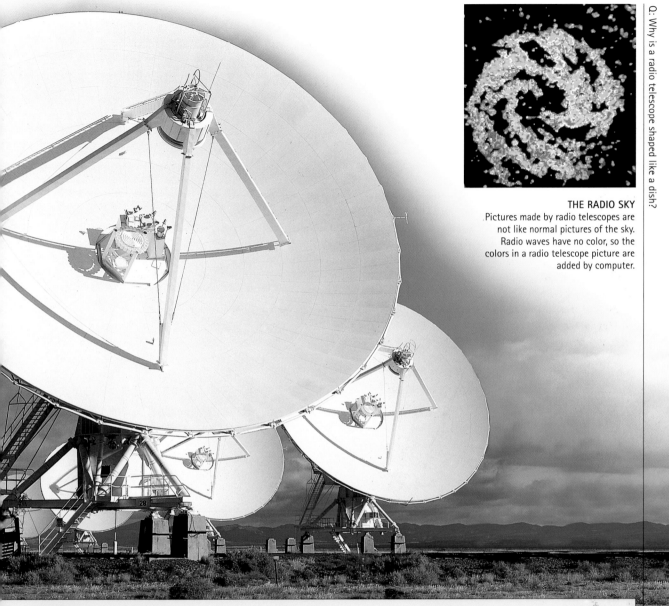

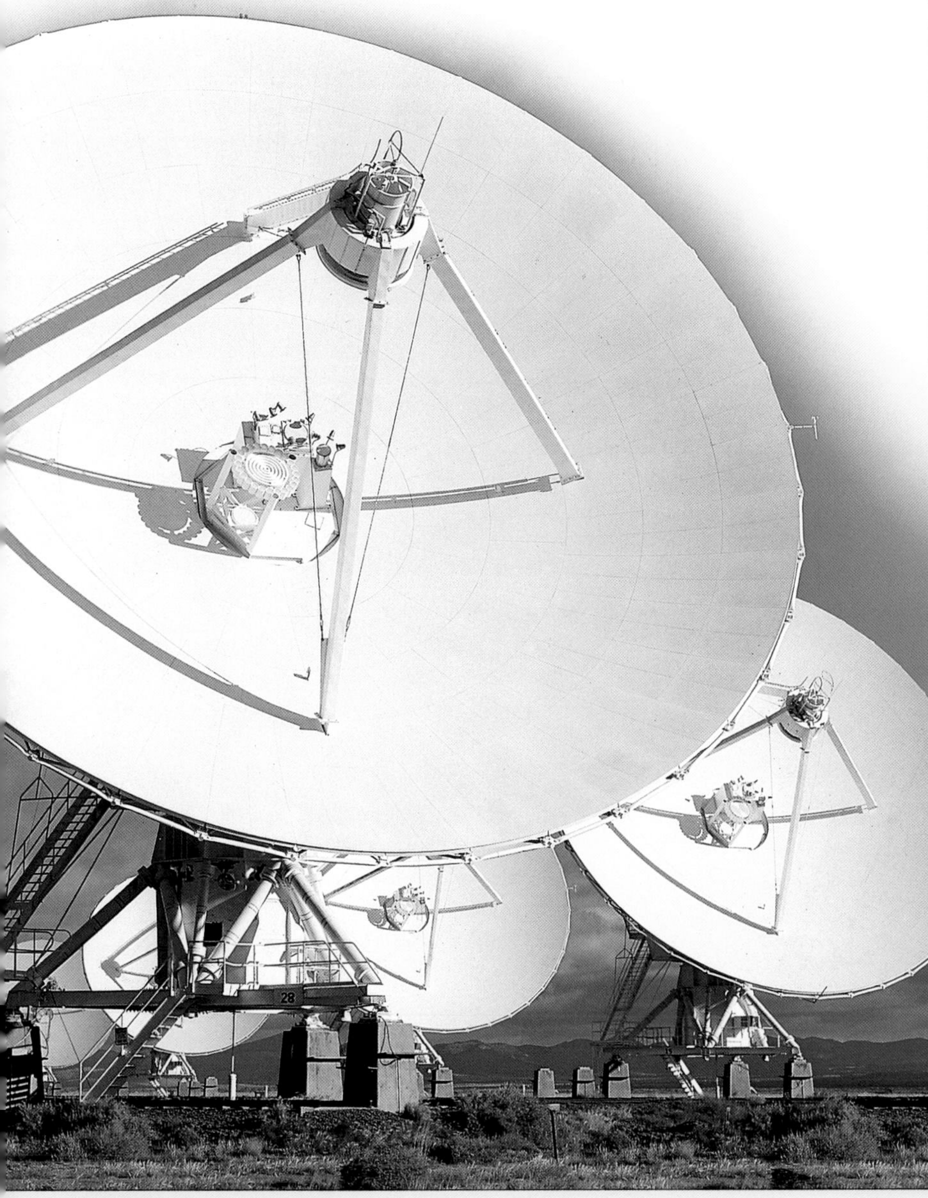

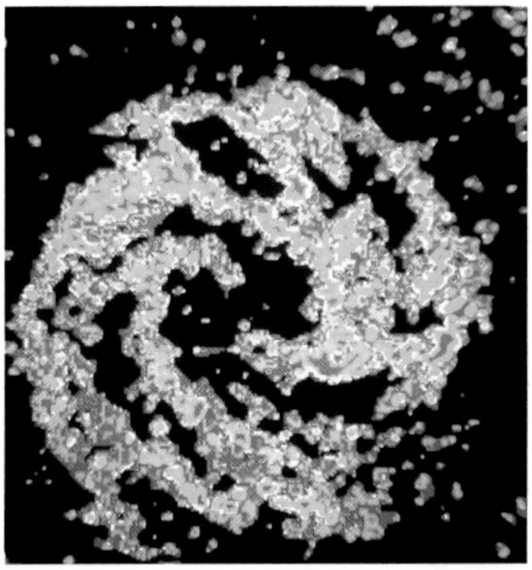

THE RADIO SKY

Pictures made by radio telescopes are not like normal pictures of the sky. Radio waves have no color, so the colors in a radio telescope picture are added by computer.

Q: Why is a radio telescope shaped like a dish?

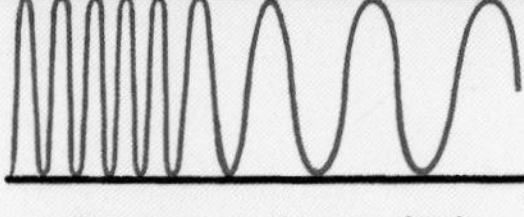

Frequency modulation (FM)

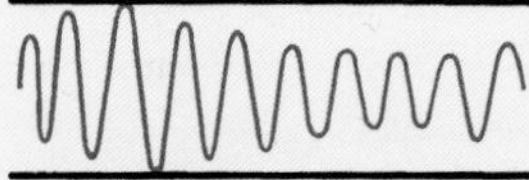

Amplitude modulation (AM)

The studio signal changes either the frequency (speed of vibration) of the carrier wave, which is called frequency modulation; or the carrier wave's amplitude (size), which is called amplitude modulation.

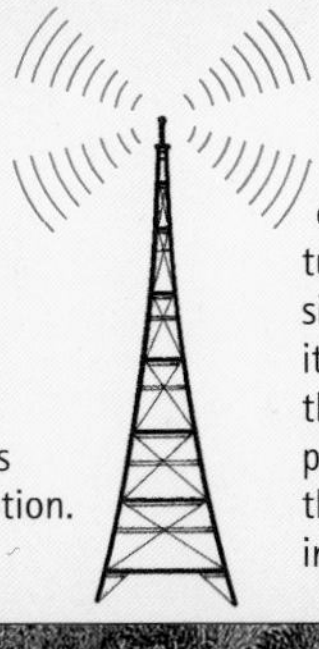

Various signals flow around a radio antenna and create tiny electrical currents. The radio is tuned into just one of these signals, which is separated from its carrier wave. The signal is then amplified (made more powerful) by the radio, and the speaker changes it back into sound.

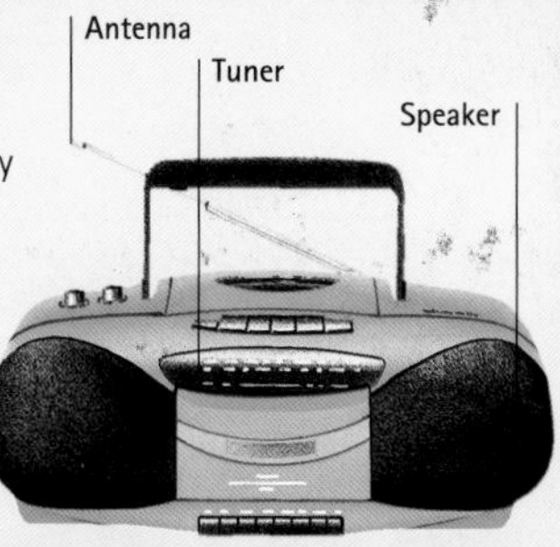

• COMMUNICATIONS •

Messages from Space

Satellites circling the Earth send us pictures of the weather and relay telephone calls and television programs around the world. They also study vast areas of the Earth and its oceans, taking photographs and measurements with their cameras and instruments and beaming them down to Earth by radio. Some satellites circle the planet from pole to pole; others circle around the equator. Most satellites orbit the Earth at a height of between 124 miles (200 km) and 496 miles (800 km) and have to travel at a speed of 5 miles (8 km) per second to stay in orbit. Communications and weather satellites are boosted to a height of 22,320 miles (36,000 km)—much higher than other satellites. At this height above the equator, a satellite circles the Earth once every 24 hours, the same time the Earth takes to spin once on its axis. This kind of orbit is called "geostationary" because the satellite seems to hover over the same spot on Earth. It takes three satellites in geostationary orbit to relay telephone calls between any two points on Earth.

In the sky
A low-flying satellite orbits at a height of about 155–186 miles (250-300 km) just outside most of the Earth's atmosphere. It can dip down to as low as 74 miles (120 km) to take close-up photographs of interesting places. Its advanced camera systems can see details as small as 2 in (5 cm) across.

Communications satellite
A communications satellite, or comsat, works a little like a mirror in the sky. It receives radio signals beamed up to it from Earth, amplifies them and sends them back to a different place on Earth.

Gas tanks
The satellite uses jets of gas from its gas tanks to stop it from drifting out of position.

Communications circuits
The satellite's communications circuits can relay tens of thousands of telephone calls at the same time.

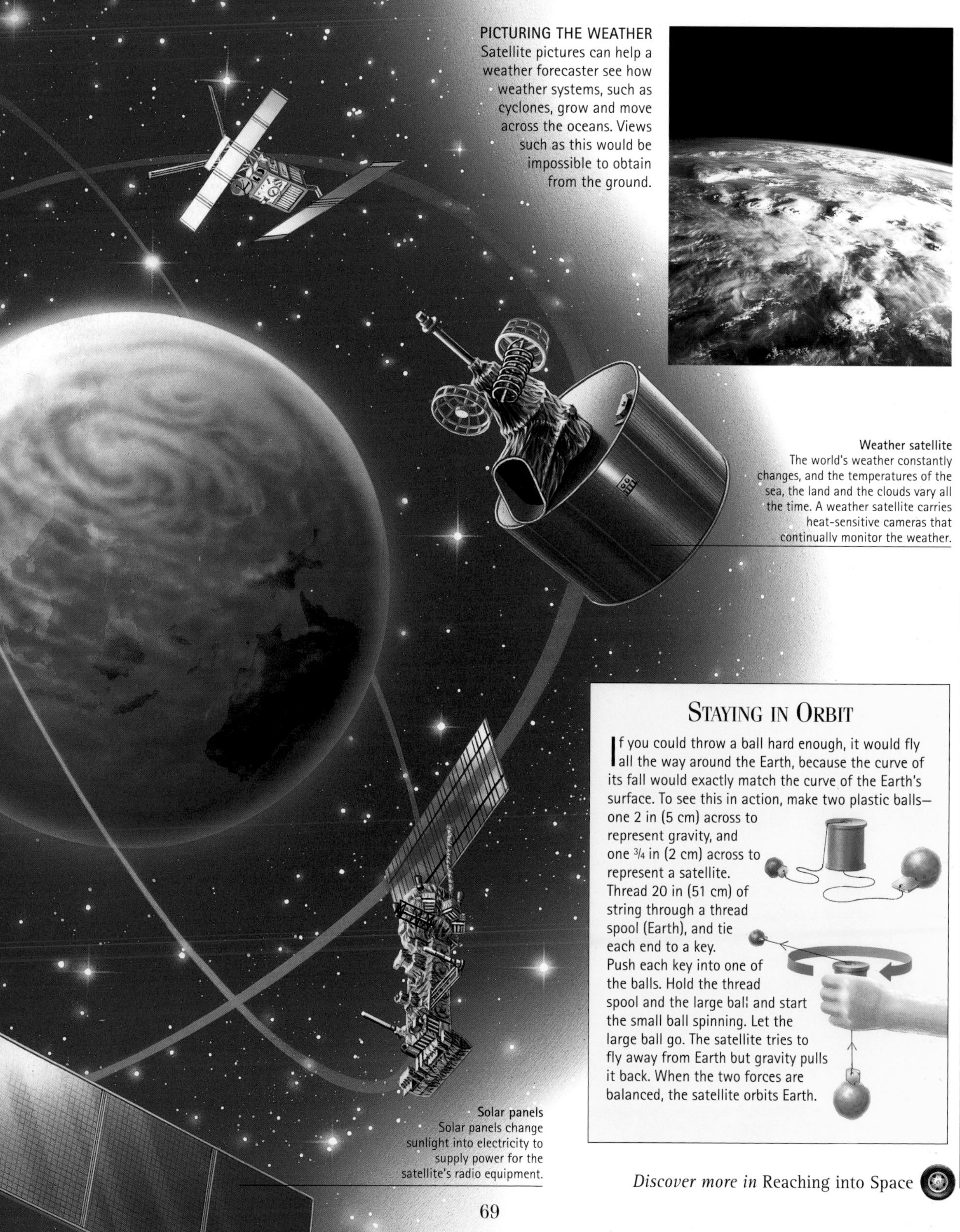

PICTURING THE WEATHER
Satellite pictures can help a weather forecaster see how weather systems, such as cyclones, grow and move across the oceans. Views such as this would be impossible to obtain from the ground.

Weather satellite
The world's weather constantly changes, and the temperatures of the sea, the land and the clouds vary all the time. A weather satellite carries heat-sensitive cameras that continually monitor the weather.

Solar panels
Solar panels change sunlight into electricity to supply power for the satellite's radio equipment.

Staying in Orbit

If you could throw a ball hard enough, it would fly all the way around the Earth, because the curve of its fall would exactly match the curve of the Earth's surface. To see this in action, make two plastic balls—one 2 in (5 cm) across to represent gravity, and one $^{3}/_{4}$ in (2 cm) across to represent a satellite. Thread 20 in (51 cm) of string through a thread spool (Earth), and tie each end to a key. Push each key into one of the balls. Hold the thread spool and the large ball and start the small ball spinning. Let the large ball go. The satellite tries to fly away from Earth but gravity pulls it back. When the two forces are balanced, the satellite orbits Earth.

Discover more in Reaching into Space

TELEPHONE
A telephone converts the sound of a caller's voice into an electric current and changes electric currents received from other telephones into sound.
Coil
An electrical signal received by the earpiece passes through a coil and creates a weak magnetic field around it.
Magnet
The magnet attracts or repels the coil and makes it vibrate.
Diaphragm
The diaphragm then vibrates to create a sound.
Diaphragm
The mouthpiece works in the opposite way to the earpiece. The caller's voice makes the diaphragm vibrate.
Coil
A coil of wire fixed to the diaphragm vibrates next to a magnet. The vibrations create an electric current that is sent on.

• COMMUNICATIONS •

Shrinking the World

Distances are usually measured in miles or kilometers, but they can also be measured in time—the time it takes to communicate over a certain distance. In past centuries, the distance to the next town might have been measured by the time it took to travel there on foot or on horseback. A more distant town might be a week away and another continent might be several months away by ship. With telephones we can now communicate with someone thousands of miles away just as quickly as we can with someone in the next room. The size of the world seems to have shrunk. Electrical communication works by changing information into electrical signals that can be sent along cables. The first telephone calls made their entire journey as electrical signals in metal cables. Today, telephone calls can also travel in the form of infrared beams along fiber-optic cables or as radio waves relayed by satellites in space.

The Path of a Telephone Call

Telephones are connected to a network of exchanges that are linked together by copper cables, fiber-optic cables or radio. Every telephone is identified by a unique number and the path a telephone call takes depends on the number that is dialed. Most telephones stay in one place and are connected to the nearest exchange by cable, but some are portable. Mobile telephones can be carried anywhere, even to another country. Every few minutes, they send out coded radio signals that identify them and let the network know where they are. This enables calls to be transmitted to the correct mobile telephone from the nearest radio antenna.

MOBILE PHONE

Mobile telephones are linked to the international telephone network by radio. Every mobile telephone contains its own radio receiver and transmitter.

STRANGE BUT TRUE

The fiber optics that carry telephone calls are made of highly refined glass. A 12-mile (19-km) block of it would be as clear to see through as an ordinary window pane. A few fibers, enough to carry 100,000 telephone calls at the same time, can pass through the eye of a needle.

FIBER-OPTIC CABLES

In many parts of the world, metal telephone cables are being replaced by fiber-optic cables made of glass. Telephone calls travel along these cables as flickering infrared beams. Fiber-optic cables are much thinner, yet carry more calls than metal cables.

Antenna
The antenna detects radio waves for the telephone's radio receiver, and also sends them out from its transmitter.
Earpiece
The earpiece changes electrical signals from the radio receiver into sound.
Display
A liquid crystal display shows the number being dialed.
Battery
A mobile telephone is powered by a battery. When the battery runs out of energy, it can be recharged (filled with more electrical energy) by a charging unit.
Keypad
Telephone numbers are dialed by pressing these keys.
Microphone
The microphone changes the speaker's voice into electrical signals.
1. Local exchange
A telephone call is sent through the caller's local exchange to the nearest main exchange by cable.
2. Main exchange
The main exchange sends the call on its way to the next main exchange via cables, optical fibers or radio signals.
3. Mobile network
Calls made to a mobile telephone are sent through the mobile telephone network.
4. Cell base station
The call is then sent to the mobile telephone from a nearby radio antenna.

Q: How do telephone calls travel through glass?

Computer Friendly

Computers have become part of our everyday lives. We use them to store a vast amount of information and process it very quickly. The processing and storage are carried out by microscopic electronic circuits called chips. The master chip, the microprocessor, controls the computer. A microprocessor may contain several hundred thousand electronic components in a space that is no bigger than your thumbnail. The chips and the rest of the equipment form only one part of a computer, the hardware, but the computer also needs instructions to tell the hardware what to do. These instructions are called computer programs, or software. Software can make a computer perform a huge range of different jobs. It may turn the computer into a word processor for writing and storing documents, a games machine for having fun, an educational tool or a very fast calculating machine.

PERSONAL COMPUTER
Every computer, whatever its size and complexity, contains four basic elements: the input device, usually a keyboard; the memory, where information is stored; the central processing unit (CPU), which carries out the instructions; and the output device, usually a monitor and printer.

Monitor
A computer monitor looks like a small television screen. It receives and displays information from the computer.

CD-ROM drive
A CD-ROM (Compact Disk Read-Only Memory) can hold all sorts of information that can be copied from the CD-ROM onto the computer, but new information cannot be recorded on it.

Ball

Wheel

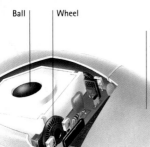

Buttons
A mouse may have one, two or three buttons.

DRIVING THE MOUSE
A mouse is used to steer a pointer around the screen. When you move the mouse, a ball underneath it rolls and makes two slotted wheels turn. As each wheel turns, a light shines through the slots and the flashes are detected by a sensor. The number and speed of the flashes show how far, how fast and in which direction the mouse is moving. When you "click" the button or buttons on the mouse, you select different options on the screen.

Floppy Disk Drive

The disk drive works like a tape recorder, but instead of recording information on magnetic tape it uses magnetic disks. With a disk slotted into the drive, which is positioned at the front of the computer, information can be copied onto the disk or from the disk onto the computer.

Read-write head
The read-write head records information onto the disk and reads it again when it is needed.

DISK
Information is stored as magnetic patterns on a paper-thin disk.

Microprocessor
The microprocessor is a personal computer's master control chip. It contains the computer's central processing unit.

Speakers
A computer often has speakers to play music, sound effects or speech.

Keyboard
This is used to put information onto the computer.

Did You Know?

The idea of the computer dates back to the 1830s when English mathematician Charles Babbage tried to build a calculating machine called the Analytical Engine. Babbage failed because the parts for his machine could not be made with enough precision. However, many of his ideas were used more than 100 years later when the first computers were built.

Discover more in Recording Sound

View of a butterfly wing with the naked eye

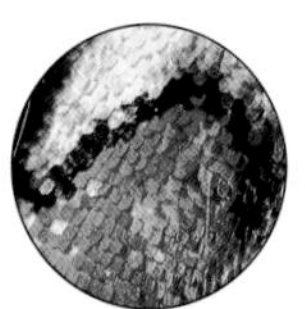

15 x magnified view of a butterfly wing

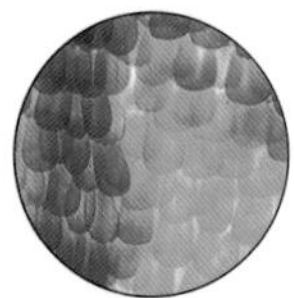

50 x magnified view of a butterfly wing

MICROSCOPE

The simplest microscope is a magnifying glass. However, a single lens can only magnify an object up to 15 times. For greater magnifications, a compound microscope with several lenses is used.

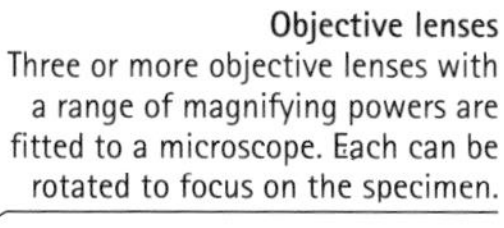

Seeing clearly
The image is seen by looking into the eyepiece. It contains one or more lenses.

Objective lenses
Three or more objective lenses with a range of magnifying powers are fitted to a microscope. Each can be rotated to focus on the specimen.

Specimen
The specimen is placed between two pieces of glass, which must be thin enough for light to pass through them.

Light source
Light is reflected up to the specimen using an angled mirror.

• LEISURE AND ENTERTAINMENT •

A Closer Look

The human eye is an amazing organ, but there are many things it cannot see because they are too small or too far away. We use instruments to magnify tiny details so they are big enough for us to see. Microscopes, for example, can make small objects look 2,500 times bigger than they really are. Telescopes and binoculars produce magnified images of objects that appear too small to see clearly because they are so far away. These instruments are built with lenses, because lenses can bend light rays and make our eyes think that the light has come from a much larger object. Light enters the instruments through a type of lens called an objective lens. This forms an enlarged image of the object. We look at this image through another lens, the eyepiece, which magnifies it a little more.

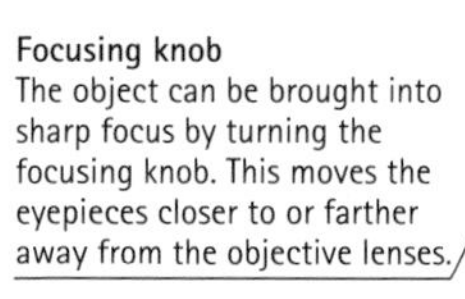

Focusing knob
The object can be brought into sharp focus by turning the focusing knob. This moves the eyepieces closer to or farther away from the objective lenses.

Eyepiece
Each eyepiece contains lenses that magnify the image. One eyepiece can be adjusted to allow for differences between the eyes.

UP CLOSE

Binoculars are two compact, portable telescopes, side by side. They allow people to see things close up with both eyes.

CLEAR VISION

Glasses are a pair of lenses placed in front of the eyes to correct poor vision.

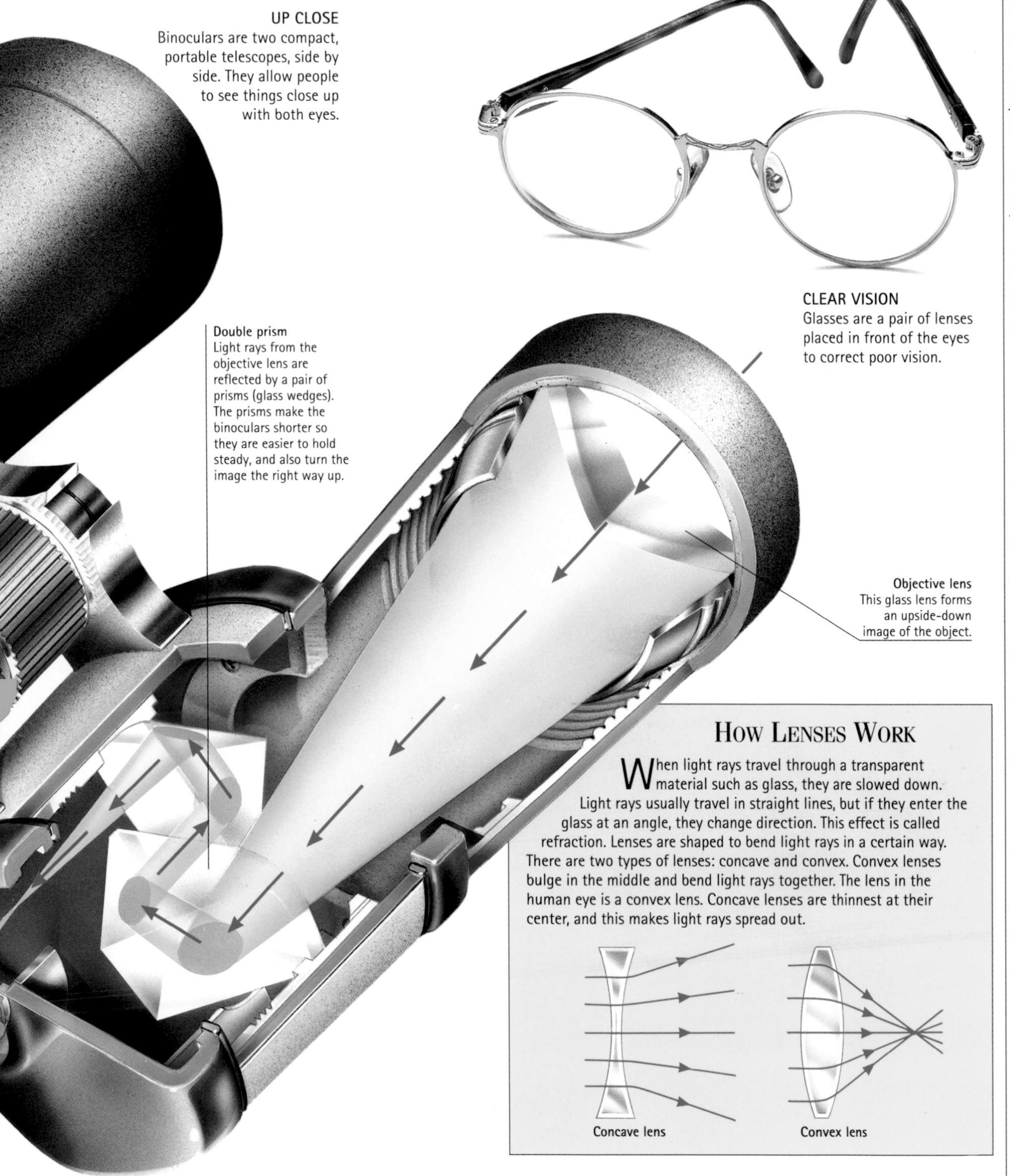

Double prism
Light rays from the objective lens are reflected by a pair of prisms (glass wedges). The prisms make the binoculars shorter so they are easier to hold steady, and also turn the image the right way up.
Objective lens
This glass lens forms an upside-down image of the object.

How Lenses Work

When light rays travel through a transparent material such as glass, they are slowed down. Light rays usually travel in straight lines, but if they enter the glass at an angle, they change direction. This effect is called refraction. Lenses are shaped to bend light rays in a certain way. There are two types of lenses: concave and convex. Convex lenses bulge in the middle and bend light rays together. The lens in the human eye is a convex lens. Concave lenses are thinnest at their center, and this makes light rays spread out.

Concave lens

Convex lens

Q: What do the prisms inside a pair of binoculars do?

In Focus

A camera allows us to take photographs of people or scenes. Cameras vary enormously in their complexity but they all operate on the same principle—light enters the camera and falls on the film inside. Light rays enter a camera through a lens, which focuses them to form a sharp image on the film. The camera is aimed by looking through a window called the viewfinder. Many cameras automatically control the amount of light entering them, which makes them simple to use. Other cameras allow you to manually control the amount of light that falls on the film, but this makes them more complicated to use. Some cameras have separate lenses for forming the image on the film and in the viewfinder. One popular type of camera, the single lens reflex (SLR), can have both automatic and manual control. It uses the same lens for both so that the photographer always sees precisely the same scene that will be photographed.

Did You Know?

The first permanent photograph was produced in 1827 by Frenchman Joseph-Nicéphore Niépce when he discovered that asphalt was light sensitive. However, posing for his photograph may not have been much fun. He took eight hours to take one photograph!

SINGLE-USE CAMERA
A single-use camera is sold complete with a film loaded inside it. When all the photographs have been taken, the whole camera is sent away for the film to be processed.

Plastic lens
To keep the camera simple to make and use, the plastic lens is set so that it does not have to be adjusted.

SLR CAMERA
A single lens reflex (SLR) camera can be fitted with a variety of different lenses. A wide-angle lens is used for broad scenes, while a macro lens is added for close-ups. A zoom lens varies the magnifying power.

Winding on
After a photograph is taken, the film winder is turned to move a new piece of film behind the shutter, ready for the next photograph.

Smile!
The shutter release button is pressed to take a photograph.

Film
A springy plate presses the film into position behind the shutter, and also keeps it flat.

Viewfinder
The photographer looks through the viewfinder to see the picture the camera will take.

Right way up
The pentaprism is a specially shaped block of glass. It reverses the image formed by the lens so that it appears the correct way through the viewfinder.

Making Photographs

When light falls on photographic film, it causes a chemical reaction in a light-sensitive layer called the emulsion. In the fraction of a second when a camera's shutter is open, the chemical reaction releases a tiny amount of silver from silver crystals in the emulsion. Only a few atoms of silver are released by each crystal, so the image is invisible. When the film is treated with chemicals, millions more silver atoms are released. The emulsion is then washed away in places where light did not fall on it. The picture formed on the film is a negative image—dark where light fell on it. This is turned into a photograph by shining light through the negative onto a sheet of light-sensitive paper and developing the image on the paper. Color film has three layers of light-sensitive chemicals. Each layer is sensitive to a different color. The three colors combine to form a lifelike color photograph.

Hinged mirror
The mirror reflects light entering the camera onto the viewing screen. Once the shutter release is pressed, the mirror flips out of the way to let light fall on the film.

Lens system
The lens in an SLR camera contains several separate lenses that work together to form a clear, sharp image.

HOW A CAMERA SEES

When a photographer presses a camera's shutter release button, the shutter opens and lets light stream in through the lens and fall on the film. The lens focuses the image on the film and a chemical reaction in the film captures the image.

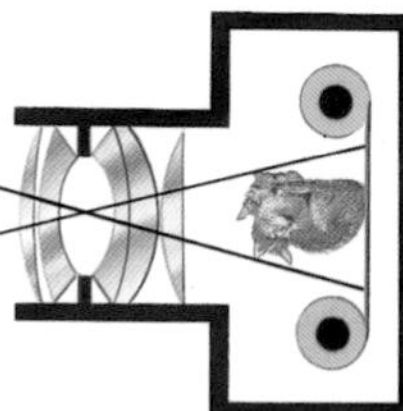

Shutter
The shutter opens to let light fall on the film, then closes again. The time it takes to do this is either set by the photographer or calculated automatically by the camera.

Q: What does a pentaprism do?

Recording Sound

Recorded sound enables us to listen to music wherever and whenever we like. Recordings can be broadcast to millions of people by radio. Small, lightweight personal stereos and compact disk players allow us to enjoy music in private, even while we are on the move. Most recorded sound depends on either magnetism or light. Personal stereos and tape recorders use magnetism. Before sound can be recorded magnetically, it must first be changed into an electrical signal by a microphone. The electrical signal is then changed into a varying magnetic force that magnetizes the recording tape. Compact disk players use light. Sound is stored on the silver-colored disk as a pattern of tiny pits (holes). When light bounces off the spinning disk, the pits make the reflections vary. The varying intensity of the reflections is changed into electricity, and a speaker then converts this into sound.

COMPACT DISK PLAYER
A compact disk player is a machine that uses light, produced by a laser, to react to a spiral pattern of tiny holes in a spinning plastic disk.

PORTABLE PERSONAL STEREO
A personal stereo is a miniature tape recorder. The pattern of magnetism on the tape creates a varying current in the playback head next to the tape. The current is amplified (made larger) and then changed into sound by the earphones.

Spindles
The portable stereo contains two spindles. They wind the tape from one spool to the other, past the tape heads.

Playback head
This detects the magnetic pattern on the tape and changes it into an electric current.

How Magnetic Tape Works

The record head and playback head of a tape recorder are electromagnets. The strength of the magnetic field set up by the record head varies as the current through it varies. As the tape moves past the head when recording, parts of the tape are magnetized to varying degrees. When the magnetized tape is run past the playback head, the fluctuating magnetism from the tape sets up tiny currents in a coil of wire. These are then amplified and fed to the headphones or to the speaker.

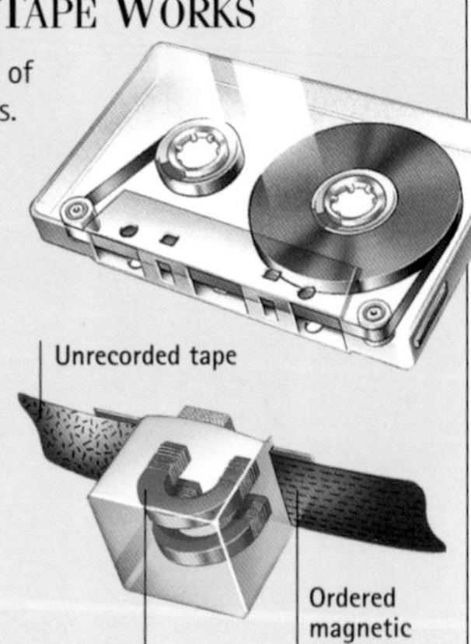

Did You Know?

The first sound recording was made by shouting at a diaphragm—a disk that vibrates in response to the sound waves of a voice. As the disk vibrated, it activated a needle attached to it. This scored a groove in a spinning cylinder covered with tinfoil. When the recording was played back, the groove made the needle and disk vibrate and recreate the voice.

MICROPHONE

Performers often wear radio microphones. The microphone changes the performer's voice into an electrical signal. Then a battery-powered radio transmitter, sometimes worn on a belt, sends it to a radio receiver, which relays it to the audience via the sound system.

Making music
On a circuit board beneath this casing, the Digital to Analog Converter (DAC) changes pulses of electricity from the photodiode (a light-sensitive conductor) into an analog (smoothly varying) electrical signal. When this is amplified, a speaker changes it into a copy of the sound recorded on the compact disk.

Laser
The laser produces an intense beam of light. A lens focuses this beam onto a spot on the disk that is one millionth of a yard across.

Photodiode
This converts reflections from the disk into an electrical signal.

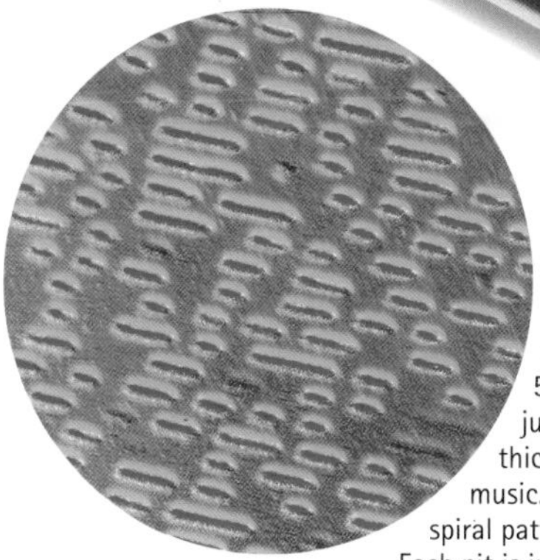

THE PITS

A standard compact disk, 5 in (12 cm) across and just over 1/25 in (1 mm) thick, can hold an hour of music. It is covered with a spiral pattern of microscopic pits. Each pit is invisible to the naked eye.

The World in View

Television programs are usually transmitted to your home by radio waves, but they can also travel via underground cables. Your rooftop antenna detects the radio waves and converts them into an electrical signal. The television converts this signal into pictures and sound. A television picture seems to be moving, but it is really a technological trick that fools your eyes and brain. The picture on the screen is made by a glowing spot that moves from side to side and up and down so quickly that the whole screen seems to glow at the same time. Television pictures appear on the screen one after another so rapidly that they look like a single moving picture. It works because of an effect called "persistence of vision." When light forms an image (picture) on the retina (the light-sensitive layer at the back of your eye), the image stays on the retina for a fraction of a second after the light that formed it has gone. This means that when images reach your eyes very quickly, one after the other, they merge together.

TELEVISION
A television converts electrical signals from a rooftop antenna or an underground cable into pictures and sound. This is a widescreen television. Its screen is one-third wider than a normal television.

Video drum
The video drum spins at an angle to the tape. Tape heads (small electromagnets) on the surface of the video drum transfer the electrical signals into a magnetic pattern on the video tape.

Video cassette
When a standard video cassette is put into the recorder, the machine automatically opens a flap on the front edge, pulls out a loop of tape, and wraps this around the video drum.

Screen
The television screen, on which pictures are formed, is the flattened end of a large glass tube.

Phosphors
The back of the screen is coated with chemicals called "phosphors." They glow in one of three colors—red, green or blue—when electrons strike them.

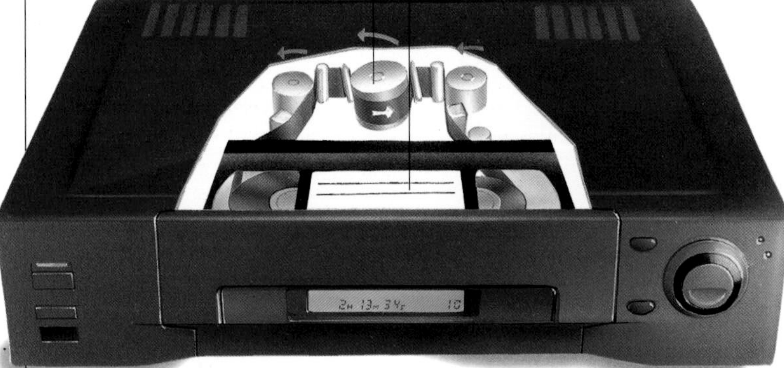

Shadow mask
The shadow mask is a metal sheet with slots in it, and three electron beams pass through it on their way to the screen. The mask ensures that each electron beam strikes and lights up only one phosphor: red, green or blue.

VIDEO CASSETTE RECORDER
A video cassette recorder can record television programs by storing the electrical signals from the television antenna magnetically on video tape.

Did You Know?

When televisions first went on sale they were sold as kits. The buyer had to put the television together. The screen was often only 4 in (10 cm) high and 2 in (5 cm) wide.

Electron beams
Three beams of electrons fly from the back of the tube to the screen. Electric fields focus them onto the screen.

Deflection coils
Electromagnets around the neck of the tube deflect (bend) the beams from side to side as well as up and down to trace out the pattern of horizontal lines that form the picture.

REMOTE CONTROL
When buttons on the remote control handset are pressed, an invisible infrared beam sends instructions to the television. The beam is a stream of coded pulses. This tells the television which buttons were pressed and what to do next.

In Color

A television can produce a picture that contains all the colors in the rainbow. The phosphors on the back of the screen that produce the picture, however, glow in only three colors—red, green and blue. Every color can be made by mixing different amounts of red, green and blue light. For this reason, they are called primary colors. Mixing these primary colors together in precisely the correct proportions produces white light. The glowing colored spots on a television screen are so small and so close together that, from a distance, they appear to merge together to form different colors.

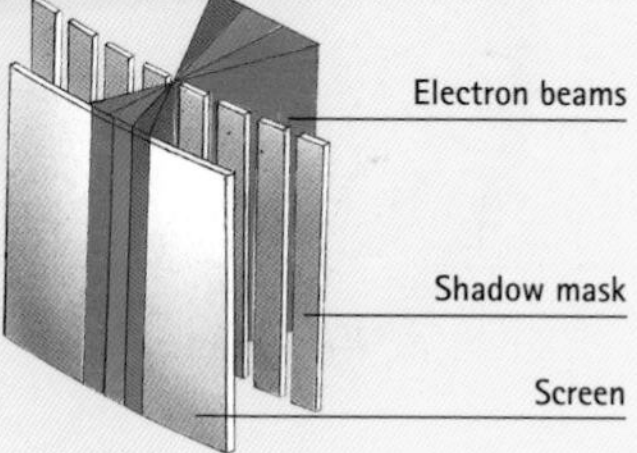

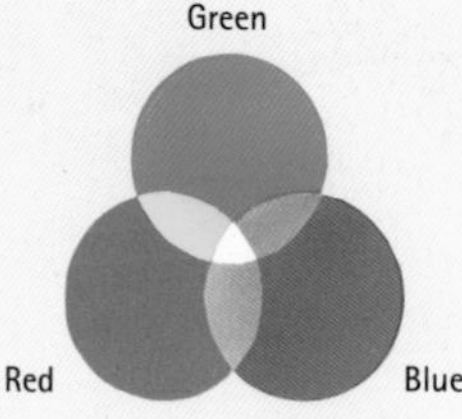

Discover more in Keeping in Touch

On the Road Again

When Carl Benz visualized the "horseless carriage" last century he could not have imagined how complex cars would become. Modern cars consist of several different mechanical and electrical systems all working together. The fuel system supplies fuel to the engine, and the ignition system provides electrical sparks at just the right moment to ignite the fuel. The transmission system transmits the power generated by the engine to the car's wheels. The lubrication system keeps all the moving parts in the engine covered with a film of oil so that they can slip over each other without sticking. The cooling system stops the engine from overheating and the braking system stops the car safely. The suspension system allows the wheels to follow bumps and dips in the road while the rest of the car glides along smoothly. Today there are more than 400 million passenger cars on roads around the world.

Suspension
A system of springs and oil-filled telescopic tubes called dampers absorbs bumps in the road and gives a smoother ride.

Fuel tank
The fuel that is burned in the engine is pumped from a tank at the rear of the car.

Tires
Pneumatic (air-filled) tires give a smoother ride over small bumps in the ground.

Brake cables
Brake cables are connected to levers on the handlebars. When the levers are squeezed, the cables compress the brake pads on the wheels and slow the bicycle down.

Chain
The chain passes around the gears and turns the rear wheel.

Gears
Gears make a bicycle easier to pedal. Low gears turn the wheel only a small amount and help the rider to pedal uphill.

Spokes
Thin wire spokes hold the wheels in place and let the wind blow through them instead of against the bicycle.

Strange but True

In 1865, a law was passed in England to limit the speed of steam cars. They were not allowed to go faster than 2 miles (3 km) per hour in cities and they also had to travel behind a man waving a red flag!

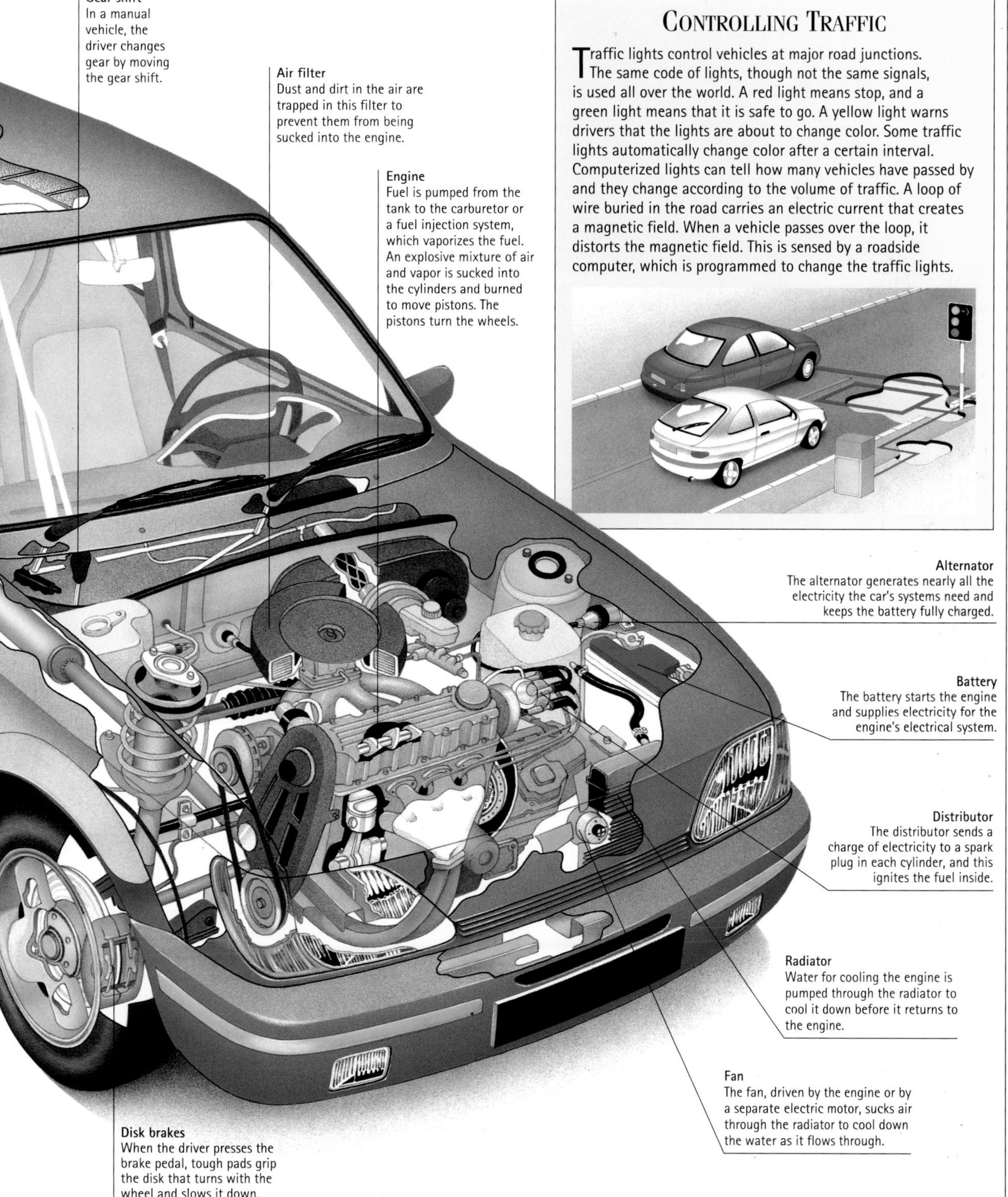

Gear shift
In a manual vehicle, the driver changes gear by moving the gear shift.
Air filter
Dust and dirt in the air are trapped in this filter to prevent them from being sucked into the engine.
Engine
Fuel is pumped from the tank to the carburetor or a fuel injection system, which vaporizes the fuel. An explosive mixture of air and vapor is sucked into the cylinders and burned to move pistons. The pistons turn the wheels.
Alternator
The alternator generates nearly all the electricity the car's systems need and keeps the battery fully charged.
Battery
The battery starts the engine and supplies electricity for the engine's electrical system.
Distributor
The distributor sends a charge of electricity to a spark plug in each cylinder, and this ignites the fuel inside.
Radiator
Water for cooling the engine is pumped through the radiator to cool it down before it returns to the engine.
Fan
The fan, driven by the engine or by a separate electric motor, sucks air through the radiator to cool down the water as it flows through.
Disk brakes
When the driver presses the brake pedal, tough pads grip the disk that turns with the wheel and slows it down.

Controlling Traffic

Traffic lights control vehicles at major road junctions. The same code of lights, though not the same signals, is used all over the world. A red light means stop, and a green light means that it is safe to go. A yellow light warns drivers that the lights are about to change color. Some traffic lights automatically change color after a certain interval. Computerized lights can tell how many vehicles have passed by and they change according to the volume of traffic. A loop of wire buried in the road carries an electric current that creates a magnetic field. When a vehicle passes over the loop, it distorts the magnetic field. This is sensed by a roadside computer, which is programmed to change the traffic lights.

Q: What does a car's lubrication system do?

Staying on Track

If you travel anywhere by train, your carriage will be pulled along by one of four types of locomotive. In a few places, steam locomotives are still used. Coal is burned to heat water and make steam, which pushes pistons inside cylinders to turn the wheels. Diesel or diesel-electric locomotives are now more common than steam engines. Diesel locomotives burn oil in a piston engine, which is like a giant car engine, to turn the wheels. Diesel-electric locomotives use a diesel engine to drive an electric generator. The generator powers the electric motors that turn the wheels. The world's fastest railway trains are pulled by electric locomotives that convert electrical energy directly into movement. The electricity for the motors is supplied by cables suspended over the track. The German InterCity Express (ICE) train is one of the world's fastest trains: its top speed is more than 248 miles (400 km) per hour, but it usually transports passengers at 155 miles (250 km) per hour.

RAILWAY SIGNALS
Colored light signals by the side of the track tell train drivers whether or not it is safe for a train to proceed.

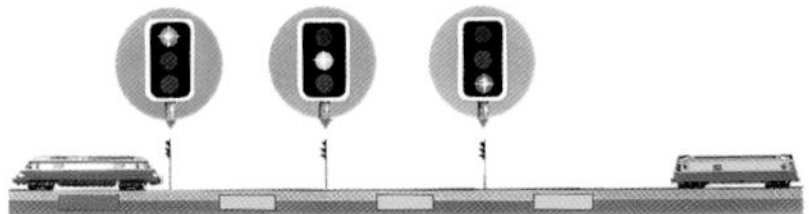

A green signal indicates that two or more sections of track ahead of a train are clear and it is safe to proceed.

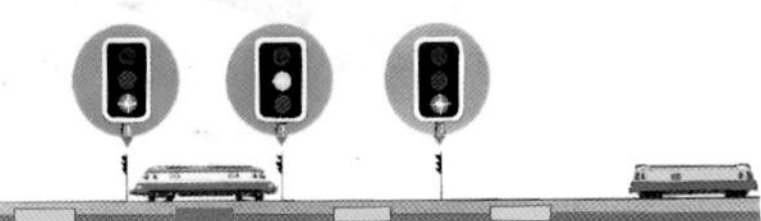

A yellow signal indicates that only one clear section of track separates two trains. As a train passes each signal, it changes to red.

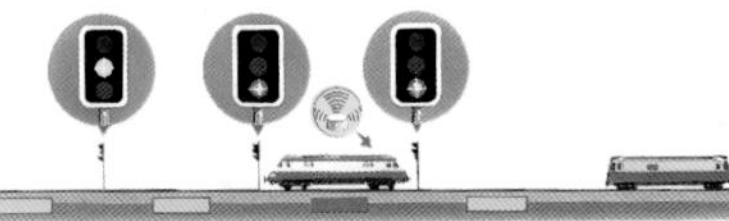

A red signal shows that the track ahead is not clear and an alarm sounds in the driver's cab.

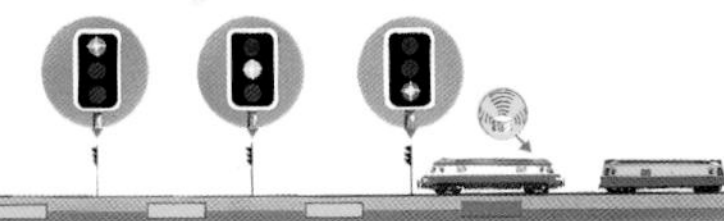

When the train has stopped, the alarm continues to sound a warning that it is not safe to proceed.

ICE TRAIN
The German ICE (InterCity Express) is an example of a modern, high-speed electric train.

Close behind
These carriages are divided into sections with seats in rows or facing each other.

Riding up front
The carriages at the front have fewer seats and more room than those behind.

Flying on Magnetism

The maglev (magnetic levitation train) is held above its track, or guideway, by powerful forces between electromagnets (electrically powered magnets) in the track and in the train. Magnets in the sides of the train hold it steady in the guideway. Magnetic fields are also used to make the train move. Magnets ahead of the train attract it, pulling it forward, and magnets behind repel it, pushing it forward. The magnetic field ripples along the guideway, pulling the train with it. There is no contact between the train and the track and passengers have a very smooth and quiet ride.

British maglev train

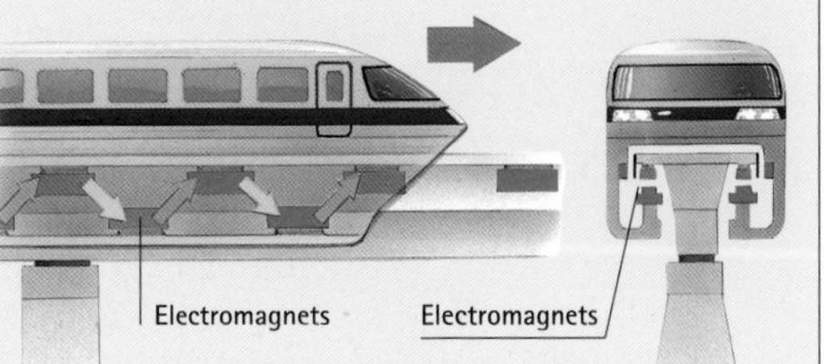

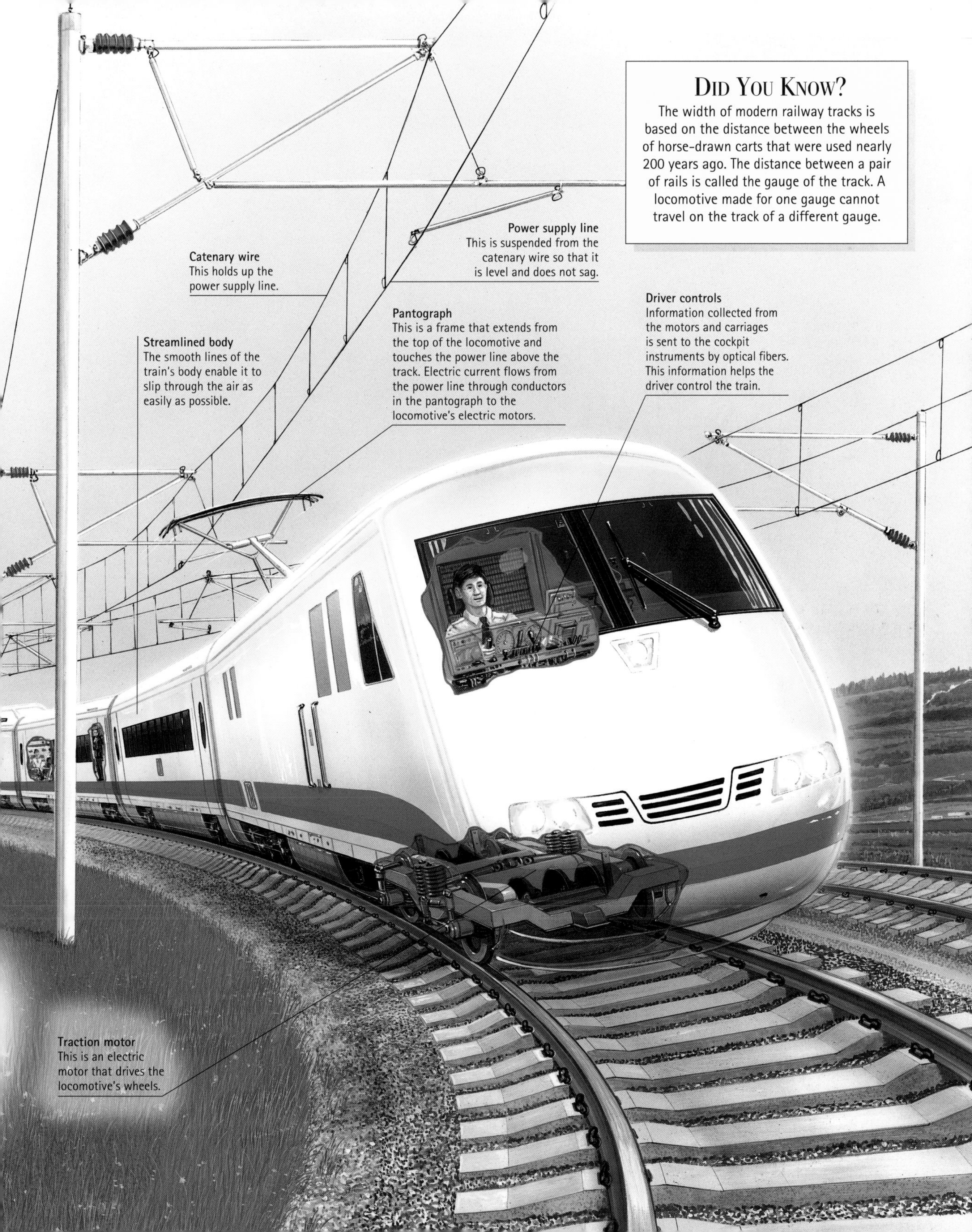

DID YOU KNOW?
The width of modern railway tracks is based on the distance between the wheels of horse-drawn carts that were used nearly 200 years ago. The distance between a pair of rails is called the gauge of the track. A locomotive made for one gauge cannot travel on the track of a different gauge.
Power supply line
This is suspended from the catenary wire so that it is level and does not sag.
Catenary wire
This holds up the power supply line.
Driver controls
Information collected from the motors and carriages is sent to the cockpit instruments by optical fibers. This information helps the driver control the train.
Pantograph
This is a frame that extends from the top of the locomotive and touches the power line above the track. Electric current flows from the power line through conductors in the pantograph to the locomotive's electric motors.
Streamlined body
The smooth lines of the train's body enable it to slip through the air as easily as possible.
Traction motor
This is an electric motor that drives the locomotive's wheels.

Did You Know?

When compasses were first used on ships, seamen did not understand how they worked and were afraid of the magical powers they seemed to possess. Compasses were hidden from the crew inside a box called a binnacle.

• TRANSPORTATION •

Roaming the Oceans

When anything tries to move through water, the water resists its movement. Boat designers try to minimize water resistance, called "drag," by making boat hulls as smooth and streamlined as possible. Water underneath a boat pushes up against its hull with a force called "upthrust." If the force of the boat's weight is equal to the upthrust of the water, the boat floats. If the boat weighs more than the upthrust of the water, it sinks. A submarine, or a smaller underwater craft called a submersible, sinks under the waves by letting water into its ballast tanks to make it heavier. It rises to the surface again by forcing the water out of the tanks with compressed air, or by dropping heavy weights to make the craft lighter. Most working boats, submarines and submersibles are powered by propellers with angled blades that push against the water as they turn.

Manipulator arm
A robot arm with a mechanical claw at the end of it picks up objects from the sea bed.

SETTING SAIL
A sail is set at an angle so that wind blowing around the sail from the side reduces the air pressure in front of it, sucking the sail and the boat forward. This means that a sail can use a wind blowing in one direction to propel a yacht in a completely different direction. But a yacht can never sail directly into the wind.

BELOW THE SURFACE
Submersibles allow scientists to explore the sea bed, study living organisms in their natural surroundings and investigate shipwrecks.

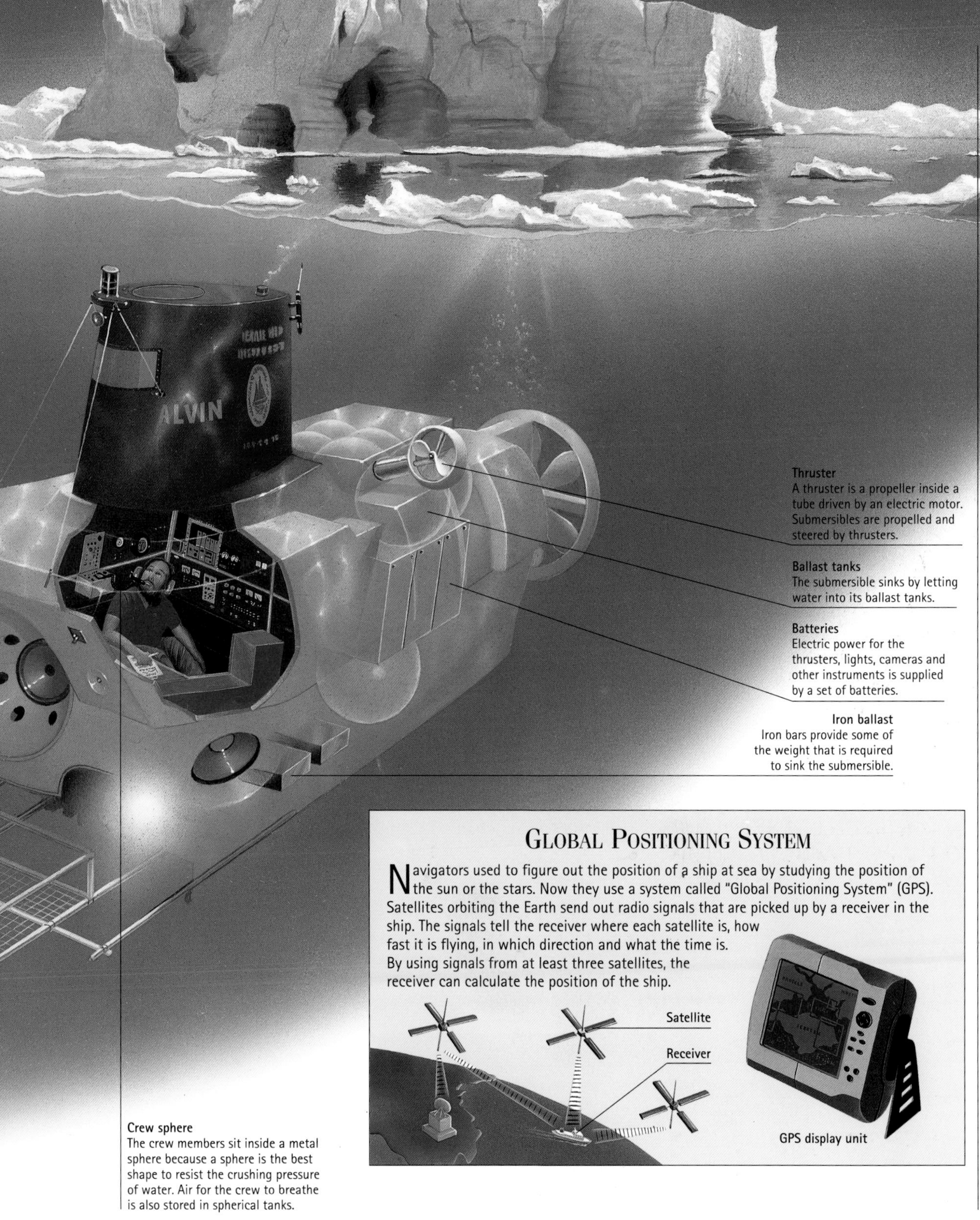

Thruster
A thruster is a propeller inside a tube driven by an electric motor. Submersibles are propelled and steered by thrusters.

Ballast tanks
The submersible sinks by letting water into its ballast tanks.

Batteries
Electric power for the thrusters, lights, cameras and other instruments is supplied by a set of batteries.

Iron ballast
Iron bars provide some of the weight that is required to sink the submersible.

Crew sphere
The crew members sit inside a metal sphere because a sphere is the best shape to resist the crushing pressure of water. Air for the crew to breathe is also stored in spherical tanks.

Global Positioning System

Navigators used to figure out the position of a ship at sea by studying the position of the sun or the stars. Now they use a system called "Global Positioning System" (GPS). Satellites orbiting the Earth send out radio signals that are picked up by a receiver in the ship. The signals tell the receiver where each satellite is, how fast it is flying, in which direction and what the time is. By using signals from at least three satellites, the receiver can calculate the position of the ship.

• TRANSPORTATION •

Reaching into Space

Technology has made it possible for us to reach into space. Special engines, for example, have been designed to power spacecraft in this airless environment. Fuel needs oxygen to burn, but because there is no oxygen in space, the rockets that propel spacecraft carry their own supply of oxygen, or a substance containing oxygen, which is mixed with the fuel before it is burned. When rocket fuel is burned, the hot gases produced expand rapidly and rush out through a nozzle. The force propels the spacecraft in the opposite direction. When the nozzle is turned, the jet of gases changes direction and this steers the rocket. In the early days of space travel, rockets and spacecraft could be used once only. In 1981, however, America launched a reusable space shuttle. It consists of an orbiter space-plane, two booster rockets and an external fuel tank. The orbiter takes off like a rocket, glides back from space, and lands on a runway, like an aircraft.

Did You Know?

In 1976, two Viking spacecraft, like the one shown here, landed on Mars to test the soil for signs of life. Although the tests failed to prove there was life on Mars, the spacecraft sent valuable data about the planet back to Earth.

Flight deck
The orbiter is controlled by its commander and pilot from the flight deck.

Thermal tiles
Tiles cover the orbiter to protect it from the intense heat it encounters when it re-enters the atmosphere.

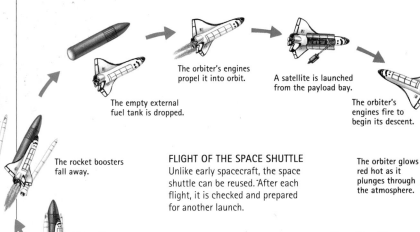

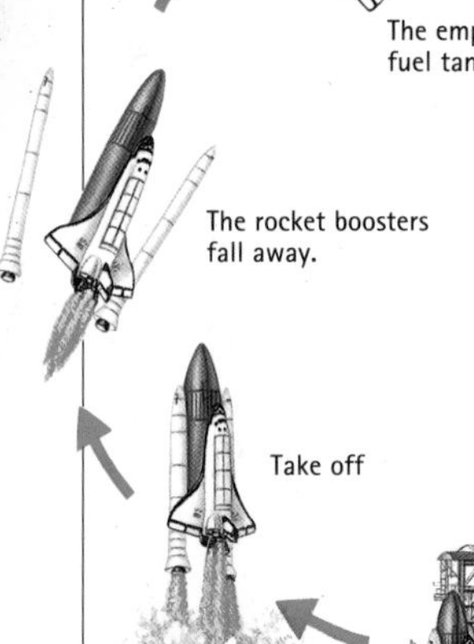

The empty external fuel tank is dropped.

The orbiter's engines propel it into orbit.

A satellite is launched from the payload bay.

The orbiter's engines fire to begin its descent.

The orbiter glows red hot as it plunges through the atmosphere.

The orbiter glides down toward the runway.

Touchdown

The space shuttle is prepared for take off.

Take off

The rocket boosters fall away.

FLIGHT OF THE SPACE SHUTTLE
Unlike early spacecraft, the space shuttle can be reused. After each flight, it is checked and prepared for another launch.

SPACE SHUTTLE

Two astronauts check a satellite before it is launched from the space shuttle orbiter's payload bay. They are linked to the orbiter by safety lines so they cannot float away into space. Small satellites are released into space by springs. Larger satellites are lifted out of the payload bay by the orbiter's robot arm. At a safe distance from the orbiter, the satellite's rocket thrusters fire to boost it into the correct orbit.

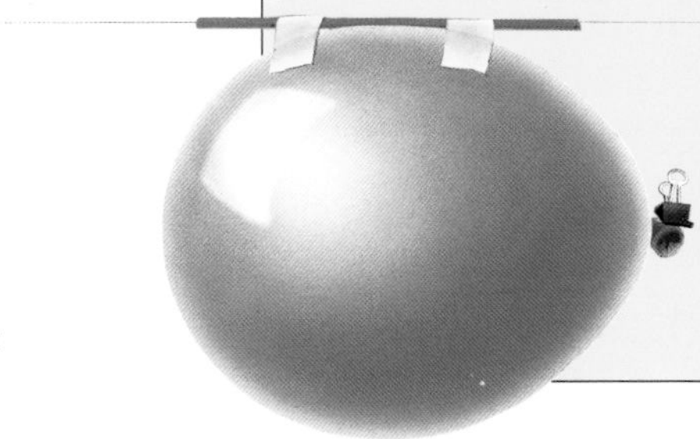

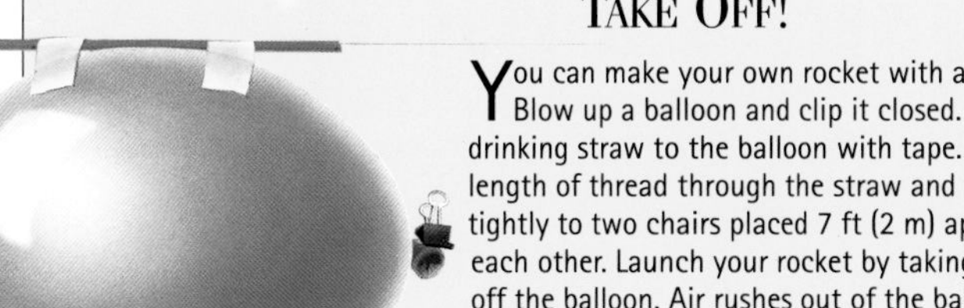

TAKE OFF!

You can make your own rocket with a balloon. Blow up a balloon and clip it closed. Attach a drinking straw to the balloon with tape. Pass a length of thread through the straw and tie it tightly to two chairs placed 7 ft (2 m) apart from each other. Launch your rocket by taking the clip off the balloon. Air rushes out of the balloon and pushes it in the opposite direction.

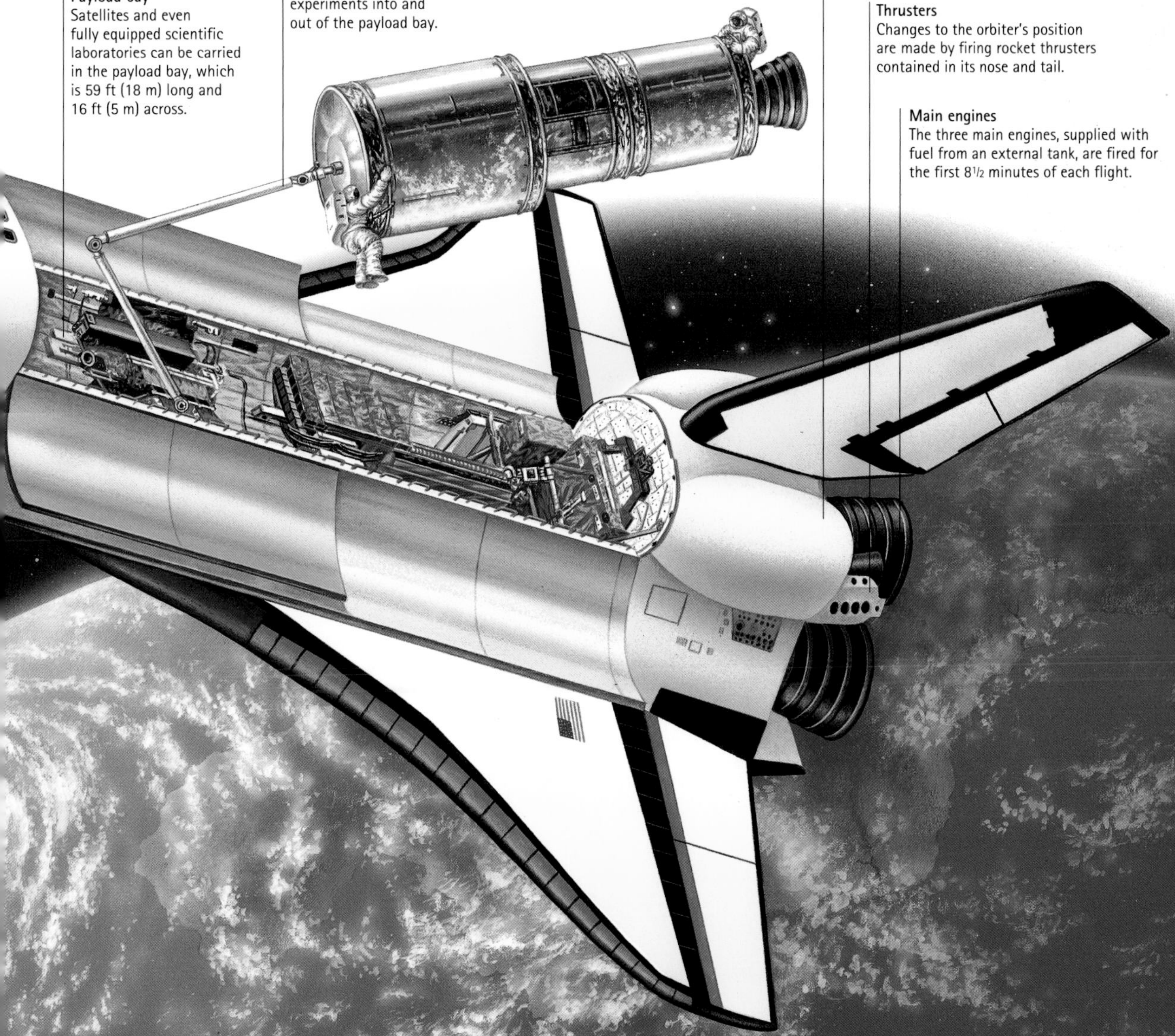

Q: Why do rockets carry their own supply of oxygen?

Robot arm
The orbiter is equipped with a robot arm for moving satellites and experiments into and out of the payload bay.

Payload bay
Satellites and even fully equipped scientific laboratories can be carried in the payload bay, which is 59 ft (18 m) long and 16 ft (5 m) across.

Orbital maneuvering engines
Two engines in the orbiter's tail move it to a higher or lower orbit and begin its descent at the end of the mission.

Thrusters
Changes to the orbiter's position are made by firing rocket thrusters contained in its nose and tail.

Main engines
The three main engines, supplied with fuel from an external tank, are fired for the first 8½ minutes of each flight.

The Principles of Things

All machines, instruments and electronic devices, from a humble office stapler or a magnifying glass to a computer or the space shuttle, make use of scientific principles. Understanding a few basic scientific principles can make it easier to see why machines are built the way they are, why some machines have a certain shape and how they work.

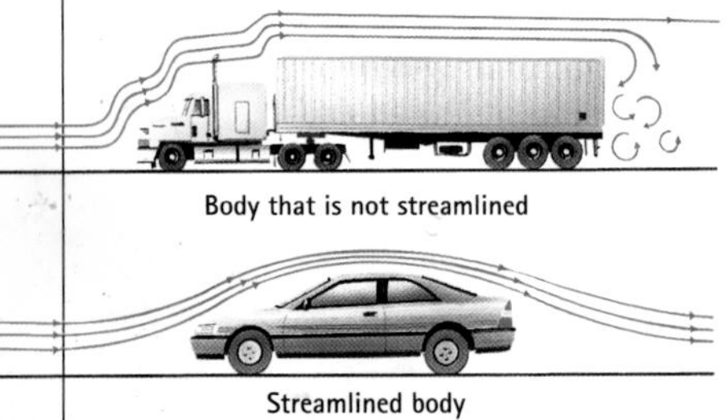

Body that is not streamlined

Streamlined body

Aerodynamics

This is the study of how air flows around objects. An object's shape affects the way that air flows around it. Air does not flow easily around a broad, angular shape, such as a truck, but it does flow easily around a slim, smoothly curved shape, such as a car. Such an object is said to be streamlined. Streamlining is particularly important for racing cars, jet airliners, rockets or anything else designed to travel at high speed.

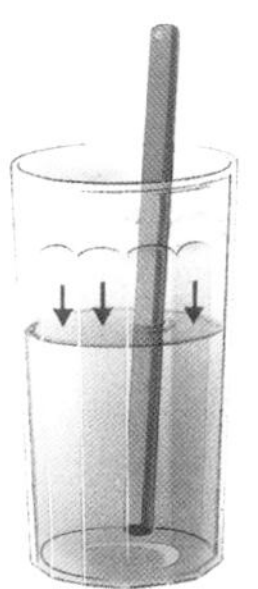

Equal air pressure

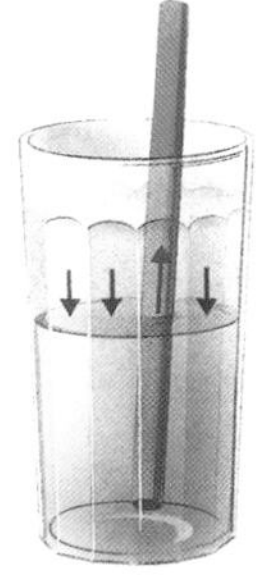

Lower air pressure in straw

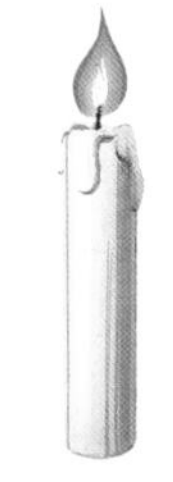

Adequate oxygen supply

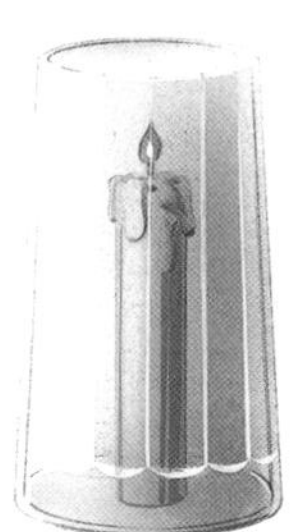

Reduced oxygen supply

Air pressure

Air pressure describes the way that air pushes back when it is squeezed. Air pressure is greatest near the Earth's surface because of the air above pressing down. High above the Earth, the air pressure is low. When you use a drinking straw you use air pressure. Sucking air out of the straw lowers the air pressure inside. The higher air pressure outside forces the drink up the straw to fill the lower pressure area.

Combustion

Combustion is another word for burning. It is a chemical reaction that gives out heat and light in the form of a flame. It occurs when a substance reacts quickly with oxygen, a gas in the air around us. A burning candle underneath an upturned glass soon uses up the oxygen in the air trapped under the glass. Its flame shrinks and goes out, while a candle outside the glass would continue to burn.

Electromagnetic radiation

Light, radio and X-rays are all examples of electromagnetic radiation. They consist of waves of electric and magnetic energy vibrating through space. The only difference between them is the length of the waves. Light is the only part of the electromagnetic spectrum that our eyes can detect. The whole spectrum is shown below, with wavelengths given in meters. Each wavelength is ten times the one before it; 10^3 meters is the same as 10 x 10 x 10, or 1,000 meters.

Electromagnetic Radiation

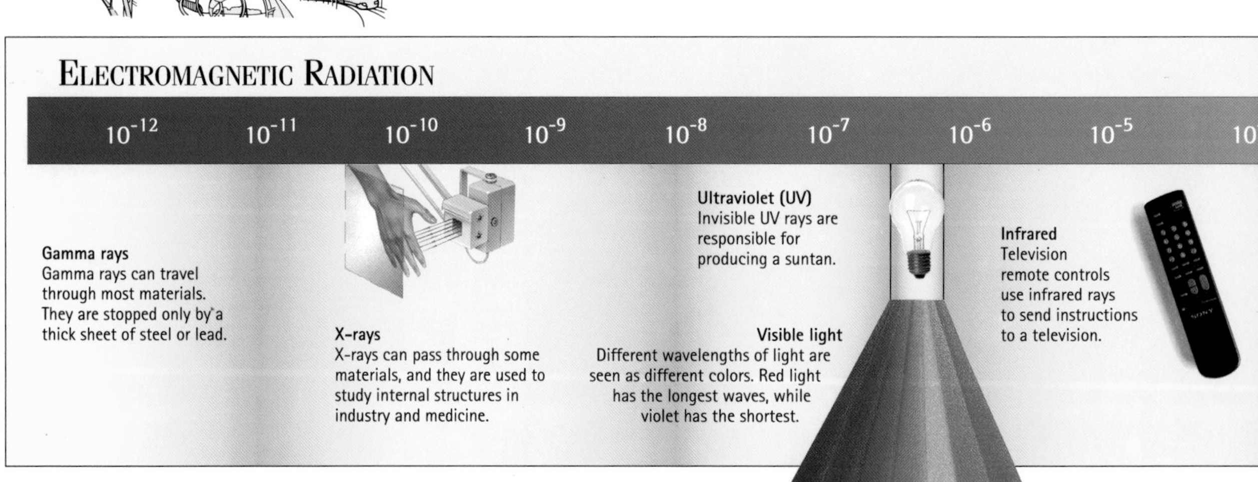

Gamma rays
Gamma rays can travel through most materials. They are stopped only by a thick sheet of steel or lead.

X-rays
X-rays can pass through some materials, and they are used to study internal structures in industry and medicine.

Ultraviolet (UV)
Invisible UV rays are responsible for producing a suntan.

Visible light
Different wavelengths of light are seen as different colors. Red light has the longest waves, while violet has the shortest.

Infrared
Television remote controls use infrared rays to send instructions to a television.

Gravity

Gravity is the force that pulls everything toward the ground, such as an apple falling from a tree. Gravity also makes the moon circle the Earth and the Earth circle the sun. The strength of an object's gravity depends on the amount of matter it is made from. Stars have a stronger gravitational pull than planets, because stars are bigger than planets.

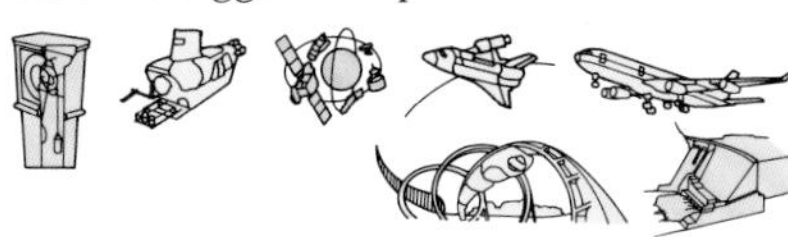

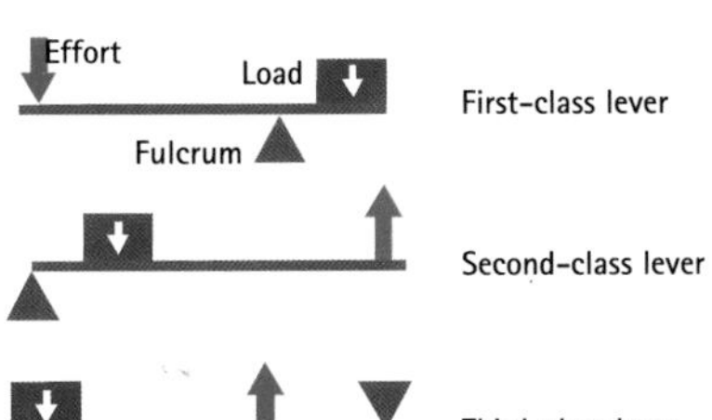

Levers

A lever is a device that transfers a force from one place to somewhere else. Every lever has a load, an effort and a fulcrum. The effort makes the lever pivot at the fulcrum, moving the load. There are three different ways of arranging the effort, load and fulcrum, called three classes of lever. A first-class lever is like a see-saw, a second-class lever is like a wheelbarrow and a third-class lever is like your own forearm.

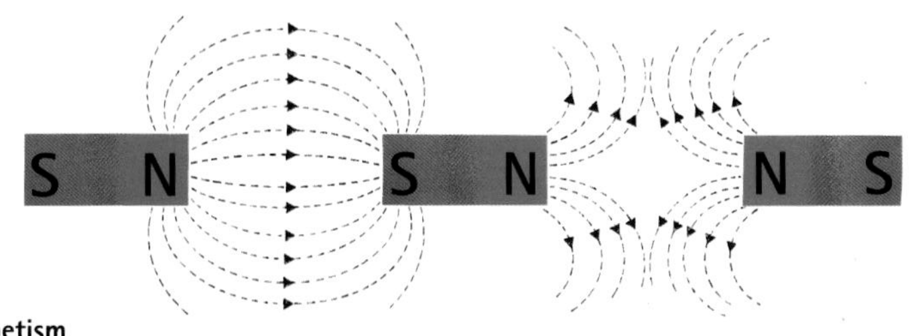

Magnetism

Magnetism is a force produced by magnets, which can attract materials such as iron, steel, cobalt and nickel. A bar magnet has a north pole and a south pole. If a north pole is brought close to the south pole of another magnet, they attract each other. If two north poles or two south poles are brought together, they push each other away. Magnetism is also produced when electricity flows. An electric current flowing along a wire creates a magnetic field around the wire.

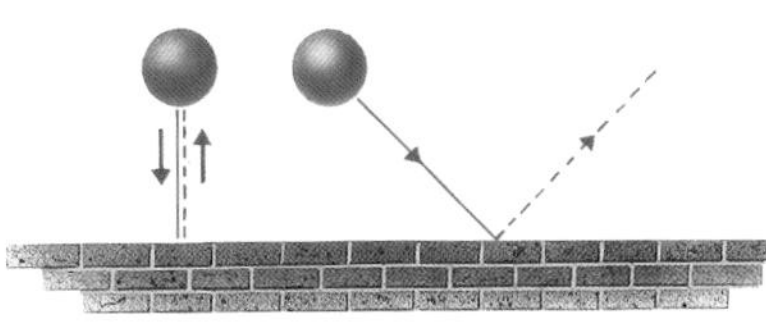

Reflection

When a wave strikes a surface it bounces back, like a ball bouncing off a wall. This rebounding effect is called reflection. We can see ourselves in a mirror because light waves are reflected by the mirror.

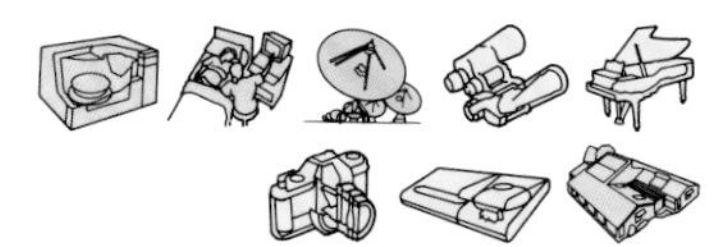

Light

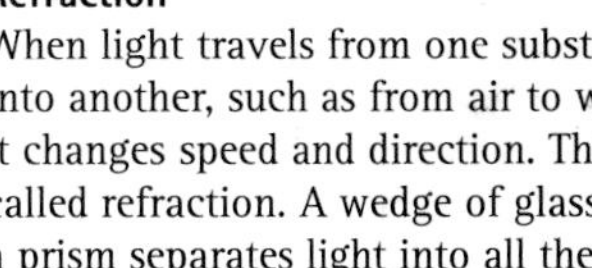

Refraction

When light travels from one substance into another, such as from air to water, it changes speed and direction. This is called refraction. A wedge of glass called a prism separates light into all the colors it contains by refraction. The different colors present in sunlight are bent by different amounts, so the colors separate and form a rainbow.

10^{-3} 10^{-2} 10^{-1} 1 10 10^{2} 10^{3} 10^{4} 10^{5}

Microwaves
Microwaves, used by microwave ovens and for communications, are radio waves between 1/25 in (1 mm) and 1 in (3 cm) long.

Radio waves
Radio waves can be as short as 1/25 in (1 mm) or as long as 62 miles (100 km).

Great Inventions

- How do inventors use natural energy?
- How can the heart of a pig save a person's life?
- Which invention was nicknamed the "literary piano"?

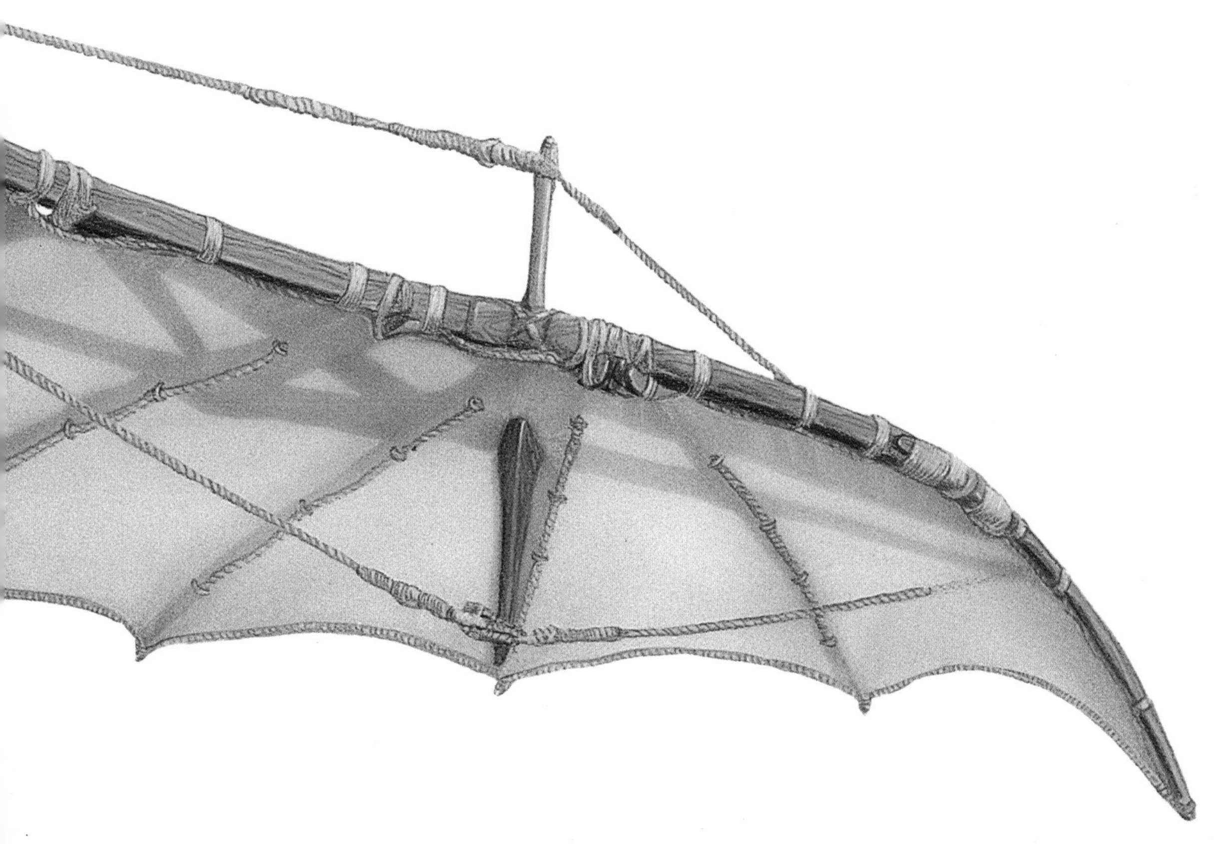

All About Invention

Inventions have shaped our world. We benefit from the work of great inventors every day: when we switch on a light, use a computer, call a friend or watch a video. Simple inventions, from buttons and zippers to Coca-Cola™ and cornflakes, make our lives easier and more enjoyable. Some inventors toil for years to perfect an idea, while others work together, sharing their discoveries and insights. The famous inventor Thomas Edison said that "genius is 1 per cent inspiration and 99 per cent perspiration." He developed the electric light bulb, after painstakingly completing 9,000 experiments! Every invention creates new knowledge, and this knowledge is used to make other inventions. Inventors protect their inventions by taking out patents—agreements with the government where inventors reveal their secrets in exchange for the right to make, use or sell their inventions. Patents can last up to 21 years, and then the invention becomes public property. During the past 500 years, a staggering 25 million products, processes and devices have been invented and patented.

Nobel Intentions

It is hard to predict all the effects an invention might have. In 1867, after three years of work, Swedish inventor Alfred Nobel made nitroglycerine safe by mixing it with a stabilizing mineral. He called this new, doughlike substance dynamite. Nobel intended that his invention would prevent accidental deaths in engineering, but when the world went to war, dynamite was used to kill and destroy. To make amends for the devastation his invention caused, Nobel put his fortune into founding the Nobel prizes. These are awarded to people who make outstanding contributions to chemistry, physics, medicine, literature, economics and peace.

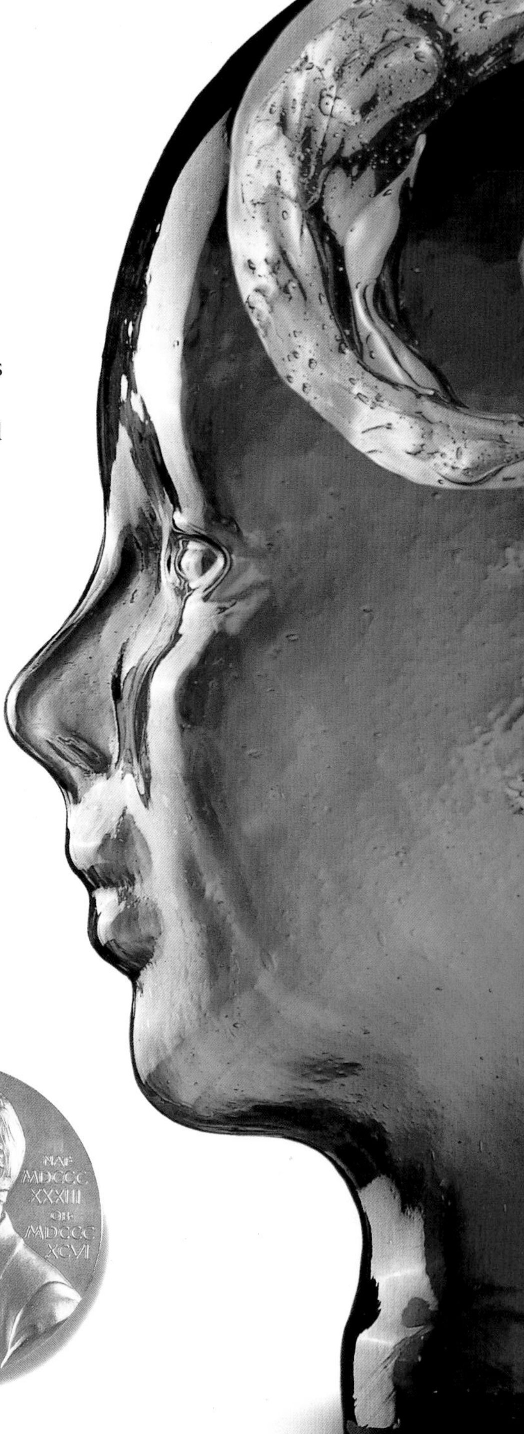

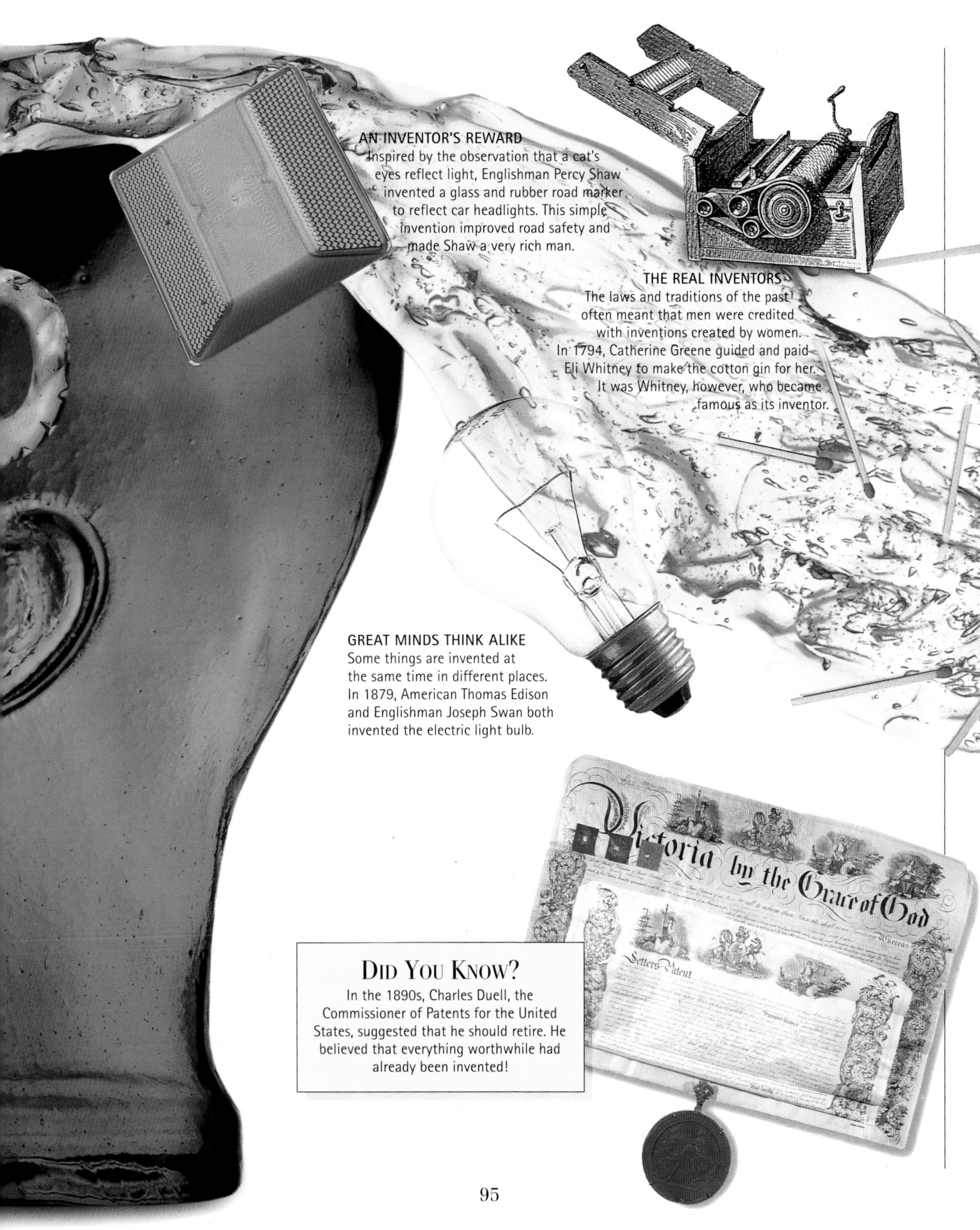

AN INVENTOR'S REWARD
Inspired by the observation that a cat's eyes reflect light, Englishman Percy Shaw invented a glass and rubber road marker to reflect car headlights. This simple invention improved road safety and made Shaw a very rich man.

THE REAL INVENTORS
The laws and traditions of the past often meant that men were credited with inventions created by women. In 1794, Catherine Greene guided and paid Eli Whitney to make the cotton gin for her. It was Whitney, however, who became famous as its inventor.

GREAT MINDS THINK ALIKE
Some things are invented at the same time in different places. In 1879, American Thomas Edison and Englishman Joseph Swan both invented the electric light bulb.

Did You Know?

In the 1890s, Charles Duell, the Commissioner of Patents for the United States, suggested that he should retire. He believed that everything worthwhile had already been invented!

LIGHT UP
Gustave Pasch of Sweden patented safety matches in 1845, but they were not manufactured until 1855. Earlier types ignited without warning, or gave off dangerous gases.

A QUICK SHAVE
In 1901, a traveling salesman named King Camp Gillette invented the disposable razor blade in the United States.

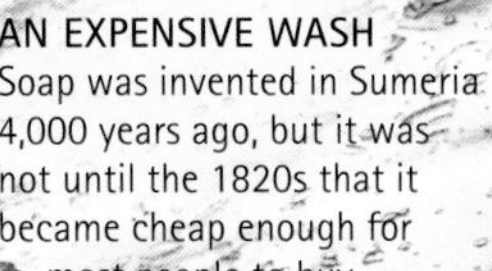

AN EXPENSIVE WASH
Soap was invented in Sumeria 4,000 years ago, but it was not until the 1820s that it became cheap enough for most people to buy.

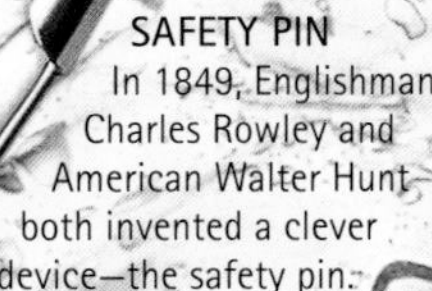

SAFETY PIN
In 1849, Englishman Charles Rowley and American Walter Hunt both invented a clever device—the safety pin.

BUTTON UP
Buttons have been used since ancient times. The modern two-holed button is thought to have been invented in Scotland about 4,000 years ago.

• EVERYDAY LIFE •

Simple Things

We use buttons, bottles, knives, nails, safety pins, combs, coat hangers and other simple inventions every day. What would we do without them? Imagine a supermarket without canned foods, bread, ice cream, cartons of milk or packets of crackers! People are constantly re-inventing simple things, such as toothbrushes and bottle caps, by using new ideas, materials and technologies. Other inventions, such as pins and coat hangers, were perfect when they were invented and have changed very little since. A special word for simple, yet ingenious, inventions was coined in New York in 1886. Frenchman Monsieur Gaget sold thousands of miniature models of the Statue of Liberty to American sightseers. The New Yorkers who bought these statues called them "gadgets," and the word has been used ever since to describe clever but simple devices.

LOCK AND KEY
In 2000 BC, the Egyptians made wooden locks and keys to secure royal treasures. These locks and keys were decorated with gold to show their importance. In 1865, Linus Yale Jr. patented a drum-and-pin lock that could be mass-produced.

ZIP UP
This ingenious device was invented by American Whitcomb Judson in 1891. But it was 19 years before the zipper became faster and easier to use than buttons.

CHOPSTICKS
Chopsticks were used by the Chinese about 4,000 years ago.

PINS
The Egyptians made pins from copper, thorns and fishbones about 4,000 years ago. In 1625, John Tilsby started the first pin factory in England.

CLEAN TEETH
Ancient civilizations had various ways of cleaning teeth, but the toothbrush as we know it was invented by William Addis in 1780.

Money, Money, Money

The first coins were probably made in ancient China. They were cast in bronze and designed to look like everyday tools, such as knives and spades. In the ancient kingdom of Lydia, round coins were used in 600 BC. They were stamped with a lion and bull imprint on one side in honour of the king. Special marks on the other side showed the weight and quality of the coins. As time went on, trade flourished and so did money. Paper money probably originated in ancient China, but paper bank notes were first issued in 1661 by the Bank of Stockholm in Sweden. In 1988, scientists in Australia invented plastic bank notes that last four times as long as paper notes and can be recycled.

COAT HANGER
Thomas Sheraton, a famous furniture maker, built permanent coat hangers into wardrobes in the 1790s. Loose coat hangers, called "shoulders," were invented 100 years later.

CANNED FOOD
Englishman Peter Durand first thought of preserving food in tin canisters. He sold his idea to John Hall and Bryan Donkin who set up a canning factory, or "preservatory," in 1811.

SUNSHADE, RAINSHADE
The umbrella was first used as a sunshade in ancient China. It was not used as a shield against the rain until much later. The term umbrella comes from a Latin word meaning "little shadow."

TABLE MANNERS
Cutlery was introduced to the world's dinner tables more than 400 years ago. The fork became part of Italian tableware in the 1500s and was used in England, France and America in the 1600s.

4000 BC
REED ROPES
Mesopotamia

1800 BC
BATHTUB
Babylonia

808
BANK
Italy

1648
SEWING THIMBLE
Netherlands

1875
SUGAR CUBES
Eugen Langen
Germany

1896
ICE-CREAM CONES
Italo Marcioni
USA

1924
PAPER HANDKERCHIEFS (tissues)
USA

1991
RECYCLED VINYL BOTTLES
USA

THE LOOKING GLASS
Glass mirrors were invented in Venice, Italy, perhaps 600 years ago. They were made by sticking a very thin layer of tinfoil onto glass using mercury.

A royal treat
Ice cream was probably first enjoyed in ancient China. It was re-invented in Europe in the 1300s and became a popular dessert among royalty.

• EVERYDAY LIFE •

Around the House

We use household inventions so frequently, it seems as if we have always had them. But these everyday items and devices were once new and exciting. Inventions for the house were designed to take the effort out of household chores. Before the vacuum cleaner, people would laboriously beat their carpets to remove the dust; before the lawn mower, cutting grass was a back-breaking task done by hand with a scythe. Before the electric refrigerator, food needed to be bought daily and any leftovers thrown away. When they were first produced, most household inventions were handmade, unreliable and expensive. Mass production made many goods cheaper, more reliable and available to everyone. Household inventions are constantly being improved and updated. What labor-saving inventions will we use in houses of the future?

FRIDGES FOR THE FUTURE
The first electric refrigerators were cooled by poisonous substances, such as ammonia. After the 1930s, manufacturers used a non-toxic substance called Freon. But Freon was found to cause the breakdown of ozone in the Earth's atmosphere. This environmentally friendly fridge was invented in Germany in 1991.

Frozen food
After observing how the Inuit (Eskimos) preserved their fish, Clarence Birdseye saw the potential for quick-freezing many foods. Birdseye introduced frozen foods to American stores in about 1930.

Margarine
A shortage of butter in France in the 1860s led Emperor Napoleon III to encourage the development of a substitute. In 1869, Hippolyte Mège-Mouriès invented a paste made from animal fats. He called it margarine.

Chocolate
Chocolate is made from the seeds of a tropical tree called *cacao*. Early Central and South Americans crushed the seeds to make a drink. The first chocolate bar was made in Switzerland in 1819 by François-Louis Cailler.

Perfect packaging
Convenient "waxed cardboard" cartons with pull-out spouts were invented in Sweden by Ruben Rausing in 1951.

"It Beats as it Sweeps as it Cleans"

In 1901, Hubert Cecil Booth was convinced he could build a machine that picked up and filtered dust using suction. He did just that, but the cleaner was so large it had to be set on a trolley and needed two people to operate it. James Murray Spangler invented a more portable model and in 1908 patented the electric Suction Sweeper. Spangler sold his idea to a man named William Hoover. His surname and the above slogan became household words in many countries.

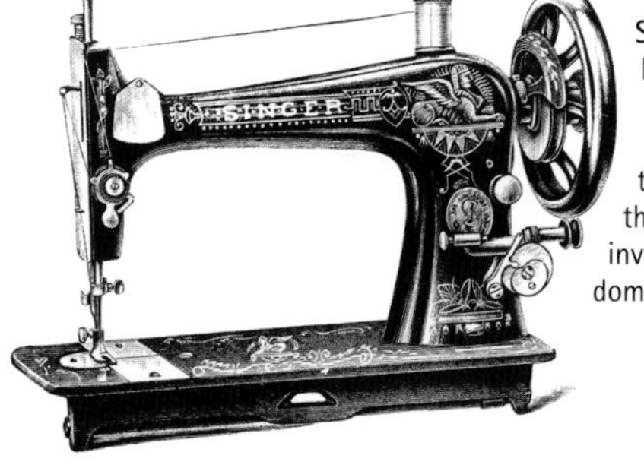

SEWING MACHINE
In the early 1800s, the first sewing machines were not welcomed by tailors, who thought their jobs were under threat. In 1851, Isaac Singer invented the first efficient domestic sewing machine.

Did You Know?

During the Second World War, two scientists developed a device to produce microwaves. Little did they know their work to improve radar would later be used to develop a new cooking appliance—the microwave oven.

RESTROOM
The flush toilet was invented by Sir John Harington in 1589. He installed one in his own house and one in the house of his godmother, Queen Elizabeth I of England. But they did not become common until nearly 200 years later.

100 BC
SAUNA BATH
Finland

1795
CORKSCREW
Samuel Hershaw
England

1857
TOILET PAPER
USA

1886
DISHWASHER
Josephine Cochrane
USA

1901
ELECTRIC WASHING MACHINE
Alva Fisher
USA

1909
ELECTRIC TOASTER
USA

1917
ELECTRIC HAND DRILL
Duncan Black and Alonso Decker
USA

1926
AEROSOL SPRAY
Erik Rotheim
Norway

1945
MICROWAVE OVEN
Percy Le Baron Spencer
USA

1985
SOAPLESS ULTRASONIC WASHER
Nihon University
Japan

At a Factory

Long ago, members of a family or tribe would make everything they needed by hand. As the population grew, people worked together in factories. In 1798, American Eli Whitney invented mass production. He received an order for 10,000 guns, but realized it was impossible for craftspeople to produce this quantity in the time available. He decided to divide the work up into separate jobs, so that different people could make different parts of the gun, which was then put together later. At the same time in England, James Watt's new steam engines were installed in factories, and soon the Industrial Revolution began. The new steam factories employed many people, but the work was dangerous, cramped, time-consuming and often boring. Many factories today offer good lighting, filtered air, protective clothing and rest breaks. Robots are used for the worst jobs, and people work fewer hours in safer conditions.

FORKLIFT TRUCK
Forklift trucks, developed in America and Australia during the Second World War, are the "worker bees" of a factory. They scurry from place to place carrying heavy loads on wood or plastic pallets.

KEEPING IT ALL TOGETHER
Handmade metal nails were first used by the Egyptians to hold coffins together 5,000 years ago. Tiny metal screws for joining wood date back to 1760. Before welding, metals were joined with pins or rivets.

PROTECTIVE CLOTHING
The heat, the cold and dangerous chemicals used in today's factories mean that suits such as this are needed to protect the worker from danger.

Work Time

The time clock was invented by American W. H. Bundy in 1885. Workers were given their own specially numbered key, which they inserted into the clock when they arrived at work. This key activated the clock to print their key number and their arrival time on a strip of paper. When the workers were ready to leave, they repeated this process, so their employer could check the number of hours they had worked. The Australian phrases to "bundy on," meaning to arrive at work, and to "bundy off," meaning to leave work, have helped to keep the inventor's name alive.

CONVEYOR BELT

The moving assembly line brings the work to the person. It was invented by Henry Ford in Detroit in 1908.

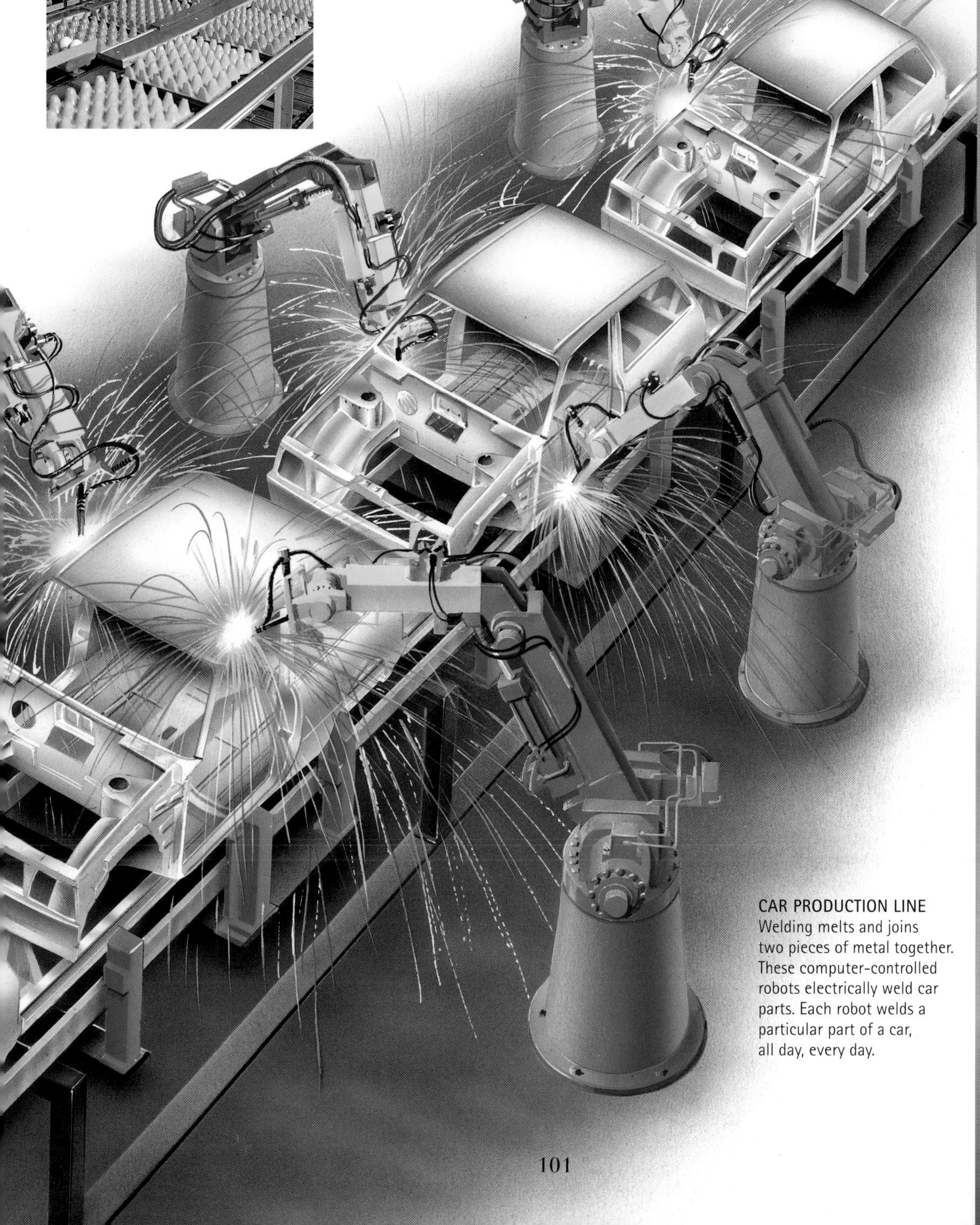

CAR PRODUCTION LINE

Welding melts and joins two pieces of metal together. These computer-controlled robots electrically weld car parts. Each robot welds a particular part of a car, all day, every day.

1500 BC

IRON SMELTING
Asia Minor

870 BC

PULLEY WHEEL
Assyria

200 BC

CRANK HANDLE
China

100 BC

BAROULKOS (CRANE)
Hero of Alexandria

1550

NUTS, BOLTS AND WRENCHES
France

1804

PATTERN-WEAVING LOOM
Joseph-Marie Jacquard
France

1856

STEEL MAKING
Henry Bessemer
England

1903

OXYACETYLENE WELDING TORCH
Edmond Fouche and Jean Picard
France

1946

ROBOT AUTOMATION
Delmar Harder
USA

1983

ROBOT-MAKING ROBOT
Japan

• EVERYDAY LIFE •

On a Farm

The plow and irrigation have tamed more farmland than any other farming inventions. People first grew crops in the Middle East about 10,000 years ago, but planting, harvesting and watering them by hand was a slow process. In Egypt and India, nearly 4,500 years later, farmers prepared the ground for planting with wooden plows pulled by oxen. The Egyptians invented a machine called a shaduf, which helped them take water from the River Nile to irrigate or water their crops. Barbed wire was another great farming invention. Farmers used it to divide huge areas of Africa, North America and Australia into separate wheat, cattle and sheep farms in the 1800s. These enormous new farms revolutionized farming. Farmers now needed faster ways of harvesting grain, wool, meat and milk. The old methods were soon replaced by machines that did the work of hundreds of people.

FORK
Iron forks were invented by the Romans. "Pitchforks" were used to "pitch" or stack hay in the field.

RAKE
Wooden rakes were invented in Europe in about AD 500 to gather grain that had been threshed or beaten off its stalks.

SPADE
Wooden spades with iron blades were invented by the Romans about 2,000 years ago.

BARBED WIRE
In 1867, American Lucien Smith invented barbed wire and made it possible for farmers to fence off their lands.

FOUR JOBS IN ONE
In 1884, Australian Hugh McKay invented the horse-drawn harvester. It combined cutting, threshing, winnowing and bagging wheat grain into one operation. Combine harvesters with gasoline or diesel engines are now used 24 hours a day, with lights at night, to harvest the crops.

Watering the Crops

The Egyptian shaduf is a little like a seesaw. A long wooden pole, balanced on a crossbeam, has a rope and bucket at one end, and a heavy stone weight to counterbalance it at the other. The weight of the rock makes it easier to lift a heavy bucket of water.

PLOW
Plows made from wood and stag antlers were invented in Egypt and India about 5,500 years ago. Simple ox-drawn plows are still used on family farms in many countries.

TRACTOR
Three-wheeled steam tractors, built by the Case company of America in 1829, were very heavy and often became stuck in the soft soil. Modern tractors were pioneered by Henry Ford in 1907.

Did You Know?

Superphosphates—artificial chemicals that enrich the soil—were invented by Sir John Bennett Lawes in England in 1842. But fertilizers often run into the rivers and oceans, killing fish and making algae grow.

1794
COTTON GIN (SEPARATOR)
Catherine Greene and Eli Whitney
USA

1831
GRAIN REAPER (CUTTER)
Cyrus McCormick
USA

1833
STEEL PLOW
John Lane
USA

1860
NUTRICULTURE
Julius von Sachs
Germany

1868
GRANNY SMITH APPLE
Maria Smith
Australia

1889
MODERN MILKING MACHINE
William Murchland
Scotland

1924
AERIAL CROP DUSTING
USA

1939
DDT PESTICIDE
Paul Müller
Switzerland

1975
AXIAL COMBINE HARVESTER
International Harvester
New Holland, USA

At School and the Office

During some stage of their lives, people in many countries spend time in schools and offices. Schools were first set up in Greece between 800 BC and 400 BC to teach boys subjects such as mathematics and astronomy. In the 1800s, people were employed in offices to monitor the staff and accounts of the first factories. Today, on a desk at school or the office you will find inventions large and small. It is hard to imagine our lives without them. Desks would be strewn with papers because we would not have paperclips or staplers to keep them together. How would write without pens and pencils and make straight lines without rulers? How would you cut paper without scissors? In fact, if the Chinese had not invented paper, there would be nothing to write on, cut or keep in an orderly pile.

BLACKBOARD
James Pillans, a Scottish teacher, invented the blackboard in 1814 so that all his students would be able to see the maps he drew.

Sticky tape
In 1939, ten years after inventing masking tape, Richard Drew invented clear sticky tape.

Rubber bands
Native South Americans used the white sap of rubber trees to make rubber bands.

Glue
In 3000 BC, the Egyptians used glue to stick furniture together.

Correction fluid
Bette Graham of the United States invented this white fluid in 1959.

Stapler and staples
Englishman Charles Gould invented these in 1868.

Scissors
Two-bladed shears were invented in 1500 BC by the Chinese. These became our modern scissors.

Eraser
This was invented in 1752 by Magellan from Portugal.

Felt pens
These were invented in 1960 by the Japanese company Pentel.

Paperclips
These were patented in 1900 by Norwegian Johann Waaler.

Did You Know?

Inventions are often simple but ingenious solutions to problems. Arthur Fry kept losing his place in a hymn book. He put some weak glue on his page markers so they could be stuck on one page, then moved to another. Sticky notes were invented.

HITTING THE KEYS
Carlos Gliddens and Christopher Sholes named their typewriter the "literary piano". In 1873, the Remington Fire Arms Company undertook to manufacture it, and in 1876, it was displayed at the Centennial Exposition in the United States.

MOVING LIGHT
The desk lamp is a little like an arm. It can be moved about for close work or kept in the same position. An adjustable desk lamp was designed by George Carwardine in 1934.

PHOTOCOPIER
The first photocopiers used messy chemicals and sensitive papers to photograph documents. In 1938, Chester Carlson invented a dry copying process that used plain paper. The first photocopiers of this kind were sold in 1959.

Pencils
Soft graphite was used for pencils in England from 1564.

Fax Machine

Around 1900, German scientist Arthur Korn invented an electric cell that could detect dark and light areas on paper. He used it to send a photograph by telephone line from Germany to England in 1907. Almost 70 years passed before people realized how useful this invention would be in the office. The fax (which is short for facsimile, meaning an exact copy or a reproduction) now plays an important part in offices. This machine makes it possible to communicate instantly with people all over the world.

Sticky notes
These were invented in 1980 by American Arthur Fry.

Discover more in From Quill to Press

800 BC
SCHOOL
Greece

1806
CARBON-COPY PAPER
Ralph Wedgewood
England

1837
SHORTHAND WRITING
Isaac Pitman
England

1858
PENCIL WITH ERASER ATTACHED
Hyman Lipman
USA

1901
ELECTRIC TYPEWRITER
Thaddeus Cahill
USA

1903
WET PHOTOCOPIER
George Beidler
USA

1959
CORRECTION FLUID
Bette Graham
USA

1990
NO-LICK STAMPS
Australia Post
Australia

At Play

People are always inventing ways to have fun. The Egyptians threw stone balls at upright pins in a game similar to bowling about 5,000 years ago. The Greeks played "soccer" with inflated animal bladders about 2,500 years ago. Some games seem timeless–hopscotch, marbles, tick-tack-toe and rope skipping are as popular today as when they were first played. Dolls have delighted young and old for centuries. They have been made of many different materials, from apples and animal skins to china and plastic. In 1823, baby dolls were made to cry. Soon, they were talking as well. Today, the games industry is booming as inventors create new and exciting games that challenge all who play them.

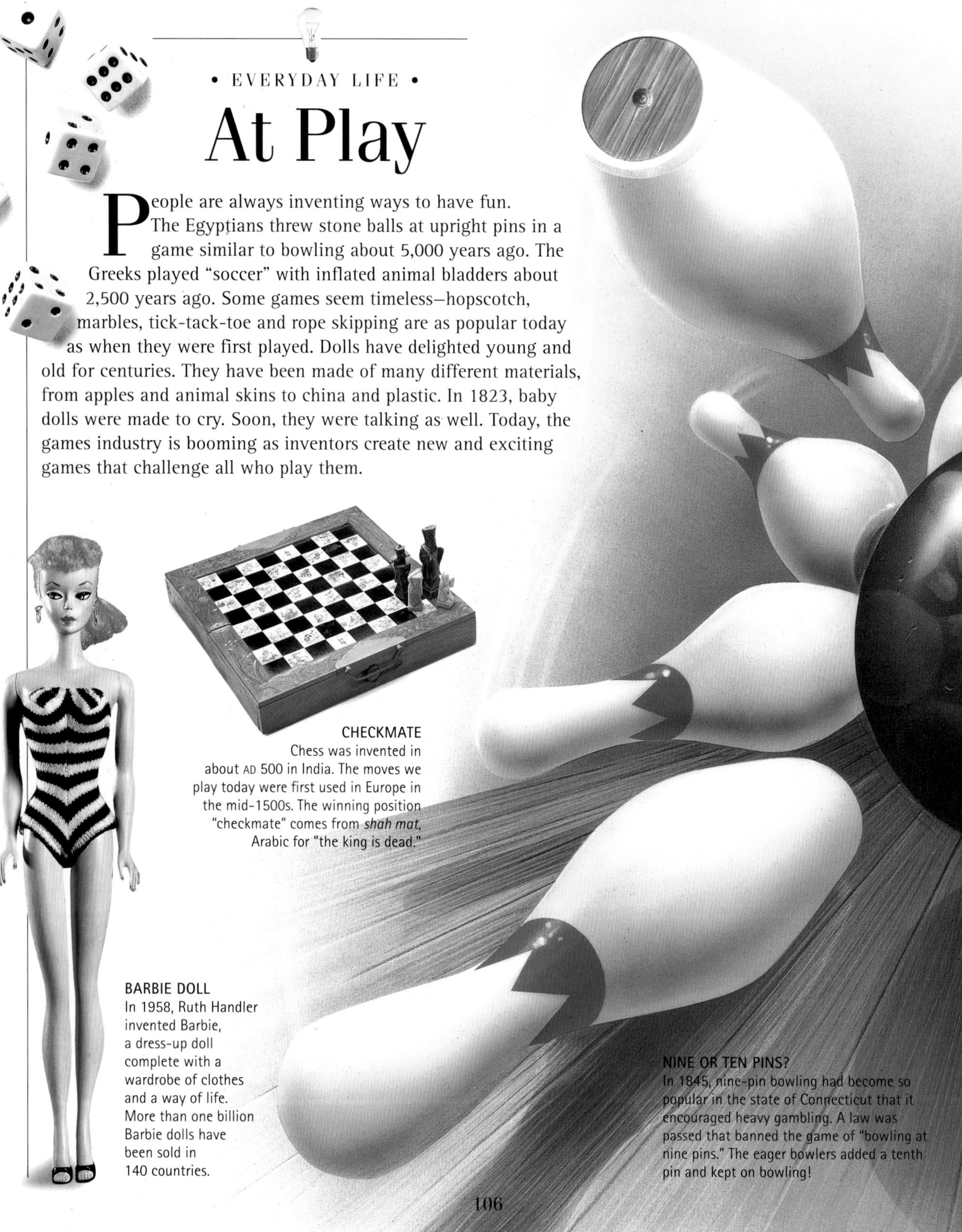

CHECKMATE
Chess was invented in about AD 500 in India. The moves we play today were first used in Europe in the mid-1500s. The winning position "checkmate" comes from *shah mat,* Arabic for "the king is dead."

BARBIE DOLL
In 1958, Ruth Handler invented Barbie, a dress-up doll complete with a wardrobe of clothes and a way of life. More than one billion Barbie dolls have been sold in 140 countries.

NINE OR TEN PINS?
In 1845, nine-pin bowling had become so popular in the state of Connecticut that it encouraged heavy gambling. A law was passed that banned the game of "bowling at nine pins." The eager bowlers added a tenth pin and kept on bowling!

Did You Know?

The very first roller skates, invented by a Belgian musician Joseph Merlin in 1760, had wheels in one line—similar to today's rollerblades.

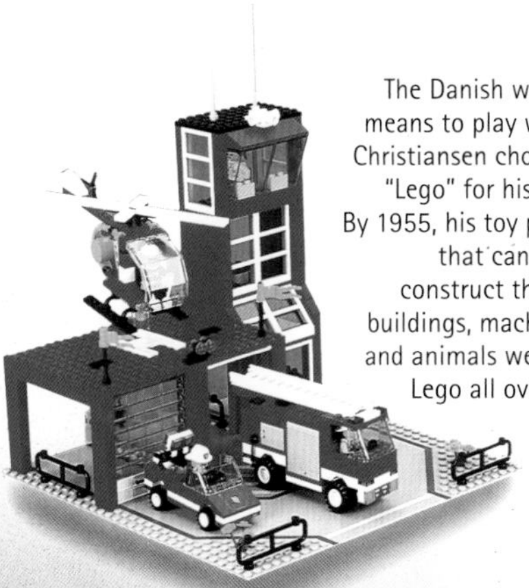

LEGO™

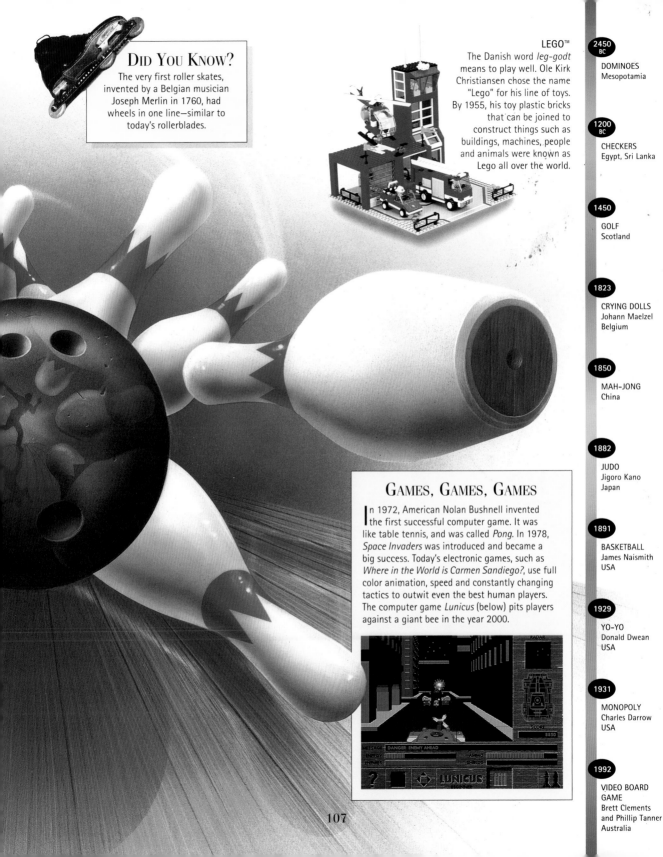

The Danish word *leg-godt* means to play well. Ole Kirk Christiansen chose the name "Lego" for his line of toys. By 1955, his toy plastic bricks that can be joined to construct things such as buildings, machines, people and animals were known as Lego all over the world.

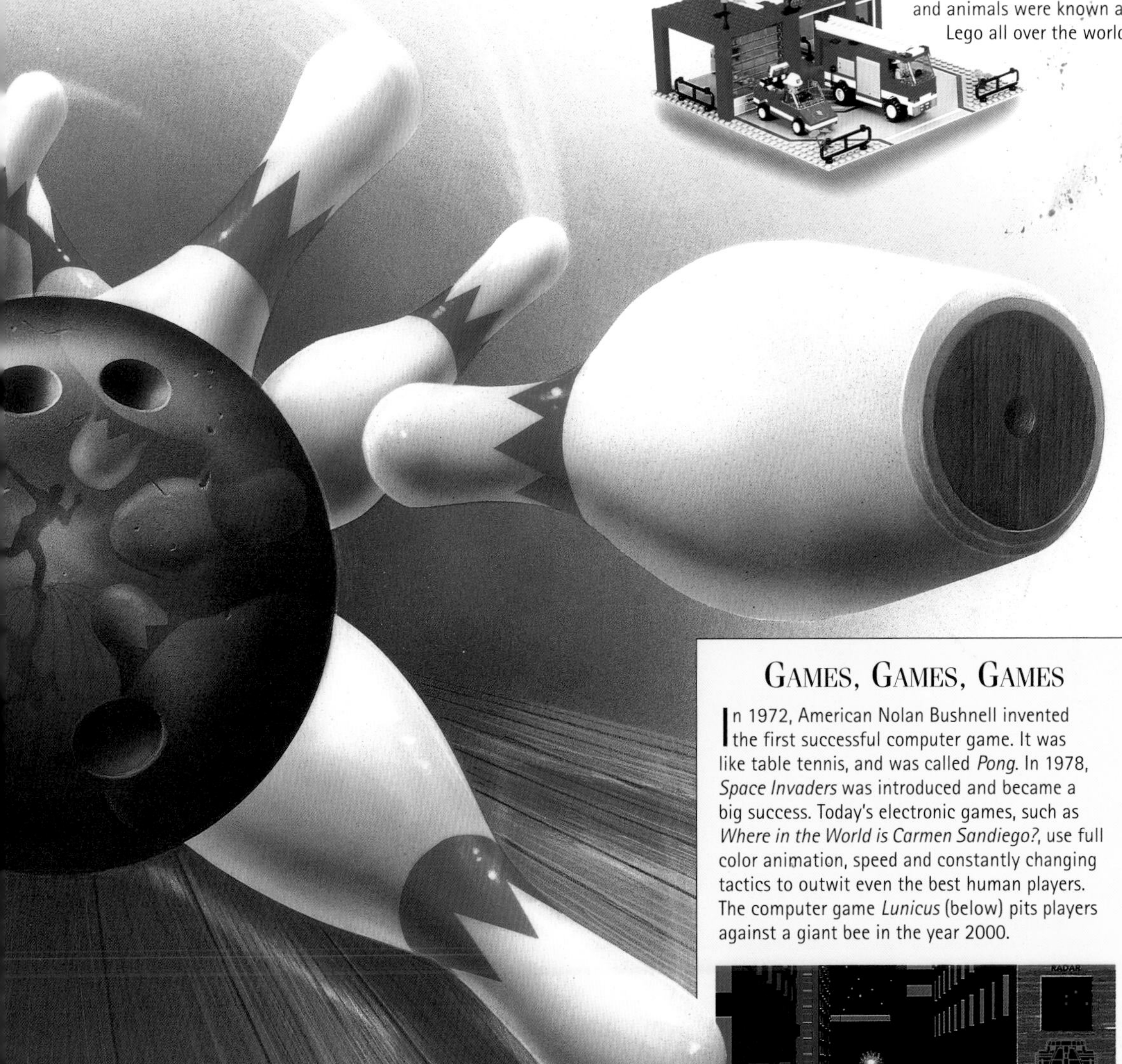

Games, Games, Games

In 1972, American Nolan Bushnell invented the first successful computer game. It was like table tennis, and was called *Pong*. In 1978, *Space Invaders* was introduced and became a big success. Today's electronic games, such as *Where in the World is Carmen Sandiego?*, use full color animation, speed and constantly changing tactics to outwit even the best human players. The computer game *Lunicus* (below) pits players against a giant bee in the year 2000.

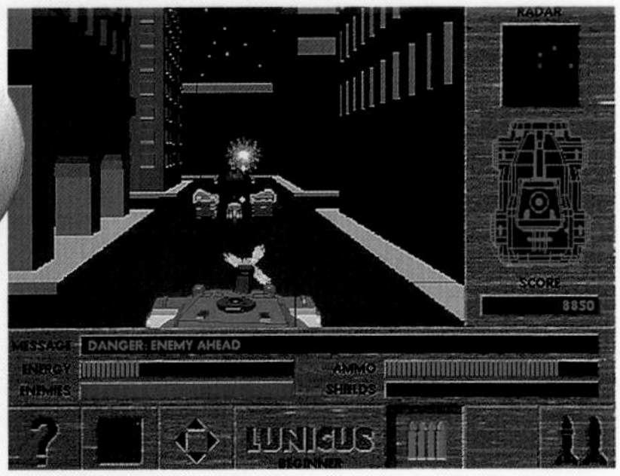

2450 BC
DOMINOES
Mesopotamia

1200 BC
CHECKERS
Egypt, Sri Lanka

1450
GOLF
Scotland

1823
CRYING DOLLS
Johann Maelzel
Belgium

1850
MAH-JONG
China

1882
JUDO
Jigoro Kano
Japan

1891
BASKETBALL
James Naismith
USA

1929
YO-YO
Donald Dwean
USA

1931
MONOPOLY
Charles Darrow
USA

1992
VIDEO BOARD GAME
Brett Clements and Phillip Tanner
Australia

REED PEN
A hollow reed can be cut to a point and used as a pen with ink or paint.

PENCIL
In 1792, Jacques Nicolas Conté invented a hard, long-wearing pencil made from clay mixed with powdered graphite and covered in cedar wood.

HIEROGLYPHS
The Egyptians developed a type of picture writing called hieroglyphs about 3000 BC. They either carved these pictures into stone, or painted them onto walls or papyrus with a pen cut from a reed from the River Nile.

FOUNTAIN PEN
This pen, which stores ink in its handle, was invented in 1884 by American Lewis Waterman.

CALLIGRAPHY BRUSH
This is used by trained writers, called calligraphers, to paint words onto rice paper and silk.

BALLPOINT PEN
In 1938, Laszlo Biro from Hungary invented a pen that used a rolling ball instead of a nib.

Did You Know?

Braille is the name of the writing for blind people, which can be felt and read with the fingertips. It took French professor Louis Braille eight years to perfect 34 "letters" made up of raised dots in soft paper.

SEAL OF APPROVAL
A seal is a device used to imprint a design or symbol that represents a family or a company. The first seals were used in Sumeria and India for signing documents.

• COMMUNICATIONS •

From Quill to Press

Technology has made it possible for us to communicate in different ways. People all over the world write with pens and pencils; many key their words into computers. About 30,000 years ago, however, people drew pictures on cave walls to tell stories or record news. The ancient Sumerians replaced this form of picture writing with shapes that they pressed into wet clay. The Chinese invented 47,000 characters that were written onto paper or silk with a brush. The first books in Europe were written with ink and a quill—a feather plucked from a goose and cut to a sharp point. The Chinese printed books by using wooden blocks. Later, they created movable, fire-baked characters that could be dipped into ink and pressed onto paper, but they wore out quickly. This problem was solved by the invention of reusable type made of hard metal. The printing press was soon in operation.

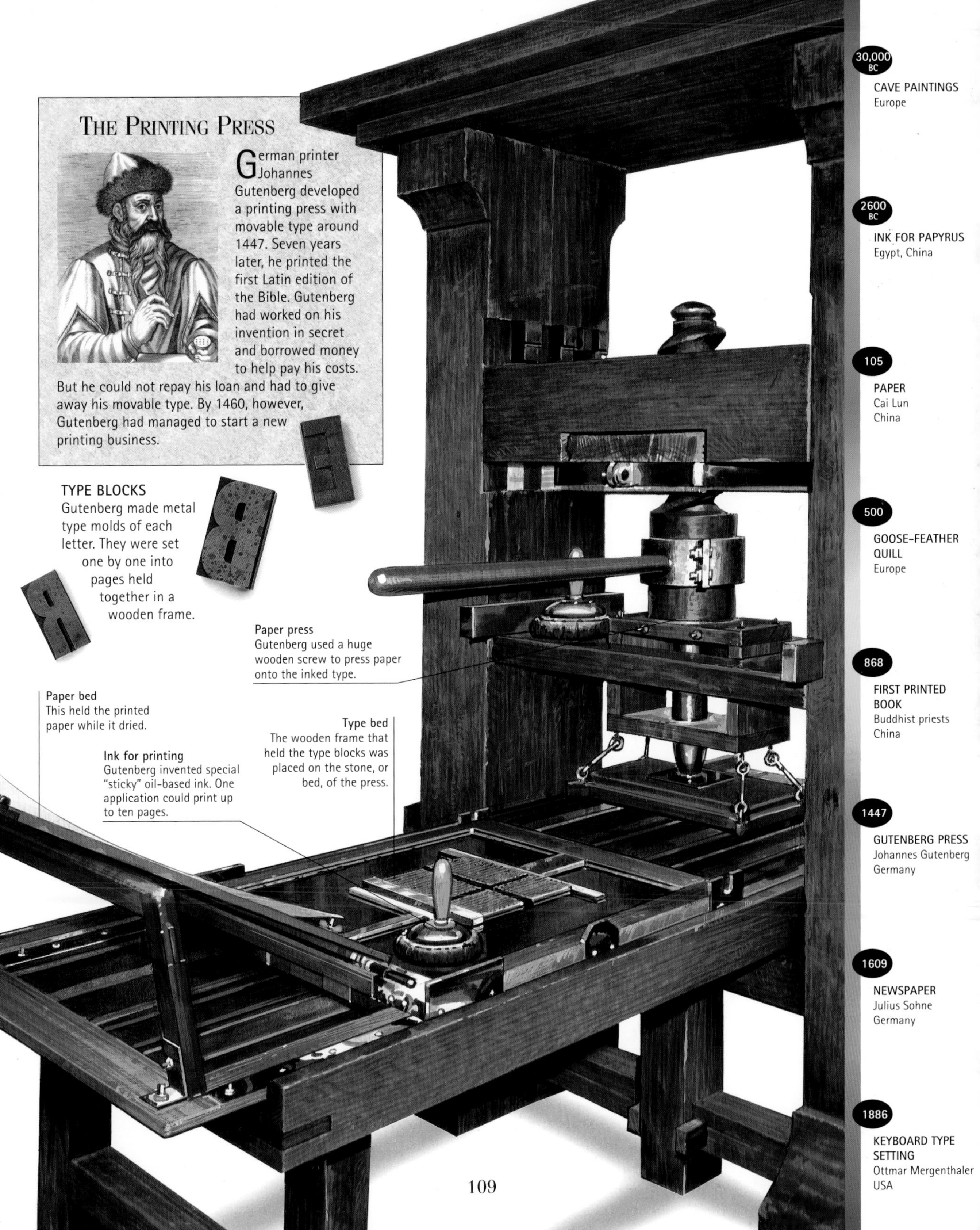

Paper press
Gutenberg used a huge wooden screw to press paper onto the inked type.
Paper bed
This held the printed paper while it dried.
Type bed
The wooden frame that held the type blocks was placed on the stone, or bed, of the press.
Ink for printing
Gutenberg invented special "sticky" oil-based ink. One application could print up to ten pages.

The Printing Press

German printer Johannes Gutenberg developed a printing press with movable type around 1447. Seven years later, he printed the first Latin edition of the Bible. Gutenberg had worked on his invention in secret and borrowed money to help pay his costs. But he could not repay his loan and had to give away his movable type. By 1460, however, Gutenberg had managed to start a new printing business.

TYPE BLOCKS
Gutenberg made metal type molds of each letter. They were set one by one into pages held together in a wooden frame.

30,000 BC CAVE PAINTINGS
Europe

2600 BC INK FOR PAPYRUS
Egypt, China

105 PAPER
Cai Lun
China

500 GOOSE-FEATHER QUILL
Europe

868 FIRST PRINTED BOOK
Buddhist priests
China

1447 GUTENBERG PRESS
Johannes Gutenberg
Germany

1609 NEWSPAPER
Julius Sohne
Germany

1886 KEYBOARD TYPE SETTING
Ottmar Mergenthaler
USA

FIBER OPTICS
In 1976, the Western Electric Company of Atlanta, Georgia used pulses of laser light to send voice, video and computer messages through fibers made of glass, which were called optical fibers.

EXCHANGING WORDS
As a telephone wire could carry only one message at a time, Bell and Gray invented the telephone exchange system in 1878. Within ten years, hundreds of wires connected houses to buildings called exchanges, where operators joined the wires so that people could speak to each other.

Making Connections

On February 14, 1876, Scottish-born Alexander Graham Bell and American Elisha Gray both applied to patent the telephone in the United States, although neither of them had made a telephone that really worked. Gray was two hours later than Bell and lost the race to claim the telephone as his invention. People were very eager to invest in this exciting new technology, and by the end of 1877, Bell was a millionaire.

ELECTRIC TELEGRAPH
In 1837, the American Samuel Morse used a magnet to interrupt the flow of electricity in a wire. This could be heard at the other end of the wire as a "beep." The beeps were formed into a code (Morse code) that operators learned to understand and translate back into words.

• COMMUNICATIONS •

Along a Wire

Messages can be passed from person to person in many ways. Voices, horns and beating drums carry messages through the air; written messages are sent by mail. All early methods of communication relied on how far people could run, see, hear or shout. The first messages to travel further and faster were sent by telegraph in the 1830s. The telegraph consisted of a special code of electric "beeps" that traveled huge distances along wires in a few minutes. At the other end, the receiver sorted the beeps into words and delivered the message in person. In 1851, the first telegraph cable was laid under the English Channel between Dover and Calais. By 1866, undersea cables provided the first transatlantic telecommunications link. Today, wires still connect millions of people by telephone, fax and computer.

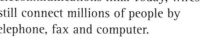

CANDLESTICK TELEPHONE
This was the most common telephone in the world for many years. The early models did not have dials, and you had to rattle the side hook to alert the operator. Frenchman Antoine Barnay invented the dial in 1923.

1832–1837

ELECTRIC TELEGRAPH SYSTEMS
Michael Faraday and Pavel Schilling
England, Russia

1837

MORSE ELECTRIC TELEGRAPH
Samuel Morse
USA

1851

UNDERWATER CABLE
Charles Wheatstone and Joseph Brett
England

1889

PUBLIC TELEPHONE
William Gray
USA

1895

WIRELESS TELEGRAPH
Guglielmo Marconi
Italy

1907

PHOTO-TELEGRAPH
Arthur Korn
Germany

1916

TELEX
Markrum Company
USA

1955

OPTICAL FIBER
Dr Narinder Kapany
England

DID YOU KNOW?

You can make a string telephone by connecting two containers, or cans, by a long length of string. Pull the string tight and speak into one container. The person at the other end should be able to hear what you say. Children have made string telephones since the 1600s.

WIRED FOR SOUND
The electric microphone, which amplifies, or increases, sound, was invented in 1916 and first tested at Madison Square Gardens, New York.

HEADPHONES
These were developed from hearing-aid technology invented in 1901 by American Miller Hutchinson.

Pictures and Sound

People told stories and cast shadow shapes on the walls of firelit caves thousands of years ago. In the 1640s they used early projectors called "magic lanterns" to shine candlelight through hand-painted glass slides. Frenchman Gaspard Robert invented the marvellous Fantasmagoria in 1798. This special kind of magic lantern projected moving pictures and shadows of ghosts and monsters onto sheets in a dark room. Audiences screamed and fainted at the sight, and quickly lined up to see it all over again. In 1891, the brilliant American inventor Thomas Edison developed a moving-picture camera called a Kinetograph and opened the way for silent movies and stars of the screen such as Charlie Chaplin. Within the next 40 years, inventions such as radio, television, film and video brought new dimensions to the quality of pictures and sound.

PUMPING THE PIANO
The Fotoplayer Company of Berkeley, California invented the Fotoplayer in 1915. This huge piano was powered by an air pump and played music programmed by a roll of punched paper. It provided sound effects for silent movies.

Light-activated sound strip

RADIO
In 1906, Reginald Fessenden broadcast voice and music on radio waves for the first time.

TIMING SOUND

Phonograph records added lifelike sound to movies. But it was difficult to match the record with the action on the movie; voices often finished after the actors had stopped mouthing the words. In the 1929 movie *Hallelujah*, sound was recorded as a pattern on the film. This pattern was "read" by a light-sensitive cell that synchronized sound with the moving pictures.

PICTURES TO EUROPE

In 1962, the first television pictures were sent from the United States to Europe. They bounced off the *Telstar* satellite in space and were collected by a dish-shaped antenna like this.

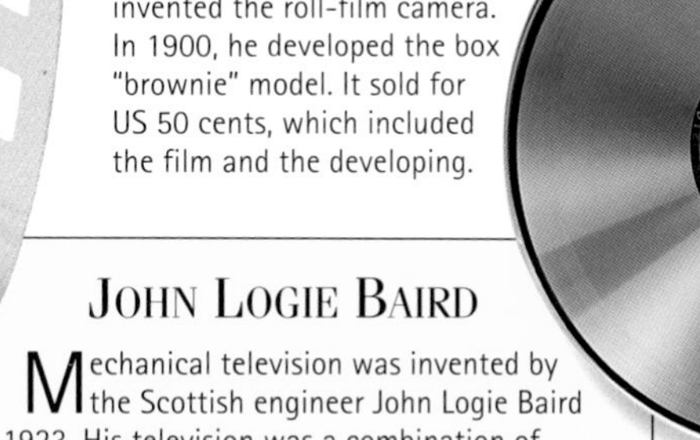

BOX "BROWNIE" CAMERA

In 1888, George Eastman invented the roll-film camera. In 1900, he developed the box "brownie" model. It sold for US 50 cents, which included the film and the developing.

COMPACT DISC

Japanese and Dutch scientists invented the CD in 1981. It records sounds as microscopic changes in the surface of a plastic disc. The changes are "read" by a laser in the CD player and changed back into sound electronically.

John Logie Baird

Mechanical television was invented by the Scottish engineer John Logie Baird in 1923. His television was a combination of inventions and discoveries by other people. Baird's cameras and receivers contained a spinning disc invented by Nipkow of Germany in 1884. The disc translated pictures into dots of light in eight lines that were focused onto a tiny television screen.

1939 German television

John Logie Baird and the first TV transmitter

TWO FOR ONE

The video camera was invented in America in 1931, but it was larger than a human and could only send pictures, not record them. In 1981, the Sony Corporation of Japan invented a hand-held video camera that records as well.

1640
MAGIC LANTERN
Athanase Kircher
Germany

1827
PHOTOGRAPH
Joseph Nicéphore Niepce
France

1877
WHEEL OF LIFE ANIMATOR
Emile Raynaud
France

1895
RADIO TELEGRAPH
Guglielmo Marconi
Italy

1906
FEATURE FILM
Charles and John Tait
Australia

1931
ELECTRONIC TELEVISION
Vladimir Zworykin
USA

1962
SATELLITE TELEVISION
Telstar
USA

1980
WALKMAN™ TAPE PLAYER
Akio Morita
Japan

2000+
3-D TELEVISION

SAXOPHONE
Adolphe Sax of Belgium invented the saxophone in 1841. He patented it in 1846 and spent the next 11 years practicing and studying before teaching students at the Paris Conservatoire.

Reed
The reed is a thin piece of wood or metal inside the mouthpiece.

Musical Instruments

Sounds are made by waves or vibrations of air. The first musical instrument was the human voice. When we sing, the air in our throat vibrates. It echoes around our mouth and nose and, hopefully, comes out as music. The first musicians learned to use objects such as shells to make their voices louder, and soon realized that musical sounds could be made by plucking the string of a hunting bow or blowing into an animal bone. Most musical instruments have evolved through the tiny improvements made by instrument makers year after year. The first wind instruments were simple animal-bone flutes; stringed instruments, such as the harp, developed into the violin and the piano. Computers now enable us to create a wide variety of sounds electronically without blowing, hitting, plucking or strumming anything at all. Music can be made by everyone.

Keys
Mechanical keys for wind instruments were invented in the 1800s by the German instrument maker Theobald Boëhm.

GUITAR
A type of guitar was played in the Middle East from about 1000 BC. The modern acoustic guitar was invented in 1850 by Antonio de Torres, a Spanish instrument maker.

INDONESIAN GAMELAN ORCHESTRA
These players use mainly percussion instruments, including the saron and bonang, to play the melody by heart. They use string instruments such as the rebab and chelempung to enhance the sound.

PAN FLUTE
The first flutes were made from the hollow bones of sheep. Leg bones were punched with holes that were covered by the fingers to alter the pitch of the notes.

PLAYING THE PIANO

In 1710, Italian Bartolommeo Christofori invented keys attached to small hammers to strike strings. He called his invention the "piano-forte," which means soft and loud.

Did You Know?

In 1993, the Yamaha company of Japan invented a saxophone connected to a computer—a MIDI controller. The instrument itself makes no sounds because the computer creates the correct note electronically.

PLAYING PERCUSSION

This Chinese instrument dates back to about 1000 BC. Different-sized sheets of metal were hung on a frame and struck with a wooden mallet.

BEATING TIME

No one knows who made the first drum. These African drums have animal skin stretched over one end, which the player hits to produce a sound.

Notating Music

Greek scholars first wrote down music in 500 BC as a line of alphabetical signs. The signs showed musicians if a note should be played high or low. Symbols called "neumes," which stood for notes or groups of notes, were introduced in AD 650. In 1026, Italian Guido d'Arezzo introduced a system whereby the neumes were placed high or low on a line to show the pitch of the note. Rhythm and timing were added in about 1500.

15th-century music score

Original Handel score

5000 BC
DIDGERIDOO
Australia

3000 BC
HARP
Sumeria, Egypt

220 BC
PIPE ORGAN
Ctesibius
Alexandria

1300
HARPSICORD
Europe

1816
METRONOME
Johann Maelzel
Germany

1821
HARMONICA
C. F. L. Buschmann
Germany

1935
ELECTRIC GUITAR
Adolph
Rickenbacher
USA

1965
SYNTHESIZER
Robert Moog
USA

THE WATER CLOCK
The Egyptians developed a water clock about 3,500 years ago to tell the time at night. Shaped like a bucket, the clock had a scale marked on the inside to mark the water level and a hole near the bottom through which water trickled.

The time that had passed could be measured by reading the scale.

ON A STRING
The Inca of Peru recorded numbers by tying knots at intervals on a series of cords. This system of cords was called a quipu.

• INSTRUMENTS AND MACHINES •

Clocks and Calculators

Humans have always been fascinated by time. The first clocks used natural rhythms such as the movement of the sun to measure time. Later, the desire to divide up the day more precisely led to the invention of mechanical clocks. Powered by the energy stored in a metal spring, or weights on a chain, these clocks relied on an important device called the escapement, which turned the energy into a regular movement. By the mid-1600s, the accuracy of clockwork cogs and gears had caught the attention of mathematicians, and counting machines were invented to take the hard work out of sums. Inventors everywhere were inspired by the mechanical clock. They imagined that clockwork could be used to power all their wonderful ideas for the future.

The Mechanical Calculator

In 1642, 19-year-old Blaise Pascal built a simple arithmetic machine for his father, whose job involved counting money. The machine used clockwork gears to automatically add (up to eight-digit figures) or subtract. Some years later, a great mathematician, Gottfried Leibniz, developed Pascal's machine into a new model that could add, subtract, multiply, divide and find the square root of numbers. This was the starting point for all true calculators, and eventually, computers.

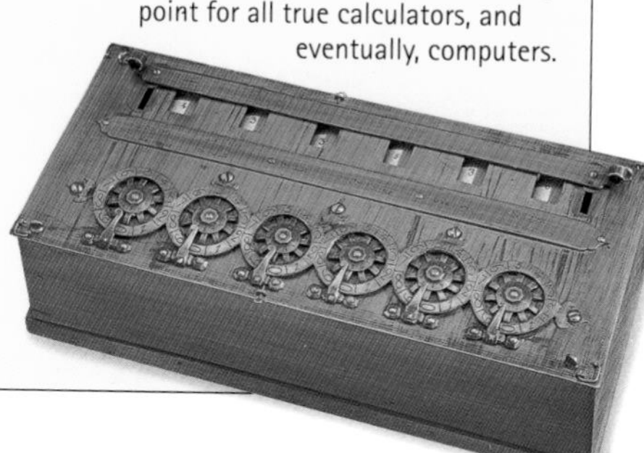

MARKING TIME

Inspired by the action of a church lamp swinging steadily during an earth tremor, Italian Galileo Galilei invented the pendulum in 1581. The first pendulum clock was made in 1656 by a Dutch scientist, Christiaan Huygens.

KEEPING THE CHANGE

In 1879, American James Ritty invented the cash register to discourage his bar staff from stealing the profits. The register used a clockwork mechanism to add, total and print transactions.

PLOTTING THE HEAVENS

The orrery is a clockwork model that shows the movements of planets around the sun. It was named after the English Earl of Orrery who had the first one built in about 1720.

ANCIENT ADDITION

Invented in Babylonia about 3000 BC, the abacus is still used throughout Asia to add, subtract, divide and multiply numbers.

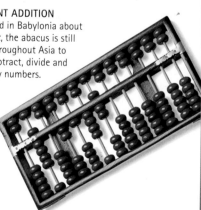

3400 BC

NUMBERS
Middle East

3000 BC

ABACUS
Babylonia

400

CANDLE AND FUSE CLOCK
Byzantium

725?

MECHANICAL WATER CLOCK
Yi Xing
China

1335

CHIMING CLOCK
Italy

1624

CLOCKWORK CALCULATOR
Wilhelm Schickard
Germany

1840

ELECTRIC CLOCK
Alexander Bain
England

1847

ALARM CLOCK
Antoine Redier
France

1907

MODERN WRISTWATCH
Louis Cartier and Hans Wilsdorf
France, Switzerland

1948

ATOMIC CLOCK
Frank Libby
USA

Computers and Robots

Two hundred years ago, people who figured out, or computed, difficult mathematical problems were called "computers." Today, computers are machines that use electronic circuits to store information such as numbers, words, pictures, sounds, shapes and calculations in code. Computers are used to control the most complex tools that have been invented—robots. These sophisticated machines are faster, more accurate and stronger than people. They can work in places and conditions where people could not survive, and they do not get bored doing the same thing every day! Virtual reality is a new invention that uses technology in a unique way. Special helmets, gloves and sensors connect a person's sight, hearing and touch to a computer. In the future, virtual reality will enable surgeons in one country to perform an operation in another country.

A SLAVE TO THE JOB
The word robot comes from the Czech "robotnik," which means "work slave." A robot can do many things faster and better than humans can.

LAPTOP COMPUTER
In 1987, Clive Sinclair of England invented a portable, or laptop, computer that weighed less than 2 pounds (1 kg).

SILICON CHIPS
Microscopic electrical circuits etched into chips of silicon were invented in 1959 by American Jack Kilby. These wafers hold hundreds of tiny silicon chips—each one powerful enough to run a small computer.

A SHEARING BREAKTHROUGH

In 1986, a robot invented by Australian farmer Lance Lines sheared the fleece of a sheep in about 90 seconds. The robot was programmed to be an efficient and safe shearer.

Did You Know?

In 1834, the Countess of Lovelace invented the first computer programs. She used a system of holes punched into paper cards to send instructions to Babbage's "analytical engine."

Robotic arm
Electric motors and hydraulic fluid move the robot's arm.

Moving robot
The robot slides along a rail.

Held tight
The sheep is gently clamped onto a platform.

Charles Babbage

In 1834, Charles Babbage invented a huge, mechanical "analytical engine"—the first mechanical computer. This machine was as big as a bus and could store and retrieve calculations from its memory. Babbage spent 40 years trying to build the machine, but he never completed it—the tools and materials of the time were not as advanced as his visionary invention.

375 BC
AUTOMATON "FLYING DOVE"
Archytas of Tarentum
Italy

1834
ANALYTICAL ENGINE
Charles Babbage
England

1859
BINARY LOGIC
George Boole
England

1907
AUTOMATIC TOTALIZATOR
George Julius
Australia

1941
COLOSSUS COMPUTER
Max Neuman and Alan Turing
England

1954
COMMERCIAL MAGNETIC MEMORY COMPUTER
IBM
USA

1962
COMMERCIAL ROBOTICS
Unimation
USA

1975
PERSONAL COMPUTER
H. Edward Roberts
USA

1985
CD-ROM
Philips/Hitachi
Netherlands, Japan

2000+
VIRTUAL SURGERY

Early Power

Hero, a mathematician in ancient Alexandria, first used steam power to make a metal ball spin. But he considered his invention a toy. More than 1,600 years later, inventors experimented with steam power again, but this time, the results of their efforts revolutionized people's lives. In the 1700s and 1800s, the steam-powered engine was adapted to do almost everything: pump water, drive factory machinery, propel ships, plow fields and even drive fairground rides. Some of the early steamships made so much smoke and noise that people were very reluctant to travel on them! The age of steam lasted for almost 200 years until the internal-combustion engine and electricity took over. Steam, however, is not as old-fashioned as you might think. Most of the electricity that gives us power today is produced by huge, steam-driven machines called turbines.

STRANGE BUT TRUE

Henry Seely of New York was ahead of his time. He invented the electric iron in 1882, but he could not sell it because nobody had electricity in their houses!

SMOOTHING OUT THE BUMPS
Without the steamroller, invented by Frenchman Louis Lemoine in 1859, roads would never have been smooth enough for the first fragile cars.

Edison and the Light Bulb

In the late 1800s, people predicted that electricity would be the power source of the future. Thomas Edison based his greatest inventions on electric power. In ten years he invented the electric light, an improved electric engine and generator, and a storage battery. In 1880, he opened the first power stations in London and New York to provide electric lighting.

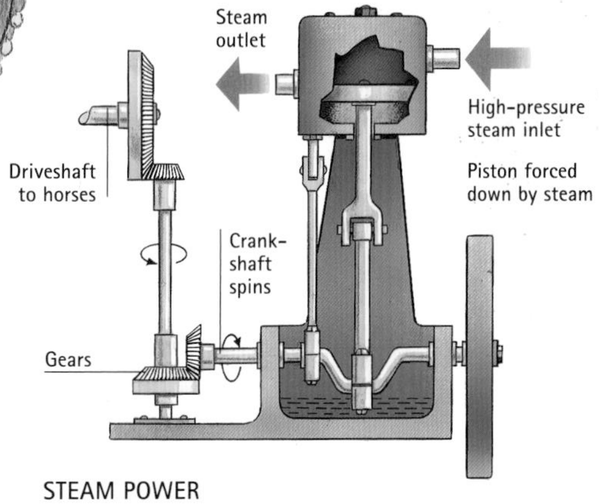

Steam outlet

High-pressure steam inlet

Piston forced down by steam

Driveshaft to horses

Crank-shaft spins

Gears

STEAM POWER

The steam for most engines was heated by burning coal or wood. The pressure of the steam from the engine above pushed a piston up and down, turning the shaft that moved the horses.

POWER FOR THE FACTORY

In 1785, James Watt invented a steam engine that could power a whole factory of machines from its single revolving shaft. The output of his engine was measured in horsepower, for the number of horses it replaced.

1690

STEAM CYLINDER ENGINE
Denis Papin
France

1698

STEAM PUMP
Thomas Savery
England

1712

ENGINE WITH BOILER
Thomas Newcomen
England

1730

STEAMBOAT
Jonathan Hulls
England

1800

VOLTAIC CELL
Allesandro Volta
Italy

1821

ELECTRIC MOTOR
Michael Faraday
England

1829

STEAM PLOW
USA

1878

ELECTRIC DC GENERATOR
Thomas Edison
USA

1882

ALTERNATING CURRENT GENERATOR
Nikola Tesla
USA

1884

STEAM-POWERED TURBINE
Sir Charles Parsons
England

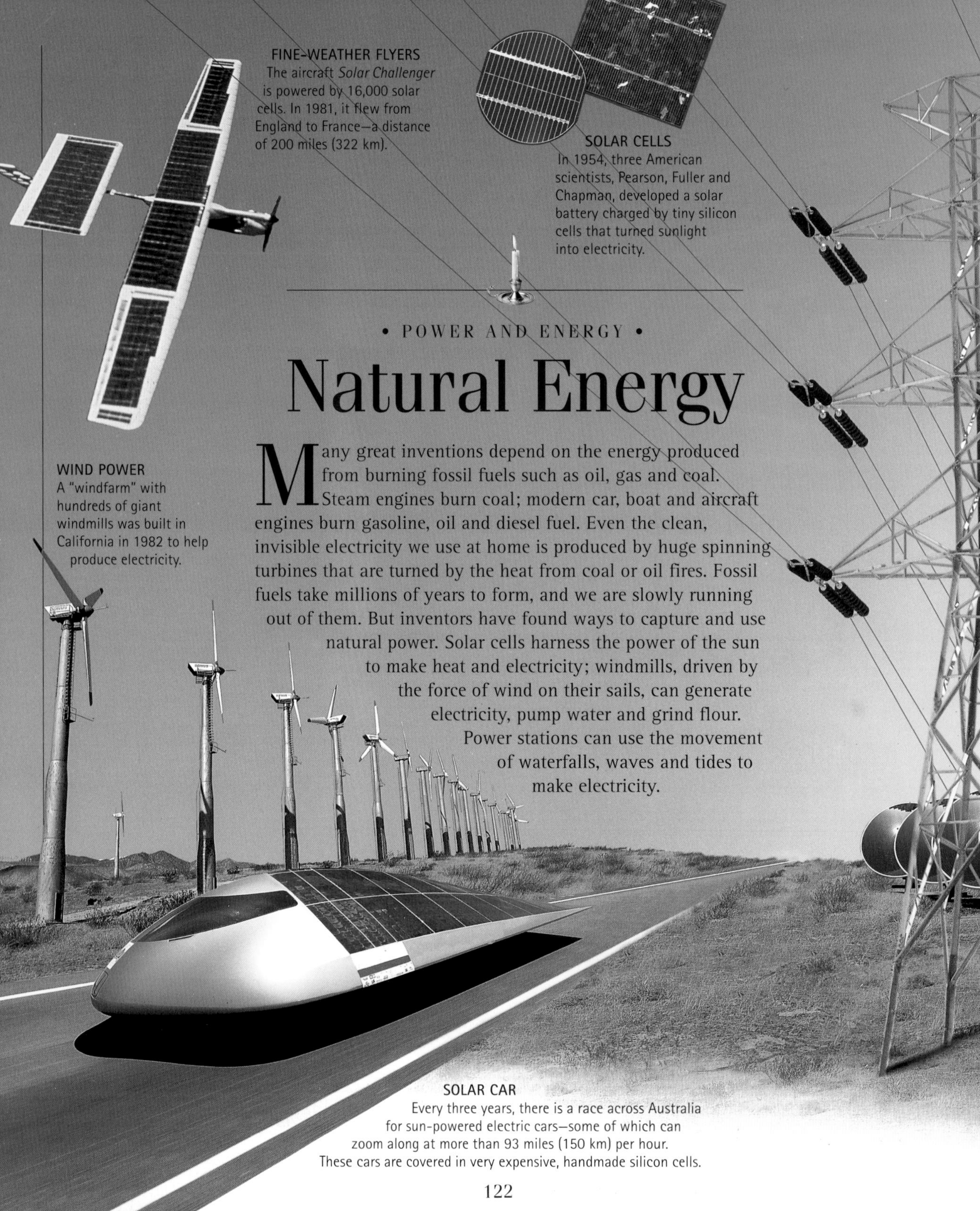

FINE-WEATHER FLYERS
The aircraft *Solar Challenger* is powered by 16,000 solar cells. In 1981, it flew from England to France—a distance of 200 miles (322 km).

SOLAR CELLS
In 1954, three American scientists, Pearson, Fuller and Chapman, developed a solar battery charged by tiny silicon cells that turned sunlight into electricity.

• POWER AND ENERGY •

Natural Energy

Many great inventions depend on the energy produced from burning fossil fuels such as oil, gas and coal. Steam engines burn coal; modern car, boat and aircraft engines burn gasoline, oil and diesel fuel. Even the clean, invisible electricity we use at home is produced by huge spinning turbines that are turned by the heat from coal or oil fires. Fossil fuels take millions of years to form, and we are slowly running out of them. But inventors have found ways to capture and use natural power. Solar cells harness the power of the sun to make heat and electricity; windmills, driven by the force of wind on their sails, can generate electricity, pump water and grind flour. Power stations can use the movement of waterfalls, waves and tides to make electricity.

WIND POWER
A "windfarm" with hundreds of giant windmills was built in California in 1982 to help produce electricity.

SOLAR CAR
Every three years, there is a race across Australia for sun-powered electric cars—some of which can zoom along at more than 93 miles (150 km) per hour. These cars are covered in very expensive, handmade silicon cells.

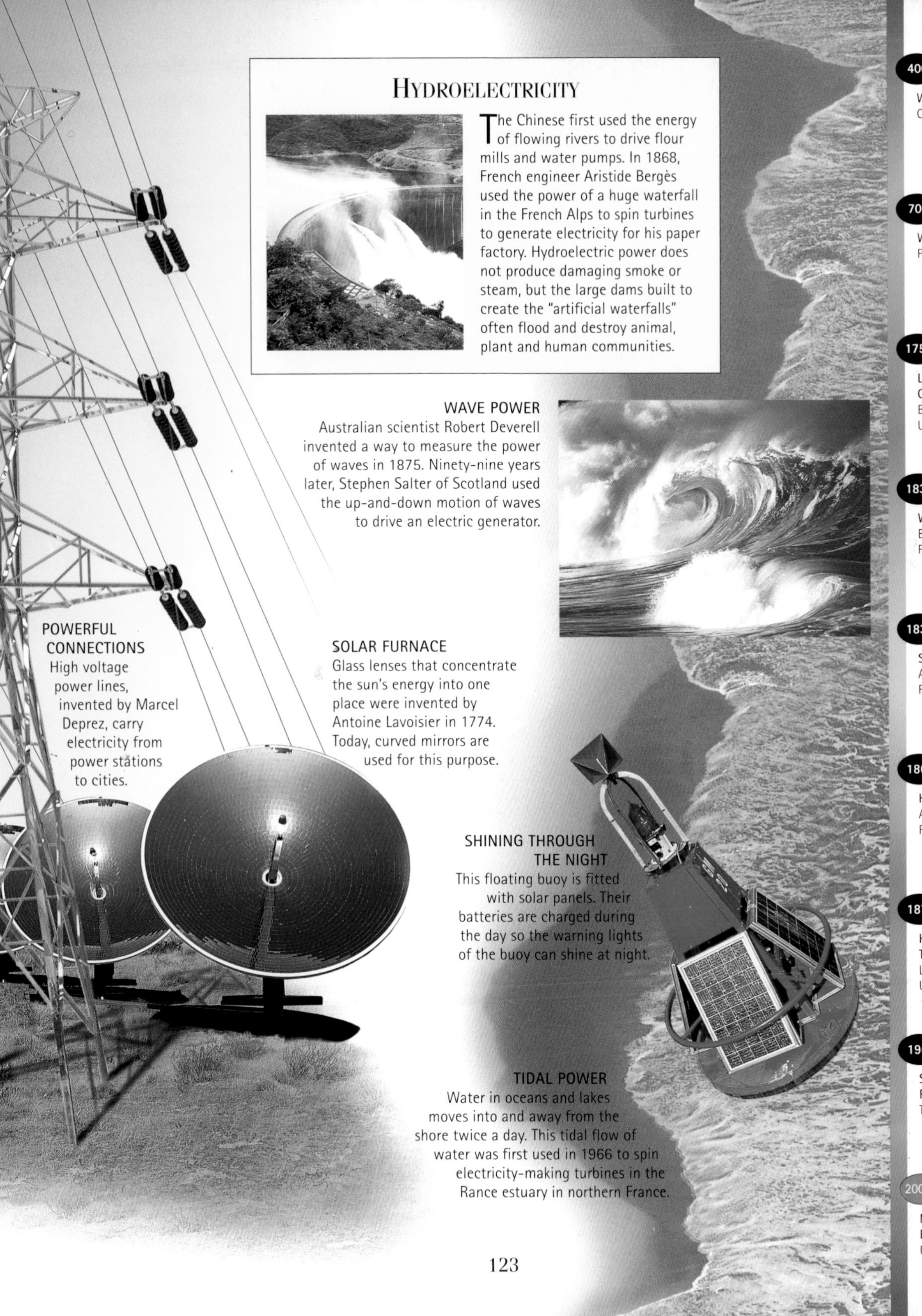

Hydroelectricity

The Chinese first used the energy of flowing rivers to drive flour mills and water pumps. In 1868, French engineer Aristide Bergès used the power of a huge waterfall in the French Alps to spin turbines to generate electricity for his paper factory. Hydroelectric power does not produce damaging smoke or steam, but the large dams built to create the "artificial waterfalls" often flood and destroy animal, plant and human communities.

WAVE POWER

Australian scientist Robert Deverell invented a way to measure the power of waves in 1875. Ninety-nine years later, Stephen Salter of Scotland used the up-and-down motion of waves to drive an electric generator.

POWERFUL CONNECTIONS

High voltage power lines, invented by Marcel Deprez, carry electricity from power stations to cities.

SOLAR FURNACE

Glass lenses that concentrate the sun's energy into one place were invented by Antoine Lavoisier in 1774. Today, curved mirrors are used for this purpose.

SHINING THROUGH THE NIGHT

This floating buoy is fitted with solar panels. Their batteries are charged during the day so the warning lights of the buoy can shine at night.

TIDAL POWER

Water in oceans and lakes moves into and away from the shore twice a day. This tidal flow of water was first used in 1966 to spin electricity-making turbines in the Rance estuary in northern France.

400
WATERMILL
China

700
WINDMILL
Persia

1752
LIGHTNING CONDUCTOR
Benjamin Franklin
USA

1832
WATER TURBINE
Benoit Fourneyron
France

1839
SOLAR CELL
Antoine Becquerel
France

1868
HYDROELECTRICITY
Aristide Bergès
France

1870
HYDROELECTRIC TURBINE
Lester Pelton
USA

1960
SOLAR THERMAL POWER PLANT
Turkmenistan

2000+
NUCLEAR COLD FUSION
USA, Russia

Healers and Healing

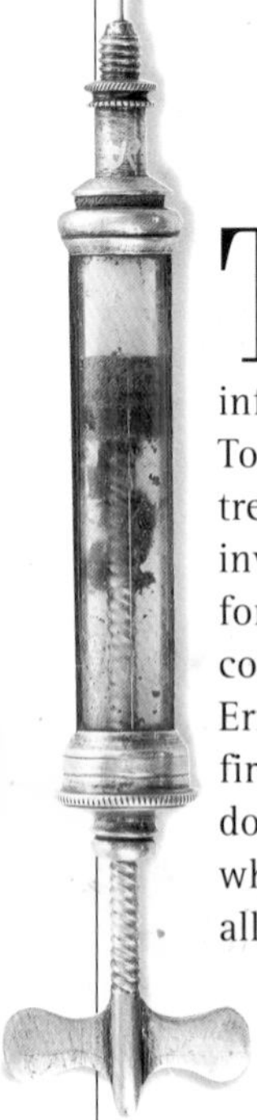

Two hundred years ago, visiting the doctor was a risky business. Operations were performed without proper anesthetic, open wounds often became infected, and many deadly diseases could not be treated. Today, doctors can vaccinate, anesthetize, sterilize and treat with antibiotics. Dramatic discoveries and ingenious inventions led to these life-saving procedures. In 1928, for example, Alexander Fleming discovered a mold that could fight germs. Twelve years later, Howard Florey and Ernst Chain developed this substance and invented the first antibiotic—penicillin. Many of the tools now used by doctors were invented in the 1800s: the stethoscope, which listens to the heartbeat; the endoscope, which allows doctors to peer inside the body; and the sphygmomanometer, which measures blood pressure.

THE POINT OF IT
A syringe is a piston in a tube that can suck up liquids and then squirt them out. The medical syringe attached to a hypodermic (beneath the skin) needle was perfected in 1853 by Scotsman Alexander Wood.

UNDER ANESTHETIC
Only 200 years ago, patients stayed awake during operations. Many had to be tied or held down. In 1846, American dentist William Morton used the chemical ether to anesthetise a patient while a tumor was removed from the man's neck.

Traditional Medicine

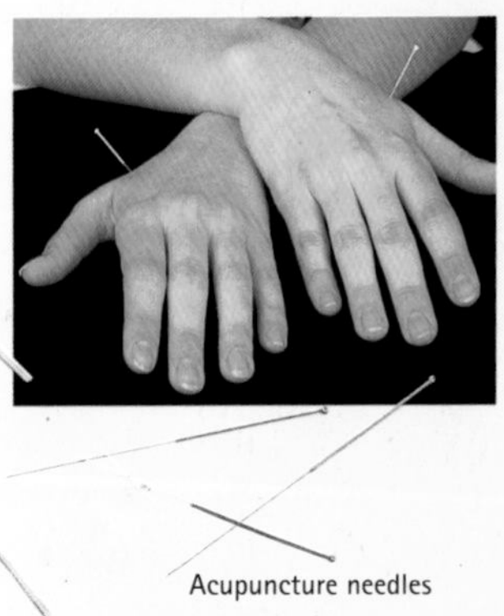

Acupuncture needles

Many cultures treat illnesses with ancient medical inventions. Aboriginal people in Australia make poultices and medicines from bush plants. Tribal shamans in South America combine plants and rituals to make people better. Chinese doctors invented acupuncture more than 4,000 years ago. Acupuncturists insert very fine needles into special points on the body to stimulate the nerves and help the body to heal itself.

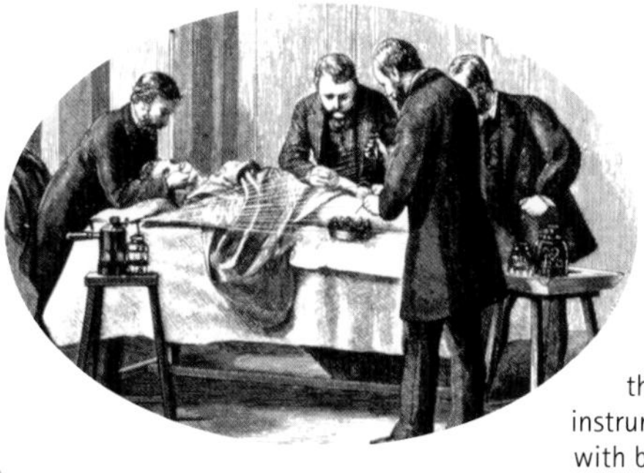

GERM FREE
Doctors once operated with their hands and instruments covered with blood from the previous operation. In 1865, Joseph Lister used carbolic acid to sterilize his hands, tools and the air during an operation.

STRANGE BUT TRUE

In 1667, a blood transfusion was carried out using a lamb as the donor. The patient, a 15-year-old boy who was bleeding to death, survived!

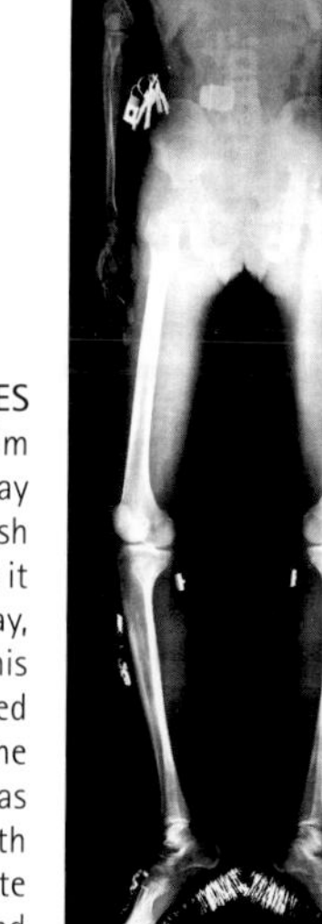

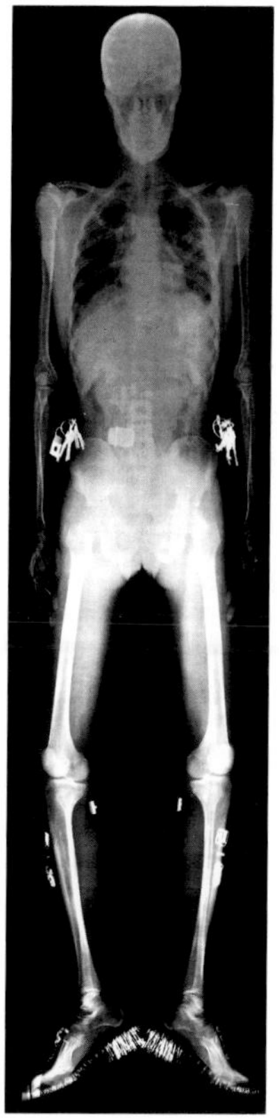

THE BARE BONES
In 1895, German Wilhelm Röntgen discovered a ray that passed through flesh but not through bone. As it was such a mystery ray, he called it X-ray. This marvellous ray was used to take pictures of the human skeleton such as this—the first full-length X-ray of a person, complete with sock suspenders and keys in the pocket.

2600 BC
ACUPUNCTURE
Emperor Huang Ti
China

1270
EYEGLASSES
Court of Kublai Khan
China

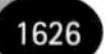

1626
MEDICAL THERMOMETER
Santorio
Italy

1796
VACCINATION
Edward Jenner
England

1816
STETHOSCOPE
Rene Laennec
France

1854
NURSING CORPS
Florence Nightingale
England

1896
SPHYGMOMANOMETER
Scipione Riva-Rocci
Italy

1899
ASPIRIN
Felix Hoffman
Germany

1928
FLYING DOCTOR SERVICE
John Flynn
Australia

AN UNLIKELY PAIR
Embryos of twins can be frozen and then implanted separately, years apart. The result: twins who are not the same age!

Freezing cells
Embryos can be frozen when they consist of only a few cells.

• LIFE AND MEDICINE •

Marvels of Medicine

Medicine has entered an exciting new stage. With today's technology, doctors can now observe the human body working on the inside without cutting it open. Vaccines and genetically engineered viruses can help the body to repair itself, and some inventions can actually replace broken and damaged organs. Artificial parts include electronic ears, plastic stomachs, mechanical hearts, heart pacemakers and ceramic hips. Doctors today use carpentry techniques and stainless steel or plastic nuts, screws and bolts to hold broken bones together. Fifty years ago, these bones never would have healed. Skin, kidneys, heart, liver, ova, sperm, lungs, corneas and bone marrow can be transplanted from person to person. Microsurgery rejoins the smallest blood vessels and nerves that have been cut in accidents.

FREEZE–THAW IVF
In 1983, an Australian team led by Carl Wood invented a way to fertilize and grow human embryos in glass tubes and then freeze and store them. The embryos can be thawed and implanted into the womb up to ten years later.

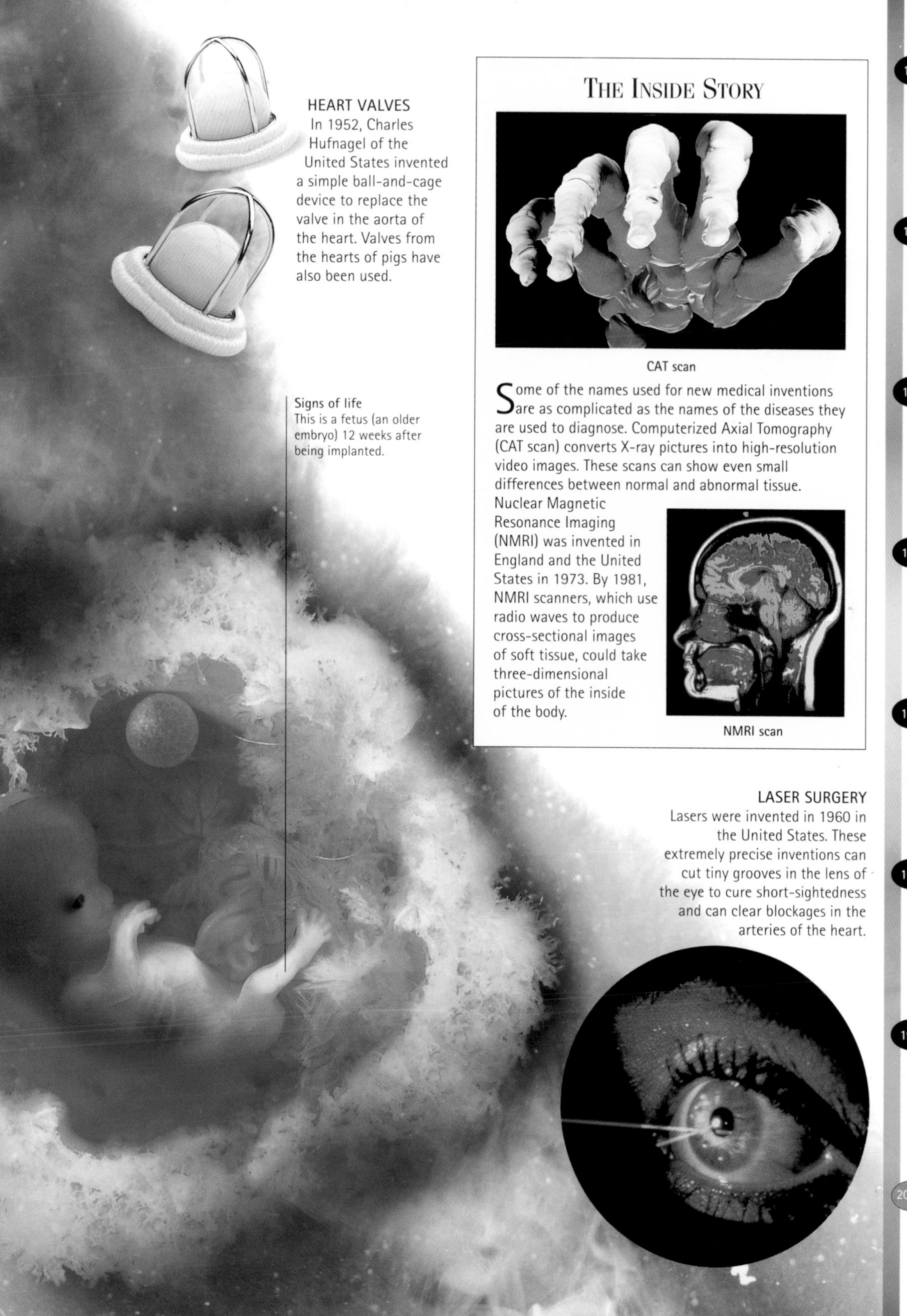

HEART VALVES
In 1952, Charles Hufnagel of the United States invented a simple ball-and-cage device to replace the valve in the aorta of the heart. Valves from the hearts of pigs have also been used.

Signs of life
This is a fetus (an older embryo) 12 weeks after being implanted.

The Inside Story

CAT scan

Some of the names used for new medical inventions are as complicated as the names of the diseases they are used to diagnose. Computerized Axial Tomography (CAT scan) converts X-ray pictures into high-resolution video images. These scans can show even small differences between normal and abnormal tissue. Nuclear Magnetic Resonance Imaging (NMRI) was invented in England and the United States in 1973. By 1981, NMRI scanners, which use radio waves to produce cross-sectional images of soft tissue, could take three-dimensional pictures of the inside of the body.

NMRI scan

LASER SURGERY
Lasers were invented in 1960 in the United States. These extremely precise inventions can cut tiny grooves in the lens of the eye to cure short-sightedness and can clear blockages in the arteries of the heart.

1900
ELECTRO-CARDIOGRAPH
Willem Einthoven
Netherlands

1927
IRON LUNG RESPIRATOR
Phillip Drinker
USA

1943
ARTIFICIAL KIDNEY MACHINE
Willem Kolff
Netherlands

1954
CONTRACEPTIVE PILL (FEMALE)
Gregory Pincus and John Rock
USA

1967
HEART TRANSPLANT
Christiaan Barnard
South Africa

1978
TEST-TUBE BABY
Patrick Steptoe and Robert Edwards
England

1979
BIONIC EAR IMPLANT
Graeme Clarke
Australia

2000+
SURGICAL ROBOTS

SPOT THE DIFFERENCE
In the future, the spot-making genes from a leopard could be mixed in with the genes of a domestic cat to produce a spotted animal.

KILLER COTTON
In 1992, an American company altered the genes in some cotton plants so that their leaves became poisonous to caterpillars but nothing else. This reduced the need for harmful insecticides.

• LIFE AND MEDICINE •

Biotechnology

We use biotechnology to alter living things. It gives us the power to create new animals, plants, foods, medicines, materials and even machines. People have used biotechnology for thousands of years to slowly breed new plants, animals and the microorganisms that make cheese, bread, beer, yogurt and wine. In 1987, geneticist Truda Straede of Australia created spotted cats after breeding tortoiseshell cats with Burmese and Abyssinian cats for ten years. Today, modern biotechnology could speed up this breeding process by altering the genetic material deep inside living cells. Scientists have already created bright blue carnations, and tomatoes that ripen on the vine without getting mushy. Biotechnology's potential is enormous. We can even use bacteria grown in laboratories to digest oil to clean up oil spills. The next hundred years will be an age of exciting "bio-inventions."

STRANGE BUT TRUE

In 1994, scientists in Australia invented a way of removing fleece from sheep without shearing. They injected sheep with a special hormone then wrapped them in lightweight hairnets. Three weeks later, the fleece could be peeled off the sheep by hand.

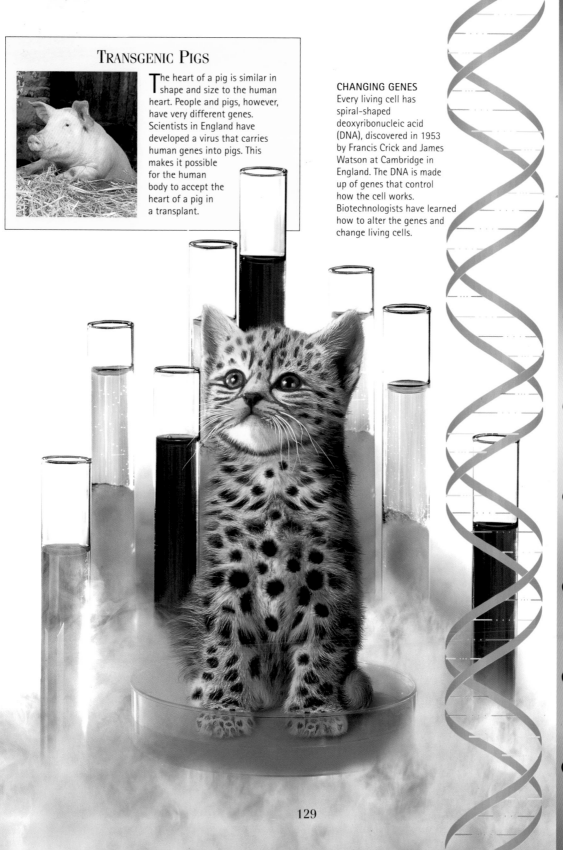

Transgenic Pigs

The heart of a pig is similar in shape and size to the human heart. People and pigs, however, have very different genes. Scientists in England have developed a virus that carries human genes into pigs. This makes it possible for the human body to accept the heart of a pig in a transplant.

CHANGING GENES
Every living cell has spiral-shaped deoxyribonucleic acid (DNA), discovered in 1953 by Francis Crick and James Watson at Cambridge in England. The DNA is made up of genes that control how the cell works. Biotechnologists have learned how to alter the genes and change living cells.

6000 BC

BEER
Mesopotamia

1000 BC

CHEESE
Nomad tribes
Middle East

1972

OIL-DIGESTING MICROBES
Dr Ananda M. Chakrabarty
USA

1975

MONOCLONAL ANTIBODY
George Kohler and Cesar Milstein
England

1984

TRANSGENIC PLANT
University of Ghent
Belgium

1986

BLACK TULIP
Geert Hageman
Netherlands

1989

GENE SHEARS
James Haseloff and Wayne Gerlach
Australia

1990

CROWN GALL BACTERICIDE
Dr Alan Kerr
Australia

1991

LONG-LIFE TOMATO
USA

Flight

- How does a jumbo-jet stay up in the air?
- Why is a Hercules used to carry cargo?
- How can a Stealth Fighter avoid being detected by enemy radar?

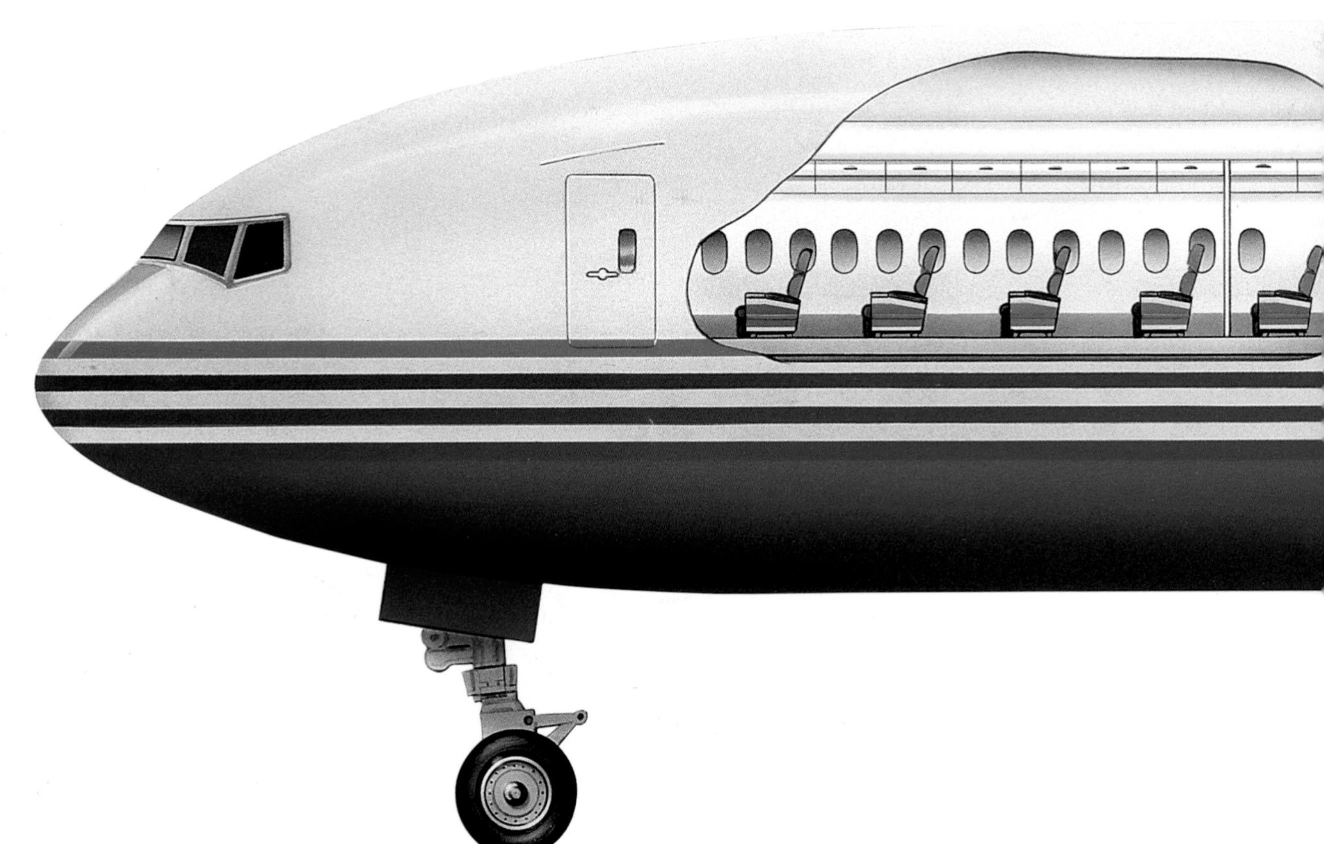

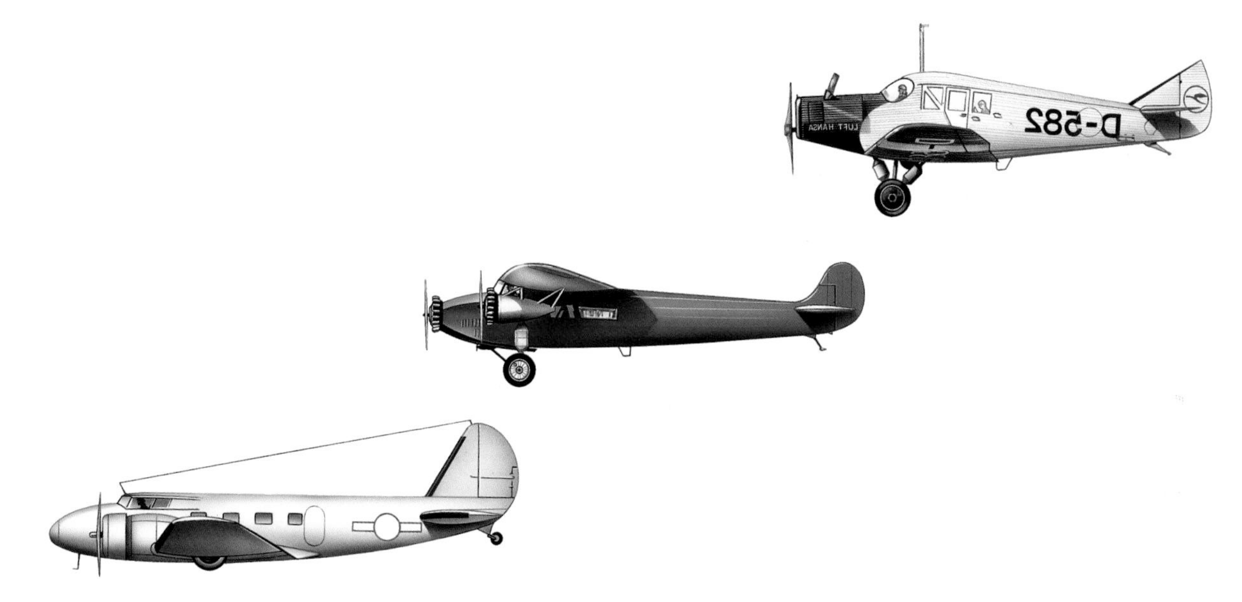
D-582
LUFT HANSA

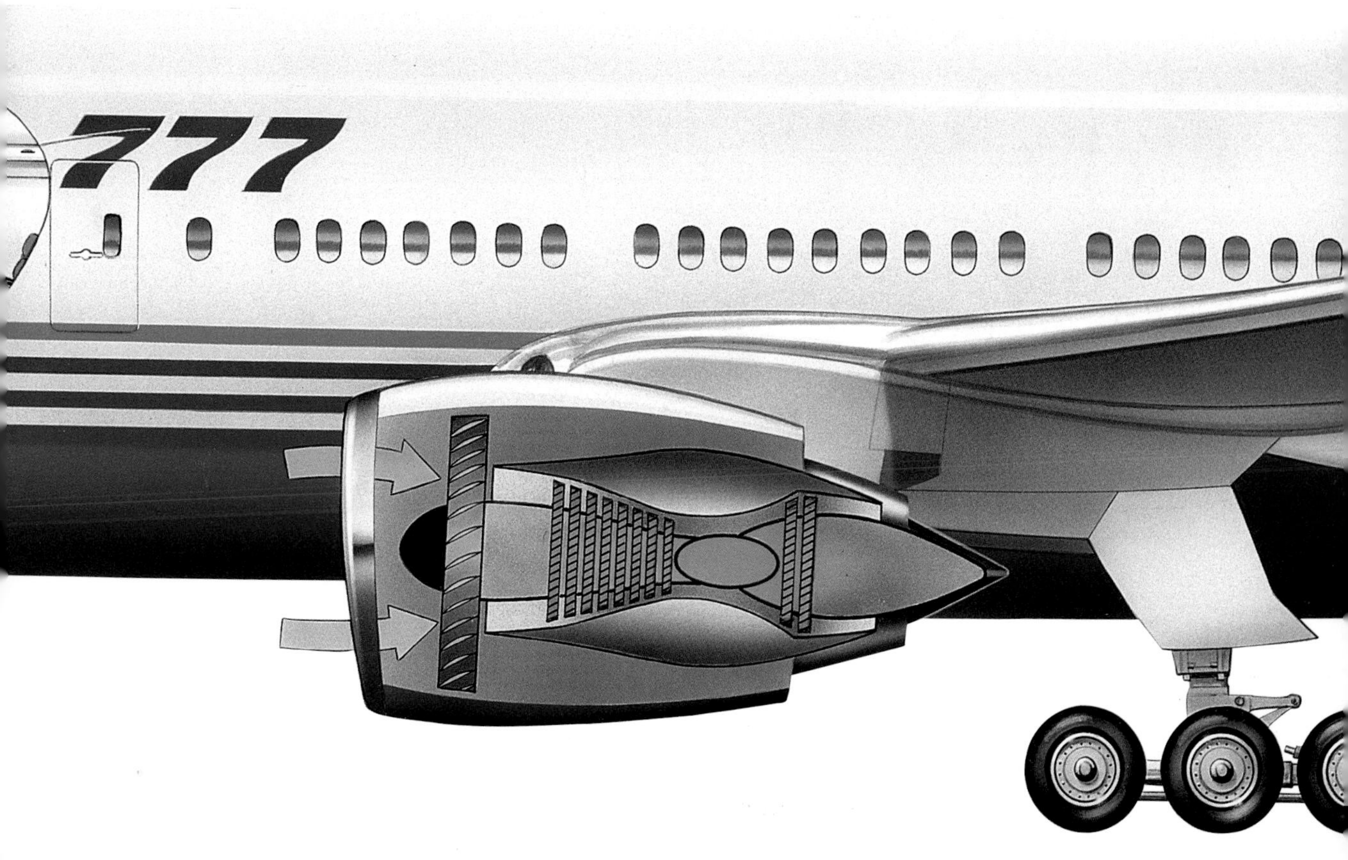

FLYING IN FORM
Geese often fly in a V formation on a long flight. The bird in front does much of the work needed to fly through the air, and the other birds benefit from this. When the bird in front tires, another takes its place as leader. It is a little like walking in freshly fallen snow. This is hard work, but if you can walk in already made footprints, it is less difficult to forge your way through the heavy snow.

TAKE OFF
Swans are heavy birds. They need to run over the water for quite a long distance before they can build up enough speed to support their great weight in the air. For the same reason, aircraft that are laden with passengers or cargo also need a long runway to become airborne.

Built for Flight

Have you ever watched birds in the sky and thought how easy it looks to fly? Centuries ago, people dreamed of joining birds in flight. Some went even further and flapped about, vainly, in wings made of feathers. But the human body is heavy and does not have the muscles needed for flight. The pioneers of aviation soon realized that before they could join the birds, they needed to understand how birds flew. They discovered that the wings of a bird are specially curved surfaces, called airfoils. When air flows over a bird's wings, a difference in air pressure is produced above and below the wings. This difference in pressure creates a force called "lift," which can overcome the weight of a bird or a plane. This is called heavier-than-air flying, and gliders and airplanes also fly this way. Balloons and airships are lighter-than-air fliers. They are filled with hot air (which always rises) or gases, such as helium or hydrogen, that are lighter than the air around them.

Did You Know?

Hydrofoils produce lift in water, just as airfoils give lift in air. This fast boat has hydrofoils, which lift it up and enable the boat to skim along the surface of the water.

Movement of airplane
Lift
Curved upper surface (airfoil)
Airflow is faster over the upper surface and decreases pressure
Airflow is slower over the lower surface and increases pressure

HEAVIER-THAN-AIR FLIERS
The wings of a swan and a giant Boeing 314 flying boat work in the same way. They produce the lift that is necessary to take off from the water.

ON THE WING
This cutaway shows the airfoil of a bird's wing.

THE SECRET OF LIFT
Hold a sheet of paper as shown here. Blow hard over its upper surface and watch the paper lift up—just like an airplane's wing.

How an Airfoil Works

This picture of an airplane wing moving through the air shows how its shape, or airfoil, affects the airflow. The airflow passing over the wing's curved upper surface is faster than the airflow passing over the lower surface. This causes a difference in pressure, which lifts or sucks the wing upwards, as shown in the experiment on the left.

Flying High

Birds fly higher, farther and faster than any other flying animals. Many species can span entire oceans and continents on their migrations. Birds are also the only flying animals that regularly use the wind as a source of lift. A bird's wings are powered by two sets of muscles on the breast. In most birds, these muscles make up about one-third of their total weight. Muscle power moves the long, stiff flight feathers. Feathers at the wing tips, called primaries, propel the bird forward, while the rest of the wing generates the lift. The wings change shape as they beat up and down. They are broad and extended on the downstroke, but tucked in tight on the upstroke.

Wing shape and how a bird lives are closely related. Long wings are more efficient than short wings, but much harder to flap. Birds with long wings are usually soaring birds. Short-winged birds have less stamina, but can build up speed very quickly.

WIDE WINGS
A spotted harrier eagle has wide wings and flies slowly over open country, looking for small reptiles, birds and mammals.

IN SLOW MOTION
The wingbeat of a European robin is a smooth alternation between the wings moving upwards (upstroke or recovery stroke) and the wings moving downwards (downstroke or powerstroke). It takes place in a cycle that is almost too fast to see. The process is broken into five stages (below) to show the details.

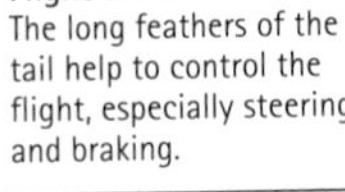

Flight control
The long feathers of the tail help to control the flight, especially steering and braking.

FEATHER CLOSE UP
Birds are the only animals that have feathers. An electron micrograph shows the intricate structure of a feather. It is held together by minute barbs and barbules like Velcro.

SPREADING OUT
The wings are high, fully spread and thrown forward. The feathers are overlapped and the feet are tucked against the body. The curled primary tips are like the angled blades of a propeller and pull the bird forward.

TUCKING IN
The wings are tucked well into the body throughout the upstroke to reduce air resistance.

BEGINNING
At the start of the upstroke, the robin's feathers are separated. This reduces air resistance and the bird uses less energy.

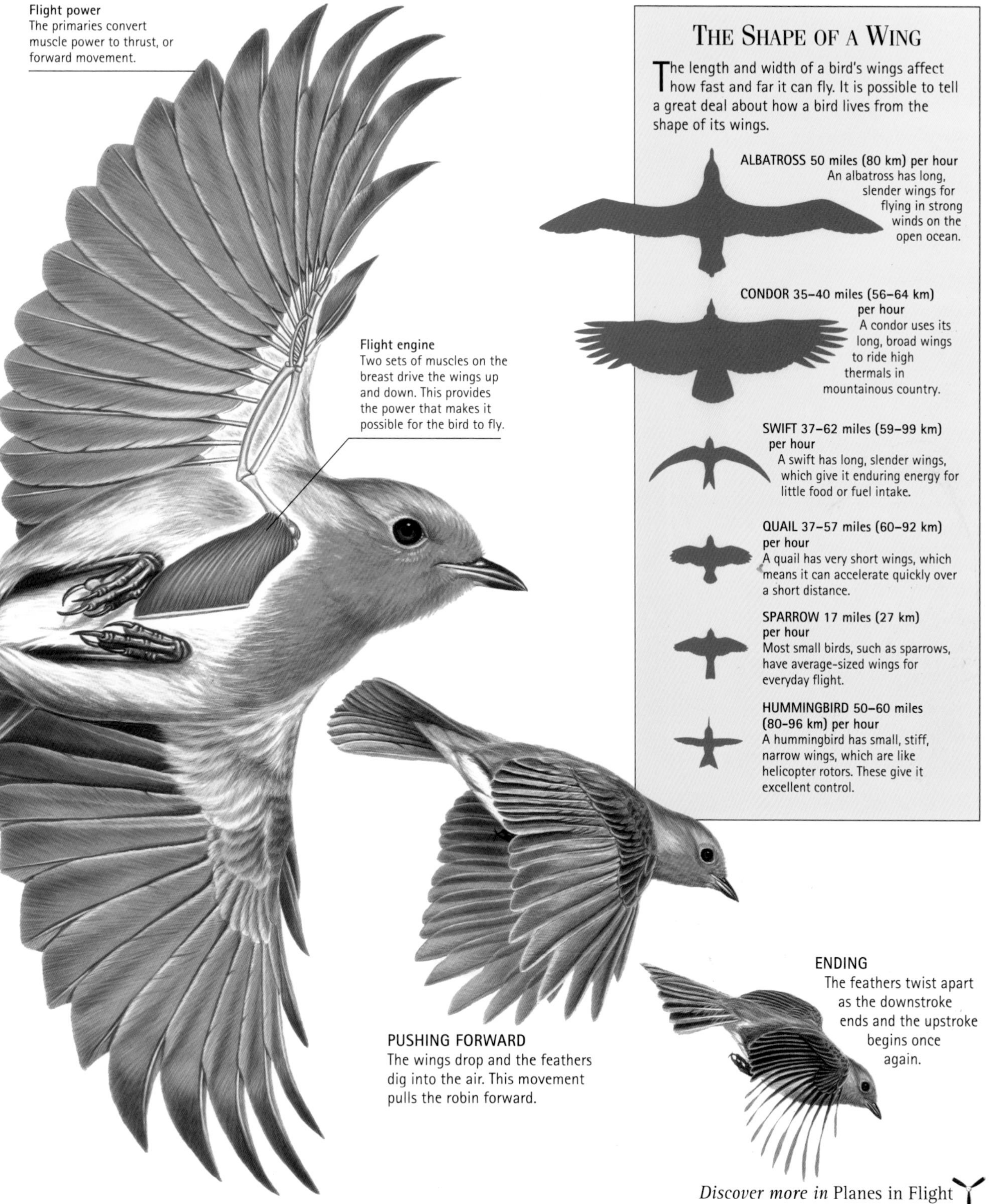

Flight power
The primaries convert muscle power to thrust, or forward movement.
Flight engine
Two sets of muscles on the breast drive the wings up and down. This provides the power that makes it possible for the bird to fly.
PUSHING FORWARD
The wings drop and the feathers dig into the air. This movement pulls the robin forward.
ENDING
The feathers twist apart as the downstroke ends and the upstroke begins once again.

The Shape of a Wing

The length and width of a bird's wings affect how fast and far it can fly. It is possible to tell a great deal about how a bird lives from the shape of its wings.

ALBATROSS 50 miles (80 km) per hour
An albatross has long, slender wings for flying in strong winds on the open ocean.

CONDOR 35–40 miles (56–64 km) per hour
A condor uses its long, broad wings to ride high thermals in mountainous country.

SWIFT 37–62 miles (59–99 km) per hour
A swift has long, slender wings, which give it enduring energy for little food or fuel intake.

QUAIL 37–57 miles (60–92 km) per hour
A quail has very short wings, which means it can accelerate quickly over a short distance.

SPARROW 17 miles (27 km) per hour
Most small birds, such as sparrows, have average-sized wings for everyday flight.

HUMMINGBIRD 50–60 miles (80–96 km) per hour
A hummingbird has small, stiff, narrow wings, which are like helicopter rotors. These give it excellent control.

Q: What is the purpose of a bird's primary feathers?

Discover more in Planes in Flight

SUSPENDED ABOVE
Hummingbirds feed mainly on nectar from flowers. This is a good source of energy and gives them plenty of fuel for their flights. They can fly in any direction or hover in midair, flapping their wings so fast it looks as if they are not flapping them at all.

• FLIGHT IN NATURE •

Gliding and Hovering

Some forest-dwelling animals can leap safely from one tree-branch to another. The southern flying squirrel glides on a furry membrane of skin. It can fly 328 ft (100 m) when there is no wind. But this is a very basic form of flight because the squirrel cannot fly for long, and its control is very limited. True flight– for animals as well as aircraft– depends on keeping a constant flow of air over a wing's surface. Animals do this in two ways: they exploit the wind by soaring; or they rely on muscle power, through flapping wings, to maintain the airflow. Hovering is an extreme example of flapping. It gives the animal great control and maneuverability, but it also demands an enormous amount of power. A hummingbird hovers with seemingly little effort. In fact, the bird is working very hard. Imagine the enormous energy Olympic athletes use at the moment of their greatest effort. The hummingbird uses more than ten times this amount of energy to hover in the air.

TREE GLIDING
The southern flying squirrel uses the furry membrane between its outstretched limbs to glide from tree to tree. The membrane acts like a parachute and makes its fall gentle and safe. The squirrel also uses its long, furry tail as a rudder to help it maneuver.

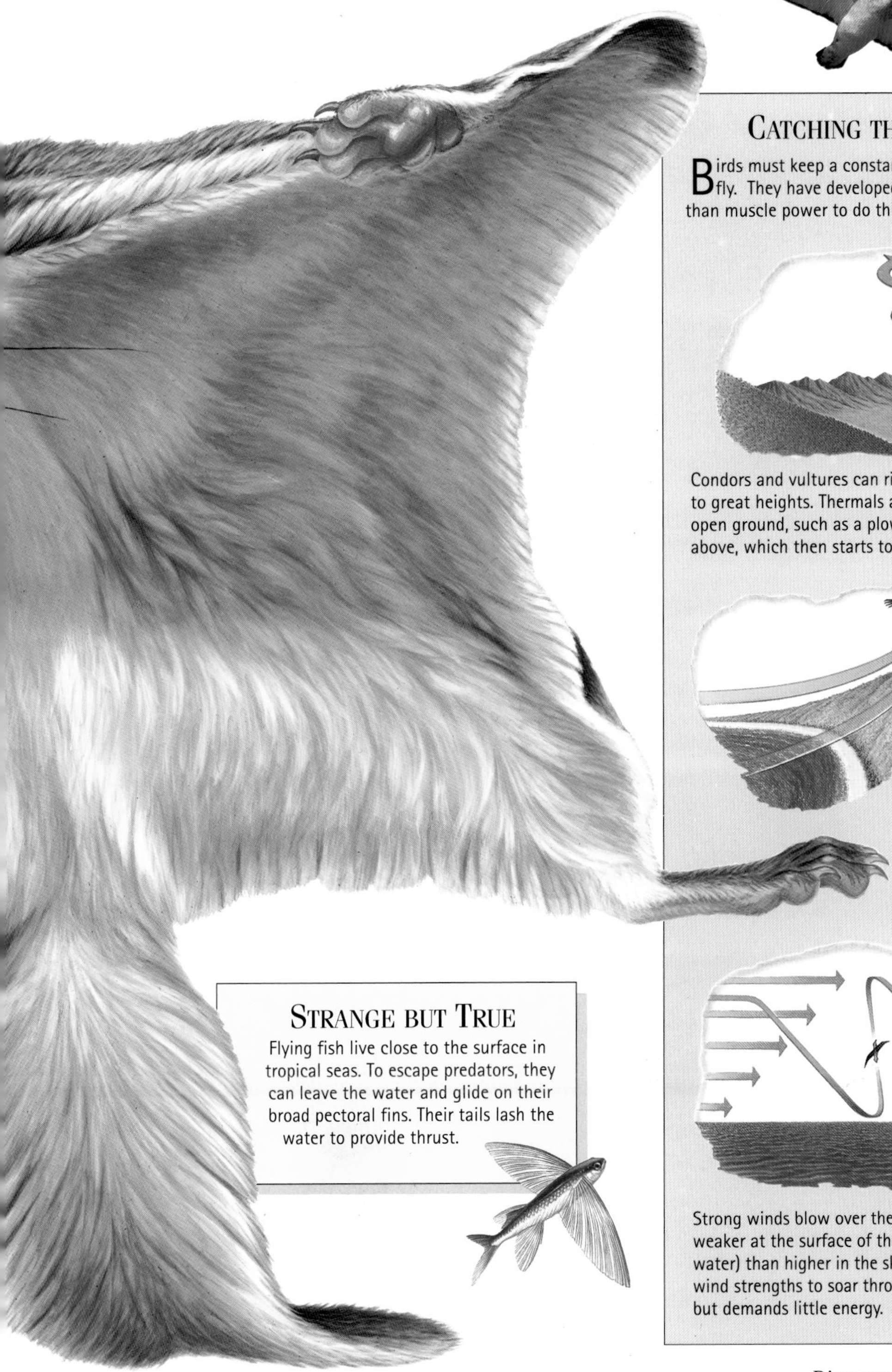

LONG-DISTANCE GLIDER
Albatrosses can fly for thousands of miles without settling on the water.

Catching the Wind

Birds must keep a constant flow of air over their wings to fly. They have developed several ways of using wind rather than muscle power to do this.

Condors and vultures can ride columns of air called thermals to great heights. Thermals are caused when the sun heats open ground, such as a plowed field. This warms the air above, which then starts to rise.

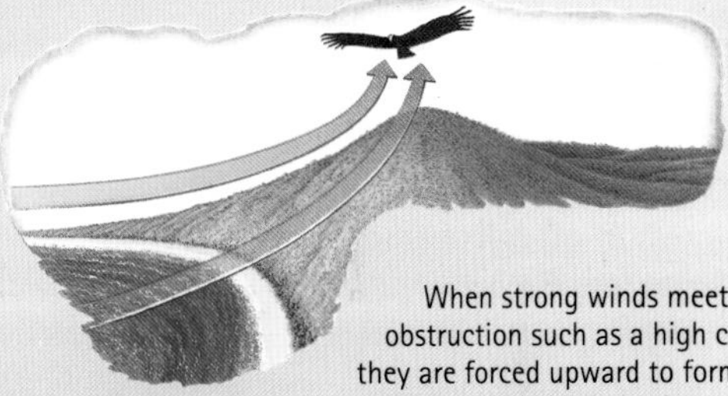

When strong winds meet an obstruction such as a high cliff, they are forced upward to form updrafts. Many birds, such as kestrels and swallows, skim along the top of these updrafts for a free ride.

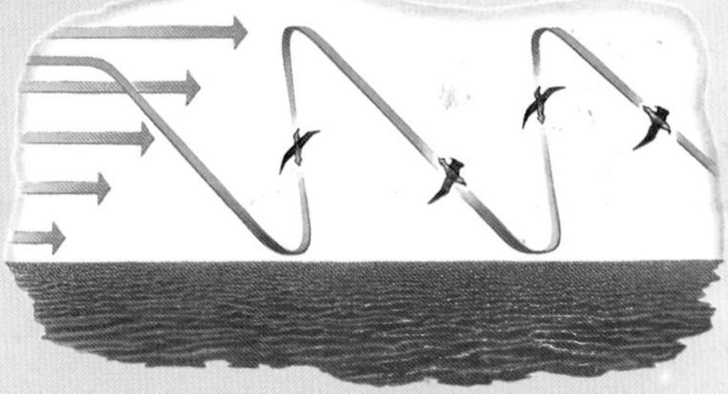

Strong winds blow over the open ocean. But these winds are weaker at the surface of the ocean (because of friction with the water) than higher in the sky. Albatrosses use these different wind strengths to soar through the air. This requires great skill but demands little energy.

Strange but True

Flying fish live close to the surface in tropical seas. To escape predators, they can leave the water and glide on their broad pectoral fins. Their tails lash the water to provide thrust.

Discover more in Kites and Gliders

Insects, Bats and Pterodactyls

Insects are the smallest of all flying animals. Their tiny muscles in tiny bodies are more efficient than large muscles in large bodies. Flying insects need less power than heavier animals such as bats and birds, and they are more maneuverable in the air. A housefly can somersault on touchdown to land upside down on a ceiling. Insects, birds and bats are the only animals alive today capable of true flight. Bats fly using a membrane of skin, reinforced with muscle and tissue, which stretches between the arms and the legs (and sometimes the tail). Most bats are the size of a mouse and catch flying moths at night, but a few species weigh as much as 3 lb (1.5 kg) and feed on fruit. Long ago, at the time of the dinosaurs, another group of animals, called pterodactyls, also flew. They included the largest of all flying animals, the *Quetzalcoatlus*.

Did You Know?

Some insects, such as flies and mosquitoes, use their flight muscles to vibrate the sides of their body wall in and out. This makes the wings vibrate up and down together and creates the familiar buzzing or whining sound of an insect.

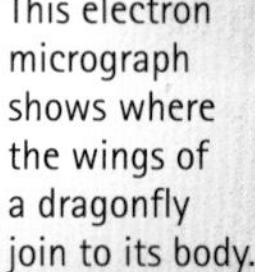

A CLOSER LOOK
A close-up of a dragonfly in flight shows some of the basic differences in the way insects, birds and bats are built for flight. Insects have two pairs of wings; birds and bats have only one. In birds and bats, the wings extend from the body, but in insects, they are entirely different structures.

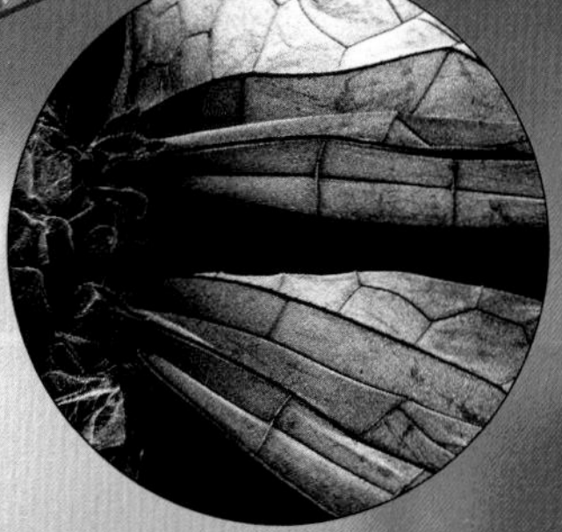

CLOSER STILL
This electron micrograph shows where the wings of a dragonfly join to its body.

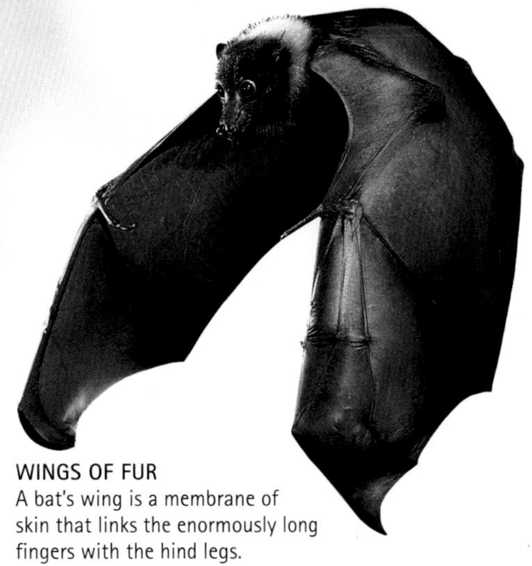

WINGS OF FUR
A bat's wing is a membrane of skin that links the enormously long fingers with the hind legs.

INSECTS' WING BEATS
The smaller the insect, the faster its wings beat. This usually means its progress through the air is also slower.

	SPEED PER HOUR	WING BEATS PER SECOND
DRAGONFLY	15 miles (24 km)	35
BUTTERFLY	14 miles (22.4 km)	10
HOUSEFLY	9 miles (14.4 km)	170
HONEYBEE	4 miles (6.4 km)	130
MOSQUITO	1 mile (1.6 km)	600

Pterodactyls

The first machine to copy the wing-flapping technique of animal flight was built as part of a study on the flight of extinct pterodactyls. A team of American scientists reconstructed a pterodactyl called *Quetzalcoatlus northropi*, which lived about 100 million years ago. Its wing span was around 19 ft (6 m) and it was equipped with a radio receiver, an onboard computer "autopilot" and 13 tiny electric motors to make the wings flap. In 1986, the model flew for three minutes over Death Valley, California.

FORERUNNER OF FLIGHT
The Japanese used vibrantly colored kites in religious ceremonies and for entertainment.

Wing shape
The main frame, called the spar, is shaped like a wing. It is stiff and curved to give the greatest lift.

HANG-GLIDING
A typical hang-glider flight begins on a high, windy ridge. Strapped into a harness, the pilot runs into the wind and is lifted by the sail (wing). The pilot holds the control bar and shifts his or her weight around to direct the hang-glider.

Control bar

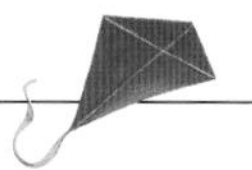

• USING AIR AND WIND •

Kites and Gliders

The kite is the ancestor of the airplane. The Chinese flew kites more than 2,000 years ago, and through the years they have been used to lift people high above battlefields on military observation, to collect weather information and to drop supplies. Kites inspired the English inventor George Cayley in his design of the world's first model glider. Pioneer fliers such as Englishman Percy Pilcher and German Otto Lilienthal used kite designs to develop the wings of their gliders. Lilienthal believed that aviators should learn to glide so they could really understand the air. The Wright brothers constructed their first glider in 1901, and this was based on a biplane kite they had built previously. Early gliders were launched from hills, but modern sailplanes are towed into the air by light planes. When they are released, they climb and soar in the sky, using thermals of hot air.

MAORI FISHING KITE
The Maoris in New Zealand flew birdmen kites. Some had special significance and were used by "tohunga" (important men) to help them make big decisions.

ON CURRENTS OF AIR

Modern, high-performance gliders are called sailplanes. They have long, slender wings and, like birds with long wings, use air currents to circle for hours. They can fly hundreds of miles and reach speeds of 149 miles (240 km) per hour in a dive.

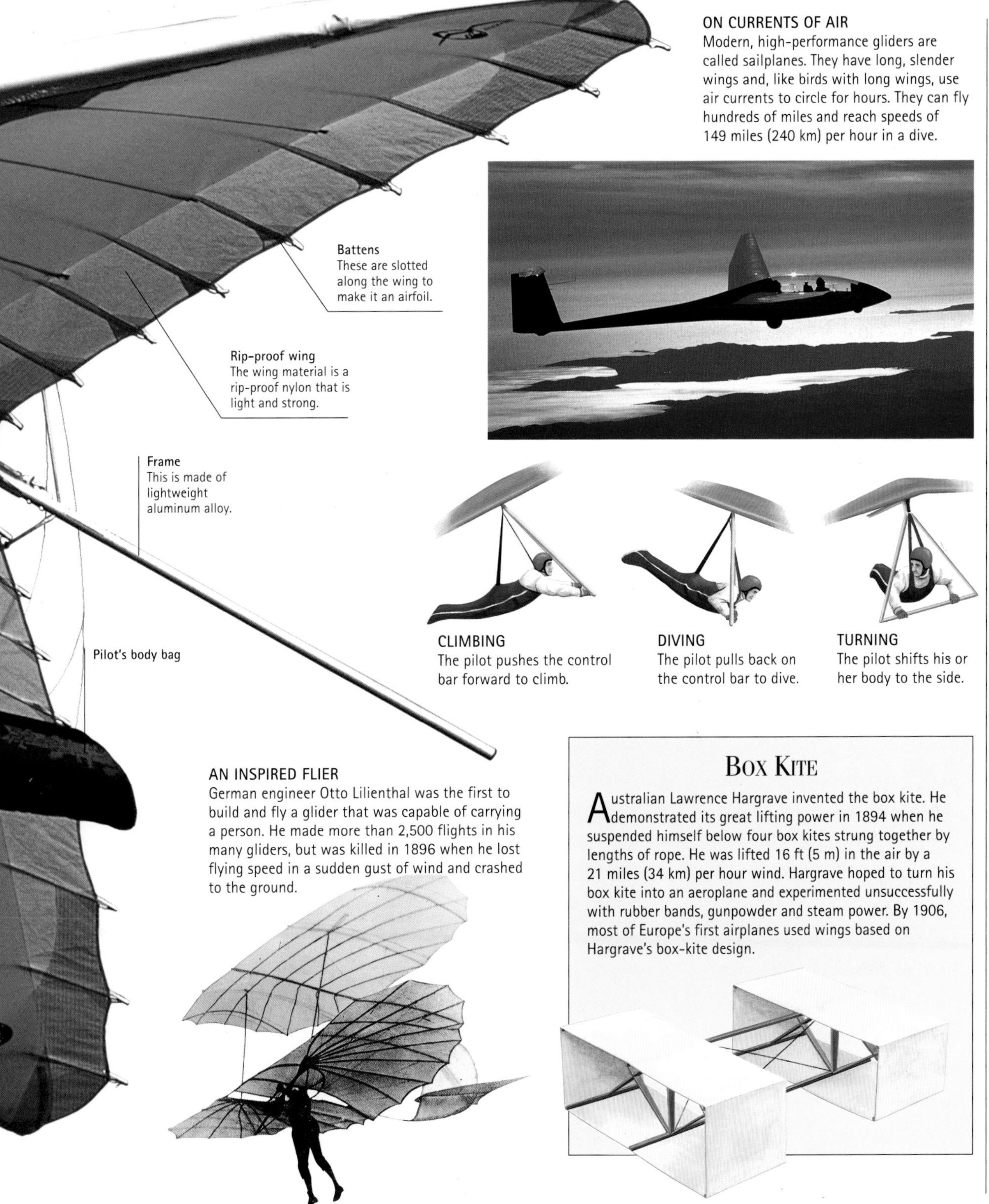

Battens
These are slotted along the wing to make it an airfoil.
Rip-proof wing
The wing material is a rip-proof nylon that is light and strong.
Frame
This is made of lightweight aluminum alloy.
Pilot's body bag

CLIMBING
The pilot pushes the control bar forward to climb.

DIVING
The pilot pulls back on the control bar to dive.

TURNING
The pilot shifts his or her body to the side.

AN INSPIRED FLIER

German engineer Otto Lilienthal was the first to build and fly a glider that was capable of carrying a person. He made more than 2,500 flights in his many gliders, but was killed in 1896 when he lost flying speed in a sudden gust of wind and crashed to the ground.

Box Kite

Australian Lawrence Hargrave invented the box kite. He demonstrated its great lifting power in 1894 when he suspended himself below four box kites strung together by lengths of rope. He was lifted 16 ft (5 m) in the air by a 21 miles (34 km) per hour wind. Hargrave hoped to turn his box kite into an aeroplane and experimented unsuccessfully with rubber bands, gunpowder and steam power. By 1906, most of Europe's first airplanes used wings based on Hargrave's box-kite design.

• USING AIR AND WIND •

Up, Up and Away

People created many elaborate flying machines in their attempts to see the world from the sky. Frenchmen Joseph and Etienne Montgolfier built a balloon of paper and cloth that rose in the hot air above a fire. Their next balloon had passengers: a sheep, a duck and a rooster. In 1783, before an astonished crowd in Paris, a Montgolfier balloon (below) carried two French noblemen into the skies and became the first successful flying craft. Hot-air and gas-filled balloons soon became popular. When Paris was surrounded by a Prussian army in 1870, the French smuggled people and mail out of the city in balloons. In 1897, three explorers vanished trying to reach the North Pole in a balloon. Fifty years later, scientists used balloons to study the Earth's upper atmosphere. Today, several groups of balloon enthusiasts are planning to fly nonstop around the world.

Burners
The pilot reaches up and pulls the trigger operating the burner blast valve. Two propane gas burners blast heat into the balloon.

Basket
Most baskets are woven of willow, because it is strong, light and flexible.

FULL OF HOT AIR
Hot-air ballooning is very popular and many balloonists operate joy flights for the public. A typical balloon is 59 ft (18 m) in diameter and holds 99,956 cubic ft (2,830 cubic m) of air. This is heated by two propane gas burners, each of which is powerful enough to heat 120 houses.

Envelope
This is made of 24 panels of polyurethane-coated, rip-proof nylon. It usually contains 10,760 sq ft (1,000 sq m) of fabric and 3 miles (5 km) of thread.
Parachute vent
Ripcord

How Hot Air Balloons Fly

Balloons travel with the wind, so balloonists have little control over their direction. But they can control the height to which they rise. If they want the balloon to climb, they turn the burner on. This heats the air in the balloon and produces lift. If a balloonist wants to descend, air in the balloon is allowed to cool, or the ripcord is pulled. Hot air then escapes from the parachute vent and is replaced by cooler (heavier) air. When the balloon has landed, the vent is opened to deflate the balloon.

BALLOON ADVENTURERS
In 1978, *Double Eagle*, an American gas-filled balloon, crossed the Atlantic in six days. Fifteen years later, a hot-air balloon (below) crossed Australia in 40 hours and 23 minutes.

BARRAGE BALLOONS
Clusters of gas-filled balloons were used to defend cities during the Second World War. They were tied to the ground by steel cables and obstructed enemy bombers that tried to fly low over the cities.

Discover more in Airships

The Groundwork

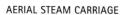

There are many stories of gallant people and the inspired flying contraptions they constructed. Most of the machines never flew, but these inventors and engineers did much of the groundwork for the aviators who were to follow. The development of the steam engine in the nineteenth century led to serious attempts to invent steam-powered aircraft. In 1874, Felix de Temple built a monoplane that managed a short, downhill hop. Clement Ader and Hiram Maxim both built machines that lifted them, briefly, off the ground. But these aircraft were difficult to control and their coal-fired steam engines were too heavy and not powerful enough for true flight. In 1896, Dr. Samuel Langley launched an unpiloted aircraft with a steam-powered engine. It did manage to fly 1 mile (1.2 km), but then ran out of steam. Steam engines were soon replaced by light and powerful gasoline engines. They made sustained flight a reality.

AERIAL STEAM CARRIAGE
In 1842, William Henson designed an airplane— the first flying invention to actually look like an airplane. It was to be powered by a steam engine, which turned two propellers. Although Henson only managed to build a model, his design had many of the features used in today's airplanes.

LANGLEY'S LUCKLESS VENTURE
American Samuel Langley made model airplanes powered by steam. They were so successful he built a full-sized version, called the *Aerodrome*, which had a gasoline engine. Its first test flight was in 1903, when the piloted aircraft was launched from a catapult on the roof of a houseboat. But the launching mechanism failed, and *Aerodrome* plunged into the Potomac River.

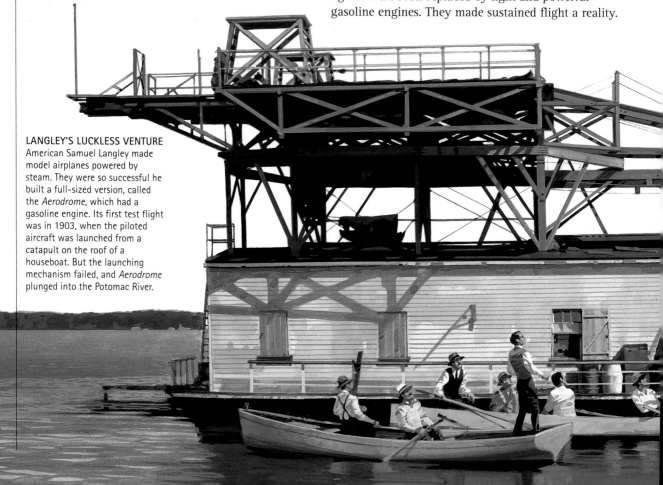

ADER'S AIRPLANE

French engineer Clement Ader built his bat-like *Avion III* in 1897. It was larger than his previous invention *Eole*, but not as successful. In 1890, *Eole* managed a short hop and rose about 8 in (20 cm) into the air. *Avion III* never left the ground.

MAXIM'S MONSTER

This flying giant, a triple biplane with a wingspan of 103 ft (31.5 m), was built in 1894 by an American, Hiram Maxim (the inventor of the machine gun). For a few seconds, its two steam engines lifted Maxim and his crew from its rail track.

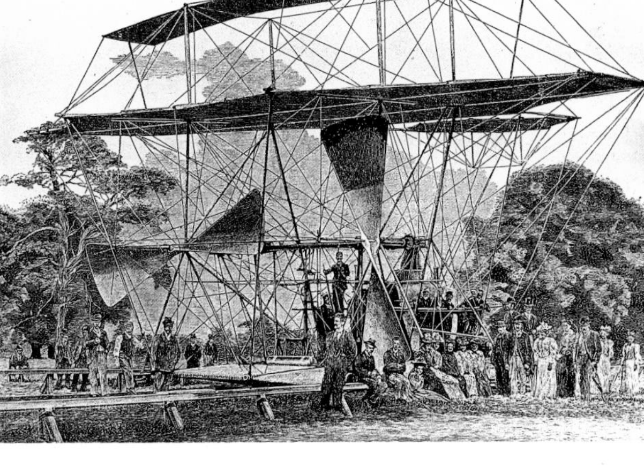

Did You Know?

Artist Leonardo da Vinci (1452–1519) was also an engineer. He believed that ornithopters (wing-flapping aircraft) were the key to powered flight. He produced many plans for ornithopters, which ranged from strap-on wings to flying chariots.

The Search for an Engine

In 1852, Henri Giffard built an airship, which was powered by the first aircraft engine— an extremely heavy, three-horsepower steam engine. Aviators searched for an alternative with more power and less weight and experimented with electric motors and engines powered by compressed air and coal gas. In the late 1800s, Otto Daimler invented the gasoline engine. This finally provided the light and powerful engine needed for heavier-than-air airplanes. The Anzani gasoline engine shown here was invented in 1909.

Q: How did gasoline engines make true flight possible?

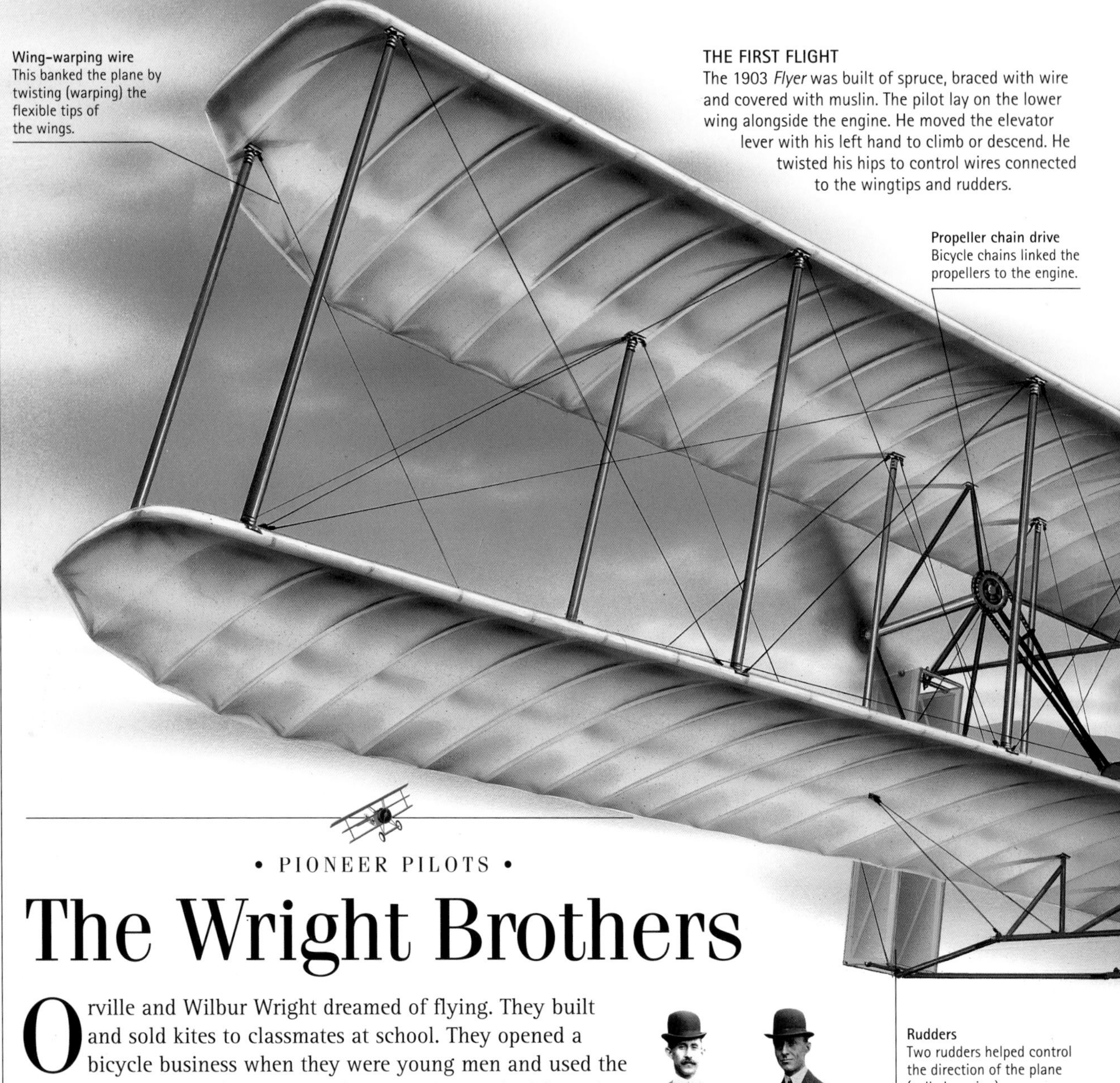
Wing-warping wire
This banked the plane by twisting (warping) the flexible tips of the wings.
Propeller chain drive
Bicycle chains linked the propellers to the engine.
Rudders
Two rudders helped control the direction of the plane (called yawing).

THE FIRST FLIGHT
The 1903 *Flyer* was built of spruce, braced with wire and covered with muslin. The pilot lay on the lower wing alongside the engine. He moved the elevator lever with his left hand to climb or descend. He twisted his hips to control wires connected to the wingtips and rudders.

• PIONEER PILOTS •

The Wright Brothers

Orville and Wilbur Wright dreamed of flying. They built and sold kites to classmates at school. They opened a bicycle business when they were young men and used the profits to build aircraft. For years they experimented with, and examined the theories of, flight. What was the clue to the mystery of flight? By 1902, they had developed a glider that could carry a person. It made more than 1,000 flights. Next, they designed and built a tiny 12-horsepower gasoline engine and connected it by bicycle chains to a pair of propellers. It turned their glider into a powered airplane– the *Flyer.* In December 1903, Orville made the world's first powered flight from Kill Devil Hill, over Kitty Hawk beach in North Carolina. The first *Flyer* flew just four times, for a total of 98 seconds. Then, it was caught in a gust of wind and crashed into the sand– severely damaged.

Did You Know?

Wilbur (left) and Orville Wright tossed a coin to decide who would be the world's first pilot. Wilbur won, but he stalled and crashed into the sand. Orville succeeded where his brother had failed.

AHEAD OF ITS TIME
Orville Wright was part of a team that designed this streamlined, 1920 Dayton Wright monoplane racer. It had retractable landing gear and extremely strong wings!

Propeller Power

A propeller is a tiny wing that spins. As it rotates, air flows around the propeller blades and moves faster over the curved leading edge. This reduces the air pressure in front of the blade and pulls the aircraft forward. Many propellers allow pilots to adjust the blade angle for climbing, cruising and descending. This improves performance and keeps engine speed and fuel consumption low— like changing gears in a car. The propeller of the *Flyer* (shown on the right) was carved out of wood. Today, propellers are made of metal or fiberglass and carbon.

Water-filled radiator

Fuel tank

Biplane elevators
These tilted up or down to make the plane climb or descend.

Gasoline-combustion engine
The 12-horsepower engine was mounted to the side to balance the pilot's weight.

Elevator lever

Skids for landing

THE UNITED STATES OF AMERICA

THAT'S MY PLANE
The Wright brothers patented their aircraft in 1906 to stop others from copying their ideas. But aviators in Europe were already designing different kinds of airplanes.

A LATER PERSPECTIVE
Orville Wright's flight covered a distance of 170 ft (51.5 m), which included the take off and landing run. The whole flight could have taken place in the passenger area of this Boeing 747-400.

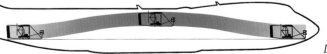

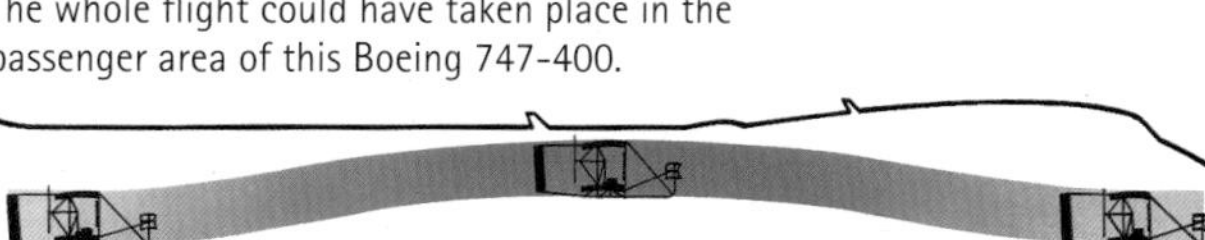

Discover more in Built for Flight 

Famous Firsts

The progress of aviation has been marked by the achievements of many pioneers determined to dominate the skies. It all began in 1783 with the Montgolfiers' hot-air balloon. In 1853, George Cayley created the first heavier-than-air aircraft. Fifty years later, the Wright brothers introduced powered flight and five years after, carried the first plane passenger. Louis Blériot flew across the English Channel in 1909 and proved that water was no longer an obstacle. Soon, time and technology would reduce flying times, and the world would be encompassed by airplanes. In 1947, Chuck Yeager blasted through the sound barrier in his Bell X-1. Aviation sights were then set even higher, and in 1961, Russian Yuri Gagarin became the first person to fly in space. Six years later, the rocket-powered X-15A-2 reached a world-record speed of 4,497 miles (7,254 km) per hour– about 6.8 times the speed of sound.

WALKING ON THE MOON
Americans Neil Armstrong and Edwin "Buzz" Aldrin landed their lunar module *Eagle* on the moon on July 21, 1969. Their tentative steps were seen by millions of people all over the world.

PEDAL POWER
American cyclist Bryan Allen pedalled his *Gossamer Condor*, the first successful human-powered aircraft, around a 1 mile (1.6 km) figure-eight course in 1977. His aircraft cruised at 10 miles (16 km) per hour, had a wingspan of 95 ft (29 m) and weighed 72 lb (32.7 kg). It was made of cardboard and aluminum tubing covered in plastic.

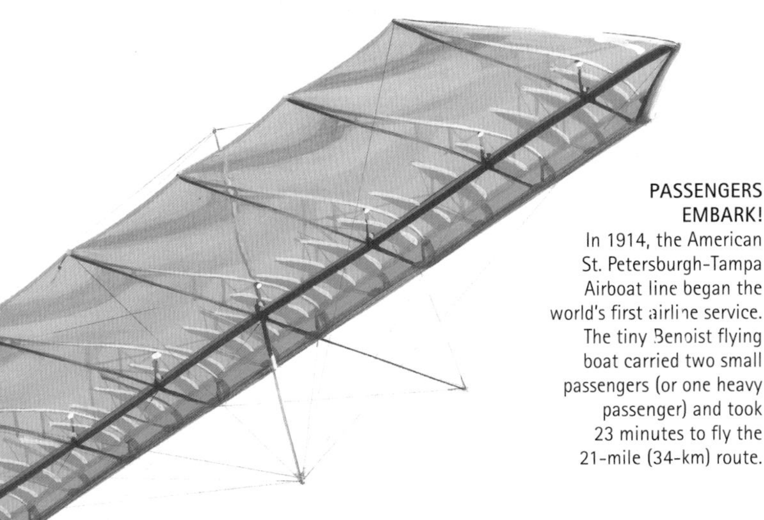

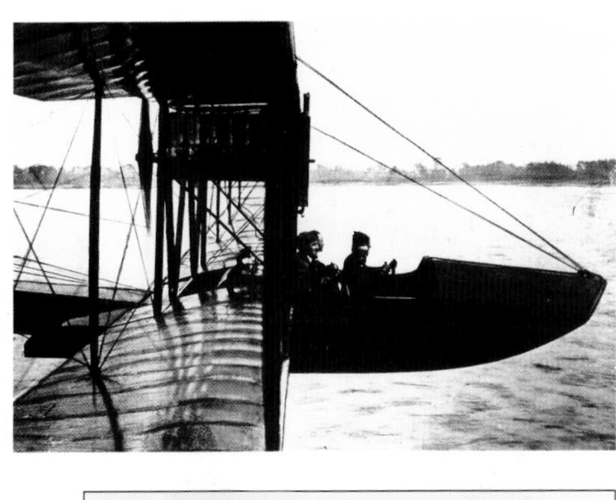

PASSENGERS EMBARK!
In 1914, the American St. Petersburgh-Tampa Airboat line began the world's first airline service. The tiny Benoist flying boat carried two small passengers (or one heavy passenger) and took 23 minutes to fly the 21-mile (34-km) route.

Women of the Air

Women pilots were among those setting aviation firsts. In 1910, Baroness de Laroche from France became the first female pilot. Two years later, American Harriet Quimby flew the English Channel. Another famous American Amelia Earhart (above) was the first woman to fly the Atlantic in 1932. Other solo, long-distance pilots of the 1930s were Amy Johnson of England who flew 12,162 miles (19,616 km) to Australia; Australian Lores Bonney who flew 18,054 miles (29,120 km) to South Africa; and New Zealander Jean Batten whose array of firsts included crossing the South Atlantic. In 1953, American Jacqueline Cochran was the first woman to break the sound barrier.

JETTING ABOUT
In 1939, the German Heinkel He 178 became the world's first jet-powered aircraft. It could reach speeds of 434 miles (700 km) per hour. These aircraft had a great impact on aviation. All future designs for fighter planes in the United States and Europe were jet-propelled.

A FLYING MILESTONE
The sleek 1912 Deperdussin monocoque racer was the super plane of its day. Its single-shelled (monocoque) fuselage made it streamlined and fast. Flown by Frenchman Jules Vedrines, it was the first aircraft to exceed 100 miles (161 km) per hour.

Discover more in Breaking the Sound Barrier

CROSSING THE PACIFIC
In 1928, Australians Charles Kingsford-Smith and Charles Ulm made the first aerial crossing of the Pacific Ocean. They averaged 89 miles (143 km) per hour in their Fokker VII/3m *Southern Cross* on the 7,400-mile (11,914-km) flight. They stopped for fuel in Hawaii and Fiji.

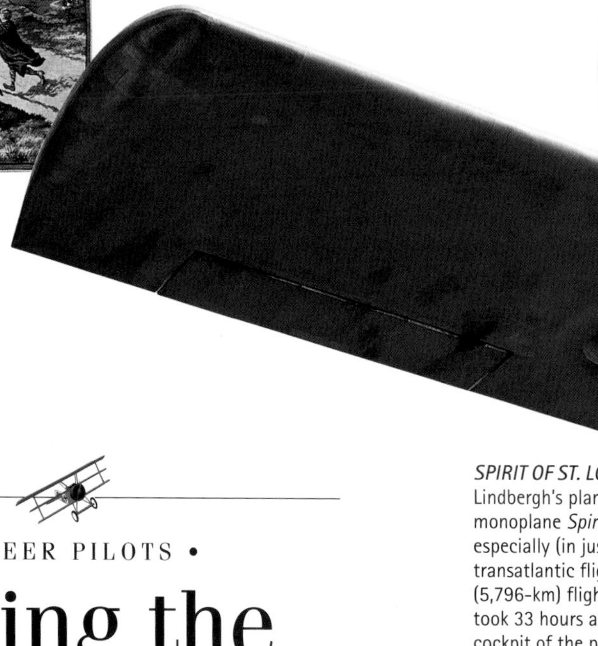

THE WHITE CLIFFS OF DOVER
Louis Blériot flew from France to England in a monoplane, powered only by a 35-horsepower engine. He crash-landed on the cliffs of Dover after his great flight.

SPIRIT OF ST. LOUIS
Lindbergh's plane, the Ryan NYP monoplane *Spirit of St. Louis*, was built especially (in just two months) for his transatlantic flight. The 3,600-mile (5,796-km) flight from New York to Paris took 33 hours and 30 minutes. The cockpit of the plane was tucked behind a huge fuel tank, and Lindbergh had to use a periscope to see in front of him.

• PIONEER PILOTS •

Making the World Smaller

As airplanes changed from rickety machines to planes that could cover huge distances, pilots dreamed of conquering large expanses of land and water. On 25 July 1909, Louis Blériot took nearly 37 minutes to become the first person to fly the 22 miles (35 km) across the English Channel. He battled wind gusts and a severely overheating engine to make a rushed downhill landing that shattered his propeller and landing gear. American Cal Rodgers survived five crashes to fly across the United States in 84 days in 1911. Ross and Keith Smith set an extraordinary record when they flew 11,426 miles (18,396 km) from England to Australia. Aviation dominated the headlines in 1927 when Charles Lindbergh flew the Atlantic, and a year later when Charles Ulm and Charles Kingsford-Smith conquered the Pacific. Jet travel eventually brought the continents less than a day's flight apart.

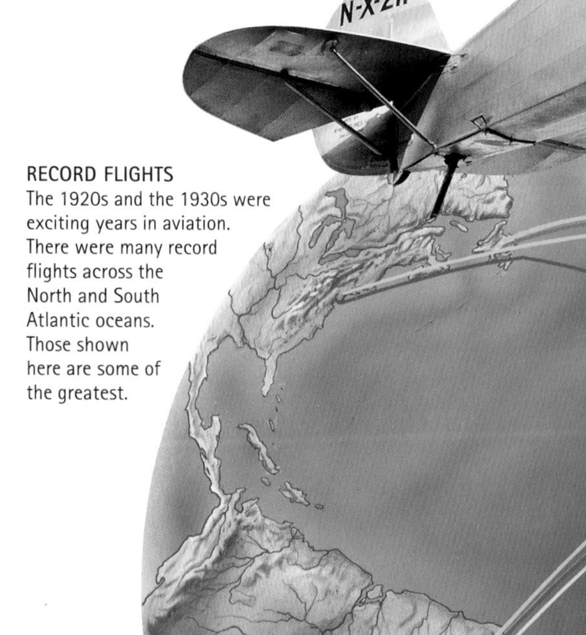

RECORD FLIGHTS
The 1920s and the 1930s were exciting years in aviation. There were many record flights across the North and South Atlantic oceans. Those shown here are some of the greatest.

AROUND THE WORLD IN NINE DAYS
A long-distance aviation record was set in 1986 when Dick Rutan and Jeana Yeager flew their plane *Voyager* nonstop around the world in nine days.

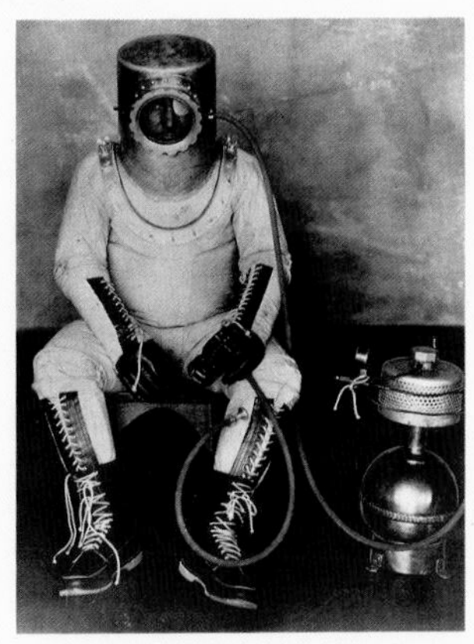

Altitude Record

After flying around the world in 1934, American Wiley Post decided to break the world's altitude record. He designed the first spacesuit which, like a deep-sea diver's suit, allowed him to breathe and work in unusual pressure situations. In 1934, he reached a record 50,000 feet (15,240 m). He wore the suit when he made the first flights in jet streams– the high altitude winds used by today's airlines to increase their speed over the ground.

FLYING FAME
Charles Lindbergh began his flying career by carrying mail across the United States. He became the world's most famous pilot after his Atlantic crossing.

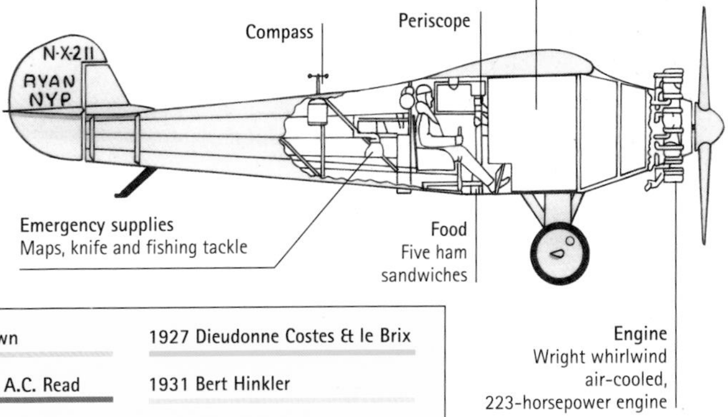

Compass
Periscope
Gasoline tanks
N-X-211
RYAN NYP
Emergency supplies
Maps, knife and fishing tackle
Food
Five ham sandwiches
Engine
Wright whirlwind air-cooled, 223-horsepower engine

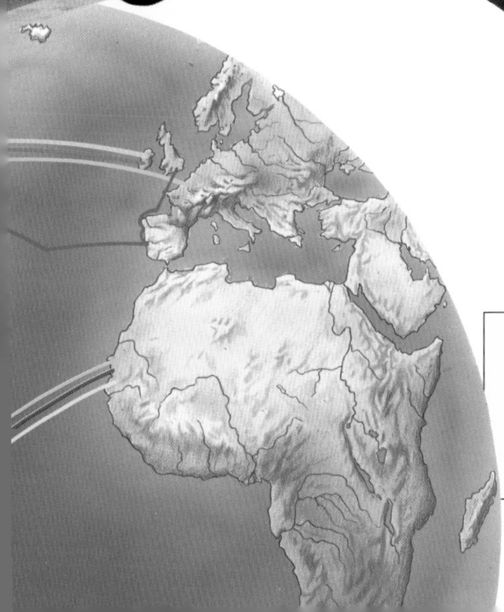

1919 Alcock & Brown
1919 Commander A.C. Read
1927 Charles Lindbergh
1927 Dieudonne Costes & le Brix
1931 Bert Hinkler
1932 Amelia Earhart
1935 Jean Batten

Q: Why were the transoceanic crossings of the 1920s so important?

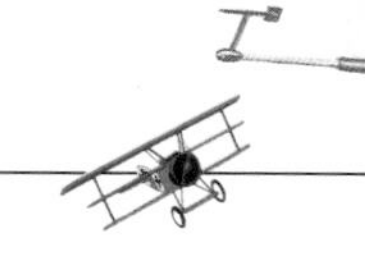

Breaking the Sound Barrier

Imagine flying through the air and striking an invisible barrier. This happened to Spitfire and Mustang fighter pilots during the Second World War. At speeds of around 545 miles (880 km) per hour, their aircraft suddenly became difficult to control. The planes shook so violently that some even broke apart. These pilots were approaching the sound barrier, which many experts believed no aircraft could penetrate. Breaking through that barrier became an international challenge, and some pilots in the early jet fighters died in their attempts. But in 1947, Chuck Yeager blasted through the sound barrier in his specially designed Bell X-1, powered by a rocket engine. An American F-86 Sabre jet fighter then exceeded the speed of sound while in a dive. Today, airplanes such as the Concorde and most military aircraft can easily fly faster than the speed of sound.

FASTER THAN THE SPEED OF SOUND
As bullets were known to be supersonic, Bell aircraft shaped the fuselage of the X-1 experimental rocket plane like a .50 caliber bullet. The aircraft was powered by a rocket motor and launched from Boeing B-29 and B-50 bombers.

THE AREA RULE
This is a method of designing an airplane's shape to reduce drag. The red dashes on the F-102 above show the width of the middle fuselage before it was trimmed according to Area Rule calculations.

GLAMOROUS GLENNIS
At an altitude of 43,000 ft (13,106 m), Captain Charles "Chuck" Yeager flew through the sound barrier at 698 miles (1,126 km) per hour in *Glamorous Glennis*, named after his wife.

High-speed probe
This gathers information on air pressure during flight.

THE SOUND BARRIER
As it moves through the air, an airplane makes pressure waves that travel at the speed of sound. They radiate like ripples from a stone dropped in a pond.

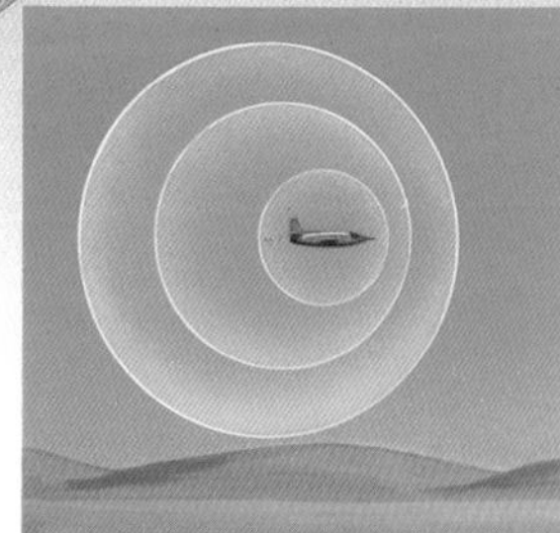

SUBSONIC: BELOW MACH 1
The pressure waves radiate in front of, as well as behind, the airplane.

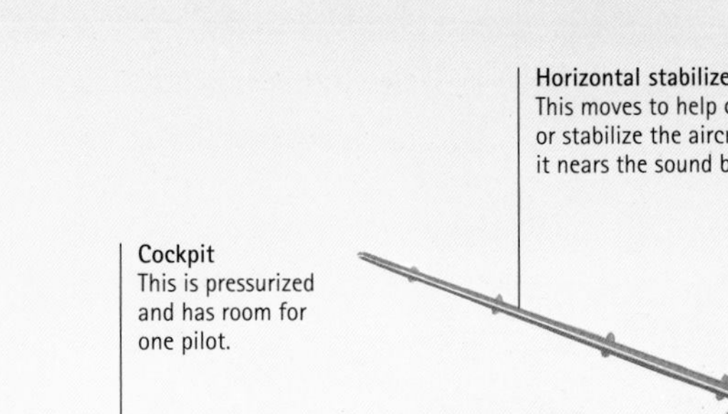

Horizontal stabilizer
This moves to help control or stabilize the aircraft as it nears the sound barrier.

Cockpit
This is pressurized and has room for one pilot.

Rocket-engine plumes
The engine is a 6,000-lb (2,722-kg) thrust rocket, powered by liquid oxygen and ethyl alcohol.

SPEEDING THROUGH AIR
A Machmeter gives the speed of air as a percentage of the speed of sound, which varies with temperature. At 40,000 ft (12,192 m), where it is very cold, Mach 1.0 is 657 miles (1,060 km) per hour.

Wings
The wings are short and very thin to reduce drag at high speed.

Did You Know?

A thunderclap, rifle shot and whip-crack are tiny sonic booms. Like the boom of a supersonic airplane, they are created by shock waves– sudden increases in air pressure.

Fuselage
This is shaped like a supersonic .50 caliber machine gun bullet.

Test Pilots

Test flying requires skill and daring– pilots call it "the right stuff." Each new aircraft, whether it is the latest glider, jumbo jet, military fighter or space shuttle, must be tested in flight to check that it is safe and reliable. Test pilots push their machines through every imaginable flight maneuver until they are satisfied that there are no problems with the aircraft. This dangerous task has now been made easier by supercomputers that can simulate the flight performance of new designs before the actual planes are ever flown.

TRANSONIC: AT MACH 1
The airplane catches up with its own pressure waves, which build up into a shock wave.

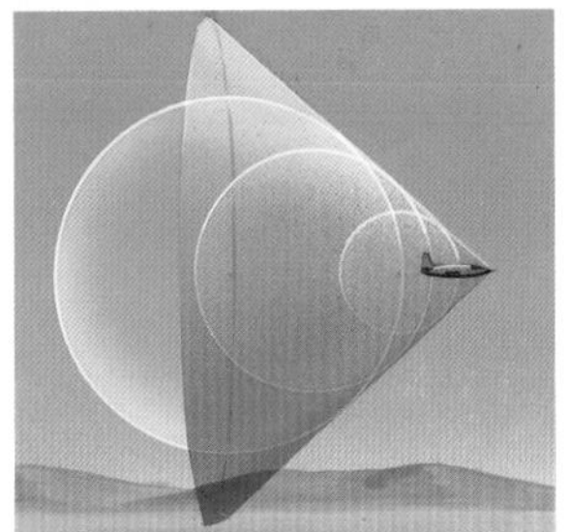

SUPERSONIC: ABOVE MACH 1
The shock waves form a cone. This causes a sonic boom when it hits the ground.

Planes in Flight

The invisible force that makes heavier-than-air aircraft fly is the flow of air around an airplane's wings. The differences in pressure above and below the wings combine to "lift" the airplane. "Lift" is one of the four forces that act upon a plane in flight, and it overcomes the plane's weight. The "thrust," or forward movement of the plane is produced by the engine, and this opposes "drag," the natural resistance of the airplane to forward motion through the air. But an airplane also needs to be stable so that it can fly smoothly and safely. Its tailplanes and the dihedral shape of its wings (which means the wings are angled upwards slightly from the fuselage) make the plane stable in the same way the tail of a kite makes it steady. The wings and tailplanes are also equipped with movable control surfaces called ailerons, elevators and rudders. These alter the airflow over the wings and tailplanes, and the pilot uses them to change the airplane's direction and height.

Rudder

Vertical tailplane (tailfin)

Horizontal tailplane

Control rods
These link the pilot's controls to the elevators and rudder.

Left aileron down

PITCHING
When the elevators are up, the airplane's nose is raised above the horizon and the airplane climbs. The rudder and ailerons are in a neutral position. When the airplane descends, the elevators are down. This up or down movement of the nose is called "pitching."

Elevators up

BANKING (ROLLING)
The left aileron is down and the right aileron is up, which makes the airplane bank to the right. The elevators and rudder are in a neutral position. This movement of the wings is called "rolling."

Right aileron up

ANGLE OF ATTACK
This is the angle at which the wing meets the airstream. As an airplane slows down, this angle must be increased to produce enough lift to equal its weight. When the angle reaches 14 degrees, the wing loses lift (called stalling) and the airplane descends.

LOW ANGLE
At high speed, the wing needs only a low angle of attack (about 4 degrees) to produce enough lift.

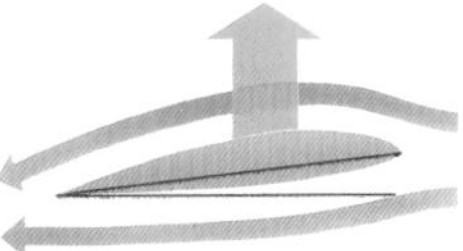

HIGH ANGLE
At low speed, a much higher angle of attack is needed to produce the same amount of lift.

STALL ANGLE
At about 14 degrees angle of attack, the airstream over the wings becomes turbulent. The plane stalls and loses height.

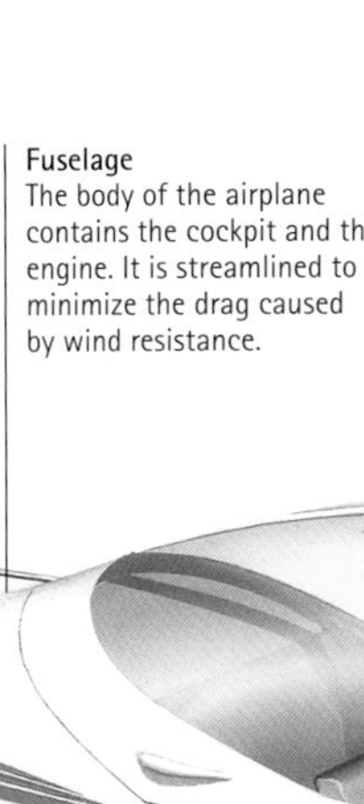

Fuselage
The body of the airplane contains the cockpit and the engine. It is streamlined to minimize the drag caused by wind resistance.

Control column
This moves backward and forward to operate the elevators, and from side to side to operate the ailerons.

Did You Know?

As an airplane flies higher, the pressure of the air outside decreases. The changes in pressure as an airplane climbs or descends can make your ears "pop." People with bad colds can experience painfully blocked ear drums.

Q: What has happened if an airplane stalls?

Propeller
This has rotating blades, shaped like airfoils, which convert the engine power into forward thrust.

Rudder pedals
These control the rudder and also operate the aircraft's brakes.

THE CONTROL SURFACES
Ailerons, elevators and the rudder are operated by the control column and rudder pedals in the cockpit. They are used to make the airplane climb or descend, roll, turn or simply fly straight and level, as shown.

Rudder right

TURNING (YAWING)
The left aileron is slightly down, the right aileron is slightly up. The rudder is moved to the right, which helps to push the airplane's nose sideways into a gentle right turn. This sideways movement of the nose is called "yawing."

Wing Flaps

When birds land, they spread their feathers and change wing shape to touch down slowly. Airplane pilots do the same thing by lowering sections of the front and rear edges of the wing, called flaps and slats. These devices produce extra lift and help big jets to land and take off at slow speeds.

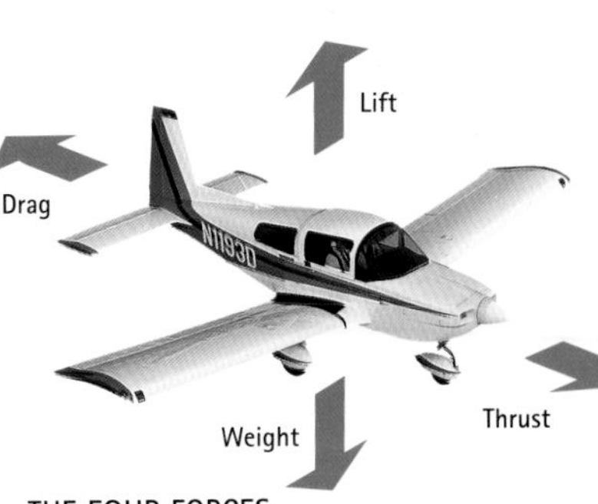

THE FOUR FORCES
When an airplane is in straight and level flight at a steady airspeed, the four forces are in equilibrium (balanced). This means that lift is equal and opposite to weight, and thrust is equal and opposite to drag.

Discover more in Airports

• THE INSIDE STORY •

The Cockpit

The cockpit is the nerve center of the airplane. It is crammed with controls, instruments and computers. Some Boeing 747 cockpits contain 971 instruments and controls. Orville Wright had none of these devices. He had to lie on the lower wing of the plane and look at the horizon to judge the plane's position in flight. Pioneer pilots navigated by comparing features on the ground with those on their maps. Pilots today do not even have to see the ground. They use navigation systems that are linked to satellites, while the computer-controlled autopilot flies the airplane far more accurately than a human ever can. The latest instrument panels have television, radar and multi-function displays that give pilots the information they need to fly their planes safely.

HAND THROTTLE
This cluster of throttle levers operates the eight engines of a giant B-52 bomber.

A PILOT'S PERSPECTIVE
The Spitfire fighter was an important player in the air battles of the Second World War. The instruments and controls shown in this Spitfire cockpit are very similar to those found in small airplanes today.

BOEING 747
The flight crew of a modern airliner sits in a spacious cockpit using sophisticated computers and instruments that are large and easy to read.

Flight Simulators

Jet airliners are very expensive to fly, so machines called simulators are used to train pilots and to practice emergency drills. These machines are built to resemble the cockpit of an airliner. They have all the instruments and controls of a real plane. To make the simulator even more lifelike, moving pictures of the sky and ground are projected onto the windshield— just like a giant video game.

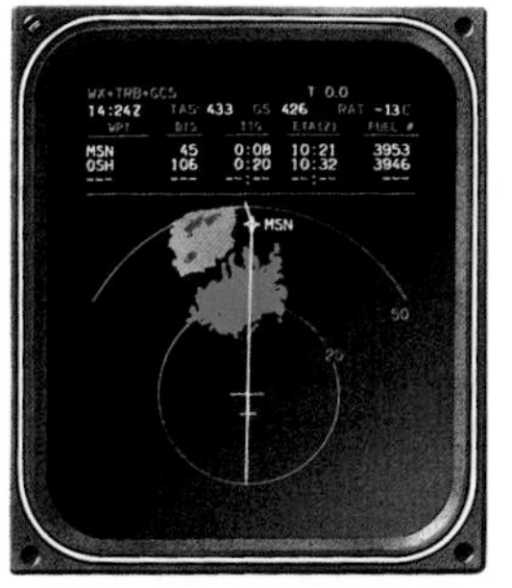

NAVIGATIONAL DISPLAY
This display shows the airplane's position on a radar picture of the ground below. It also gives the airplane's speed, fuel flow, and the time and distance to the next position along the air route.

PRIMARY FLIGHT DISPLAY
In modern airplanes, all the instruments needed for "blind" flying are combined in this single display. It has replaced the cluttered flight instrument panel that was used in airplanes such as the Spitfire.

Q: Why was it important for the early pilots to have detailed maps?

• THE INSIDE STORY •

Airports

The first commercial airports were built in the 1920s. They usually consisted of a large grass field with a few small buildings, a hangar and a rotating searchlight beacon to help pilots find the airport in bad weather. Airports today are miniature cities, surrounded by a web of taxiways and runways that can be more than 13,120 ft (4,000 m) long. The busiest airport in the world is O'Hare Airport in Chicago– more than 2,000 airplanes land and take off every day. Huge numbers of passengers and large amounts of baggage pass through airports. When passengers first began traveling by air, they were weighed along with their luggage! The ground staff at airports look after the equipment needed to keep the airplanes flying safely. Movement of planes through an airport is regulated by air traffic controllers, who watch and use radar to monitor the planes' flight paths.

NETWORKING
To keep airplane traffic flowing, busy airports such as San Francisco International Airport need a network of runways, taxiways and parking bays.

CONTROL TOWER
The Control Tower provides a bird's-eye view of the airport and the surrounding sky. Its staff control the movement of all airplanes on the ground and in the air near the airport.

Stacking
Aircraft circle over a radio beacon as they await their turn to land.
Outer marker
Shows that the airplane is 5 miles (8 km) from touchdown on final approach.
Middle marker
Marks the midway point of the final approach.
Glide-slope beam
Shows that the airplane is descending to the runway at the right angle.
Localizer beam
Shows that the airplane is properly in line with the runway.
Inner marker
At this point, close to touchdown, pilots should be able to see the runway.

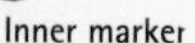

Instrument Landing System

In bad weather, pilots use the Instrument Landing System (ILS) to land safely. Two narrow radio beams are transmitted from the touchdown point on the runway. One is called the Glide-slope, the other is called the Localizer. If pilots follow the position of these two beams on an instrument in the cockpit, they can approach the runway and land the plane without seeing the runway until the final moment.

RUSH HOUR

Airport staff rush around this 375-passenger Airbus at the terminal. In just 90 minutes, the airliner must be unloaded, cleaned, restocked with food and drinks, refueled and boarded by new passengers.

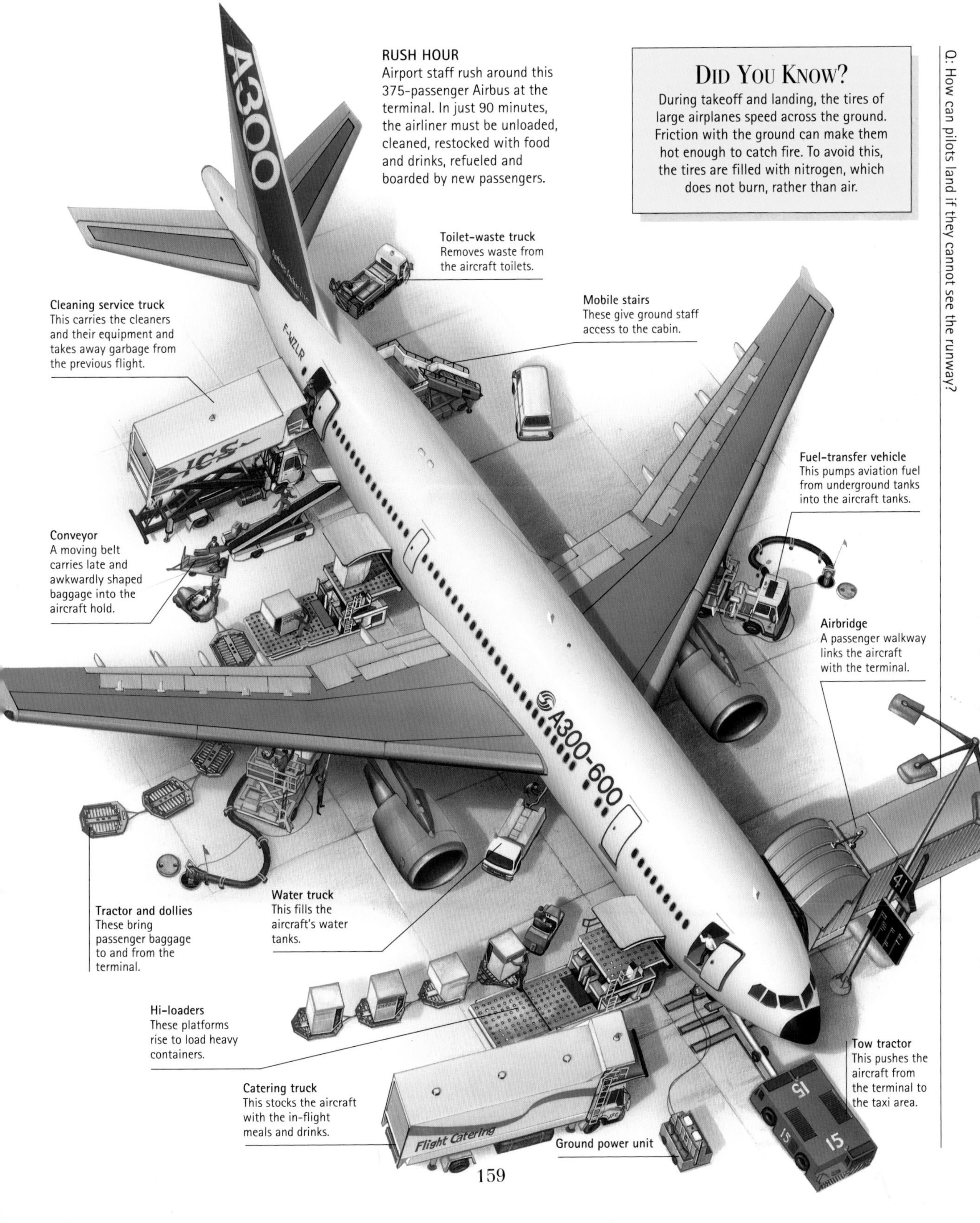

Did You Know?

During takeoff and landing, the tires of large airplanes speed across the ground. Friction with the ground can make them hot enough to catch fire. To avoid this, the tires are filled with nitrogen, which does not burn, rather than air.

Toilet-waste truck
Removes waste from the aircraft toilets.

Cleaning service truck
This carries the cleaners and their equipment and takes away garbage from the previous flight.

Mobile stairs
These give ground staff access to the cabin.

Fuel-transfer vehicle
This pumps aviation fuel from underground tanks into the aircraft tanks.

Conveyor
A moving belt carries late and awkwardly shaped baggage into the aircraft hold.

Airbridge
A passenger walkway links the aircraft with the terminal.

Tractor and dollies
These bring passenger baggage to and from the terminal.

Water truck
This fills the aircraft's water tanks.

Hi-loaders
These platforms rise to load heavy containers.

Tow tractor
This pushes the aircraft from the terminal to the taxi area.

Catering truck
This stocks the aircraft with the in-flight meals and drinks.

Ground power unit

Q: How can pilots land if they cannot see the runway?

Airships

The first airship was a sausage-shaped balloon. It was built in 1852 by French engineer Henri Giffard, who fitted his new aircraft with a small steam engine and a rudder for steering. It flew 17 miles (27 km) but did not have enough power to fly against the wind. In 1900, Count Ferdinand von Zeppelin from Germany built the first rigid airship. It was longer than a football field and had a lightweight framework that contained huge gas bags or cells, each of which was filled with hydrogen– a highly flammable gas. Between 1910 and 1913, Zeppelin airships carried more than 30,000 passengers on sightseeing flights over Germany. They were also used to bomb London in night raids during the First World War. The luxurious *Graf Zeppelin* and the *Hindenburg*, the largest rigid airship, carried thousands of passengers across the Atlantic between the two world wars. In 1937, however, the world was stunned when the *Hindenburg* exploded. The airship era came to an abrupt and tragic end.

A DRAMATIC END
The *Hindenburg* approached its mooring mast at Lakehurst, New Jersey. Suddenly, flames and smoke billowed into the sky– the airship had exploded! Amazingly, 62 of the 97 people on board escaped from the blazing airship.

TRAVELING IN STYLE
The *Graf Zeppelin* was the world's most successful airship. It was powered by five engines and had a top speed of 79 miles (128 km) per hour.

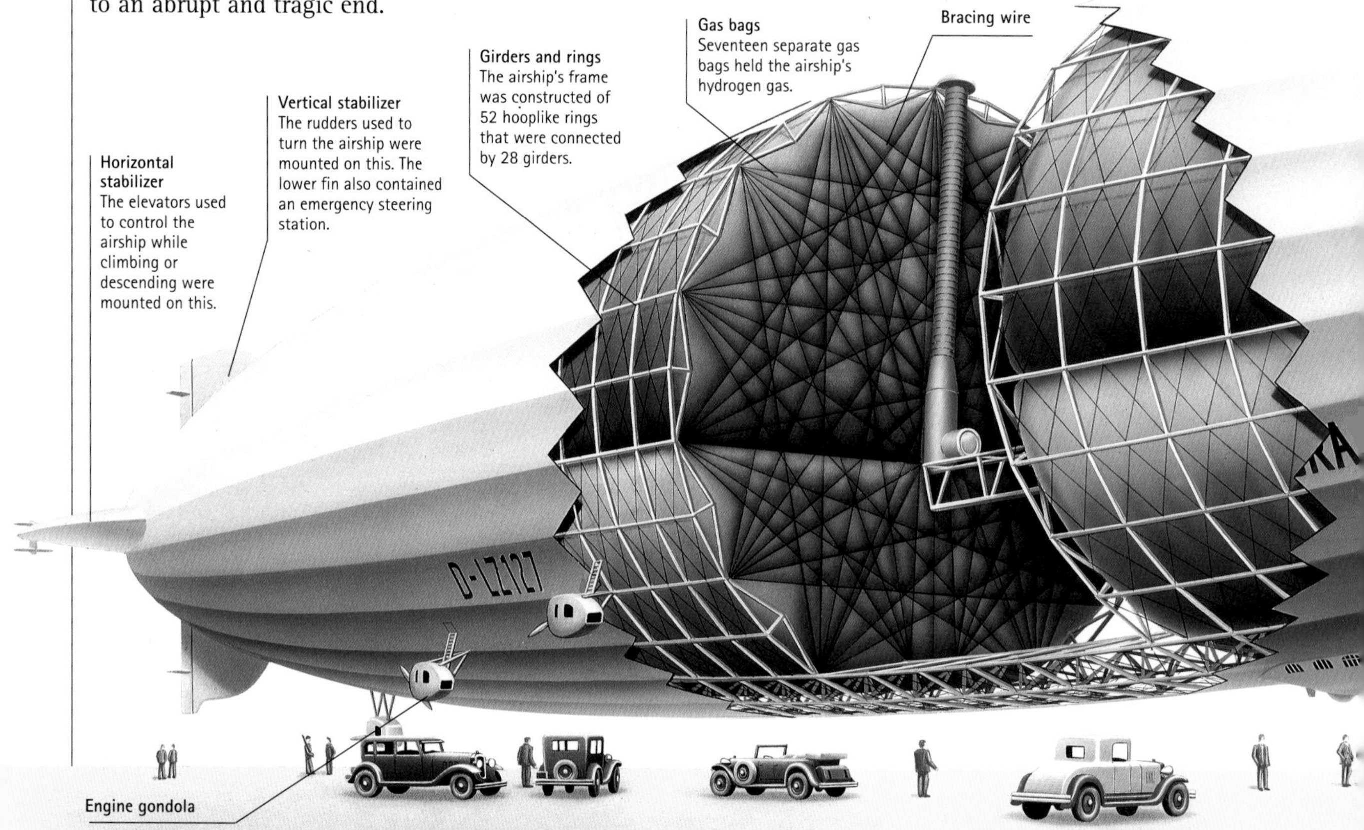

Bracing wire

Gas bags
Seventeen separate gas bags held the airship's hydrogen gas.

Girders and rings
The airship's frame was constructed of 52 hooplike rings that were connected by 28 girders.

Vertical stabilizer
The rudders used to turn the airship were mounted on this. The lower fin also contained an emergency steering station.

Horizontal stabilizer
The elevators used to control the airship while climbing or descending were mounted on this.

Engine gondola

D-LZ127

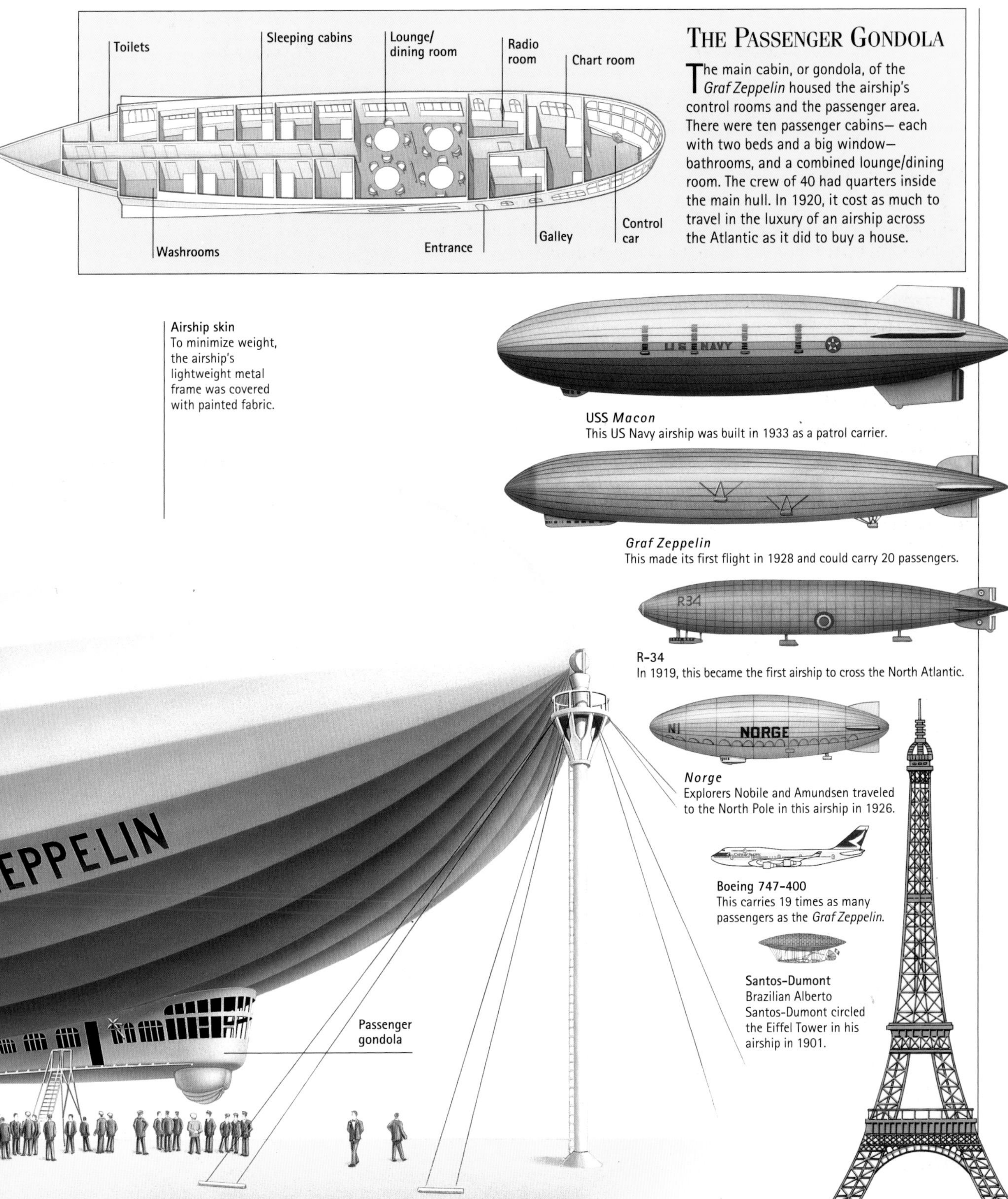

THE PASSENGER GONDOLA

The main cabin, or gondola, of the *Graf Zeppelin* housed the airship's control rooms and the passenger area. There were ten passenger cabins— each with two beds and a big window— bathrooms, and a combined lounge/dining room. The crew of 40 had quarters inside the main hull. In 1920, it cost as much to travel in the luxury of an airship across the Atlantic as it did to buy a house.

Airship skin
To minimize weight, the airship's lightweight metal frame was covered with painted fabric.

USS *Macon*
This US Navy airship was built in 1933 as a patrol carrier.

Graf Zeppelin
This made its first flight in 1928 and could carry 20 passengers.

R-34
In 1919, this became the first airship to cross the North Atlantic.

Norge
Explorers Nobile and Amundsen traveled to the North Pole in this airship in 1926.

Boeing 747-400
This carries 19 times as many passengers as the *Graf Zeppelin.*

Santos-Dumont
Brazilian Alberto Santos-Dumont circled the Eiffel Tower in his airship in 1901.

• A PARADE OF AIRCRAFT •

Seaplanes

The 1930s was the age of the seaplane. People believed these aircraft were a safe way to cross stretches of water during a time when aircraft engines were thought to be unreliable. The luxurious flying boats, designed to compete with ocean liners, introduced people all over the world to the exotic reality of long-distance air travel between continents. Many airlines were now able to extend their services beyond Europe and North America. Pan American's Clipper flying boats provided the first passenger services across the Atlantic and Pacific. The Boeing 314 Clipper was the largest airplane of its day. It could carry 74 passengers and a crew of eight, and had 40 sleeping berths. Some flying boats were used to patrol the oceans for submarines during the Second World War. But the war also helped to bring about the end of the great flying boats. Land aircraft had improved enormously and airfields had been built all over the world.

TRANSPACIFIC

BY SEA AND AIR
Pan American Airways called their flying boats Clippers after the fast sailing ships that crossed the oceans of the world a century earlier.

PASSENGER COMFORT
The enormous Boeing 314 had four massive engines and could cruise at a speed of 174 miles (280 km) per hour. It could also fly 3,472 miles (5,600 km) without refueling.

Radio operators

Engines
600 hp Wright double-cyclone engines.

Lounging and dining
At meal times, the lounge became a restaurant where diners were served by waiters.

Wing walkway
The engineer could walk along here to make minor repairs during the flight.

Anchor
A ship's anchor was used when a mooring dock was not available.

Galley
Meals were prepared and cooked on board. On modern airliners, food is reheated.

Sponsons
These stabilizers balanced the aircraft on the water and were used to hold fuel.

AN AVIATION FAILURE
This Italian flying boat, a 9-winged Caproni Noviplano, was designed to carry 100 passengers. Instead, it crashed on its first test flight in 1921.

TYPES OF SEAPLANE

Amphibian
This has retractable landing gear and operates from land or water.

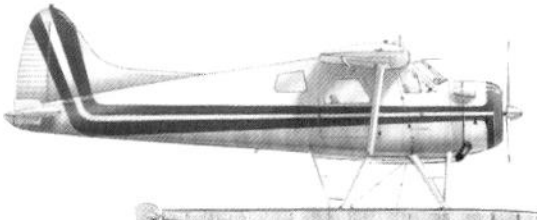

Float plane
This operates only from the water and uses floats.

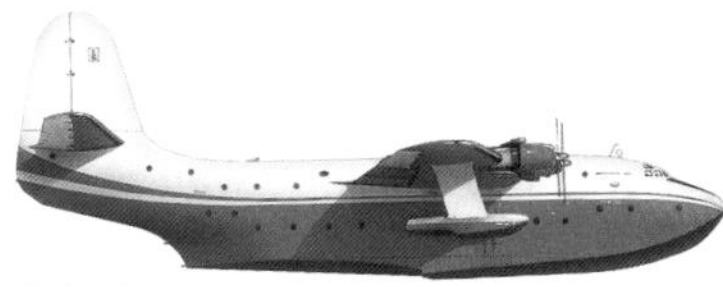

Flying boat
The large hull of the flying boat is shaped like that of a boat.

GLOBAL TRAVEL

Flying boats were used on the early transoceanic airline services. Pan American Airways pioneered long-range flying boat services in the mid-1930s when its Commodores and S-42s flew to South America and Martin M-130s crossed the Pacific. In 1938, Short S-23s operated the England-to-Australia service. In 1939, a Boeing 314 made the first transatlantic airline run. Catalinas were used during the Second World War.

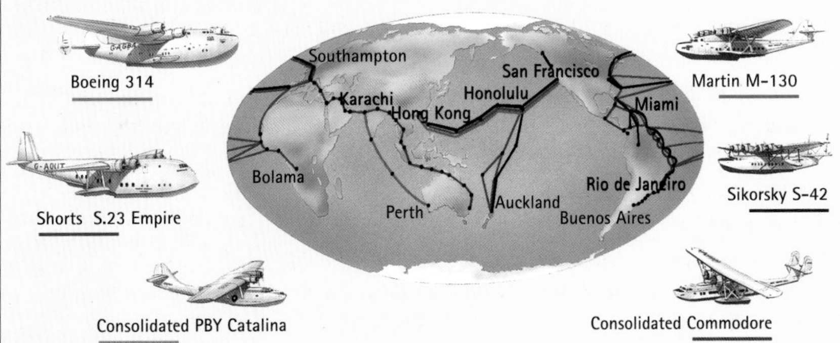

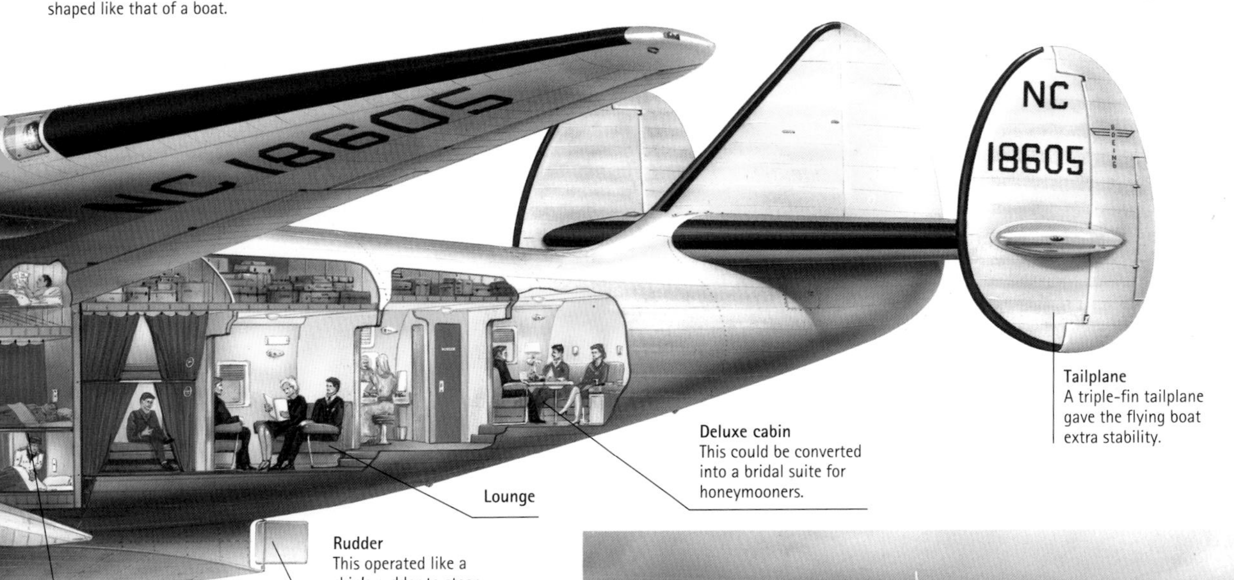

Tailplane
A triple-fin tailplane gave the flying boat extra stability.

Deluxe cabin
This could be converted into a bridal suite for honeymooners.

Lounge

Rudder
This operated like a ship's rudder to steer the plane when it taxied on water.

Day/night cabin
Fold-down bunks in the cabin converted it into sleeping quarters.

A VALUABLE CARGO
The Martin Mars flying boat is used today to fight forest fires. It can skim over water and take 60,500 gallons (275,000 liters) of water on board in 30 seconds.

Planes at Work

Pilots were inventive in the ways they used their wonderful new flying machines. In 1911, Frenchman Henri Pequet began an airmail service in India. Two weeks later, similar services were started in France, Italy and the United States. During the First World War, a French company built a huge biplane, which contained a portable operating theater. It landed on the battlefields carrying surgeons and nurses, who carried out emergency operations amid the chaos of war. The Huff Daland Dusters began dusting crops from airplanes in rural areas of the United States in 1924. When goldmines were built in New Guinea, all the supplies and materials were delivered by adventurous bush pilots. They landed on dangerous airstrips, carved from the jungle, in Junkers monoplanes. As the world's airplane industry grew, so too did the jobs airplanes performed. They are now used to fight fires, herd cattle, guard coasts and look for sharks, drop supplies to the victims of floods, storms and famines, and carry cargo.

A CLEAR VIEW
The slow-flying Edgely EA 7 Optica has a glass cockpit. This makes it ideal as an aerial spotter.

AIR WATCH
The coastlines in America are patrolled by specially equipped observation planes, such as this high-speed Falcon jet.

ON THE LAND
Helicopters are efficient and effective alternatives to traditional ways of rounding up horses and cattle.

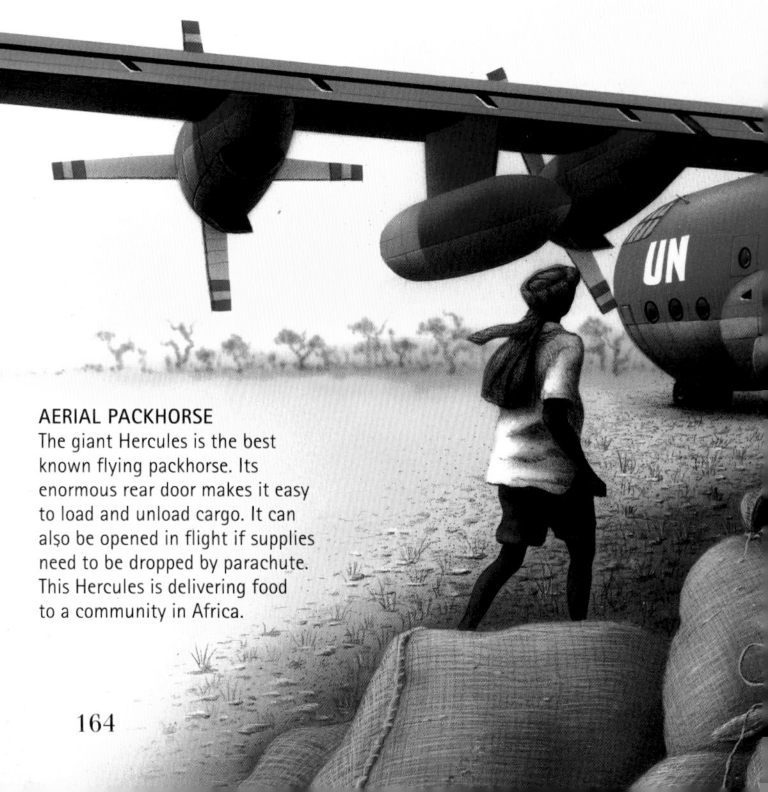

AERIAL PACKHORSE
The giant Hercules is the best known flying packhorse. Its enormous rear door makes it easy to load and unload cargo. It can also be opened in flight if supplies need to be dropped by parachute. This Hercules is delivering food to a community in Africa.

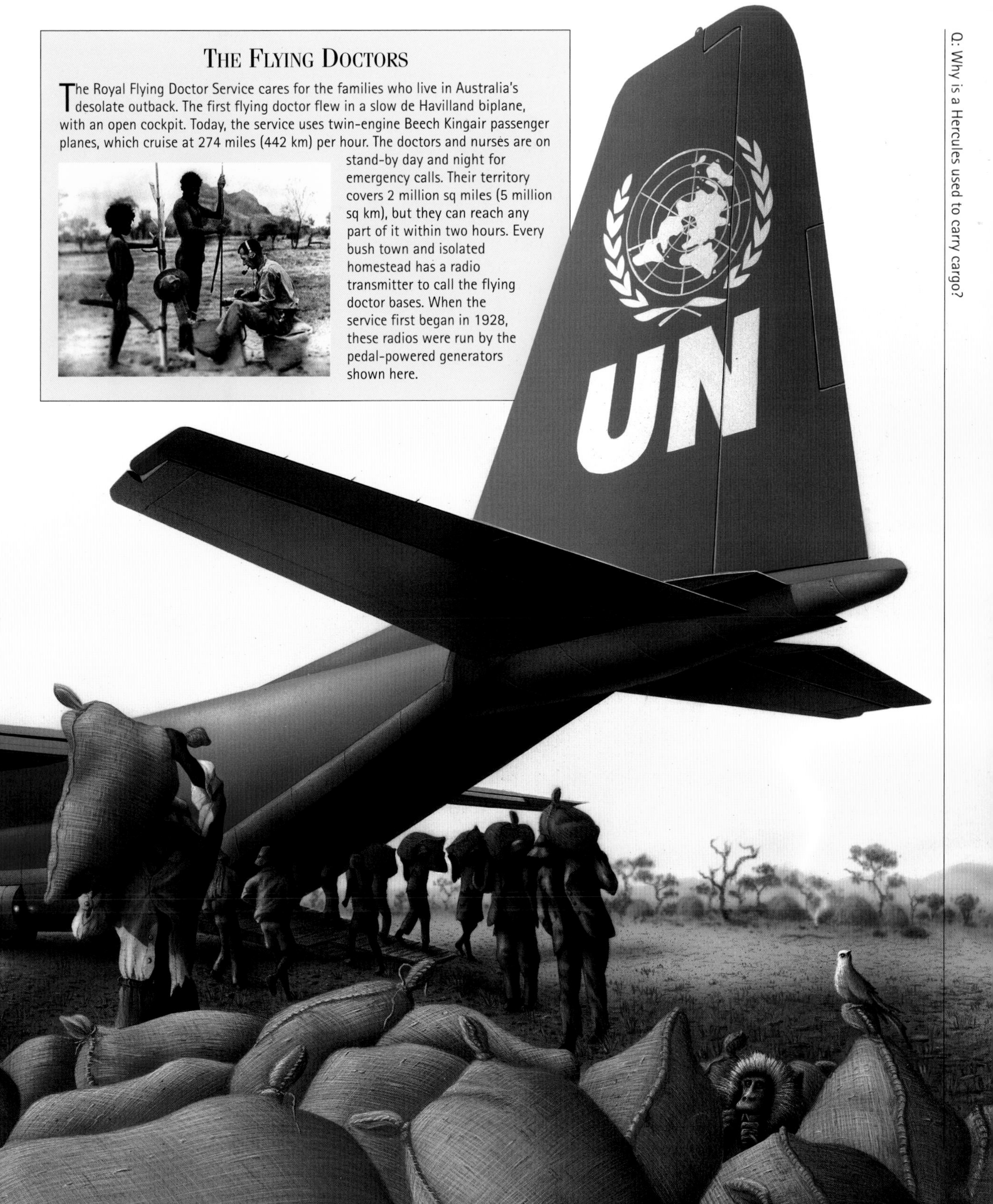

The Flying Doctors

The Royal Flying Doctor Service cares for the families who live in Australia's desolate outback. The first flying doctor flew in a slow de Havilland biplane, with an open cockpit. Today, the service uses twin-engine Beech Kingair passenger planes, which cruise at 274 miles (442 km) per hour. The doctors and nurses are on stand-by day and night for emergency calls. Their territory covers 2 million sq miles (5 million sq km), but they can reach any part of it within two hours. Every bush town and isolated homestead has a radio transmitter to call the flying doctor bases. When the service first began in 1928, these radios were run by the pedal-powered generators shown here.

Q: Why is a Hercules used to carry cargo?

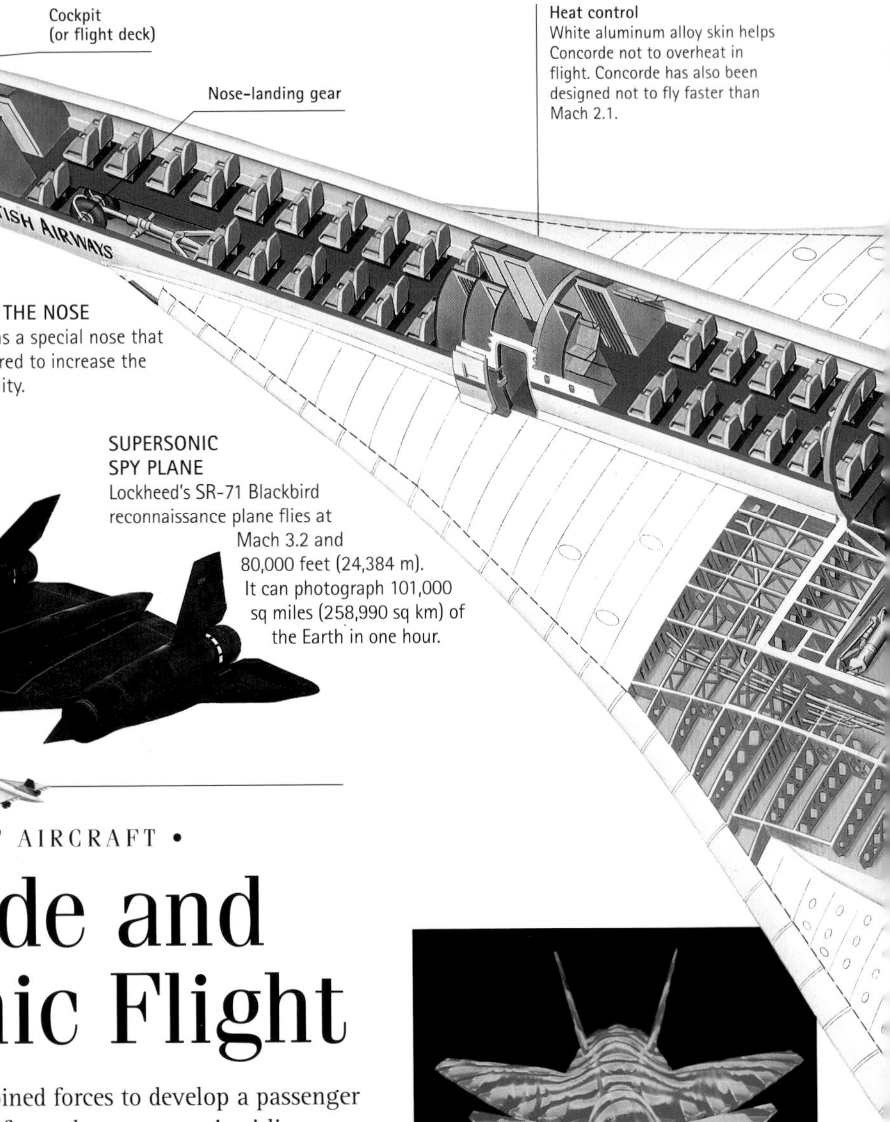

Cockpit (or flight deck)

Nose-landing gear

Heat control
White aluminum alloy skin helps Concorde not to overheat in flight. Concorde has also been designed not to fly faster than Mach 2.1.

BRITISH AIRWAYS

The nose fully raised above 286 miles (461 km) per hour means Concorde is totally streamlined.

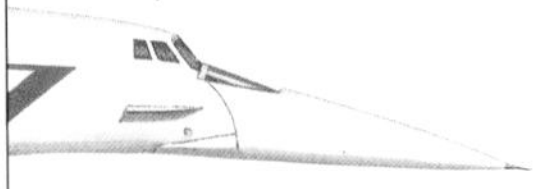

The nose 5 degrees down improves crew visibility for taxiing and take off.

The nose $12^1/_2$ degrees down improves crew visibility when landing.

LOWERING THE NOSE
Concorde has a special nose that can be lowered to increase the pilot's visibility.

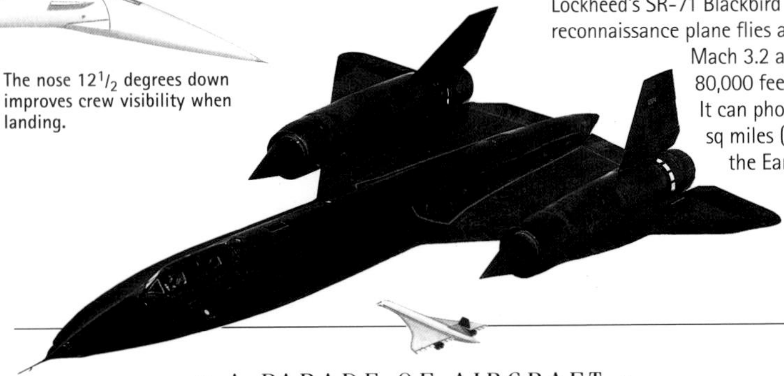

SUPERSONIC SPY PLANE
Lockheed's SR-71 Blackbird reconnaissance plane flies at Mach 3.2 and 80,000 feet (24,384 m). It can photograph 101,000 sq miles (258,990 sq km) of the Earth in one hour.

• A PARADE OF AIRCRAFT •

Concorde and Supersonic Flight

In the 1960s, Britain and France joined forces to develop a passenger plane that could fly at the speed of sound– a supersonic airliner. America also began to design such a plane, but abandoned it when costs skyrocketed and concentrated instead on building large subsonic jumbo jets. In 1969, Concorde, the world's first commercial supersonic plane, made its debut flight. The 14-plane Concorde fleet started service with British Airways and Air France in 1976. By then, the Soviet Union had built a supersonic airliner called the Tu-114. It crashed tragically at an airshow and never flew passenger services. Concorde has not been a great commercial success. It is expensive to operate, seats only 100 passengers, and is banned from many cities because of its sonic boom. It is, however, a technological triumph. Cruising at twice the speed of sound, Concorde can fly from New York to London in three-and-a-half hours.

WIND TUNNELS
Airplanes are tested in wind tunnels, which imitate the airflow they will experience in flight. This model is covered with fluorescent paint, which will highlight the airflow and any problem areas.

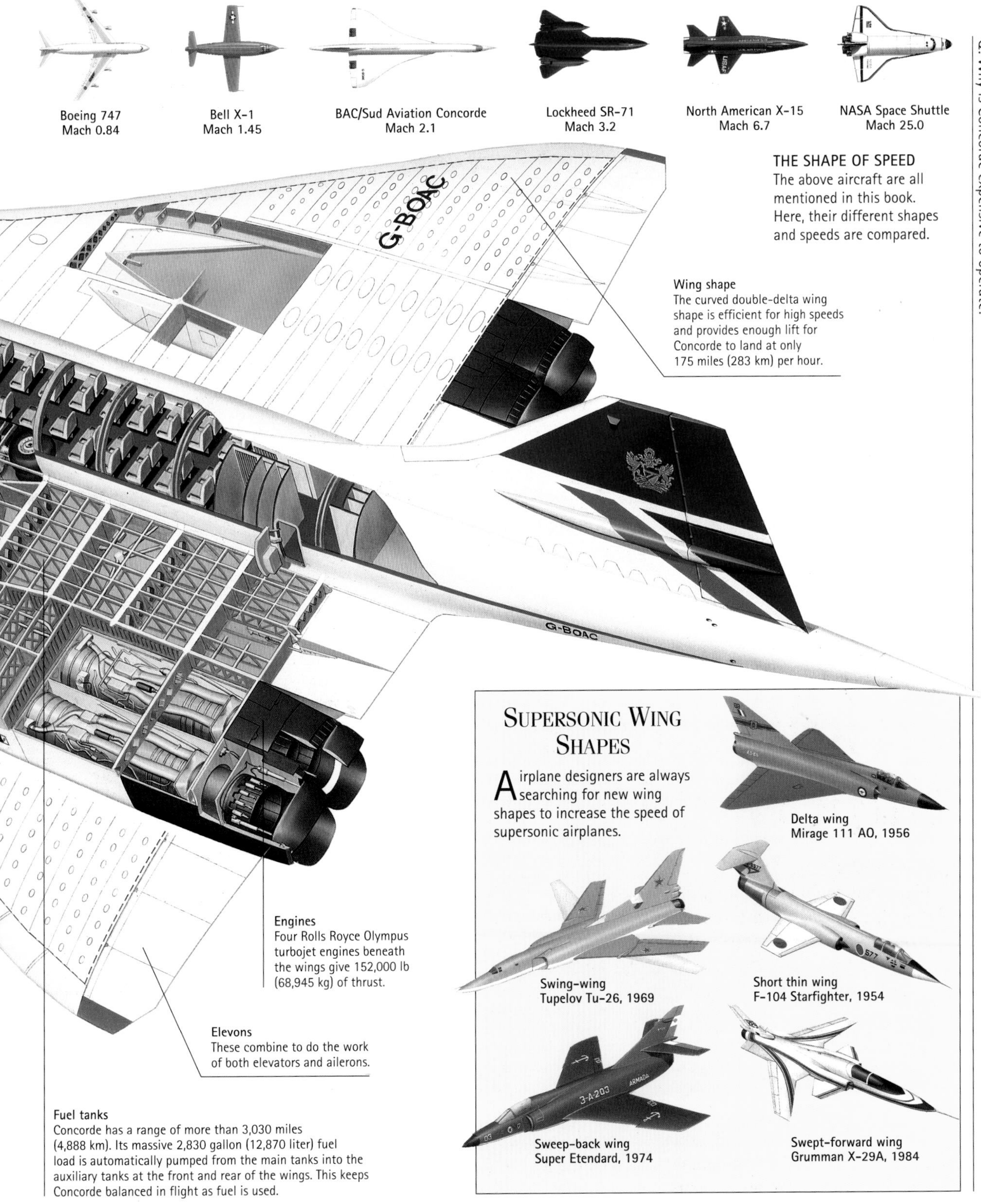

Q: Why is Concorde expensive to operate?

THE SHAPE OF SPEED

The above aircraft are all mentioned in this book. Here, their different shapes and speeds are compared.

Wing shape
The curved double-delta wing shape is efficient for high speeds and provides enough lift for Concorde to land at only 175 miles (283 km) per hour.

Engines
Four Rolls Royce Olympus turbojet engines beneath the wings give 152,000 lb (68,945 kg) of thrust.

Elevons
These combine to do the work of both elevators and ailerons.

Fuel tanks
Concorde has a range of more than 3,030 miles (4,888 km). Its massive 2,830 gallon (12,870 liter) fuel load is automatically pumped from the main tanks into the auxiliary tanks at the front and rear of the wings. This keeps Concorde balanced in flight as fuel is used.

SUPERSONIC WING SHAPES

Airplane designers are always searching for new wing shapes to increase the speed of supersonic airplanes.

Delta wing
Mirage 111 AO, 1956

Swing-wing
Tupelov Tu-26, 1969

Short thin wing
F-104 Starfighter, 1954

Sweep-back wing
Super Etendard, 1974

Swept-forward wing
Grumman X-29A, 1984

Military Aircraft

Wars have accelerated the development of aircraft. At the beginning of the First World War, most planes could not fly further than 100 miles (161 km) and had a maximum speed of around 62 miles (100 km) per hour. The first military planes were used only for observing enemy activity from the air, but they were soon adapted for fighting. By the end of the war, bombers could travel almost 2,000 miles (3,220 km) and reach speeds of 150 miles (241 km) per hour. The most famous war planes of the Second World War were the piston-engine Spitfire, Mustang and Messerschmitt 109 fighters, the Flying Fortress and Lancaster bombers. Rocket-powered planes and jet fighters were also introduced, and the first all-jet air battle took place during the 1950–53 Korean War. Military planes today are controlled by onboard computers and can fly at supersonic speeds.

Jet nozzles
Wide, flat jet nozzles reduce and disperse exhaust to make the aircraft less visible to infrared missiles at night.

AIR-TO-AIR MISSILES
Modern fighter pilots do not even need to see their enemy. They can destroy other aircraft with deadly missiles guided by electronic or infrared devices.

UNDETECTABLE
Lockheed's F-117A Stealth Fighter is designed to be invisible on enemy radar screens. Most airplanes are rounded, but the surfaces of this plane are faceted (like a diamond) and highly polished to deflect and disperse radar signals.

A TIMELY EXIT
A pilot escapes in a rocket-powered ejection seat as his fighter explodes. Moments later, a parachute will open and bring him safely to the ground.

1915 German Fokker E.1 Eindecker
This could fly at 79 miles (128 km) per hour and was the first fighter equipped with a real forward-firing machine gun.

1917 French Spad X11
This great biplane fighter was flown by French, American and British airmen. It could fly at 129 miles (208 km) per hour.

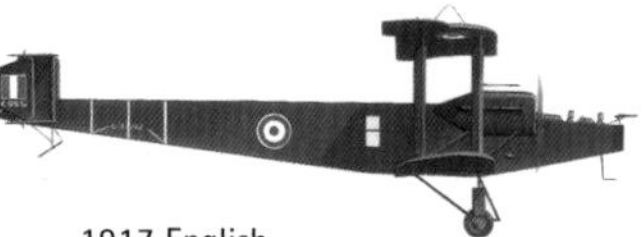

1917 English Handley Page 0/400
This giant bomber could carry a 2,002-lb (906-kg) load of bombs and travel at 79 miles (128 km) per hour.

1938 English Supermarine Spitfire
More than 20,000 Supermarine Spitfires were built during the Second World War. This model could fly at 357 miles (576 km) per hour.

Jump Jets

This McDonnell Douglas AV-8B version of the British Harrier jump jet is flown by the United States Marine Corps. It is called a V/STOL (Vertical/Short Take Off and Landing) airplane because it can hover, land and take off like a helicopter. Its jet exhausts shoot out horizontally to the rear like an ordinary fighter plane when it is flying normally. The jet nozzles direct the exhaust vertically downwards for landing and taking off. The Harrier takes a short run to help it "jump" into the air when it has a heavy load.

VIEWING ON SCREEN

When fighter pilots are in combat, they need to be able to look around and react quickly. Important instrument information is displayed on the visor of this special helmet, which means the pilot does not have to look down at the instrument panel.

Q: What are the special design features of the Stealth Fighter?

V–tail
This V–tail replaces the usual vertical and horizontal tailplanes. It is slanted back to deflect or inhibit enemy radar and infrared sensors.

Cockpit
Serrated edges around the cockpit deflect enemy radar.

Infrared sensor
A grill covers the F-117A's own infrared sensors and deflects radar.

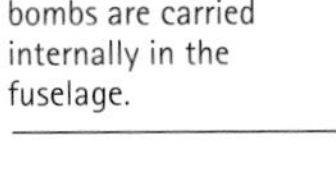

Smart bombs
Two laser-guided smart bombs are carried internally in the fuselage.

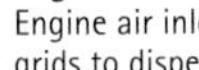

Engine intake
Engine air inlets have grids to disperse enemy radar.

Faceted pilot tubes
These provide airspeed and altitude readings for the pilot.

1943 English Gloster Meteor
This was powered by two engines and was the first British jet fighter. It could fly at 600 miles (969 km) per hour.

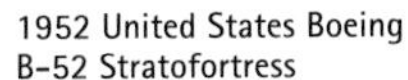

1952 United States Boeing B-52 Stratofortress
This giant bomber was powered by eight jets and flew a record 12,421 miles (20,034 km). It could fly at 595 miles (960 km) per hour.

1974 German, English and Italian Panavia Tornado
This strike aircraft has variable sweep wings. It can travel at 1,446 miles (2,333 km) per hour.

1978 United States McDonnell Douglas F/A 18C Hornet
This is also used by Australia, Canada, Spain and Kuwait. It can fly at 1,317 miles (2,124 km) per hour.

Aircraft Carriers

A coal barge was the first, and perhaps most unlikely, aircraft carrier. It towed observation balloons during the Civil War. In 1910, American stunt pilot Eugene Ely flew his Curtiss biplane from a platform on the cruiser USS *Birmingham*. The first true carrier, however, was built by the British during the First World War. Its narrow landing deck was very dangerous and returning pilots were forbidden to land. They had to ditch their planes in the sea. Aircraft carriers did improve, and by the Second World War they had replaced battleships as the most important naval ships. The bombers from a Japanese carrier force made a devastating attack on Pearl Harbor in 1941, and the major sea battles in the Pacific were fought by squadrons of carrier-based planes. Today, huge nuclear-powered carriers are the most powerful ships in the world.

COUNTING DOWN
The plane is in launch position on the carrier. The catapult crew, wearing green jackets, are in place. The catapult officer (the "shooter"), wearing a yellow jacket, gives the signal to launch the plane.

THE LANDING PATTERN
Carrier pilots fly 5-mile (8-km) wide circles at different heights while "hawking" (watching) the carrier, waiting to land. When the last aircraft are ready to launch, the pilots take turns to join the approach pattern. They time their descent to land the moment the deck is clear.

LAUNCHING
A holdback device on the catapult's shuttle (launcher) stops a plane from rolling forward, even when it is under full power, until the catapult is fired.

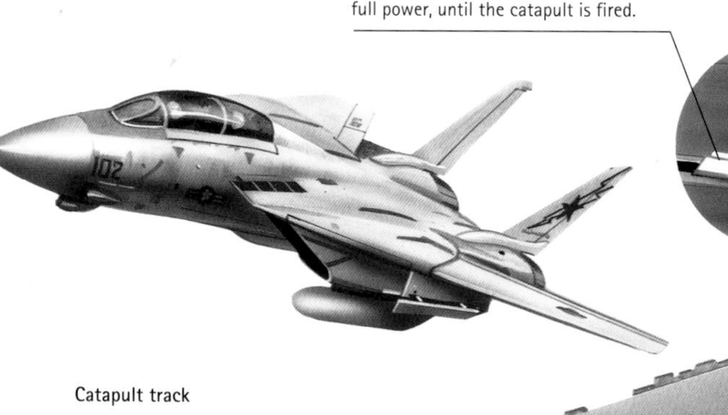

Jet-blast deflector
Retractable steel walls deflect the jet exhaust away from the deck.

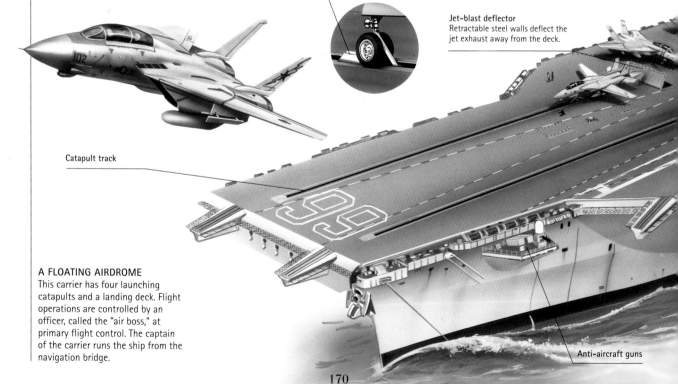

Catapult track

A FLOATING AIRDROME
This carrier has four launching catapults and a landing deck. Flight operations are controlled by an officer, called the "air boss," at primary flight control. The captain of the carrier runs the ship from the navigation bridge.

Anti-aircraft guns

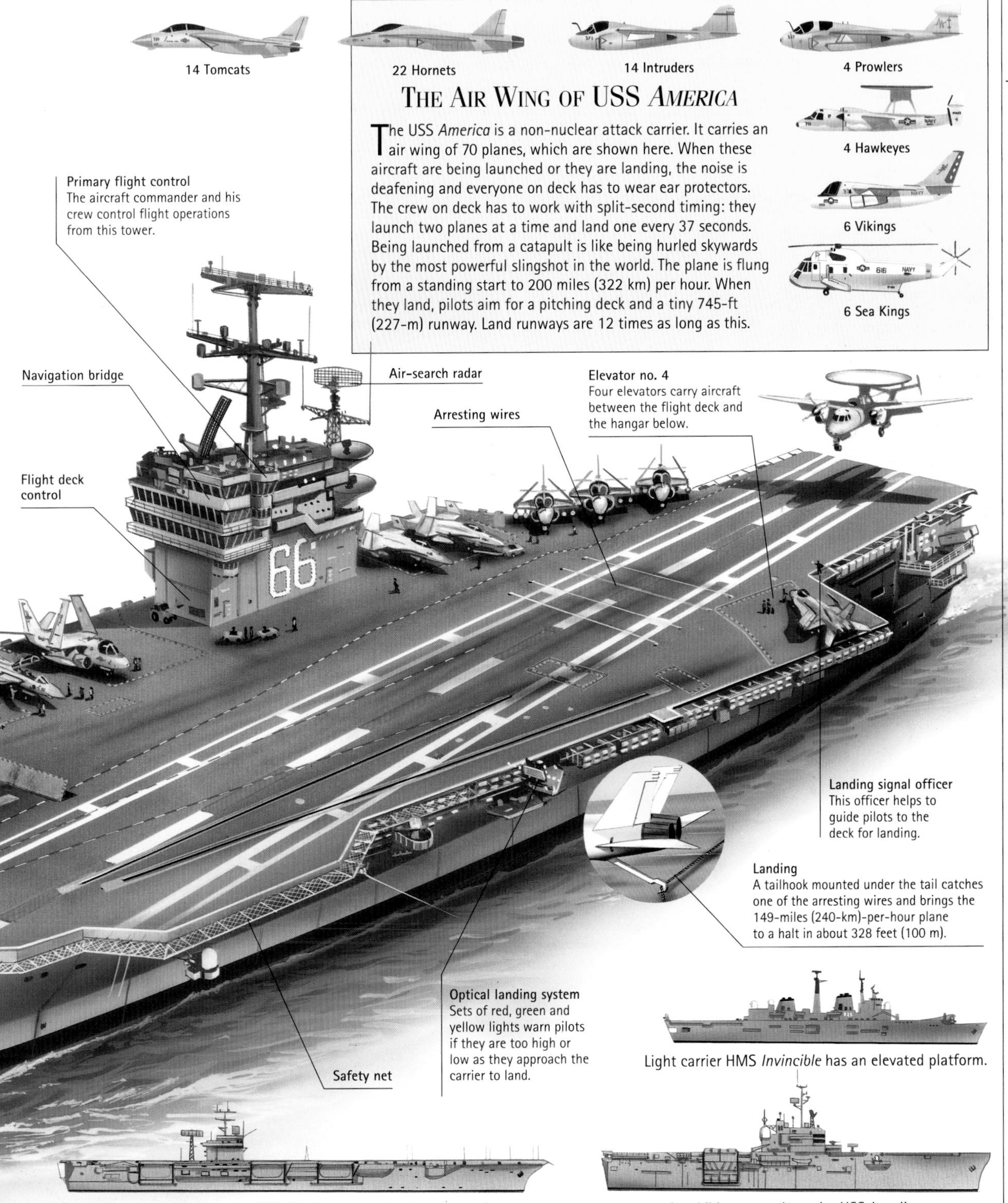
14 Tomcats
22 Hornets
14 Intruders
4 Prowlers
4 Hawkeyes
6 Vikings
6 Sea Kings
Primary flight control
The aircraft commander and his crew control flight operations from this tower.
Navigation bridge
Air-search radar
Flight deck control
Arresting wires
Elevator no. 4
Four elevators carry aircraft between the flight deck and the hangar below.
Landing signal officer
This officer helps to guide pilots to the deck for landing.
Landing
A tailhook mounted under the tail catches one of the arresting wires and brings the 149-miles (240-km)-per-hour plane to a halt in about 328 feet (100 m).
Optical landing system
Sets of red, green and yellow lights warn pilots if they are too high or low as they approach the carrier to land.
Safety net

THE AIR WING OF USS *AMERICA*

The USS *America* is a non-nuclear attack carrier. It carries an air wing of 70 planes, which are shown here. When these aircraft are being launched or they are landing, the noise is deafening and everyone on deck has to wear ear protectors. The crew on deck has to work with split-second timing: they launch two planes at a time and land one every 37 seconds. Being launched from a catapult is like being hurled skywards by the most powerful slingshot in the world. The plane is flung from a standing start to 200 miles (322 km) per hour. When they land, pilots aim for a pitching deck and a tiny 745-ft (227-m) runway. Land runways are 12 times as long as this.

Light carrier HMS *Invincible* has an elevated platform.

Attack carrier USS *Nimitz* carries 85 aircraft.

Amphibious assault carrier USS *Iwo Jima*.

Completing the Picture

It is difficult to get a really good view of an airplane when it is on the ground or flying noisily overhead. This page, however, shows three-way views of 12 of the airplanes that have appeared as main images in this book. A three-way view is a standard aviation drawing that allows you to inspect and identify the plane's vital statistics: its shape; the number, type and position of the engines; and its wingspan.

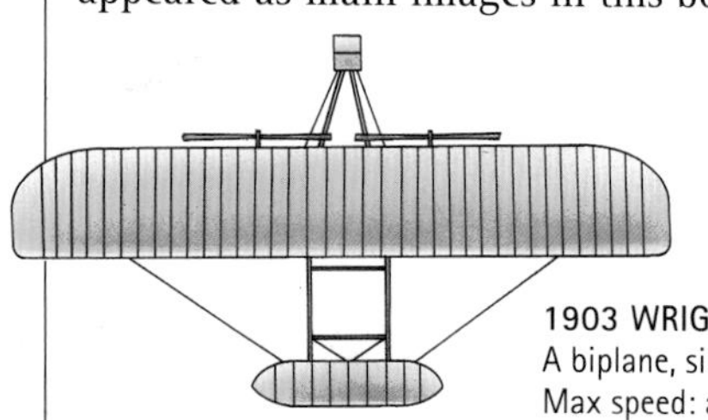

1903 WRIGHT *FLYER*
A biplane, single-piston engine.
Max speed: approx 30 miles (48 km) per hour.
Wingspan: 40 feet (12.3 m).

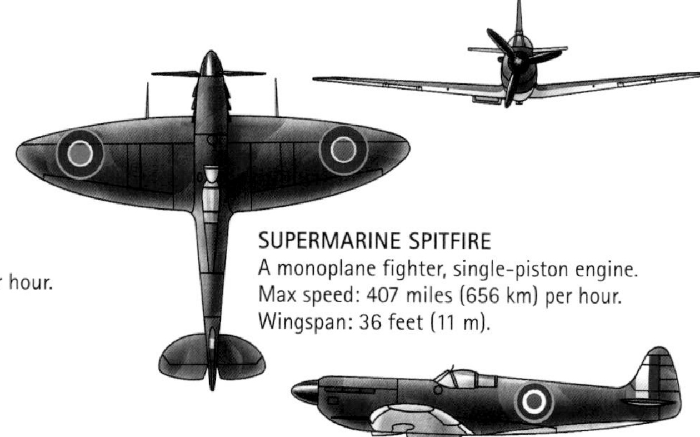

SUPERMARINE SPITFIRE
A monoplane fighter, single-piston engine.
Max speed: 407 miles (656 km) per hour.
Wingspan: 36 feet (11 m).

BOEING 314 CLIPPER
A monoplane flying boat, four piston engines.
Max speed: 192 miles (309 km) per hour.
Wingspan: 141 feet (43 m).

GRAF ZEPPELIN
An airship, five piston engines.
Max speed: 79 miles (128 km) per hour.
Length: 774 feet (236 m).

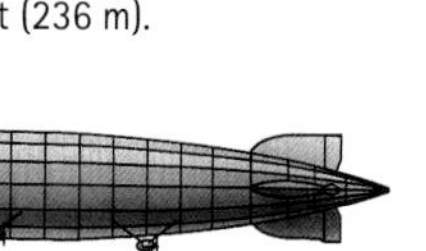

SUPERMARINE S.5
A monoplane float plane, single-piston engine.
Max speed: 282 miles (454 km) per hour.
Wingspan: 27 1/2 feet (8.4 m).

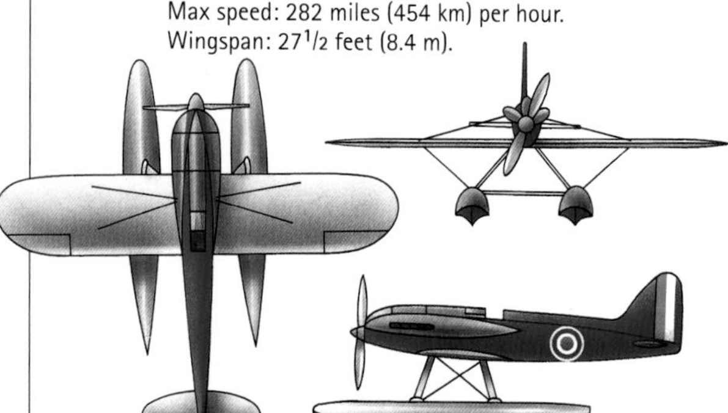

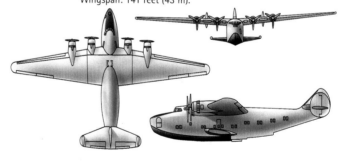

BELL X-1
An experimental monoplane, single-rocket motor.
Max speed: Mach 1.45, 949 miles (1,531 km) per hour.
Wingspan: 28 feet (8.5 m).

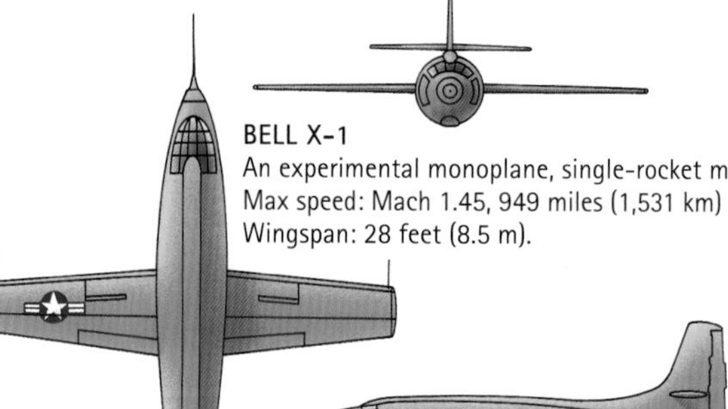

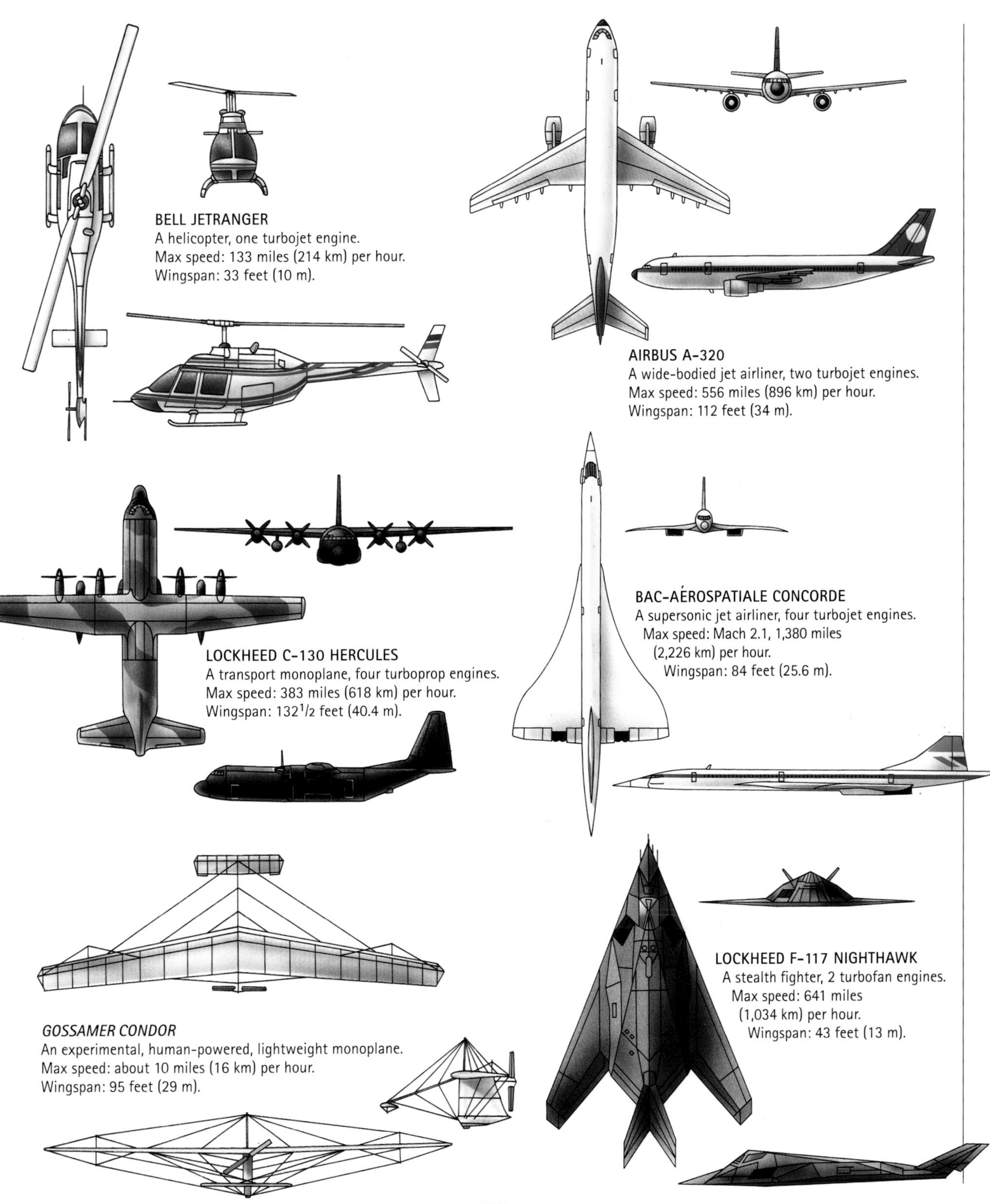

BELL JETRANGER
A helicopter, one turbojet engine.
Max speed: 133 miles (214 km) per hour.
Wingspan: 33 feet (10 m).

AIRBUS A-320
A wide-bodied jet airliner, two turbojet engines.
Max speed: 556 miles (896 km) per hour.
Wingspan: 112 feet (34 m).

LOCKHEED C-130 HERCULES
A transport monoplane, four turboprop engines.
Max speed: 383 miles (618 km) per hour.
Wingspan: 132 1/2 feet (40.4 m).

BAC-AÉROSPATIALE CONCORDE
A supersonic jet airliner, four turbojet engines.
Max speed: Mach 2.1, 1,380 miles (2,226 km) per hour.
Wingspan: 84 feet (25.6 m).

GOSSAMER CONDOR
An experimental, human-powered, lightweight monoplane.
Max speed: about 10 miles (16 km) per hour.
Wingspan: 95 feet (29 m).

LOCKHEED F-117 NIGHTHAWK
A stealth fighter, 2 turbofan engines.
Max speed: 641 miles (1,034 km) per hour.
Wingspan: 43 feet (13 m).

Great Buildings

- Is it easier to defend or attack a castle?
- How can you build a house without any tools?
- Why did the early Russians build domes shaped like onions?

• IN THE BEGINNING •

A Place to Live

People must have shelter to survive. They will die without protection from the sun, rain, wind and cold. Today, people can live in almost every part of the world because they have learned to build walls and to put a roof over their heads. For centuries, people had no tools to cut or move trees and large stones, so the first houses were built from materials that were easy to handle, such as grasses, vines and small stones. They discovered that hard rocks with sharp edges could cut trees and other rocks, and these became the first building tools. Many centuries later, people melted metals from rocks to make stronger, sharper tools. In places with little stone or wood, people made sun-dried bricks out of mud to build their houses. Some of the earliest cultures in history were the first to discover and use many of the basic building materials still used today.

Did You Know?

The basic methods used to support the roofs of many great buildings were first developed in ancient villages to hold up the roofs of huts.

The roof
A waterproof roof is made from grass by thatching. Bundles of swamp grass are tied to a wooden frame so that each bundle overlaps the ones next to it and below it.

STONE HUT

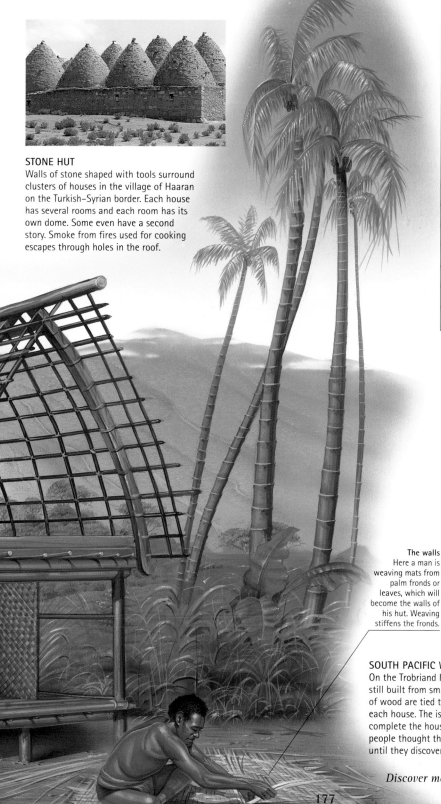

Walls of stone shaped with tools surround clusters of houses in the village of Haaran on the Turkish–Syrian border. Each house has several rooms and each room has its own dome. Some even have a second story. Smoke from fires used for cooking escapes through holes in the roof.

Making Bricks

Sun-dried mud bricks were perhaps the first synthetic building material ever made. A mixture of mud and straw is pressed into molds then laid out in the sun to dry, as seen here. The straw holds the bricks together so they do not crumble. As rain will dissolve sun-dried bricks, a coating of lime is added or a wide roof is built to protect the walls.

Q: How can you build a house without any tools?

BEEHIVE HUT

This hut on Dingle Peninsula in Ireland looks like a beehive. It was built centuries ago by a monk who piled up small flat stones cleared from his fields. He stacked each circle of stones on top of the circle below and made each stone slope downwards slightly towards the outside, so rain could not get in.

The walls
Here a man is weaving mats from palm fronds or leaves, which will become the walls of his hut. Weaving stiffens the fronds.

SOUTH PACIFIC WOVEN HUTS

On the Trobriand Islands of Papua New Guinea, houses are still built from small trees cut with stone tools. The pieces of wood are tied together with vines to form the frame of each house. The island people use plant materials to complete the house. Grass and leaves bend easily and people thought they seemed too weak to use for building until they discovered how hard it was to pull them apart.

Discover more in Games and Entertainment 

Early American Empires

The oldest architectural monuments in the Americas are found in present-day Mexico and along the west coast of South America. Early civilizations there had neither iron tools nor animals that could be trained to pull carts, yet the people constructed enormous stone buildings. The Olmecs and later civilizations in Mexico such as the Toltecs and Aztecs lived in scattered farm villages. These peoples had one religion and their religious centers were cities of stone such as Teotihuacán, where temples stood on top of tall pyramids. The peace-loving Mayan people lived in the rainforests of the Yucatan Peninsula in Mexico and they also built their religious centers of stone. In the fifteenth century, the Incas ruled an empire 2,480 miles (4,000 km) long in the Andes mountains of Peru. Their many towns were united by paved roads and a fast mail system. Incan stonemasons cut, polished and fitted stones together so tightly that a knife blade will not slide between them even today.

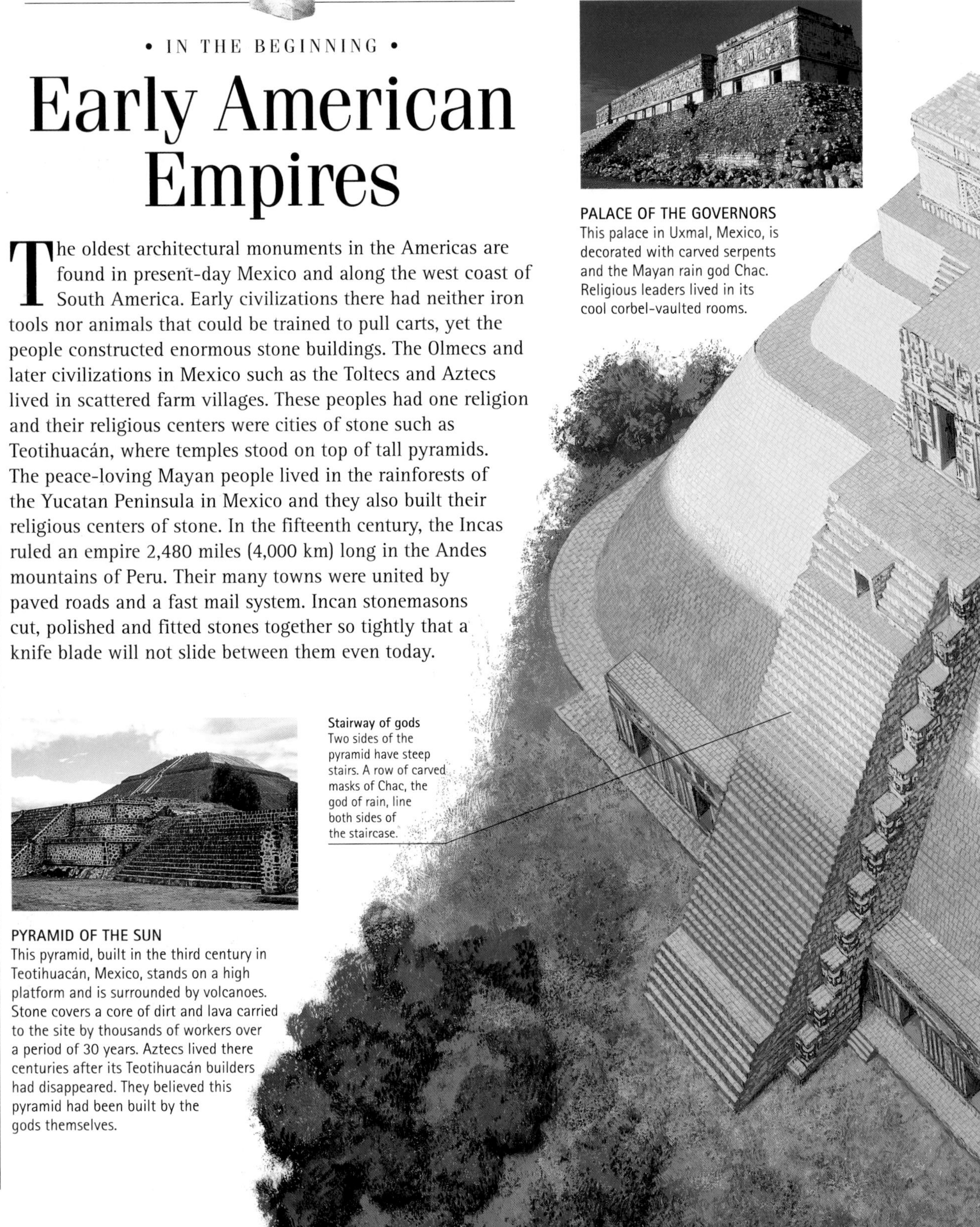

PALACE OF THE GOVERNORS
This palace in Uxmal, Mexico, is decorated with carved serpents and the Mayan rain god Chac. Religious leaders lived in its cool corbel-vaulted rooms.

Stairway of gods
Two sides of the pyramid have steep stairs. A row of carved masks of Chac, the god of rain, line both sides of the staircase.

PYRAMID OF THE SUN
This pyramid, built in the third century in Teotihuacán, Mexico, stands on a high platform and is surrounded by volcanoes. Stone covers a core of dirt and lava carried to the site by thousands of workers over a period of 30 years. Aztecs lived there centuries after its Teotihuacán builders had disappeared. They believed this pyramid had been built by the gods themselves.

PYRAMID OF THE MAGICIAN
The Mayans built this pyramid in Uxmal, Mexico, in the ninth century. It has an unusual oval shape and two temples at the top. The peoples of Mexico built high platforms, or pyramids, for their temples so they would be closer to the gods in the heavens.

At the top
The temples on the pyramid are stone replicas of Mayan thatched huts. Gifts were offered before statues of gods inside the corbel-vaulted rooms.

THE CITADEL
Offerings were placed on this Chac Mool, a god sculpted as a man lying on his back, which sits near an eleventh-century Toltec pyramid in Chichen Itza, Mexico. The pyramid has a steep staircase on each side and a temple at the top.

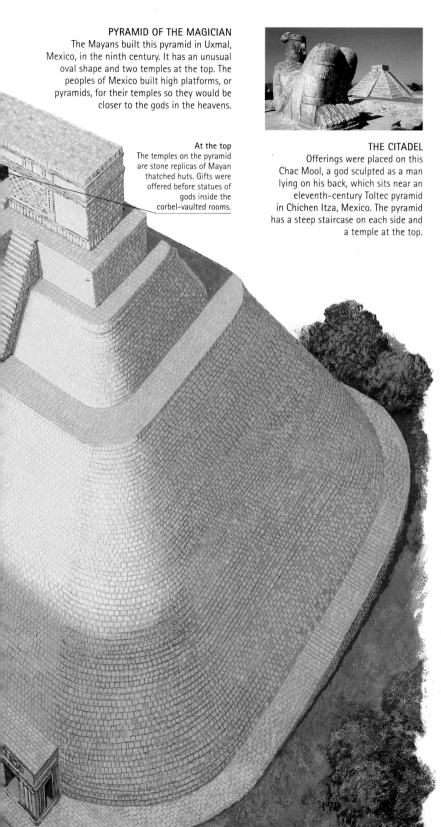

Corbeled Roofs

A building constructed of stone posts and horizontal beams will collapse if the beams have to support heavy walls or if the posts are not set close enough together. Stone doorways and stone roofs or vaults, such as the one shown here, can be built with small stones called corbels. Each stone lies on top of the last stone and has one end sticking out over the opening. Once the stones or corbels from both sides of the opening meet at the top, stones placed on top of the roof will hold it in place.

Did You Know?

The Pyramid of the Magician encloses three older temples. In Mexico, a new pyramid and temple often encased an earlier one. A completely furnished temple ready for use was discovered within the Pyramid of the Sun.

INCAN RUINS
Important religious ceremonies took place in Machu Picchu, an Incan town high in the Andes mountains of Peru. The plain stone walls of important Incan buildings were covered with plates of pure gold.

Q: Where can you find ruins of early American civilizations?

Early Civilizations

More than 5,000 years ago, a great civilization developed in Mesopotamia, the land between the Tigris and Euphrates rivers, then spread eastward along the north coast of the Indian Ocean. The Egyptian civilization developed beside the River Nile soon after. People traveled between the two areas and brought new ideas and inventions with them. Egypt had many workers and plenty of stone, and the Egyptians built huge pyramids and temples using simple tools and techniques. Because they did not have the wheel, 20 men pulled each stone to the pyramid on a wooden sled. Both stone and wood were scarce in Mesopotamia. The people there invented new materials such as bricks molded from clay and baked in an oven or dried by the sun. They then built wheeled carts to transport the bricks.

THE PYRAMIDS OF GIZA
These three pyramids were built more than 4,500 years ago as tombs for Egyptian pharaohs. The largest of the three, the Great Pyramid of Pharaoh Khufu, contains nearly two-and-a-half million stone blocks.

TEMPLE FOR A GOD
The huge columns of Egyptian temples still stand like stone forests in the desert above the banks of the Nile. This complex at Karnak was built over a period of 1,200 years. Here a statue of a pharaoh and his daughter stands outside the temple.

Did You Know?

Some Egyptian architects today are also building vaulted structures out of sun-dried bricks. The buildings stay cool and the materials do not damage the environment.

Steers and dragons
The symbols of the Babylonian weather god Adad and of the city's protector, the god Marduk, decorate the Ishtar Gate.

ISHTAR GATE

In the sixth century BC, King Nebuchadnezzar built a road called the Processional Way. This road led from his palace in the city of Babylon, the main city of Mesopotamia, to a ceremonial hall for New Year's celebrations. The Processional Way passed through the city's double walls at the Ishtar Gate.

PARADE OF LIONS

Every animal lining the walls of the Processional Way was brick, cast from special molds so that the bodies curved out from the wall. Each of the lions was made up of 46 specially molded and glazed bricks.

INVENTING THE ARCH

A stone laid across an open space like a doorway is brittle and will break if a heavy weight is placed on it. To avoid this, the supports of ancient stone buildings were set close together. Mesopotamians invented the arch so they could build wide, open rooms. Bricks or small stones set in a curve form an arch. The weight of each stone pushes it against the next until one pushes against a thick wall, called a buttress. The buttress presses the stones together and holds the arch in place. A vault is a ceiling built with arches.

Q: How did the people in Mesopotamia make their bricks?

Glazed bricks
The bricks on the walls were painted with a glasslike mixture then baked to produce glowing colors.

An arched vault
The passage through the gate was 13 ft (4 m) wide, which was only possible because it was covered by an arch.

Monuments to the Gods

In the fifth century BC, most Greeks lived in small city-states on islands in the Aegean Sea and in mountain valleys near its coast. The Greeks built temples as homes for their gods so the gods would live among them and defend their cities. The first temples were built of timber and sun-dried brick and looked like the Greeks own huts. Later temples were built on top of a three-stepped platform and surrounded by columns. When the wooden temples decayed they were replaced by stone temples, which looked exactly the same. The main goal of the Greeks was to make their temples look perfect. They built with the purest white marble and architects used geometry to design the temples so that all the proportions fit together in harmony.

GREEK ORDERS
The Greeks built in three styles called orders. You can recognize the different orders by the style of the wide section at the top of each column, which is called a capital.

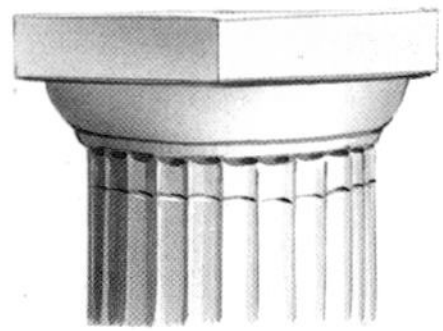

Doric order
This style has thick columns and plain capitals.

Ionic order
The thinner columns of this style are topped by a capital with two wide spirals called volutes.

Corinthian order
This order is more elaborate, and the capital is decorated with acanthus leaves.

TEMPLE OF ATHENA NIKE
The design of this small temple, dedicated to the goddess Athena, is based on a typical Greek hut. It was built in the Ionic style.

Under the roof
Walls and columns set close together hold up the timber frame for the tiled roof. There is little floor space in a Greek temple.

Frieze
A narrow band of carving encircles the top of the temple wall and shows the procession on Athena's festival day.

The goddess Athena
The tall wooden statue of Athena had an ivory face, arms and feet. She wore clothing made of gold plates that weighed 2,500 lb (1,134 kg).

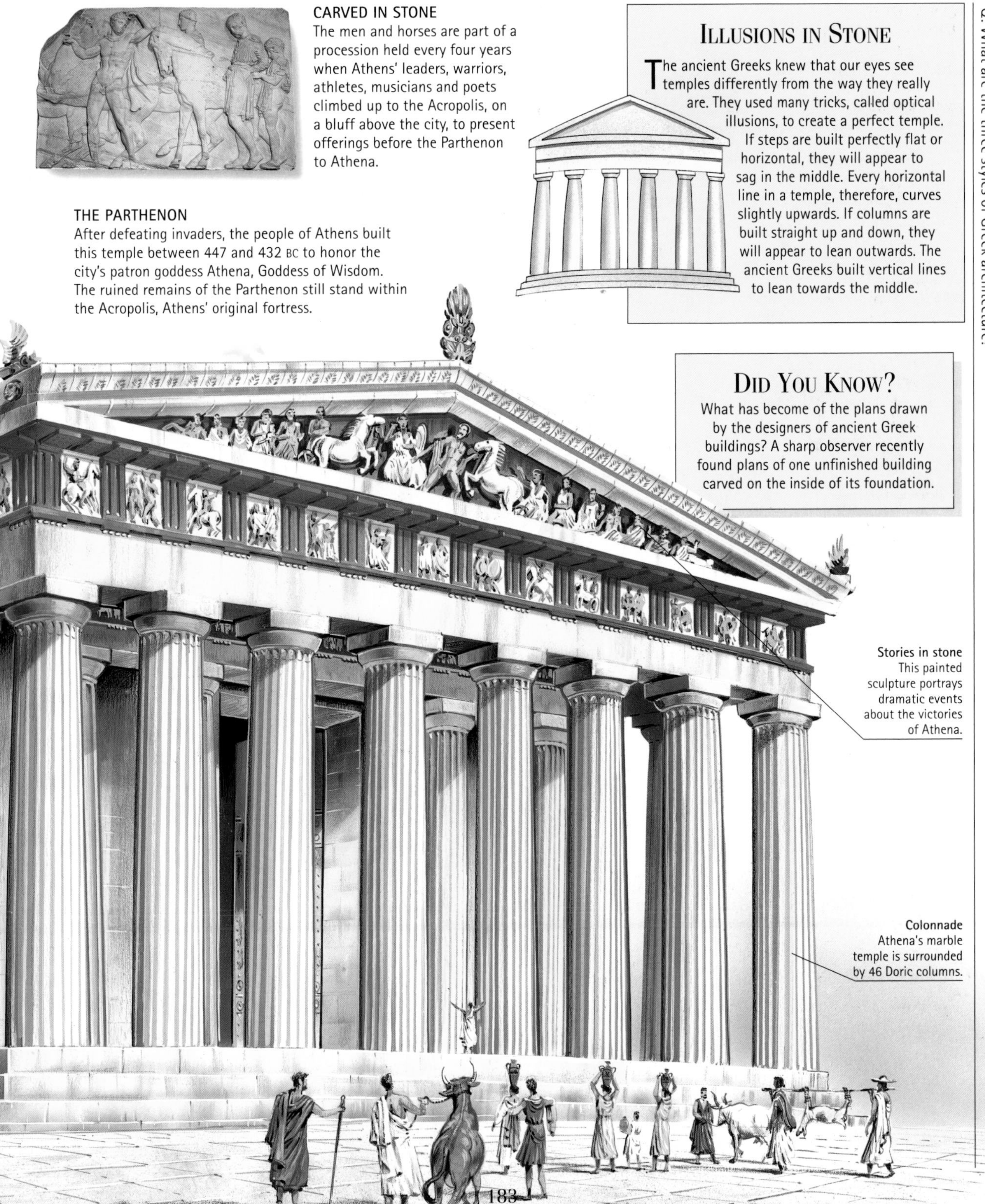

CARVED IN STONE
The men and horses are part of a procession held every four years when Athens' leaders, warriors, athletes, musicians and poets climbed up to the Acropolis, on a bluff above the city, to present offerings before the Parthenon to Athena.

THE PARTHENON
After defeating invaders, the people of Athens built this temple between 447 and 432 BC to honor the city's patron goddess Athena, Goddess of Wisdom. The ruined remains of the Parthenon still stand within the Acropolis, Athens' original fortress.

Illusions in Stone

The ancient Greeks knew that our eyes see temples differently from the way they really are. They used many tricks, called optical illusions, to create a perfect temple. If steps are built perfectly flat or horizontal, they will appear to sag in the middle. Every horizontal line in a temple, therefore, curves slightly upwards. If columns are built straight up and down, they will appear to lean outwards. The ancient Greeks built vertical lines to lean towards the middle.

Did You Know?

What has become of the plans drawn by the designers of ancient Greek buildings? A sharp observer recently found plans of one unfinished building carved on the inside of its foundation.

Stories in stone
This painted sculpture portrays dramatic events about the victories of Athena.

Colonnade
Athena's marble temple is surrounded by 46 Doric columns.

Q: What are the three styles of Greek architecture?

PONT DU GARD
The Pont du Gard is part of an aqueduct that carried water from mountain springs to baths and homes in Nimes, France, which was once a Roman city. The water channel stayed almost level as the aqueduct crossed mountains and valleys.

Take-out food shop and viewing gallery

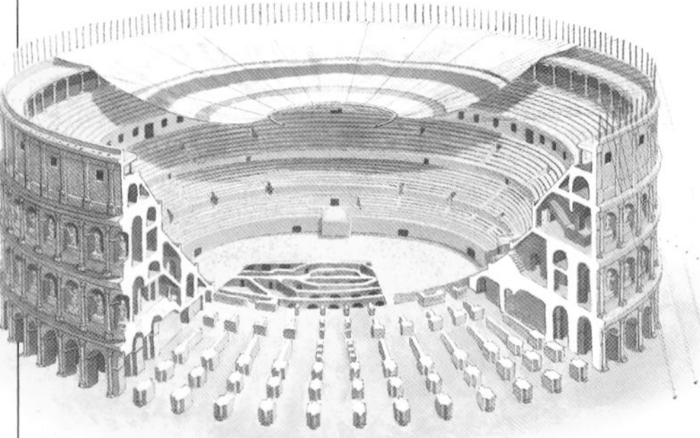

COLOSSEUM
The 50,000 seats at the Colosseum in Rome stood on rings of concrete-vaulted passages, which were reached by stairs. Every spectator could leave the Colosseum in five minutes through exits called vomitoria. The Colosseum was used for many activities. It was flooded for mock sea battles, and gladiators tested their skills against lions that leapt into the arena when hidden doors snapped open.

Swimming pool
Every Roman boy was expected to be able to read and to swim. Baths in colder parts of the empire had indoor, heated swimming pools.

Frigidarium
The Frigidarium was at the center of the baths and was a popular place to meet friends. Four baths filled with cold water gave the room its name.

WORKING OUT
A mosaic on the floor of the baths in the Villa Casale, a private country house in Piazza Armerina, Sicily, shows women exercising. Many public baths had a separate bathing area for women.

Roman Recreation

By the first century AD, Rome was a great empire. It reached from the Caspian Sea in the east and the British Isles in the north, to North Africa in the south. The Romans built roads with hard surfaces to connect their many cities. Aqueducts brought water to the cities from mountain springs. Luxury goods arrived in Rome's large harbors from every part of the known world. Romans in the cities bought food in take-out restaurants to eat in apartments with glass windows. They spent their free time watching plays or sporting events such as chariot races. They gathered at public baths to exercise and relax. Roman emperors ordered the construction of lavish buildings for public recreation to make themselves popular with the citizens. Roman engineers used synthetic materials such as concrete to construct these buildings, which were decorated with statues, mosaics and imported marble.

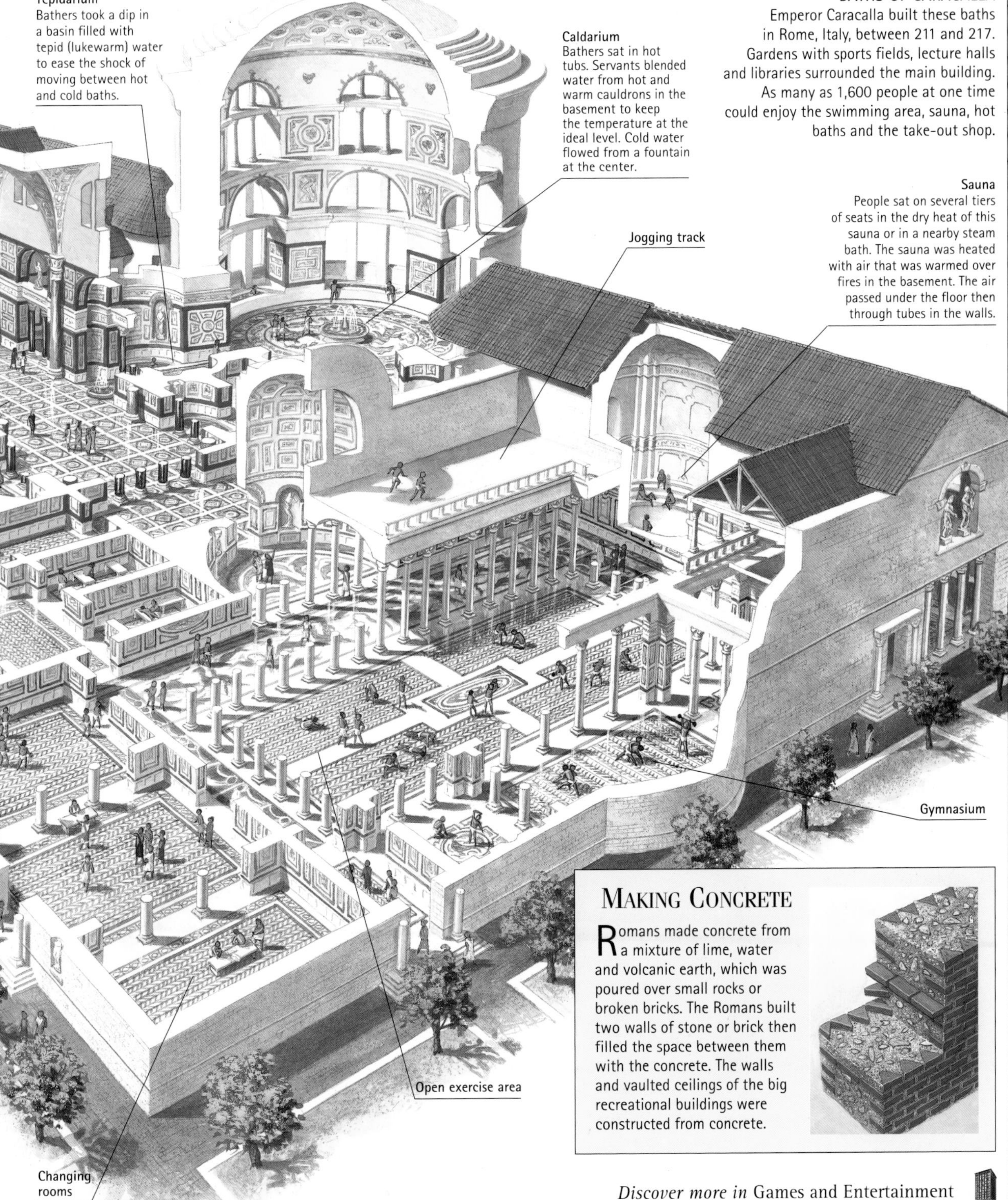

Tepidarium
Bathers took a dip in a basin filled with tepid (lukewarm) water to ease the shock of moving between hot and cold baths.
Caldarium
Bathers sat in hot tubs. Servants blended water from hot and warm cauldrons in the basement to keep the temperature at the ideal level. Cold water flowed from a fountain at the center.
Jogging track
Sauna
People sat on several tiers of seats in the dry heat of this sauna or in a nearby steam bath. The sauna was heated with air that was warmed over fires in the basement. The air passed under the floor then through tubes in the walls.
Gymnasium
Open exercise area
Changing rooms

BATHS OF CARACALLA

Emperor Caracalla built these baths in Rome, Italy, between 211 and 217. Gardens with sports fields, lecture halls and libraries surrounded the main building. As many as 1,600 people at one time could enjoy the swimming area, sauna, hot baths and the take-out shop.

Making Concrete

Romans made concrete from a mixture of lime, water and volcanic earth, which was poured over small rocks or broken bricks. The Romans built two walls of stone or brick then filled the space between them with the concrete. The walls and vaulted ceilings of the big recreational buildings were constructed from concrete.

Discover more in Games and Entertainment

Spiritual Journeys

Many different peoples live on the islands and peninsulas of Southeast Asia and they all have unique lifestyles. From early times, traders from all parts of Asia sailed along these coastlines and seaways. They traded goods and spread new ideas. Hinduism and Buddhism arrived from India, and Islam and Christianity came from further west to join the many local religions. Some of the greatest buildings in the area were built for Buddhist worship. Siddhartha Gautama, called the Buddha or the Enlightened One, founded Buddhism in India in the sixth century BC. He taught that every person could hope to achieve nirvana—a peaceful life beyond death where there is no suffering. Buddhists build stupas over relics of their spiritual leaders. A stupa is usually shaped like a dome and often stands on a square platform. Pilgrims walk along a path on the platform and meditate on the spiritual journey they will have to make to achieve nirvana.

Did You Know?

Despite the great expense and effort of building Borobudur, it was abandoned after it was finished. Jungle plants soon covered it from sight.

BOROBUDUR
This Buddhist shrine has stood in a jungle on the island of Java in Indonesia since the beginning of the ninth century. It was built to look like a mountain. The stupa has eight stories or terraces. Pilgrims walk around each one on their way to the top.

ENTRY PAVILION
This magnificently carved gatehouse at Angkor in Cambodia leads to Angkor Wat, a twelfth-century Hindu temple. This temple may be the world's largest religious structure.

At the top
A statue is hidden under the highest stupa.
The goal
At each compass point, pilgrims can look up a long flight of steps and glimpse their goal at the top.

SMALL BUDDHAS
Statues of Buddha meditating under corbeled vaults line the corridors on the square terraces of Borobudur. The walls are carved with events from Buddha's life.

Corbeled Domes

A simple corbeled dome is built by laying circles of stones flat on top of each other. One end of each stone juts out slightly over the room that is being domed. Pressure below and above one end of each stone holds it in place. A wide, heavy stone set on top locks all the layers below it in place.

ANANDA
This cluster of stupas in Pagan, Burma, partially hides Ananda, a white marble stupa rising in tiers above Pagan. This stupa shelters Buddhist relics.

WAT PRA KEO
The Royal Pantheon stands at the center of Wat Pra Keo in Bangkok, Thailand, the Buddhist area in the grounds of the royal palace. Ceremonies are held in the Royal Pantheon, which has eight gold statues of kings inside.

THE GREAT WALL OF CHINA
In the third century BC, the Chinese completed their first wall to keep out invaders from the north. This wall was rebuilt in the fourteenth century during the Ming dynasty. Five horses could walk side by side along the top. The wall still stretches for 1,500 miles (2,400 km) across northern China.

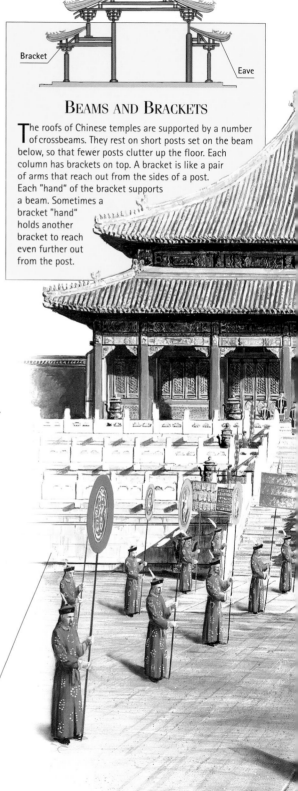

Beams and Brackets

The roofs of Chinese temples are supported by a number of crossbeams. They rest on short posts set on the beam below, so that fewer posts clutter up the floor. Each column has brackets on top. A bracket is like a pair of arms that reach out from the sides of a post. Each "hand" of the bracket supports a beam. Sometimes a bracket "hand" holds another bracket to reach even further out from the post.

• EMPIRES OF THE EAST •

Center of the Universe

China is a unique country with a single civilization that has flourished for centuries in an area as large as Europe. The Chinese are known for their silk and porcelain and for their philosophies, Confucianism and Taoism. Philosophy and building have close ties in China. Both deal with how a person finds his or her place in the universe. Everyone is at the center of their own universe. A family's house marks the center of the family's universe. The palace of the Emperor stood at the center of China and of the universe as a whole. The Chinese were also influenced by other countries. Traders and travelers brought Buddhism from India along with Buddhist techniques for building with wood. Few ancient buildings survive today but we can still see what they looked like because important wooden buildings were later copied in stone. These buildings have elaborate wooden roofs covered with glazed tiles.

TEMPLE OF HEAVEN
At the beginning of each spring, the Emperor prayed for an abundant harvest at this round hall with its three tiled roofs.

The Earth
The hall, like all important buildings, stands on a platform that represents the Earth.

HALL OF SUPREME HARMONY

The Emperor arrives at the Hall of Supreme Harmony in the Forbidden City. The hall was originally built in the fifteenth century during the Ming dynasty as part of the Imperial Palace. The building as it stands now was rebuilt in 1696 during the Qing dynasty. The hall and the Emperor's seat face south because the Chinese believe that a south-facing seat shows honor and respect.

THE FORBIDDEN CITY

The Imperial Palace was called the Forbidden City because few people were allowed inside its powerful fortifications. This 600-year-old painting shows government officials gathering outside the gates of the city.

The heavens
The wide eaves are turned up at the ends and seem to make the roof float above the hall. The elaborate roof of a Chinese building represents the heavens.

Q: Why are beams and brackets important in Chinese architecture?

HIMEJI CASTLE
Castles were built for the nobility in the sixteenth century. Himeji, in Hyogo, has a tall central tower, or keep, surrounded by smaller towers linked by corridors. Soldiers, called samurai, defended the castle with guns and arrows.

In Harmony with Nature

The Japanese have learned to appreciate the beauty of natural things from a religion called Shinto—the way of the gods. Shinto teaches that simple things in nature, such as a tree or waterfall, may embody the forces of nature. The Japanese have also learned from the Chinese. In the sixth century, Buddhism reached Japan from China by way of Korea. Chinese and Korean carpenters brought woodworking skills with them, which the Japanese soon adapted to their own taste. The Japanese Buddhists also embraced the Shinto love of nature. Japanese wooden buildings are very delicate and have complicated details. Houses and temples are designed so they blend into nature, not stand apart from it. The people inside a building never feel cut off from the outdoors. A wall is often built so that it can be pushed to the side to open the room to a garden outside.

Did You Know?

When early Japanese governments moved to a new capital, they ordered that the most sacred temples be taken apart, moved and reassembled at the new location.

Brackets
These simple brackets make it possible to build this wall between the two roofs with just a few wooden posts set far apart.

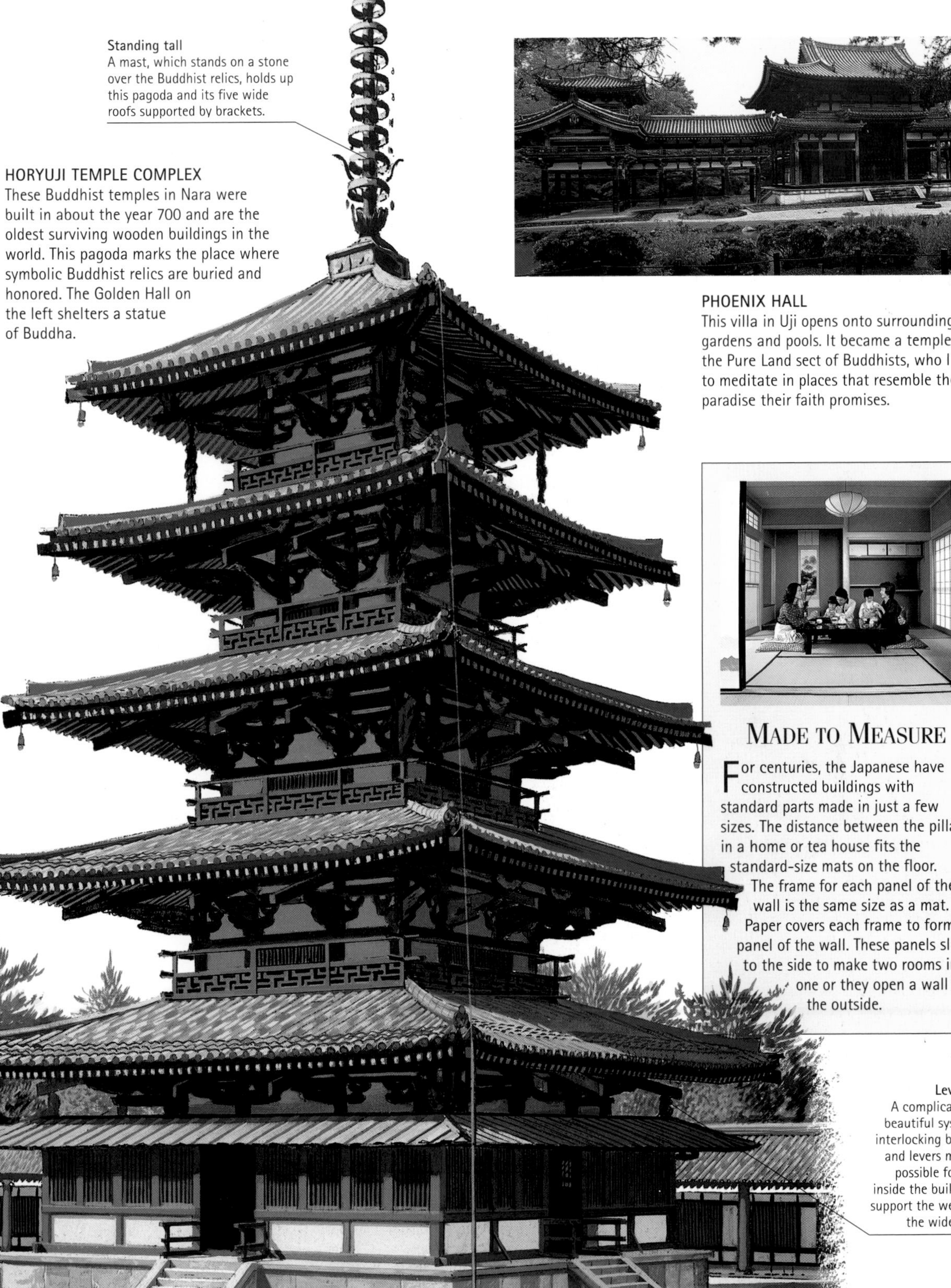

Standing tall
A mast, which stands on a stone over the Buddhist relics, holds up this pagoda and its five wide roofs supported by brackets.

HORYUJI TEMPLE COMPLEX
These Buddhist temples in Nara were built in about the year 700 and are the oldest surviving wooden buildings in the world. This pagoda marks the place where symbolic Buddhist relics are buried and honored. The Golden Hall on the left shelters a statue of Buddha.

PHOENIX HALL
This villa in Uji opens onto surrounding gardens and pools. It became a temple of the Pure Land sect of Buddhists, who like to meditate in places that resemble the paradise their faith promises.

Made to Measure

For centuries, the Japanese have constructed buildings with standard parts made in just a few sizes. The distance between the pillars in a home or tea house fits the standard-size mats on the floor. The frame for each panel of the wall is the same size as a mat. Paper covers each frame to form a panel of the wall. These panels slide to the side to make two rooms into one or they open a wall to the outside.

Lever arm
A complicated yet beautiful system of interlocking brackets and levers makes it possible for posts inside the building to support the weight of the wide eaves.

Heaven Meets Earth

Christians believe in Jesus, the son of God, and their religion is based on his life and teachings. Christians were persecuted for many years during the Roman Empire, but in AD 313 Emperor Constantine made the religion legal. He then left the city of Rome and moved east to Byzantium and established a new Christian capital named Constantinople, which is now Istanbul in Turkey. The Roman Empire later split into east and west. The western empire collapsed after it was invaded many times by nomadic tribes from central Asia, but the eastern part survived to become the Byzantine Empire. Christianity as it developed there is called Orthodox Christianity. Hagia Sophia was the magnificent Orthodox church in Constantinople and it inspired builders of Orthodox churches for centuries. The great dome at the center of the church represented the heavens. The floor below represented life on Earth.

THE PANTHEON
For many years, the dome of the Pantheon, in Rome, Italy, baffled modern engineers. They did not know how the ancient Romans managed to build such a large dome. Then they discovered that the dome was made of concrete that becomes lighter as it gets higher because each level is mixed with lighter stones such as volcanic pumice.

Did You Know?

For many hundreds of years the dome of the Pantheon was the largest in the world. It measures 142 ft (43 m) across and is the same in height. Walls 16 ft (5 m) thick buttress the base of the dome.

A new technique
Byzantine architects learned to construct round domes over square rooms. They used four pendentives, triangles cut from a circle, to provide a round base on which the dome rests. The pendentives shift the weight of the dome to the four supports below.

THE CHURCH TODAY
Four towers called minarets surround Hagia Sophia. They were added when the Islamic Ottoman Turks, founders of modern Turkey, conquered the Byzantine Empire and converted the church into a mosque.

Central dome
The large, lightweight dome is built of a single layer of brick and is 107 ft (33 m) wide. It has a row of arched windows cut into its base.

THE CONGREGATION
There were no seats in Hagia Sophia. Worshippers stood in the space beyond the columns—the men in the aisle below and the women in the gallery above—to listen to the singing of the Orthodox church service.

Half domes
A half dome at each end lengthens the nave to 250 ft (76 m) and buttresses the main dome by pressing against its base.

Decorating with Mosaics

A mosaic is a design or picture made up of small pieces of colored glass or stone that are mounted on a wall or ceiling. Mosaics seem to glow in the dimmest light. At one time, many colorful mosaics covered the ceilings of Hagia Sophia. Jesus (right) and other great leaders and heroes of Christianity were portrayed in mosaics against a gold background, which symbolized Heaven.

HAGIA SOPHIA
Byzantine architects began this church in Constantinople in 532, during the reign of Emperor Justinian. They finished it six years later and it soon became the model for future Orthodox churches. The clergy, as God's representatives, met the emperor, the worldly ruler, under the great domes, where the teachings of Jesus were read.

Q: What new building technique was developed by Byzantine architects?

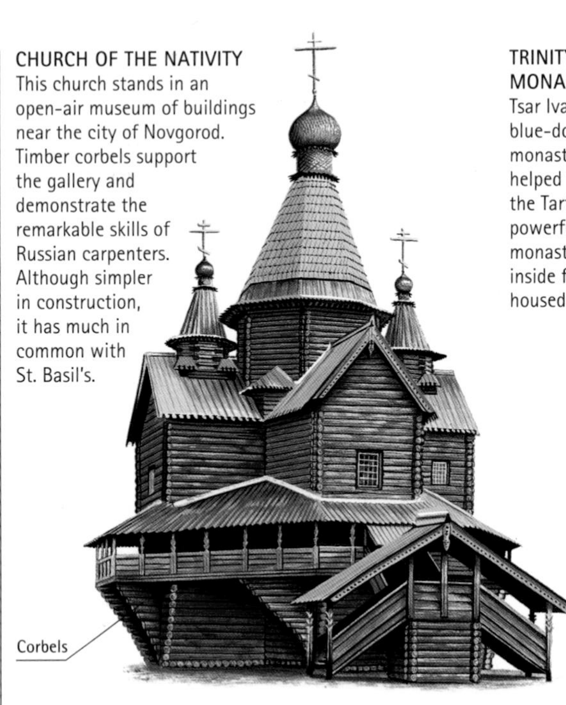

CHURCH OF THE NATIVITY
This church stands in an open-air museum of buildings near the city of Novgorod. Timber corbels support the gallery and demonstrate the remarkable skills of Russian carpenters. Although simpler in construction, it has much in common with St. Basil's.

TRINITY ST. SERGIUS MONASTERY
Tsar Ivan the Terrible built the blue-domed cathedral for this monastery after the monks helped to fund his war against the Tartars. It was the most powerful of the Russian monasteries that were built inside fortifications, and it housed soldiers.

• EAST MEETS WEST •

The Russian Heritage

The first Russian people lived in the forests west of the Ural Mountains, where Europe meets Asia. Russian merchants traveled down the long rivers and across the Black Sea to trade furs with their powerful neighbor, the Byzantine Empire. They later adopted the religion of Byzantium and became Orthodox Christians. Mongol Tartars, nomads from Asia, conquered the area in the thirteenth century and ruled it for 200 years before the Russians succeeded in regaining their independence. In the sixteenth century, Tsar Ivan the Terrible attacked two Tartar states and took over their lands. He then set out to make Russia a great power. Russian carpenters were skilled builders of wooden houses and boats and learned from the Byzantines how to build with stone and brick. Both Russian and Byzantine churches have many domes, but Russian domes are mounted high above the roofs and shaped like onions to shed the heavy snow and rain that falls so far north.

THE KREMLIN
The city of Moscow grew out from this kremlin, or fortress. Palaces and cathedrals stand within its walls, as does a tall bell tower built by Tsar Ivan the Terrible.

A LOOK INSIDE
Frescoes of plants in colorful abstract patterns flow across the walls and ceiling of St. Basil's. These frescoes were rediscovered in 1954, hidden beneath layers of plaster.

Did You Know?

St. Basil's is named after Basil the Fool, a holy man who dared to criticize Tsar Ivan the Terrible. He was so popular that Ivan did not dare punish him.

Central tower
The tall towers in the center of early Russian churches were inspired by the high-roofed tents of the earliest Russians.
Onion domes
Eight colorful domes, each with a unique shape, surround the tower. Each dome crowns a small chapel.
Chapels
Access to the chapels is from a gallery around the cathedral, which is reached by two covered stairways.

ST. BASIL'S CATHEDRAL
When Tsar Ivan the Terrible conquered the Tartars he celebrated by ordering his architects to build a cathedral that would be a "hymn of joy." Construction on St. Basil's in Moscow began in 1554. This colorful building was originally painted white.

Making Frescoes

A fresco painter spreads wet plaster on a wall or ceiling then paints it quickly so the paint sinks into the plaster before it dries. The only way to correct a mistake is to scrape off the layer of plaster and begin again. Sunlight slowly bleaches the color from frescoes, and moisture can cause the plaster to flake off. Shown here are frescoes painted on the outside of Voronet Monastery in Moldavia, Romania. They are unusual because they have survived the weather for more than three centuries.

Q: Why did the early Russians build churches with domes?

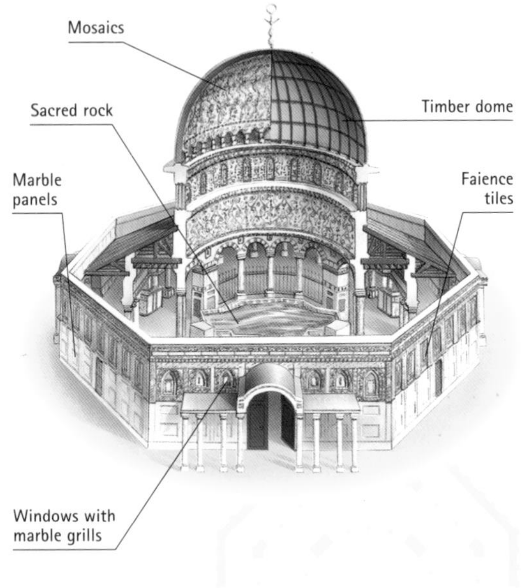

Birth of Islam

In the seventh century, Mohammed, an Arab trader, founded a new religion called Islam, which means "surrender to the one God." Mohammed urged his followers to care for the poor and weak. He spent his life teaching in the cities of Medina and Mecca and converted most Arabs to his beliefs by the time of his death. Those who believe in Islam are called Muslims, and they stop whatever they are doing five times each day to pray. A leader calls them to prayer from the minaret, or tall tower, of the nearest mosque, an Islamic place of worship. Mosques are decorated with flowing Arabic script and geometric patterns. Pictures of animals or people never appear on a mosque because Mohammed was determined to stop the worship of false gods. The tall, arched doorways of mosques and their high domes are often pointed or in the shape of a horseshoe.

DOME OF THE ROCK
This mosque in Jerusalem, Israel takes its name from the high dome built over a rock at a site that is sacred to Muslims. Pilgrims kneel to pray under the low roofs surrounding the rock. The mosque was completed in 691 and is the oldest surviving Islamic building. The decoration has been added in more recent centuries.

Garden paradise
The tomb opens onto a garden because Mohammed, who lived in a desert land, pictured paradise as a beautiful garden cooled by fountains.

RESTING STOPS
Resting places for caravans were built along trade routes and in cities. Camels, donkeys and horses rested in the stables while merchants showed their goods.

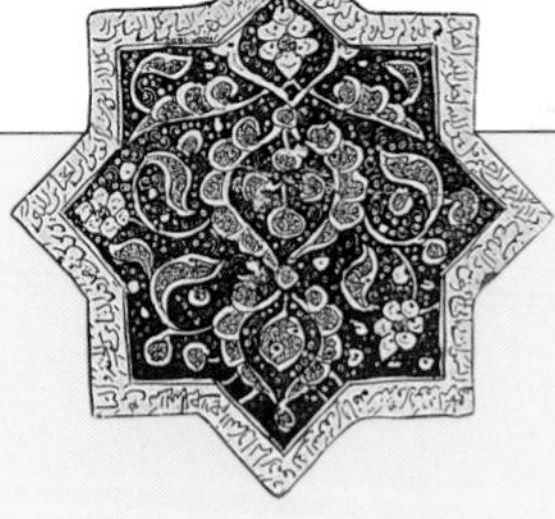

Protective Tiles

Since ancient times, people in the Middle East have made tiles from baked clay. They glazed or covered the tiles with a mixture of liquid and glass and baked them again. These tiles were waterproof and were first used to protect sun-dried brick buildings from the rain. This picture is made up of faience tiles, which are tiles painted with pictures or other patterns before they are glazed.

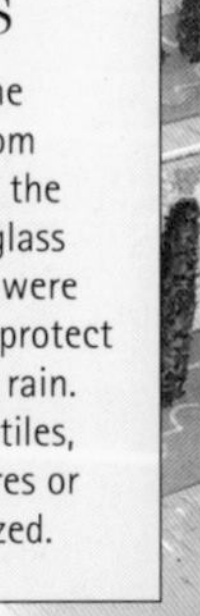

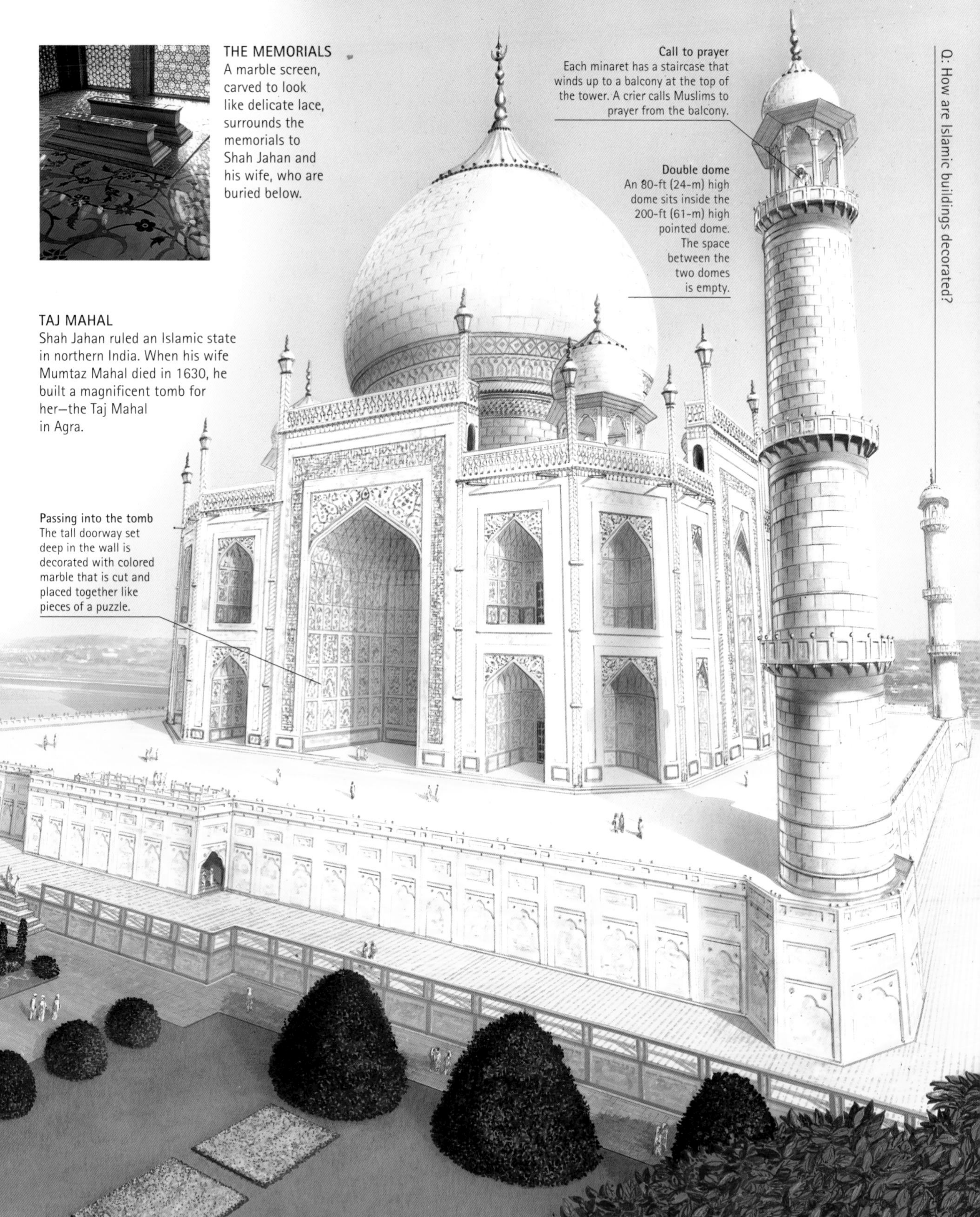

THE MEMORIALS
A marble screen, carved to look like delicate lace, surrounds the memorials to Shah Jahan and his wife, who are buried below.

TAJ MAHAL
Shah Jahan ruled an Islamic state in northern India. When his wife Mumtaz Mahal died in 1630, he built a magnificent tomb for her—the Taj Mahal in Agra.

Call to prayer
Each minaret has a staircase that winds up to a balcony at the top of the tower. A crier calls Muslims to prayer from the balcony.

Double dome
An 80-ft (24-m) high dome sits inside the 200-ft (61-m) high pointed dome. The space between the two domes is empty.

Passing into the tomb
The tall doorway set deep in the wall is decorated with colored marble that is cut and placed together like pieces of a puzzle.

Q: How are Islamic buildings decorated?

A PALACE FORTRESS
The Alhambra in Spain was such an intimidating fortress that few of the ruler's subjects suspected a beautiful palace lay inside its walls.

Tower of the Ladies

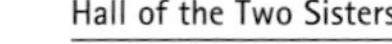

Hall of the Two Sisters

TALAKARI MADRASA
This high archway leads into an Islamic university, or madrasa, built in the seventeenth century in Samarkand, Uzbekistan. The dome rises over the mosque. Glazed tiles decorated and protected buildings, many of which were built of sun-dried brick.

• EAST MEETS WEST •

Spread of Islam

From the eighth century, the Islamic faith spread out along the trade routes. Islam reached China along with the camel caravans that brought Chinese jade and silk west along the Silk Road through Samarkand in the deserts of Central Asia. Islam spread along the north coast of the Mediterranean Sea where Arab traders exchanged Indian cotton and spices for glass and cloth to sell in India, where the new faith also took root. Strong Islamic states grew up along these trade routes. Rulers there built powerful fortresses on hills overlooking their cities. The luxurious palaces were designed to be cool during the heat of the long summers. They had large courtyards filled with colorful flowers, pools of water and fountains. The spray of the fountains kept the air fresh and cool. Shady rooms opened onto the courtyards and were separated from the outside by rows of columns.

COURT OF THE LIONS
Shaded walks surround this courtyard in the Alhambra. The fountain is surrounded by carved lions. The ruler held court in the Hall of Judgment at the end.

THE ALHAMBRA
The Alhambra, or red castle, was built in the fourteenth century on a high ridge above the city of Granada in Spain. Low buildings and garden courtyards form a palace at its center. Complicated geometrical patterns and religious sayings in graceful Arabic script are carved into the stucco on the walls.

Carved Decoration

Patterns carved into stucco decorated many surfaces. During this time, stucco was made from marble dust, wet lime and egg white. It was spread on a surface then allowed to dry before additional layers were added. The rows of small stalactites on the underside of the arch seen here were carved into seven layers of stucco.

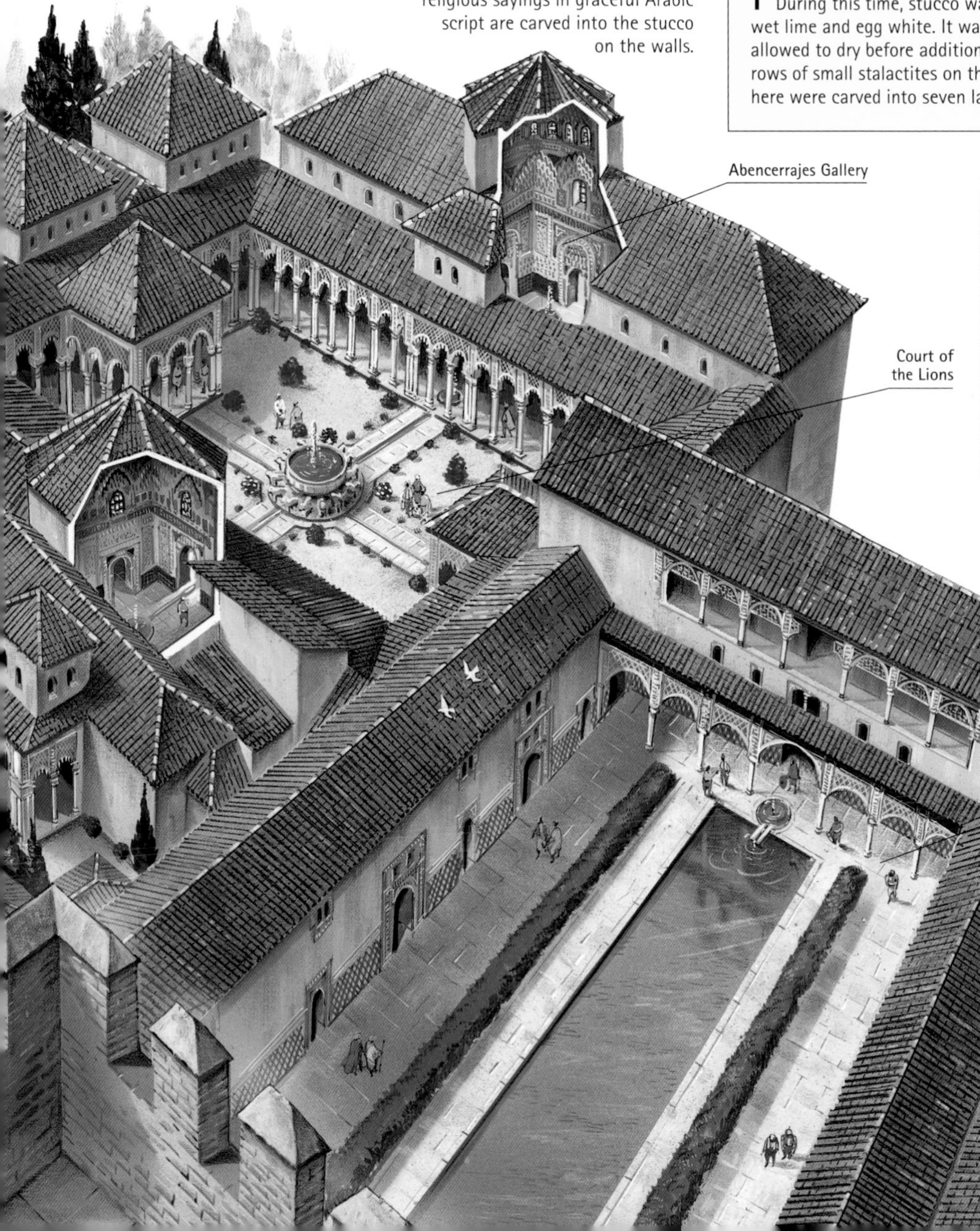

Abencerrajes Gallery

Court of the Lions

COUNTRY ESTATE
The ruler of Granada also built a small country palace with large gardens. The royal apartments face the Canal Court shown here.

Court of the Myrtles

Q: How did the Islamic religion spread to other areas?

A Monastic Life

Religious communities lived in monasteries or abbeys and these were the chief centers of art and learning in Europe between the tenth and twelfth centuries. A single community often included several hundred men called monks, or women called nuns, who lived in a walled settlement. The monks and nuns divided each day between worship, study and work. Monasteries were often located in the frontier areas of Europe among various nomadic tribes. Monks built churches that looked like fortresses because they were seen as strongholds of God in an evil world. People came there seeking peace from the violence and wars around them. Living areas of a monastery opened off a cloister—a covered walkway built around a square garden. After the fall of the Roman Empire in the fifth century, many building techniques were forgotten. Stonemasons had to rediscover how to build arched stone vaults so the churches had fireproof roofs. These vaults were like those built by the Romans, so the style is called Romanesque.

SLEEPING QUARTERS

This dormitory in the abbey at the cathedral in Durham, England, has a trussed roof built from thick, roughly cut timbers. Light from large windows allowed the monks to read during their afternoon rest period.

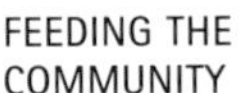

FEEDING THE COMMUNITY

On feast days, the monks roasted a wild boar over a fire in the center of the floor of this kitchen at Glastonbury Abbey in Somerset, England. They cooked other dishes for the large community over the four fireplaces in the corners of the room.

Dormitory
In the winter, the monks sat by a fire in the warming room then went to bed in the unheated dormitory upstairs. A door in the dormitory led into the church because the monks worshipped in the middle of the night.

Refectory
Twice a day, monks sat down in the refectory to eat their simple meals.

Toilets

Growing food
The monks worked in the fields of the farm outside the monastery walls. They also cultivated a small herb garden where they grew the plants used to make medicines.

Making Pilgrimages

People rarely traveled in these times, but they did make a trip, or pilgrimage, to pray at the burial place of a Christian saint. Some pilgrims walked hundreds of miles to reach their goal, such as Santiago de Compostela in Spain shown here. They slept in monastic guest houses and prayed at churches along the way. Pilgrims brought home new ideas from their travels, including new ways to build churches.

Did You Know?

People liked living near a monastery. It often provided the only hospital or school in an area and travelers stayed at guest houses located within the monastery.

Q: What did monks do during the day?

Cellar
The monks made cheese and candles, cured hams and brewed ale to stock their cellar with all the things the community needed.

MARIA LAACH ABBEY
This twelfth-century Romanesque abbey west of Koblenz, Germany, has six towers decorated with dark stone. This scene reconstructs a typical monastery cloister next to the abbey church.

SEGOVIA ALCAZAR
Large towns often built fortified castles to protect them. This alcazar, or castle, in Segovia, Spain, guarded the town from the top of an isolated rock.

NEUSCHWANSTEIN CASTLE
King Ludwig of Bavaria was fascinated by castles. He built this country palace, which looks like a medieval castle, in the 1800s.

CONWAY CASTLE
King Edward I of England built Conway castle in Conway, Wales. A workforce of 1,500 men completed most of the castle between 1283 and 1287. The king often arrived at the castle's water gate by boat, while townspeople and knights entered across the drawbridge.

This section is the outer courtyard of the castle.

MOTTE AND BAILEY CASTLE
A simple castle was built by digging a ditch around a piece of land then surrounding it with a wooden fence made of stakes called a palisade. A hill, or motte, was built with dirt from the ditch and might also have a palisade or ditch around it. The knight of the castle lived on top of the motte in the keep.

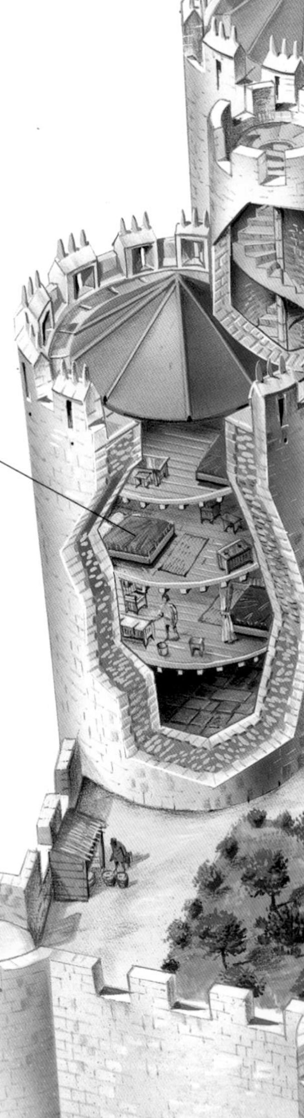

A place to sleep
Royal bedchambers took up two floors of the king's tower. Treasure was hidden in a cellar reached through a trap door in the floor.

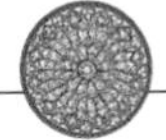

Royal Fortresses

For hundreds of years after the collapse of the Roman Empire in the fifth century, Europeans were often at war. Tribes fought tribes, and knights fought among themselves until strong kings conquered them. The first royal fortresses, or castles, were built of wood. The earliest stone castles were single square towers called keeps, built on high ground and surrounded by fences and ditches. As weapons changed, so did the design of castles. People built stone walls 16 ft (5 m) thick to shield them from battering rams, arrows, stones and a kind of burning tar. They filled their ditches with water, turning them into moats, so the enemy could not dig a tunnel under the wall and make it cave in. Archers positioned themselves in round towers that bulged out from the walls. This enabled them to fire their arrows on attackers from three sides.

A hasty exit
Prisoners were often taken to the dungeons of the prison tower through a hidden door in the Great Hall.
Great Hall
Banquets were held here and prisoners were brought before the king.
Arrow loops
Drawbridge
Repair work
A man climbed stairs mounted on the inside of a large wheel to wind a rope around a small wheel at its center and slowly lift stones tied to the end of the rope.

Lifting Things

People and animals can lift very heavy weights without powered equipment by using levers. Here a page steps onto the long end of a board on a support called a fulcrum. His weight pushes his end of the lever to the ground and lifts the heavier knight a short distance into the air. The wheel that hoisted stone to the top of a castle tower also used the principle of the lever.

SALON DE MARS
Louis XIV received his court of royal attendants three evenings a week in a suite of six rooms including the Salon de Mars. Mars was the Roman god of war, and battle scenes decorate the ceiling of the room.

PALACE CHAPEL
The king sat in this private balcony in the palace's own church. Members of the court gathered below him before the altar.

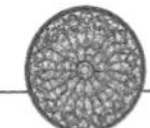

Grand Palaces

By 1660, a century of destruction from invasions and civil wars had come to an end in Europe. In several countries, kings took all political and military power for themselves, and claimed the credit for peace. These rulers were called absolute monarchs as they claimed absolute, or unlimited, power over their people. Absolute monarchs were popular if they used their power to bring peace. Kings moved out of the cities that had rebelled against them, and built huge palaces in the countryside for their governments. These palaces had magnificent staterooms built for court ceremonies. They were decorated with tapestries, paintings and statues that praised the king's victories or recalled the glorious deeds of powerful Roman emperors and mythical Greek gods. The most skilled workers in each nation decorated their ruler's palace, which became a showplace of the country's finest products.

PALACE OF VERSAILLES
The Palace of Versailles was the first unfortified residence built in Europe since the fall of the Roman Empire. In 1661, Louis XIV began to build the palace around a hunting lodge he loved to visit as a boy. He demanded that the most powerful men in the kingdom live under his control there. Festivities and military ceremonies took place in the courtyards, as shown in this painting.

HALL OF MIRRORS
The long, narrow stateroom in the Palace of Versailles has tall windows on one long wall matched by mirrors on the opposite wall. The bright sunlight and reflections moving across the mirrors dazzle the eyes so that it is hard to see what is at the opposite end of the room. This room inspired a hall of mirrors in every palace in Europe for more than a century.

The Sun King

Louis XIV, France's absolute monarch, chose the sun as his symbol. He believed his government was as valuable to France as the sun is to the Earth, where life is only possible because of the sun's light and heat. Scientists had only recently recognized that the sun and not the Earth was the center of the solar system. At Versailles, all roads and garden paths radiate from the palace, much like the rays of the sun.

A GRAND ENTRY
Rulers of small countries tried to look more powerful by building impressive palaces much like the Palace of Versailles. A coach pulled by four horses could drive right into this palace at Würzburg in Germany, where its occupants would descend and sweep up the stairs to the staterooms above.

Discover more in Age of Happiness

THE AMALIENBURG
In the 1730s, the ruler of Bavaria built this hunting lodge in the gardens of the Nymphenburg Palace in Munich, Germany for his wife Maria Amalia. A stairway led from her bedroom to her shooting terrace on the roof.

NYMPHENBURG PALACE
Three cube shapes linked by bridges make up this palace in Munich, Germany, which is built in the Baroque style. The Amalienburg is hidden among the trees to the right.

Age of Happiness

The eighteenth century was an optimistic and light-hearted age. New ideas in science had convinced people that famine and disease could be conquered. Happiness was the highest goal in life. Statues of saints dancing or angels swinging from vines sometimes decorated churches. People no longer feared nature and they enjoyed the ever-changing plant and animal life around them. Some retreated from the busy city life to houses in the countryside. They invited friends there to enjoy the surroundings, listen to music, discuss science or play games. These country retreats were built in a delicate new architectural style called Rococo. Pink, yellow and other pastel colors made every room look cheerful. Rococo architects wanted buildings to look light and weightless. One way they achieved this was by covering walls and ceilings with delicate vines made of stucco—a type of plaster they could mold by hand into shapes. Stucco birds and butterflies flew across ceilings.

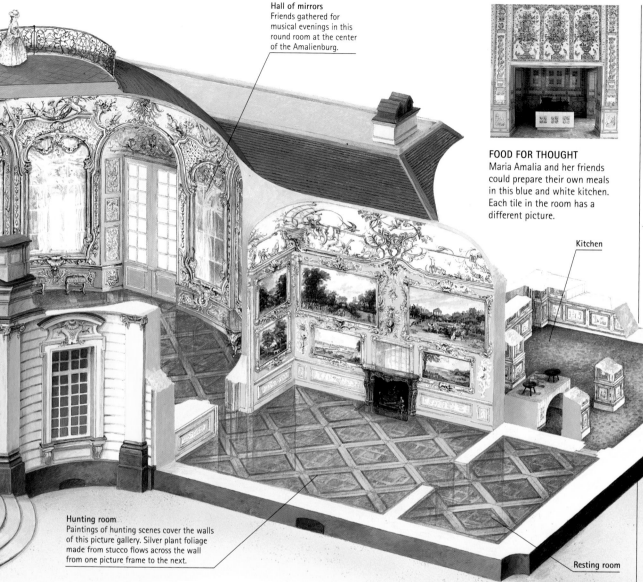

Hall of mirrors
Friends gathered for musical evenings in this round room at the center of the Amalienburg.

FOOD FOR THOUGHT
Maria Amalia and her friends could prepare their own meals in this blue and white kitchen. Each tile in the room has a different picture.

Kitchen

Hunting room
Paintings of hunting scenes cover the walls of this picture gallery. Silver plant foliage made from stucco flows across the wall from one picture frame to the next.

Resting room

Q: Why did people retreat to houses in the countryside?

Decorating with Mirrors

Glass was invented in Mesopotamia in ancient times. The Romans were the first to use glass for windows. In the seventeenth century, the French made plate glass by pouring liquid glass out onto a table and rolling it flat. Once the glass hardened, it was ground smooth and polished to make mirrors and large windowpanes. Mirrors often decorated the inside of Rococo buildings.

DE LUXE KENNELS
Hunting dogs slept in the kennels at the base of the walls in this room in the Amalienburg. Guns were stored in the cabinets above.

Discover more in Inspired by Nature

Reach for the Sky

Skyscrapers are a product of the Industrial Revolution, which began in England in the eighteenth century. New inventions revolutionized the way people lived. Steam engines, and later electricity, made enough energy available to do many more times the work that people and animals had done before. A new method of smelting iron produced huge quantities at low prices. Other inventions gave builders steel, a material even stronger than iron. Cities grew and skyscrapers provided a solution to the problems of overcrowding because they take up little space on the ground. Skyscraper frames were first built with iron, then with steel. New engines powered elevators to hoist people to the top. The weight of a tall building can easily cause it to sink or lean, so the early skyscrapers were usually built on solid rock. This is why so many were built on Manhattan, a rocky island in New York City.

COALBROOKDALE BRIDGE
The world gained a new construction material when inexpensive iron was developed. In 1779, the English built Coalbrookdale bridge in Shropshire, which was the first iron bridge to be constructed.

Did You Know?

The first skyscraper was built in 1884 in the city of Chicago, Illinois. It was only ten-stories high.

EIFFEL TOWER
This iron and steel tower was built for the Paris Exposition of 1889. When radio was invented, the tower began its long career as an antenna. It carried the first transatlantic radio–telephone call.

St. Peter's Basilica, Italy 1612	Great Pyramid of Khufu, Egypt 2700 BC	Eiffel Tower, France 1889	Empire State Building, USA 1931	Sears Tower, USA 1974	CN Tower, Canada 1976
453 ft (138 m)	479 ft (146 m)	984 ft (300 m)	1,250 ft (381 m)	1,453 ft (443 m)	1,804 ft (550 m)

The Tallest of Them All

For more than 4,500 years, the Great Pyramid of Khufu in Egypt was the tallest building in the world. Then the Eiffel Tower was built in France in 1889. In many parts of the world today, skyscrapers and towers continue to grow taller and taller.

Crown
The Art Deco style, a novelty of the 1930s, inspired the triangle-shaped windows. These are set within tiers of arches on the crown.

LIFE AT THE TOP

Native Americans were some of the earliest construction workers on skyscrapers. They worked at great heights while standing only on 8-in (20-cm) wide steel beams.

Q: Why did buildings start to get taller?

GOING UP?

Steam engines powered the first elevators, which were used only for freight. The first passenger elevators were installed in 1857 after a way was found to stop them from falling if a cable broke. By 1889, they were powered by electric motors. The elevator doors of the Chrysler Building (above) are decorated in the Art Deco style.

Core
A strong frame is built inside the building for the elevators. This frame also helps the building resist the pushing and twisting forces of the wind.

CHRYSLER BUILDING

Walter Chrysler built this 77-story skyscraper in New York City during the worldwide Depression of the 1930s. It provided much-needed employment for many construction workers. The building was the headquarters for his automobile empire and a monument to his success.

Inspired by Nature

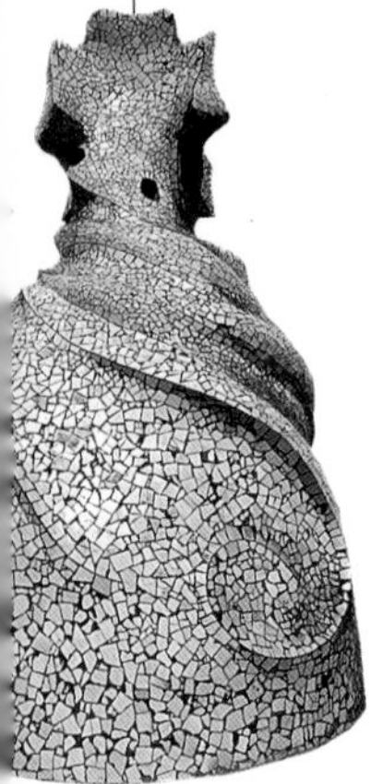

New inventions had brought conveniences such as street lights and railways to many cities in Europe by the turn of the twentieth century. Railway stations, parks and houses were often built in an original new style the French called Art Nouveau or "New Art." Germans named it Jugendstil or "Style of Youth" and Spaniards simply said "Modernismo." Art Nouveau architects were inspired by nature. Stained-glass ceilings came alive with brightly colored birds and flowers, and the iron in balcony railings was twisted and tangled like vines. The Modernismo architect Antonio Gaudí copied nature by avoiding straight lines and right angles in his buildings, which seem to have been sculpted from lumps of clay. Such unique shapes were possible because the Industrial Revolution gave builders iron, steel and concrete to work with.

THE PARIS METRO
The glass shell of the roof and the iron frame of this subway entrance are molded to look like the trunk and branches of a tree. This is just one of the many subway entrances in Paris, France, which were built in the Art Nouveau style.

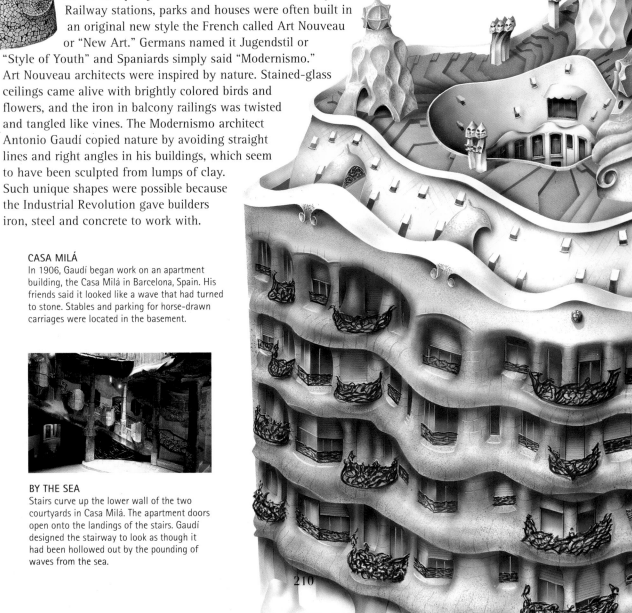

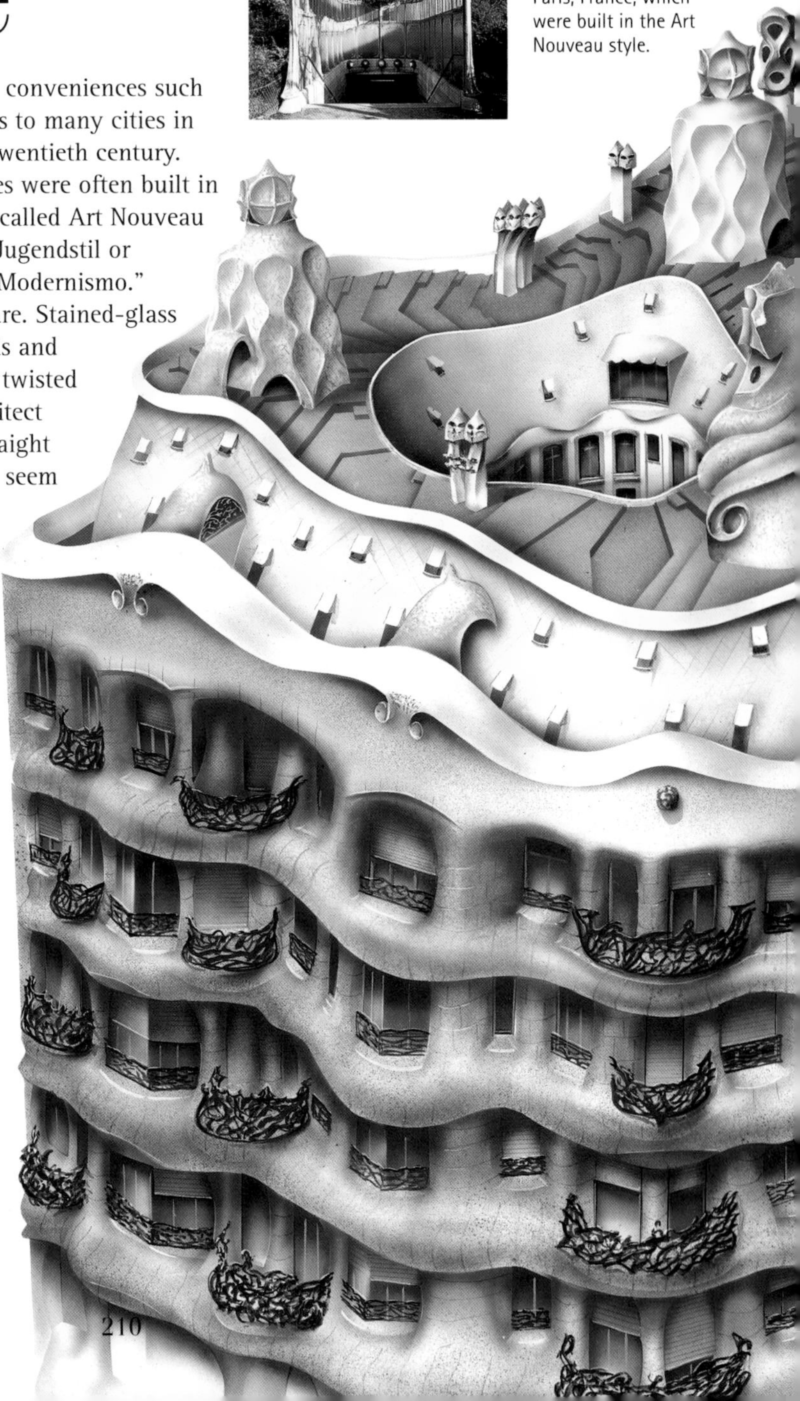

CASA MILÁ
In 1906, Gaudí began work on an apartment building, the Casa Milá in Barcelona, Spain. His friends said it looked like a wave that had turned to stone. Stables and parking for horse-drawn carriages were located in the basement.

BY THE SEA
Stairs curve up the lower wall of the two courtyards in Casa Milá. The apartment doors open onto the landings of the stairs. Gaudí designed the stairway to look as though it had been hollowed out by the pounding of waves from the sea.

COME INSIDE
In this Casa Milá apartment, the walls of the parlor curve around corners and up into the ceiling. The ceiling was inspired by the ripples left by the tide in the sand.

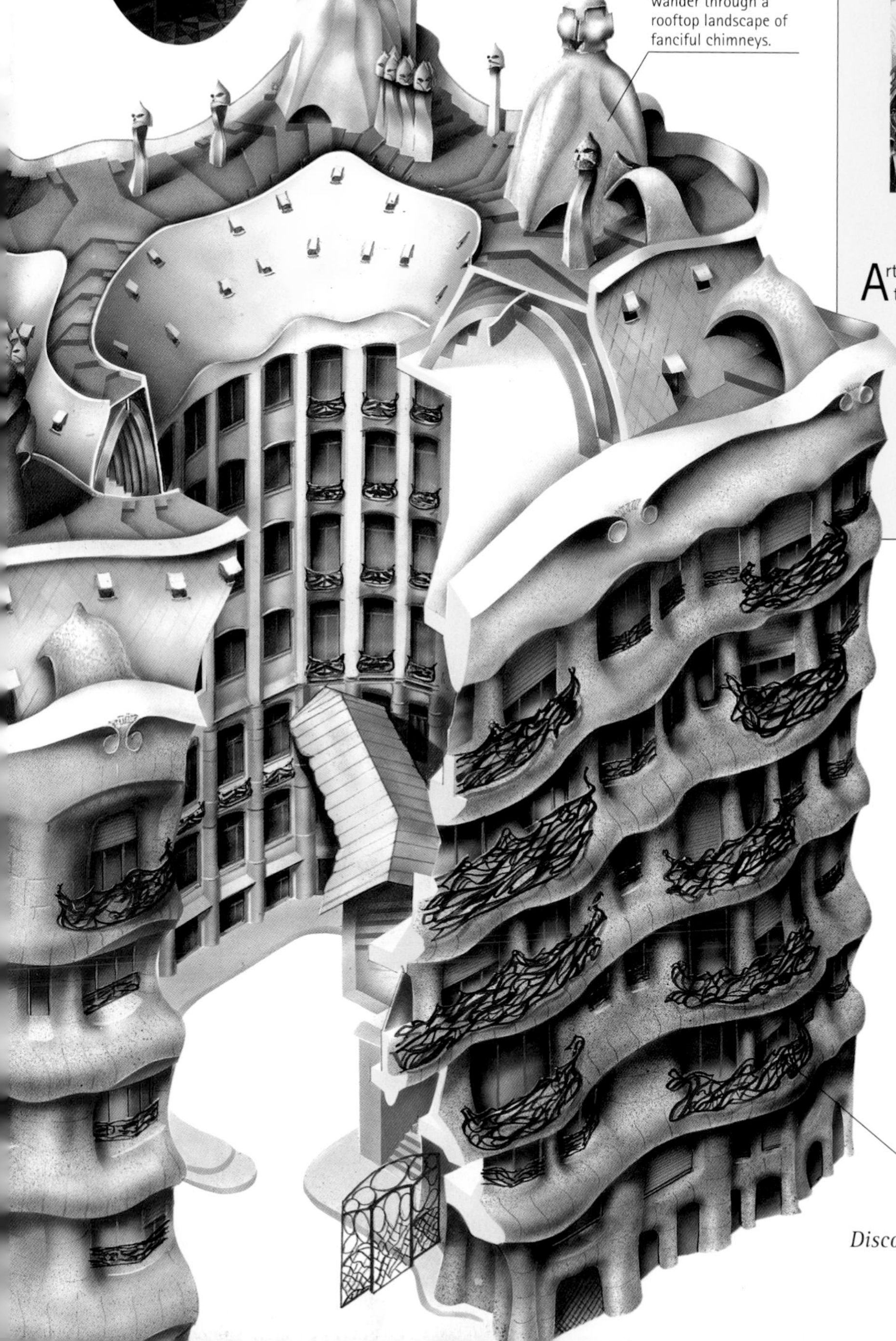

Rooftop
Residents step out onto the roof terrace through stairwell exits twisted into crosses at the top. They can then wander through a rooftop landscape of fanciful chimneys.

Sculpting a Building

Art Nouveau architects rebelled against the practice of copying historic buildings such as the Parthenon in Greece. They studied nature and copied the shapes they saw there. The Belgian Victor Horta, a founder of Art Nouveau, imitated plant life in glass and metal. At Horta's Tassel House in Belgium, shown here, light from a colorful glass dome shines down on the twisted metal vines in the stairwell.

NOTRE DAME DU HAUT
The shape of the surrounding hills inspired the design of Notre Dame du Haut in Ronchamp, France. The Swiss architect Le Corbusier built this church in the 1950s.

Balconies
Casa Milá was inspired by the seashore. The iron guards on the balconies look like bundles of seaweed.

Q: Why are there so few straight lines in an Art Nouveau building?

Discover more in Age of Happiness

FALLINGWATER
The architect of the Guggenheim, Frank Lloyd Wright, also designed houses that nestle into their natural surroundings. Fallingwater in Bear Run, Pennsylvania, copies the shelves of rock over which the waterfall beneath it flows.

GUGGENHEIM MUSEUM
The Solomon R. Guggenheim Foundation built its museum of modern art between 1956 and 1959 in New York City. The museum is constructed from a spiral of reinforced concrete in the shape of a hollow funnel. Its unusual shape contrasts sharply with the straight lines of the skyscrapers built around it.

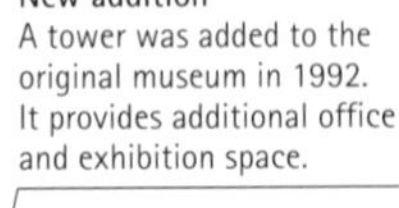

New addition
A tower was added to the original museum in 1992. It provides additional office and exhibition space.

Adventurous Shapes

After the Second World War, many nations around the world made great economic recoveries. People felt confident and full of adventure. Architects of the 1950s and 1960s designed buildings with unusual shapes to reflect this new confidence. Some buildings have simple geometric shapes, while others look like huge abstract sculptures. Many of these structures could not have been built without the invention of a new material called reinforced concrete. A roof of reinforced concrete will bridge a wide room without any other supports in between. Steel and reinforced concrete are so flexible that walls and ceilings can be built into any shape. Sometimes the walls of a room or ceiling were built so they curved away from the people inside the building. This was done to give people a feeling of exhilaration–the spirit of the times in which these buildings were designed and constructed.

ROCK AND ROLL HALL OF FAME
This museum in Cleveland, Ohio, was designed by I. M. Pei and opened in 1995. It has rectangular bridges and circles and triangles of glass, granite and white-painted steel.

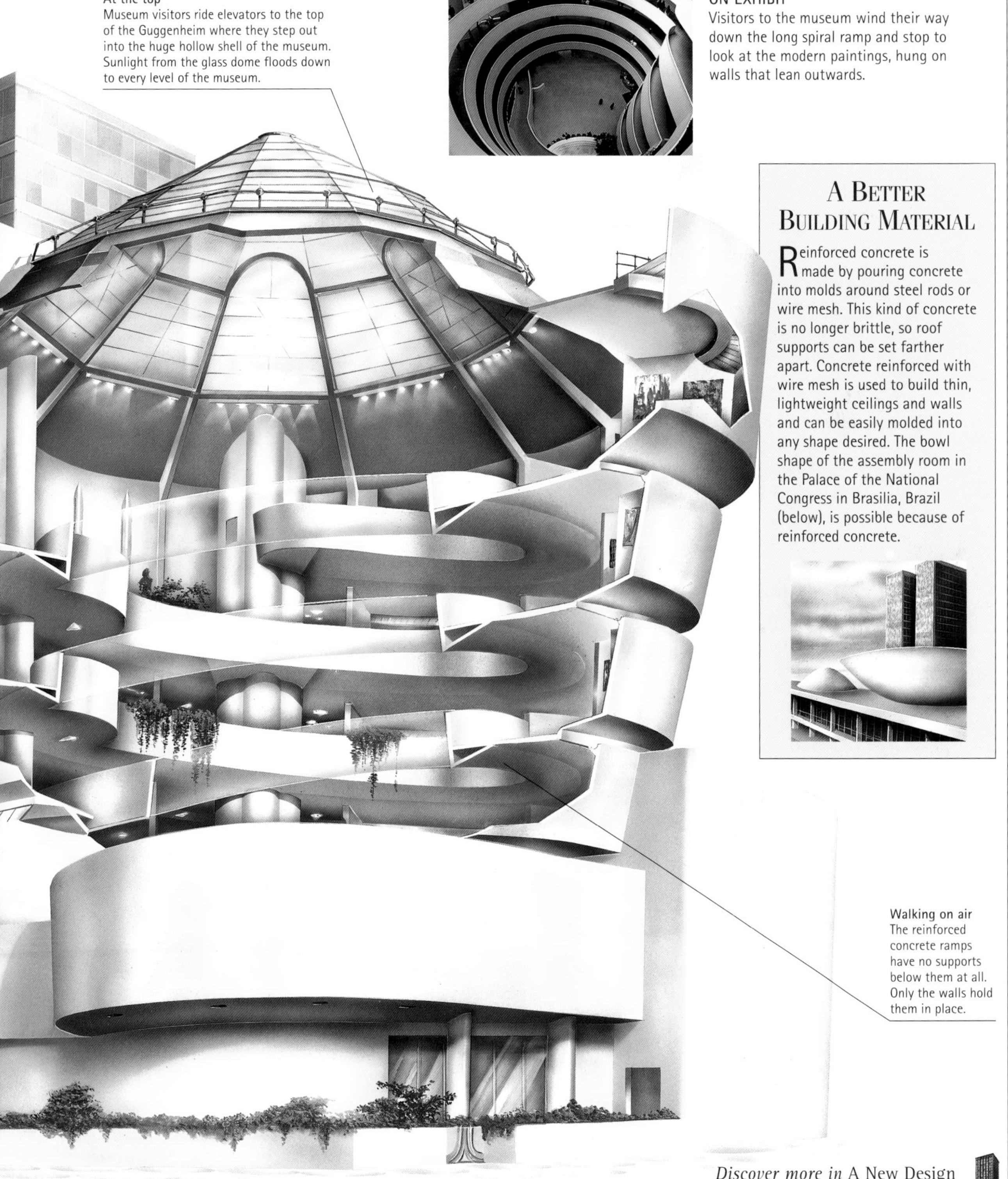

At the top
Museum visitors ride elevators to the top of the Guggenheim where they step out into the huge hollow shell of the museum. Sunlight from the glass dome floods down to every level of the museum.

ON EXHIBIT
Visitors to the museum wind their way down the long spiral ramp and stop to look at the modern paintings, hung on walls that lean outwards.

A Better Building Material

Reinforced concrete is made by pouring concrete into molds around steel rods or wire mesh. This kind of concrete is no longer brittle, so roof supports can be set farther apart. Concrete reinforced with wire mesh is used to build thin, lightweight ceilings and walls and can be easily molded into any shape desired. The bowl shape of the assembly room in the Palace of the National Congress in Brasilia, Brazil (below), is possible because of reinforced concrete.

Walking on air
The reinforced concrete ramps have no supports below them at all. Only the walls hold them in place.

Q: What is unusual about the design of the Guggenheim Museum?

Discover more in A New Design

Keeping warm and dry
Spectators enjoy indoor comfort during Toronto's long, cold winters. The SkyDome's roof is in four sections and is made of a plastic fabric stretched on thin metal frames.
The best position
The two, arched, center sections of the SkyDome roof slide on rails to a new position at one end of the stadium.
Tucked away
The half dome at the end swings on its rails around the side of the stadium and disappears under the other roof sections.

Did You Know?

The building technique used to roof many large stadiums was first used by ancient nomads. They used it to build tents, which were huts made from poles and ropes with animal skins stretched across them.

• THE INDUSTRIAL WORLD •

Games and Entertainment

Since ancient times, people have gathered in large public stadiums or arenas for entertainment. Crowds still flock to these large buildings to watch sporting competitions, concerts and other special events. Many stadiums are open to the sky and spectators are at the mercy of the weather. They face the heat in summer and the freezing cold in winter. Events can be canceled if it rains or snows. But people in many countries no longer have to consult the weather report before an event, because some stadiums are now covered by roofs. The development of new synthetic materials, particularly plastics, has made these roofs possible. Tough, lightweight plastics are stretched tight on thin frames, much like umbrellas. These roofs, which come in many shapes and sizes, can cover even the largest stadiums. They shelter the crowds and the players or performers, and no-one's view is blocked by roof supports standing on the playing field.

SPORTS COMPLEX
Many large stadiums are built originally for special events. This stadium in Seoul, South Korea, was built for the 1988 Summer Olympic Games. It seats 100,000 spectators.

OLYMPIC STADIUM
Spectators in the Olympic Stadium in Munich, Germany, sit under a clear canopy of panels made from glass and plastic. The panels hang from a square mesh made of steel cable and are attached to cables that are stretched between 56 reinforced concrete poles and the ground.

THE SKYDOME

The SkyDome in Toronto, Canada, covers 8 acres (3 hectares) and includes a hotel. Several sections of seats move on rails to the best positions for watching each event. The grass for the playing field is artificial turf that is rolled out and zipped together with 8 miles (13 km) of zippers. This arena has a movable roof that can be opened and closed according to the weather.

Roofing a Stadium

Some of the largest stadium roofs hang from steel cables. As any tightrope walker knows, a cable that is stretched tight is as sturdy as a steel beam. A stretched cable is said to be under tension. Roofing made of glass and plastic can hang from steel cables stretched between poles and the ground to create a great tent such as the Olympic Stadium in Munich, Germany (above). Roof cables hold upright the frame of the J. S. Dorton Arena in Raleigh, North Carolina (below). The cables in the roof hold the arches of the frame up and the walls hang from the frame.

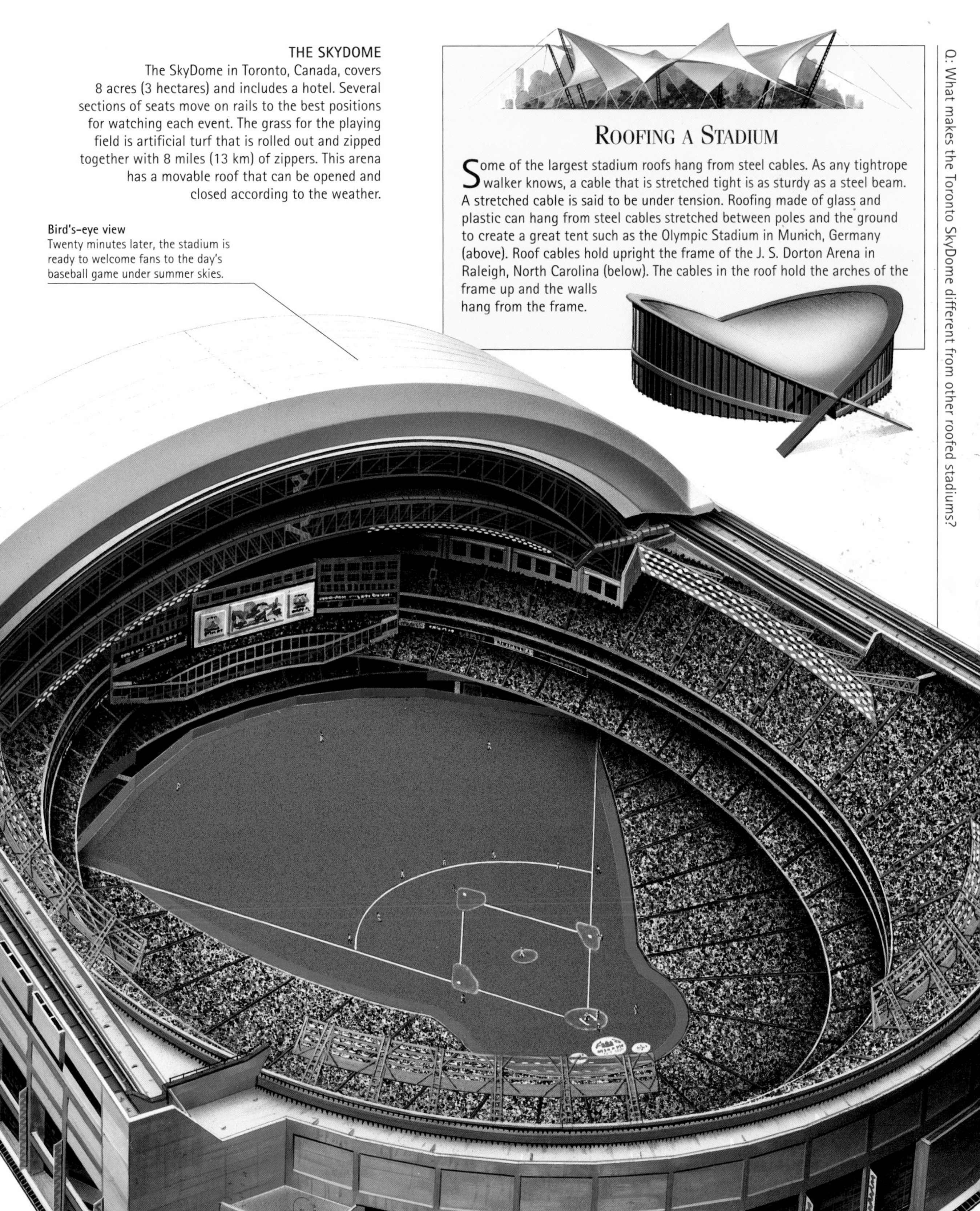

Bird's-eye view
Twenty minutes later, the stadium is ready to welcome fans to the day's baseball game under summer skies.

Q: What makes the Toronto SkyDome different from other roofed stadiums?

SYDNEY OPERA HOUSE

In 1957, a Danish architect Jørn Utzon won a contest to design the Opera House in Sydney, Australia. But it took him six years and the help of engineers and early computers to come up with a way to actually build it. Here the building is shown during different stages of construction.

Giant cranes

Three cranes arrived from France. Each required 30 trucks to transport it to the building site where they were assembled.

Roof ribs

Computers showed that the roof originally planned might have collapsed, so the design changed. The prestressed concrete roof was made by casting concrete pieces that were placed on the building before steel cables were threaded through them and pulled tight.

A New Design

The construction of an innovative building is difficult and often requires new techniques and special building materials. Many unexpected problems arise no matter how careful the advance planning may be. The architects and engineers building the Opera House in Sydney, Australia, faced major obstacles. The design was so innovative that it took several years for engineers to work out a way to actually build it. Specialists in sound, called acoustical engineers, advised on how the chosen building materials would affect the quality of sound. Metal, plastic and glass from around the world was used in the building. Manufacturers designed essential new equipment and construction workers learned new skills to build the Opera House. There were many unexpected costs and delays in construction. Sixteen years later, the architect's imaginative design became a unique masterpiece, which today is recognized throughout the world.

Prestressed Concrete

The Opera House roofs were designed to be made of prestressed concrete much like the Trans World Airline building at Kennedy Airport in New York City, seen here. The steel in prestressed concrete is stretched tight so that it squeezes the concrete around it. The Trans World Airline building has a thin, lightweight roof, which was made by pouring concrete over a tightly stretched wire mesh.

Concrete sections

Each rib was assembled from concrete sections cast at the building site in reusable molds.

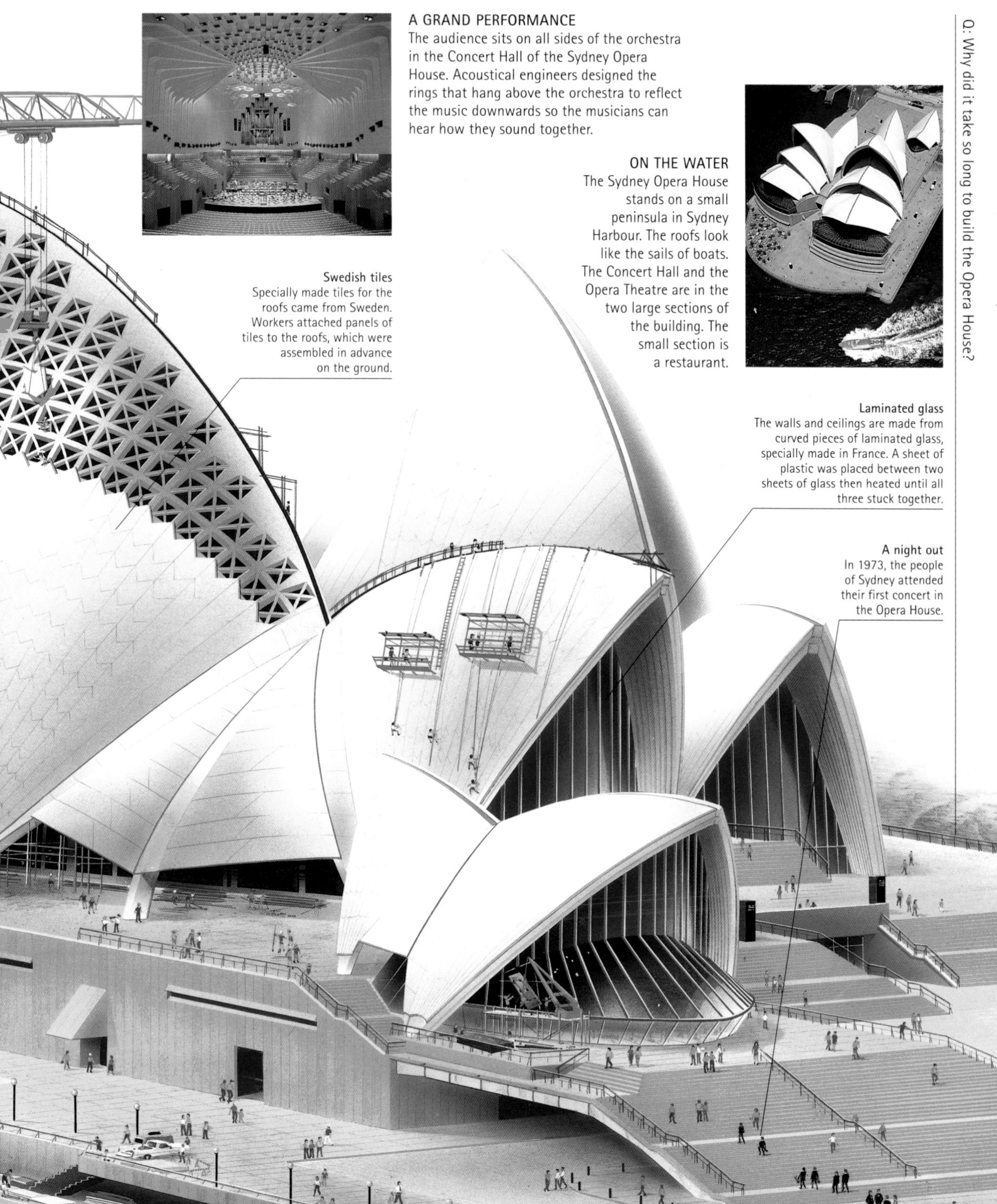

A GRAND PERFORMANCE

The audience sits on all sides of the orchestra in the Concert Hall of the Sydney Opera House. Acoustical engineers designed the rings that hang above the orchestra to reflect the music downwards so the musicians can hear how they sound together.

ON THE WATER

The Sydney Opera House stands on a small peninsula in Sydney Harbour. The roofs look like the sails of boats. The Concert Hall and the Opera Theatre are in the two large sections of the building. The small section is a restaurant.

Swedish tiles
Specially made tiles for the roofs came from Sweden. Workers attached panels of tiles to the roofs, which were assembled in advance on the ground.

Laminated glass
The walls and ceilings are made from curved pieces of laminated glass, specially made in France. A sheet of plastic was placed between two sheets of glass then heated until all three stuck together.

A night out
In 1973, the people of Sydney attended their first concert in the Opera House.

Q: Why did it take so long to build the Opera House?

Glossary

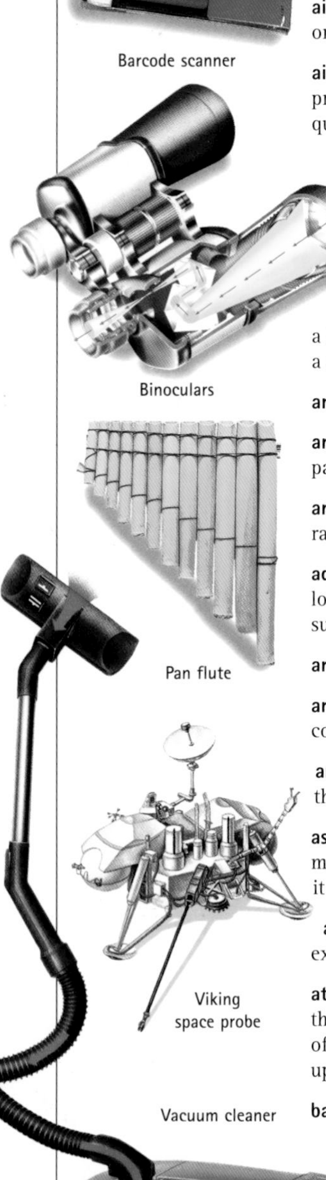
Barcode scanner

Binoculars

Pan flute

Viking space probe

Vacuum cleaner

aerodynamics The science that deals with air and how aircraft fly.

air pressure The force of the air inside a container or in the Earth's atmosphere.

airfoil A structure such as a wing, tailplane, or propeller blade that develops lift when moving quickly through the air.

airplane A powered, heavier-than-air aircraft.

airship A lighter-than-air aircraft that is driven by an engine and able to be steered.

altitude An aviation term for height.

amplitude The size of a wave. A sound wave with a large amplitude is louder than a sound wave with a small amplitude.

anatomy The scientific study of the body's structure.

anesthetic A drug that keeps the body from feeling pain and other sensations.

antenna A device that receives or transmits radio waves.

aqueduct A channel built for moving water across long distances. It can also be a bridge that carries such a channel across a valley or river.

arch A curved structure built over an opening.

architect A person trained to design and oversee the construction of buildings.

artery A blood vessel that carries blood away from the heart.

assembly line Part of the mass-production method of manufacturing. Workers fit one part to a product as it moves past them on a conveyor system.

atom A particle of matter. It is the smallest existing part of an element.

atrium A small courtyard completely surrounded by the rooms of a house, or a walled courtyard in front of a church. Also, one of the two small, thin-walled upper chambers of the heart.

bailey An open area inside the walls of a castle.

ballast A weight used to stabilize a ship, submersible, or submarine.

beam A long, squared piece of wood, stone, or metal that has a support under each end. The beams between two walls hold up the ceiling.

biotechnology The process of changing or controlling living things to make new products.

biplane A fixed-wing airplane with two sets of wings.

bone A hard, tough type of body tissue that provides strength and support for the body.

brick A molded block of clay baked in an oven so that it hardens and becomes waterproof.

calculator A machine that can add, subtract, multiply, and divide numbers.

capillary The smallest type of blood vessel, which is much thinner than a hair. Substances such as oxygen and nutrients can easily pass through its very thin walls.

cardiac Relating to the heart.

cartilage A smooth, slippery, slightly soft body tissue. It covers bones where they touch in joints, and forms the framework of body parts such as the ears and nose.

castle A fortified building designed to hold off enemy attacks.

CD-ROM An abbreviation for "compact disc read-only memory." This refers to a compact disc used with a computer system.

cell The basic living unit, or building block, of the human body (and all other living things).

cerebral Relating to the main part of the brain, the cerebrum.

chapel A room in a large building where religious services are held.

chromosome A dark, X-shaped structure inside a cell that carries genetic information in the form of the chemical DNA.

civilization A human society that has developed social customs, government, technology, and culture.

cockpit The compartment where the pilot or crew sit to control the aircraft.

column A tall, thin cylinder with a capital at the top and in some cases a wide, round base at the bottom. Columns are used to support a roof or the upper story of a building.

computer A machine that automatically performs calculations according to a set of instructions that are stored in its memory.

concave lens A lens that is thinner in the middle than at the edges.

concrete A synthetic building material made from a mixture of cement, lime, sand, pebbles, and water.

convex lens A lens that is thicker in the middle than at the edges.

courtyard An area surrounded on several sides by walls or buildings and open to the sky.

data Information. Computer data may include numbers, text, sound, or pictures.

dermis The inner layer of skin. It contains tiny blood vessels, nerves, sweat glands, hair roots, and other microscopic parts.

digestion The process of breaking down food, by physical and chemical means, into tiny pieces that are small enough to be absorbed by the body.

disk drive The part of a computer that is used to read or write data.

DNA Stands for deoxyribonucleic acid, the chemical that makes up the chromosomes inside cells. It carries the genes.

dome A curved roof that covers an area the shape of a circle. Most domes are made from arches. Domes built with corbels are called corbeled domes.

electromagnetic wave A wave of energy made of vibrating electric and magnetic fields. Light, radio, and X-rays are examples of electromagnetic waves.

electronic circuit The pathways and connections followed by electrons to control computers, robots, and modern domestic appliances.

embryo An animal in the very early stages of development in the womb. In humans, this is from three to eight weeks after fertilization.

environmentally friendly Used to describe machines, appliances, and materials that do not damage the natural resources and features of the Earth.

epidermis The outer layer of skin, made up mainly of tough, hard, dead cells.

fertilization The joining of an egg cell and a sperm cell. This leads to the development of a new animal.

fetus An animal in the later stages of development in the womb. In humans, this is from eight weeks after fertilization to birth.

filament A thin wire inside a bulb. The filament glows when an electric current flows through it.

fin The fixed, vertical part of the tail unit that helps keep an airplane flying straight ahead.

floppy disk A magnetic disk used for recording computer data.

focus The point where light rays bent by a lens come together.

fossil fuels The remains of animals and plants left in the earth that form coal, oil, and natural gas over millions of years.

frequency The rate of vibration of any wavelike motion, including light, radio, or water waves.

fuselage The body of an aircraft.

Nerve cells

gallery A long, narrow room that is open on at least one side.

genes The information or instructions that tell the body how to develop, grow, maintain, and repair itself. They are in the form of a chemical code carried by the DNA.

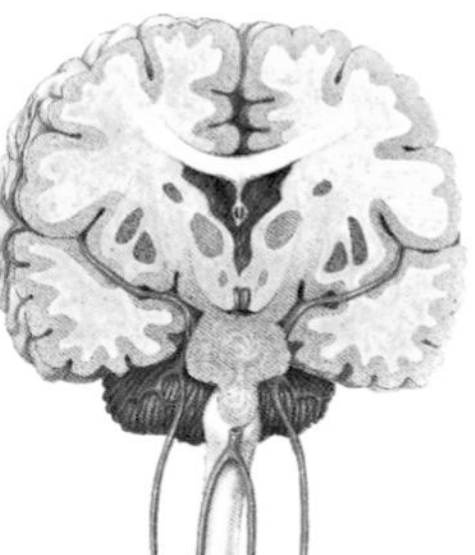

Cross section of the brain

gland A body part that makes a useful product. Endocrine glands make hormones, and exocrine glands make products such as saliva and sweat.

glider An unpowered, heavier-than-air aircraft.

gravity The force that pulls us down to the ground and also keeps the Earth and the other planets circling the sun.

gunpowder A mixture of potassium nitrate, sulfur, and charcoal used as an explosive and in fireworks.

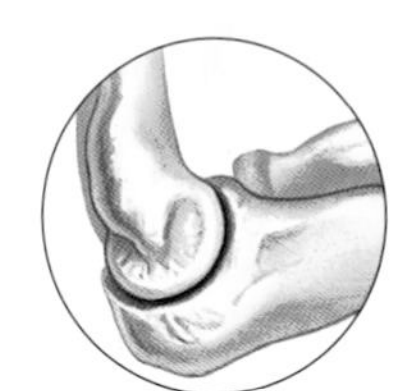

helicopter An aircraft that gets its lift from a powered rotor.

hydroponics The growing of plants by placing their roots in nutrient-rich water rather than in soil.

immune Able to fight and destroy certain bacteria, viruses, or other germs, so that they cannot multiply in the body and cause infectious disease.

Hinge joint

Industrial Revolution A change in the way people produced the goods they used. It began in England in the late eighteenth century. Engines powered by wood, coal, oil, or water replaced much of the work once done by people and animals.

inflammation The reaction of the body to infection. An inflamed area becomes red, hot, swollen, and sore.

internal combustion engine An engine in which the fuel is burned inside the engine, such as in a car.

invention An original or new product or process.

iron A strong metal used to make tools and parts of some buildings. It is found in certain types of rocks and is removed by very high temperatures.

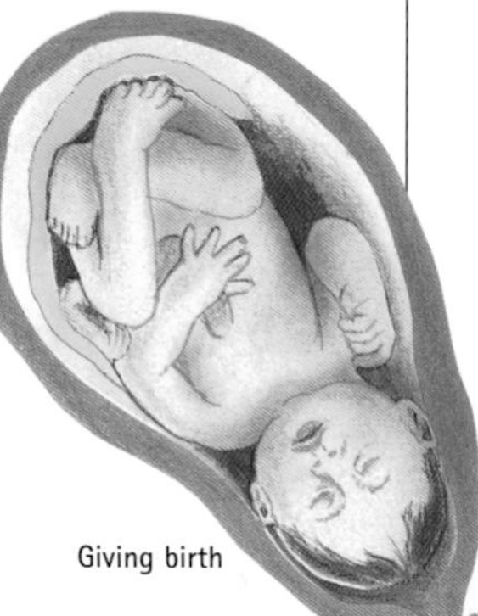

Giving birth

Mythical Garuda bird

Aerial Steam Carriage

Butterfly

Wilbur and Orville Wright

Space shuttle

jetstream Winds exceeding 99 miles (160 km) per hour that blow at very high altitudes.

keep A tall tower that is a castle, or the tall tower within a castle where the defenders retreat. The entry is usually high in a wall so it can only be reached by a ladder.

landing gear The name for the wheels that support an airplane on the ground.

laser A very intense light of one wavelength and frequency that can travel long distances. It is used to cut materials, carry television transmissions, print onto paper, and guide machines.

lift The force that enables an aircraft to fly. Lift is produced when a bird's or an aircraft's wings or a helicopter's rotor blades cut through the air.

light Electromagnetic waves that the human eye can detect. Different wavelengths are seen as different colors—red is the longest and violet is the shortest.

locomotive A self-powered vehicle that runs on a railway track.

Mach number The speed of an airplane compared with the speed of sound. Mach 1.0 is the speed of sound. A plane that flies at Mach 0.75 is flying at 75 percent of the speed of sound.

marble A popular building stone found in many colors. It can be polished until it is as smooth and shiny as glass.

mass production A method of manufacturing large quantities of goods, often using a number of machines. Each worker or machine in a factory works on just one part of a product.

membrane A thin, sheetlike layer, covering, or lining, such as the cell membrane around a cell, or the mucous membrane lining the nose, mouth, airways, and digestive tract.

microphone A device for changing sound into a varying electrical current.

microsurgery Surgery conducted using special microscopes and tiny instruments to repair the smallest parts of the body.

minaret A tall tower built outside a mosque that has a staircase inside and a platform at the top.

moat A ditch filled with water outside the walls of a castle designed to keep attackers out.

molecule A group of atoms linked together. Chemical substances are made from molecules.

monoplane A fixed-wing airplane with one set of wings.

motor A device for changing electricity into movement, such as the spinning motion of a shaft.

mucus A sticky, thick substance made by the body to protect and moisten areas, such as the lining of the nose and airways.

muscle A part of the body that can contract or relax to produce movement. Muscle is also the name given to the tissue that makes up this body part.

nerve A long, thin, pale, stringlike body part that carries nerve signals.

nucleus A cell's control center, which contains the genes that tell the cell how to work.

nutrient A food substance digested and used by the body for energy, growth, and repair.

objective lens The lens, or group of lenses, which forms the image in a microscope, telescope, or a pair of binoculars.

orbit The path of a planet around the sun, or a satellite around the Earth.

organ A main, self-contained part of the body, such as the heart, lung, kidney, liver, or brain.

oxygen The gas that is essential for life and also for combustion. Oxygen makes up 20 percent of the air around us.

patent A law that guarantees inventors the exclusive rights to perfect, build, sell, and operate their inventions for a number of years.

persistence of vision The illusion of movement produced when viewing a film or television. Our eyes see a series of still pictures moving as one.

piston A movable, solid cylinder that is forced to go up and down inside a tube by the exertion of pressure.

pitch How high or low a musical note is when compared to other musical notes.

plasma The pale, watery part of the blood.

pregnancy The time when a baby develops in its mother's womb, or uterus. This time is also called gestation.

prism A wedge-shaped block of glass used to refract or reflect light.

program Instructions given to and stored in the memory of a computer so that it can carry out a particular task.

propeller A set of blades driven by an engine that pull or push an airplane through the air.

radar Stands for "radio detecting and ranging." This is a way of locating an object by measuring the time and direction of a returning radio wave.

radio waves Invisible electromagnetic waves that carry information such as Morse code "beeps" and the human voice.

reflex A quick, automatic reaction, done without conscious thought.

Renaissance The period in Europe between 1300 and 1500 when science, invention, art, and education were strongly encouraged.

renal Relating to the kidneys.

rivet A metal pin or bolt used for holding two or more pieces of a material together.

rocket A vehicle propelled by burning a mixture of fuel and a substance containing oxygen.

rotors The parts of a machine that rotate. Also, two or more long narrow wings (called blades) that provide lift for a helicopter.

rudder A movable control fixed to a boat or the tail fin of an airplane that helps control direction.

saliva The watery fluid inside the mouth that softens and moistens food and contains enzymes to begin its chemical digestion. Another name for saliva is spit.

satellite An object that orbits a star or planet. Satellites may be natural, for example moons, or artificial, for example spacecraft.

silicon A common substance found in sand and clay. It is used in computer chips and solar cells.

software Another word for computer programs, the instructions that make computers work.

solar cell A device that converts sunlight directly into electricity.

sonar Stands for "sound navigation and ranging." A device that sends sound through water and then detects echoes as they bounce off the sea floor and other objects.

sound barrier An invisible, aerodynamic barrier that was once thought to prevent airplanes from traveling faster than the speed of sound.

space shuttle A reusable aircraft that is used to travel into space.

speed of sound At high altitudes, this is 662 miles (1,065 km) per hour; at sea level the speed of sound is 760 miles (1,223 km) per hour.

steam engine A machine that changes steam into the energy used to power equipment and tools.

steel A strong metal made from iron and carbon melted together at a very high temperature.

streamlining This gives an aircraft a smooth shape to reduce its air resistance, or drag.

submarine A large craft that can travel underwater for long distances unaided by any other craft.

submersible A small craft that can dive to great depths underwater. A submersible is much smaller than a submarine, and it is carried to and from its dive location on the deck of a ship.

Padlock

synthetic Something that is made by humans and does not exist naturally.

technology The tools and methods for applying scientific knowledge to everyday life.

thrust The force of a jet engine or rocket engine that drives an engine forward or an airplane through the air.

tile A thin slab of baked clay. Tiles are used to cover roofs and floors and are often glazed.

Dandy horse

tissue A group of cells similar in form and function, such as muscle tissue and nerve tissue, that work together to do the same job.

transonic Flying through the sound barrier.

transplant To move a natural body part (such as skin) from one site in the body to another, or from one body to another (as with a heart).

turbine A wheel with many blades that is made to turn by a gas such as steam, or a liquid such as water. It is used to power machines or to generate electricity.

Electric iron

valve A flap that allows substances to pass through one way, but not in the opposite direction.

vein A blood vessel that carries blood back to the heart.

ventricle One of the two large, thick-walled chambers of the human heart.

String telephone

virus A microorganism that can only reproduce inside a living cell.

weight The heaviness of an object, caused by gravity pulling on it.

X-rays Electromagnetic waves that can pass through soft parts of the body. X-rays are used to create images, on photographic film or a computer screen, of the inside of the body.

Pitchfork

Index

Picture Credits

(t=top, b=bottom, l=left, r=right, c=center, i=icon, Bg=background)
Ad-Libitum, 25tr, 34bc, 47tr, 49tr, 51tr, 54cl, 55br, 55c, 59cr, 60cl, 61tr, 62bl, 63br, 63tr, 64bl, 72tl, 73cr, 75tr, 76bl, 81tr, 82bl, 82tl, 86tl, 90bct, 90br, 94–95c, 94–97, 96i, 97tr, 98i, 100c, 100i, 101i, 102i, 102tl, 102tr, 103tc, 103tl, 104–105c, 104i, 104tl, 106i, 106c, 106tl, 108l, 109c, 110bl, 112tc, 112l, 113br, 113cr, 113tl, 114–115c, 114lc, 116i, 117br, 117tr, 118l, 118i, 118cr (N. Vinnicombe), 120i, 120cl (S. Bowey), 122i, 124bl, 124i, 126i, 128i, 129c, 192cl, 205br, 207bc, 210tr (E. Lessing). **A.G.E. Fotostock**, 210bl, 211tl. **Air Portraits**, 164tr. **Ancient Art and Architecture Collection**, 115cr. **AKG London**, 180tl (H. Bock), 198tr. **AKG, Berlin**, 97tl (Wurttembergisches Landesmuseum), 113bl (E. Bohr), 132cl, 142bl. **Heather Angel**, 74cl, 74tcl, 74tl. **Angelo Hornak Library**, 200tr (Wells Cathedral), 209c, 209tl, 216bl. **Arcaid**, 195cr, 195tr (M. Fiennes), 207tr (N. Barlow), 211tr, 212tl (S. Francis), 214br (R. Bryant). **Auckland Museum**, 140br. **Auscape**, 36c (Ferrero/Labat), 37cr (E. & P. Bauer), 134tr (H. & J. Beste), 136bl, 137tr (J. P. Ferrero). **Austral International**, 68bl (FPG International), 36tl, 148tr (Rex Features), 126tl (Rex Features London/The Sun), 144tl, 145t, (L'Illustration/ Sygma), 164bl (P. Schofield/Shooting Star.), 198tl (Camerapress/C. Osborne). **Australian Picture Library**, 79tr (M. Smith/Retna Pictures), 66/67, 190tl (S. Vidler), 32tl, 99cr, 105tr, 146br, 209tcr, 209tr, 214bl, 202tl, (Bettman), 36cl, 37tl (Minden Pictures), 23tr (West Stock), 111bl, (M. Adams), 100bl (Archive Photos), 95br (E.T. Archives), 122/123c, 180cl (D. & J. Heaton), 120tl. 141tr (B. Desestres/ Agence Vandystadt), 155bl (G. Hall), 152bl (UPI/Bettmann), 202tl, 217tl (D. Ball), 188bl (K. Haginoya), 198tcl (B. Holden), 202tc (R. Price/West Light). **Australian Geographic**, 143bl (P. Smith). **Bildarchiv Foto Marburg**, 207br. **Bilderberg**, 211cr (E. Grames), 210tl (M. Horacek). **Biophoto Associates**, 21tcr, 24tr, 40tr. **Black Star**, 117cr (M. Balderas), 115c. **The Bodleian Library, Oxford**, (MS. Ashmole 399, fol. 11r, 12r). **The Boeing Company**, 157tl. **Bridgeman Art Library**, 114bl (British Museum, London), 115br (British Library), 200cl (J. Bethell), 196bc (Courtesy of the Board of Trustees of the Victoria & Albert Museum), 204br (Lauros-Giraudon), 205c (Johnny van Haeften Gallery, London). **Brilliant Images**, 107br. **The British Museum**, 189tr. **British Film Institute**, 112tr, 112/113c (BFI Stills). **Bruce Coleman Ltd**, 46bl (M. Ide/Orion Press), 103cr (D. & M. Plage), 122tc (J. Cancalosi), 128tl (J. Foott), 128bl, 129tl (H. Reinhard). **Caroma Industries**, 99br. **Check Six**, 153br, 155br (M. Fizer), 156tr, 166c, 170tr (G. Hall), 164cr (J. Towers). **Christine Osborne Pictures**, 177tr. **C.M. Dixon**, 199cr, 204cl, 204tl, 181tc (Berlin Museum). **Coo-ee Picture Library**, 112bl (R. Ryan). **Crown Equipment**, 100tr. **CSIRO**, 138br. **Culver Pictures**, 95tr. **Deutsches Museum Munich**, 125br. **Edison National Historic Site USA**, 121tr. **Chris Elfes**, 140/141c. **E.T. Archives**, 110c (Science Museum). **The Granger Collection**, 40cl, 149cr, 150tl. **Robert Estall**, 184t. **George Gerster**, 186–187c. **Terry Gwynn-Jones**, 133tl, 147tl, 149br, 150tr, 162tr, 165tl (Royal Flying Doctor Service). **Sally Greenhill**, 34tl. **Timothy Hursley**, 212bl. **Hoover Co**, 99tr. **The Image Bank**, 25bc (D. de Lossy), 71cl, 105i, 108i, 110i, 112i, 114i, 123cr, 158c, 158tr, 213tc, 179br, 205bl, 178cl, 194c. **Image Select/Ann Ronan**, 39bcl, 39cl, 110cl, 145cr. **Imax Corporation**, 139br. **International Photographic Agency**, 77cr (SuperStock). **International Photo Library**, 168l. **International Photo Library. Medical Images, Inc**, 16bc (H. Sochurek). **Lockheed**, 166br. **Lego Australia**, 107tr. **Magnum**, 186bl, 187tl. **Mansell Collection Ltd**, 109tl. **Mattel Toys**, 106bl. **Loren McIntyre**, 116tr. **Melbourne Muscular Dystrophy Association of Victoria** (Neurology Department, Royal Children's Hospital), 21br. **Jenny Mills**, 187br. **National Museum of Roller Skating, Lincoln, Nebraska**, 107tl. **NHPA**, 134l (G. I. Bernard), 138tl, 139tr (S. Dalton). **Lennart Nilsson**, 40–41c, 126–127c. **Nobel Foundation**, 94i, 94l, 94r. **Oxford Scientific Films**, 136tl (S. Osolinski). **Panos Pictures**, 49br (J. Dugast). **Peter Arnold, Inc**, 35tr (L. Dwight). **Petit Format**, 42bc, 42bl, 42br, 43bc, 43bl, 43br (A. Chaumat), 41tl (Guigoz). **The Photo Library, Sydney**, 19cr, 21c, 22c, 22–23c, 24bl, 27tc, 28cl, 30tc, 30tl, 33tc, 40tcr, 40tl, 40tcl, 42tl, 50tr, 55tr, 64tl, 67tr, 69tr, 79bl, 84l, 86bc, 88tl, 97cr, 113bc, 118bl, 118tr, 122–123c, 122tr, 123br, 123r, 124cl, 126–127c, 126cl, 127br, 127br, 127tr, 128tr, 129c, 129r, 134cl, 151cr, 157tr, 179tc, 179cr, 182tr, 188tl, 191cr, 200bl, 206tl. **Photo Researchers, Inc**, 21bcr, 21tr, 24cl, 28tl, 30cl, 43tl, 48bl, 100tl, 114br. **Picture Media**, 168bl (R. Richards/ Liaison/Gamma). **Powerhouse Museum, Sydney**, 108tr, 110tl, 115tr, 120bl. **Rainbow**, 41br (C. Dittmann), 35tc, 37bc (D. McCoy), 17br (H. Morgan). **Robert Harding Picture Library**, 177cr, 187cr, 193tr, 208bl, 208tl, 217tr, 194tr (G. Campbell), 178tr (R. Frerck), 197tl (J. H. C Wilson), 177tl, 193br (A. Woolfitt). **Royal Aeronautical Society**, 143c. **Royal North Shore Hospital, Sydney**, 127tl. **Scala**, 204/205t. **SCR Library**, 194br (D. Toase). **Science Museum**, 119br (D. Exton), 124tl, 141bl, 145br, 153tr (Science & Society Picture Library), 117tl, 117bl, 121br. **Phil Schofield**, 163br. **Sextant Avionique**, 169cr. **Smithsonian Institution**, 122tl, 147r, 147br, 149cl, 149tr, 150–151c, 152c, 162bl. **Sonia Halliday Photographs**, 192bc, 196bl (L. Lushington). **Spectrum Colour Library**, 103br. **Sport The Library**, 27bc (D. McNamara). **Stock Photos**, 18cl (The Stock Market/ H. Sochurek), 102/103c (P. Steel). **Topham Picture Source**, 151tr. **TRH Pictures**, 160tr (US Navy). **Dr. John Tyler**, 38tl, 39bl, **Robert Harding Picture Library**, 101tl (R. Evans), 54tl, 113tr, 116l, 123t. **Tom Stack & Associates**, 53tc (G. Vaughn). **Victa**, 98bl. **Visions**, 151tl (M. Greenberg).**Werner Forman Archive**, 108lc, 184bl, 199tl, 199tr, 183tl (British Museum, London). **Wheels Magazine**, 122/123c (W. Kent). **Xerox Corporation**, 105br, 105cr. **Yamaha Japan**, 115tl, **Michael S. Yamashita**, 191tr.